P9-DEF-472

ARNULFO L. OLIVEIRA MEMORIAL LIBRARY
1825 MAY STREET
BROWNSVILLE, TEXAS 78520

Second Edition

Clients & Consultants

Meeting and Exceeding Expectations

Second Edition

Clients &
Consultants

Meeting and Exceeding Expectations

*Editors: Chip R. Bell
and Leonard Nadler*

Gulf Publishing Company
Book Division
Houston, London, Paris, Tokyo

ARNULFO L. OLIVEIRA MEMORIAL LIBRARY
1825 MAY STREET
BROWNSVILLE, TEXAS 78520

Clients and Consultants:
Meeting and Exceeding Expectations

Copyright © 1979, 1985 by Gulf Publishing Company, Houston, Texas. Printed in the United States of America. All rights reserved. This book, or parts thereof, may not be reproduced in any form without permission of the publisher.

First Edition, March 1979
Second Edition, January 1985

Library of Congress Cataloging in Publication Data

Main entry under title: Clients and consultants.

Bibliography: p.
Includes indexes.

1. Business consultants. I. Bell, Chip R.
                              II. Nadler, Leonard.
HD69.C6C545 1985   658.4'6   84-10917

ISBN 0-87201-119-4

Building Blocks of Human Potential
Leonard Nadler, Series Editor

Contents

Preface

The business world is growing in complexity, and one byproduct of this growth is an increasing reliance on professional helpers—consultants. In our own experience as clients as well as consultants, we have found the real key to effectiveness in those encounters to be the quality of the rapport between the parties involved, i.e., the nature of the human relationship between client and consultant. This book is dedicated to the improvement of such relationships.

When we assembled the first edition of this book five years ago, we commented on the paucity of writing devoted to the relational aspects of consultation. We still are surprised at the limited printed resources available on the topic. We have compiled the best of the available literature on the client-consultant relationship, one third of which has not appeared in any other publication.

We believe the client-consultant relationship is the most crucial and the most vulnerable aspect of the consulting process. Thus, the key to meeting and exceeding expectations in a client-consultant relationship is attaining mutual understanding as well as self-understanding. We have assembled articles useful to both clients and consultants. It is not unusual for consultants to train their clients to use a consultant, and this puts the client in a potentially dependent position that can ultimately doom the consultation to mediocrity. This book was compiled to prevent that dependence and to enhance the effectiveness of consultation.

The book was written for people who use or plan to use the services of an internal or external consultant. It provides insight and understanding for professionals who devote all or part of their working lives to helping clients. There are suggestions and techniques throughout the book aimed at achieving and maintaining a positive and productive client-consultant relationship.

Graduate students in behavioral science, management, human resource development adult education, and organizational psychology will find this to be a practical tool for understanding the subtle issues involved in managing such a complex interpersonal relationship.

We wish to express our appreciation to the authors and publishers who so kindly gave us permission to reprint their works. We are also grateful to Bruce Fritch for his creative editing and to Nancy Chapman and Ellen Suite for typing and proofing the manuscript. We wish to thank Melissa Lewis for her fine expertise as our editor. Finally, we express our warm appreciation for the love and patience of Nancy Bell and Zeace Nadler.

Chip R. Bell
Leonard Nadler

Second Edition

Clients & Consultants

Meeting and Exceeding Expectations

Part I

Introduction to the Client-Consultant Relationship

Consultation is fundamentally the act of helping. As such, it holds the dramatic vibrance and reality which characterizes life itself. Consultation is not simply the mechanical tossing of expertise toward a painful client; it is an experience in shared resources. There is an appropriate place for technique, tactic, and form. However, it is the substance and spirit in the helping process which gives consultation its unique humanness.

The core of the act of helping is the interaction of two or more people relating in order to improve some person, situation, or thing. The quality of those dynamics determines if the encounter results in more help than harm, more joy than sorrow, and more growth than death.

Many years ago there were tribes who ceremonially ate the raw meat of a mountain lion before embarking on a hunt. They believed that in the process of integrating with the lion they would assume some of the lion's strength and cunning. The analogy characterizes the client–consultant relationship in its most ideal form — the consultant and client becoming so integrated (Martin Buber called it an I–Thou relationship) that the client discovers personal power through the strength of the consultant.

The ingredients in an ideal client–consultant relationship are many. Each is not easy to come by. Even if attained, they remain slippery; all parties involved must work constantly to keep them at hand. This book is anchored to the belief that as one increases sensitivity to the dynamics of helping, the chances for effectiveness likewise climb.

The book has been assembled with the primary purpose of assisting insight and facilitating discovery by the players currently in the consultative drama and those desiring to learn it's character. It is our opinion that growth occurs in serving, as well as in being served. This book is therefore as much about growing as it is about helping.

An Overview of Consulting

Consultation has come to be a broad label for a variety of relationships. Principally, it is a two-way process of seeking, giving, and receiving help. We use the word consulting in a very specific sense. It is the provision of information or help by a professional helper (consultant) to a help-needing person or system (client) in the context of a voluntary, temporary relationship which is mutually advantageous.

The plea for professional help is precipitated by the client's recognition that he or she lacks certain kinds of resources. It may be that the specialized expertise required to solve some current or potential problem is not readily available within the client system and must thus be secured outside. It may be that the client needs a type or level of objectivity which only an outsider could provide. It could be that the client simply lacks the time to do what he or she could normally do and hires an outsider with available time.

The words "client," "client system," "consultant," and "outsider" are used in very specific ways and thus require additional clarification. Client refers to the person responsible for the outcome of the consultation. This may be a different person from the individual who served as the initial contact, go-between, or sponsor in securing a particular consultant. Client system refers to the organizational unit most directly affected by the consultation and is generally lead by the client.

The consultant is the person who, because of competence, experience, status, reputation, or a combination of these, is deemed by the client to be capable of providing needed information or help. The consultant is always external to the client system, but may be internal to the organization in which the client is an employee. The consultant is therefore sometimes a physical outsider and always a psychological outsider.

The many varied types of consultation add to the confusion of words. Throughout the following readings, authors may refer to organization development consulting (OD), management consulting, human resource development consulting (HRD), and a few others. We prefer to combine these and use the broader label of behavioral science consulting. If someone is contracted to run a training program for an organization, we would not call such an activity consulting. If, on the other hand, a person was hired to help solve a problem and if a diagnosis revealed that a training program was a solution, we would be more likely to label the activity consulting.

There are numerous ways of perceiving the consulting process. Writers differ on their words for process steps and on the models or conceptual framework they utilize. Most agree there is entry, some type of diagnosis, some response or action, and, at a point, termination of the consultation. Most agree there is a defined beginning and a defined end.

The model we have elected to use (Figure I-1) is a straightforward, simple five-step process. While the model reflects distinct phases, we would underscore that in reality these distinctions are less precise. We also should point out that the model is not intended to be a blueprint, but rather an overview of the consulting process.

The following is a brief review of the meaning of each phase and the tasks which are typically associated with each of these phases.

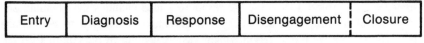

| Entry | Diagnosis | Response | Disengagement | Closure |

Figure I-1. The five phases of the consulting process.

Entry

Because of some pain or disequilibrium experienced or expected to be experienced by the client and/or client system, a consultant is called onto the scene. The entry phase begins with some contact of one by the other. Problems are jointly explored, perceived needs and symptoms are discussed, relationships are clarified, goals and roles are defined, resource parameters are identified, methodology is clarified, and ultimately a contract (written or psychological) is negotiated.

The time which elapses during entry may range from a brief telephone call to numerous meetings. Throughout the entry phase, both parties are scouting to ascertain the degree to which the consultation will be a potentially advantageous relationship.

Diagnosis

Diagnosis is essentially the process of determining by examination the cause and nature of a problem. It generally begins with the understanding of the problem as perceived by the client. It includes an appreciation of the client's goals, resources, and the client system's culture, values, norms, and beliefs.

The consultant is charged with identifying the subsystem(s) in which the problem is perceived to be located and the interrelationships between that subsystem and the other parts of the system. Another important issue in the diagnosis phase is the extent and degree to which the client system is willing to commit its resources to a resolution of the problem.

Questionnaires, interviews, observation, and analysis of previous performance data are the most common methods used in obtaining an assessment of the situation.

Response

The literature in social and behavioral science is unclear regarding when diagnosis stops and response begins. Many models of consulting place a planning phase between the two to separate them more distinctly. Should the feedback of the diagnosis be in the diagnosis phase or response phase? Technically, data feedback is, in fact, a response and may be all that was contracted. We chose to place data feedback and presentation of alternative responses in the diagnosis phase.

The response or action phase includes the selection of a course of action, redefinition of the consultative goals, and identification of appropriate objectives, strategies, and roles. Likewise, the response phase includes the planning and engagement of structured activities or interventions employed to correct the problem or improve the situation which was spelled out in the contract.

Disengagement

This book combines disengagement and closure since most writers treat them as one phase. Despite this, we feel the actions undertaken in the disengagement phase and closure phase are sufficiently different to warrant separating them into two distinct phases. The model (Figure I-1) shows a dotted line separating the two phases. This reflects the confusion regarding whether they are indeed separate. We believe writers at some point in the future will view disengagement and closure as related, but different, phases in consultation.

The disengagement phase includes the evaluation of results conducted to determine not only if the response has been successful and is progressing as planned, but also whether there is a need for response revision or additional resources. Based on that evaluation, planning for continuous process maintenance is conducted to insure permanent integration and lasting change.

An effort is made to decrease the client's dependency on the the consultant and develop within the client system the ability to use self-generated data by involving the client system in monitoring progress and evaluating results. Change can only be sustained if the client and client system attain sufficient growth during the consultation.

Closure

Presuming the consultant has taken steps during disengagement to insure continuity and internal support, he or she should be ready for a mutually satisfying termination of the working relationship. Termination may mean leaving the client system or may mean ceasing one effort and starting another. The challenge of the helpers is to bring the party being helped to a point at which a helper is no longer necessary.

Organization of the Book

The major foundation of this book is the presentation of relevant theory and practice pertinent to the client–consultant relationship. The book begins and ends with an issues look at the relational consultant and chapters on the relationship dimensions of each phase of consulting.

In our search for material, we tried to find articles which most clearly presented a particular phase. Few articles did in total what we wanted an article to do. Many were written specifically for this book and have not been previously published. Where gaps appeared, we have attempted to fill them in with the introductions to each part.

An effort was also made to present articles from diverse journals, including some not likely to be read by the practitioner (client or consultant). Most articles were published in the last few years. The exceptions are considered classics in their particular areas. Despite the proliferation of material on consultation (reflected in the Bibliography), surprisingly few articles dealt with the relationship aspects.

The part introductions provide a major service beyond filling voids caused by the scarcity of subject-related works. They are designed to serve as mental-setting devices to enhance the growth derived from the articles. The articles provide a wide diversity of thought within each chapter. We have not attempted to resolve the conflict in positions. Hopefully, the part introductions will quell some of the abruptness inherent in diversity.

Uses of the Book

This book was written for clients who currently use or plan to use the services of a consultant. The behavioral sciences have been inundated with theory and practice texts for the consultant; those for the client are few and far between. We hope this book provides insight and understanding useful to clients in managing a very complex relationship.

This book is also for the growing number of professionals who devote a portion of their working lives to providing help to clients. We feel this particular group will gain from this book a deeper appreciation for the world of the client. We have made sure there are many suggestions and techniques throughout the text that will prove useful in more effectively achieving and maintaining a positive and productive client–consultant relationship.

Finally, we view this as a comprehensive textbook dealing with the client-consultant relationship, particularly for graduate students in the fields of human resource development, behavioral science, business management, adult education, and organizational psychology. We believe the text will enhance their perceptiveness of the subtle issues surrounding the relationship of client and consultant.

For all readers, the book was designed as a ready reference. Reading the book through will provide a comprehensive view of the subject. We trust that some chapters will prove sufficiently helpful to elicit a second and third reading. The Bibliography includes most of the major works (and many of the minor works) related to consultation. All were reviewed for possible inclusion in this work.

The Bias of the Authors

Our deepest bias related to the client–consultant relationship is reflected in the old story of the grasshopper and owl. A grasshopper, having suffered during two cold winters, went to an expert owl for assistance. The owl listened carefully to the grasshopper's problem and then prescribed a solution. "All you have to do is turn yourself into a cricket and hibernate throughout the winter," the owl said. The grasshopper happily departed only to return later to the owl disappointedly. "Look," said the owl curtly when the grasshopper asked how one performs metamorphosis, "I gave you the principle, it's up to you to work out the details."

Our conviction is that the extent to which knowledge can be effectively used by clients depends in a large measure on the nature of the relationship between the client and consultant. We suspect that too frequently clients, in their frantic search for a solution, and consultants, in their drive to demonstrate their expertise, pass each other in the night without realizing that at the root of giving and receiving help is the richness of human encounter.

We believe with Carl Rogers that the only learning which significantly influences behavior is self-discovered learning — truth that has been personally assimilated in experience. This puts the helper in the role of the facilitator of discovery rather than the dispenser of information.

Lastly, we think consultants have a responsibility to be impeccably ethical in their dealings with clients. By ethical, we mean the consultant should be up front regarding his or her motives with the client. Central to his or her motives is taking to heart the best interests of the client.

Introduction to the Readings

The introductory readings are either etched in consultative issues or provide thoughts useful as a frame of reference. We felt it would be helpful to begin with a macroview of the client–consultant relationship before consultation was diced up in later chapters for a close look at smaller pieces.

At the bottom of the first page of each reading, we have provided its source. A brief statement about the author(s) has been placed at the end of each article. We have been as accurate as possible in stating the correct title and organization for each author. However, given the mobility of the practitioners in this field, some biographical data is likely to be dated.

Chapter 1
"Developing a Successful Client–Consultant Relationship"
Charles H. Ford

Clarity is a primary theme in the writing of Ford. He succinctly uncovers key causes for client-consultant disharmony.

The lack of consultant competence is the source of poor relationships on the consultant side of the equation. Failure to identify the real problem, promising too much too soon, failure to specify role, recommending actions not feasible — each are samples of consultant inadequacies Ford discusses.

The lack of effective communication lies at the heart of most of client-caused causes of poor relationships. Failure to clarify what his or her money will buy, failure to clarify how the consultant will operate, failure to inform his or her client system of the consultant's role and goals and failure to explain resource limitations are some of the problems outlined.

The article provides a useful opening piece in its pragmatic treatment of common pitfalls which doom client–consultant relationships to failure. Both clients and consultants can find helpful hints for optimizing consultation.

Chapter 2
"Explorations in Consulting-Client Relationships"
Chris Argyris

Chris Argyris is a giant in the field of behavioral science consulting. This classic article, which first appeared in 1961, was one of the first to examine relationship issues in consulting. Using two cases as a backdrop for his discussion, he surfaces the thorny problems most consultants and clients encounter and offers helpful insight into their resolution. Woven throughout his work is emphasis on the importance of authenticity, openness, accurate information flow, trust, and an attitude that values experimentation and risk taking.

Chapter 3
"The Characteristics of a Helping Relationship"
Carl Rogers

Carl Rogers defines a helping relationship as one in which at least one party has the intent of promoting the growth, development, maturity and improved functioning of the other. The definition is very compatible with the definition of a consulting relationship. This reading is among the most notable of Rogers' works and is taken from his classic *On Becoming a Person*.

It is widely known that Rogers is occupationally a psychotherapist. His writings were primarily focused on helping practitioners in one-to-one counseling develop greater genuineness, openness, and warmth in their counseling. The article is included here because we feel it has a cogent message for clients and consultants applicable to their developing a mature, positive and creative relationship.

Chapter 1

Developing a Successful Client-Consultant Relationship

Charles H. Ford

The next time you are with a group of say, ten businessmen and the conversation begins to lag, try slipping in the word "consultant" and watch the conversation pick up as passions heat. No doubt, the words "crooks" and "incompetents" and "conmen" will be the more printable ones used. One of the participants is bound to throw in the old cliche, "A consultant is nothing more than an unemployed executive with a briefcase." Almost everyone will have had either an unfortunate experience with a consultant or, more likely, will have *heard* of someone who has.

In short, as more businesses operating in today's complicated, ultra-competitive, shortage-ridden business climate can profitably use a consultant's services, the profession's reputation is sliding down hill.

Let's try to add some perspective to the situation: Business has become and is becoming even more compartmentalized in terms of specialized functions. Ten years ago, for example, few businesses were concerned with the ecological impact of their operations. Equality of employment opportunity was on the basis of race; today sex must be considered as well. OSHA is a new force to contend with. New computer applications appear almost daily. Shortages have introduced both new production problems and marketing problems.

Couple all this with the on-going situation of new marketing and new product opportunities and new manufacturing techniques, both procedural and equipmental; throw into the equation the pervasive problem of in-bred management whose perspective is sometimes obscured by being too close to a problem and whose frames of reference are based on "What we've always done," and a pretty good case can be made for the outsider who has a high level of expertise in one or more fields, whose experience is based on the experience of a multiplicity of companies, and whose frames of reference are not bound by in-bred company habits and attitudes.

Reprinted from *Human Resource Management*, Vol. 13, No. 2, Summer, 1974, pp. 2-11, Graduate School of Business Administration, University of Michigan, Ann Arbor, MI 48109.

Why, then, the rancor? The answer is two-fold. First, an increasing number of client–consultant relationships have simply not worked out. And as the cost of most everything else has gone up, so has the cost of this failure. In very simple terms, in those cases which did not work out, either the consultant did not do what he should have done or the client did not do what he should have done. More likely, the answer lies in a combination of mutual culpability.

Secondly, one does not hear with the same expression of heat and passion of successful client–consultant relationships for the same reason that newspapers do not bother to print good news. Thus, the failures take on added significance and tend to tarnish the whole aspect of consulting.

We here, of course, are concerned with why these relationships are not successful and what a client should do to insure that they will be.

We cannot help, unfortunately, the fact that most of the reasons for failure once stated appear painfully obvious. Even though the reader might conclude that "This couldn't happen to me," one must remember that client–consultant relationships are often new experiences for the client, and thus he lacks the perspective of previous experience. The obviousness of failure becomes first a product of 20–20 hindsight and second, is often lost in the welter of recrimination that follows an unsuccessful relationship.

The examples we will use are typical of what has and is happening. They will not tax the reader's imagination — nor are they meant to. Rather they seek to serve by illustration the pitfalls that client companies fall into and how they can be avoided. Let the reader be assured that if the causes of failure were profound, we would illustrate our points by profundities, but to do so in the light of reality would only serve to obscure the real simplicities of the problem. Now let us examine the causes of failure based on what the consultant should have done or did not do.

The Consultant Fails to Identify the Real Problem. A large ladies lingerie manufacturer found its sales slipping. Its salesmen complained that its high prices were making the line noncompetitive.

"Not so," humphed the president. "These guys have had it too soft too long. Now that things have gotten rough competitively, they've forgotten how to sell. We'll get them back to fundamentals."

Enter the Sales Engineering Consultant. After analyzing the situation he agreed with the president's conclusion. He went to work holding sales meetings, setting up incentive programs and quotas, holding classes in salesmanship. "We don't need him to teach us how to sell," the salesmen complained. "Some of us were selling before he was out of diapers." For emphasis, four of the company's twelve salesmen promptly quit. Sales continued to slide. Exit the sales engineer.

"Perhaps," thought the president, "I'd better look into my costing procedures." Enter the Cost Consultant. He was appalled at the simplicity and looseness of the present costing system and agreed that the problem must be there.

He proceeded to set up an elaborate costing and cost control system that would have required two extra people to administer. No one could fault his in-depth approach but when his unit costs came out approximately the same as what the company was already using, he too got his walking papers.

"That's it for consultants," said the president. "All I've got to show for them is four less salesmen and a bigger hole in my bank account." "Try one more," suggested his worried banker. "Let's try a manufacturing specialist." Enter the manufacturing specialist. "Your plants are ten years behind the times," he suggested. He laid out a program for modernizing equipment, methods, and cost controls. The company and the bank went along with the program. Result: Costs came down, prices followed; sales went up.

Two consultants (and the company president) had attacked the symptoms of the problem rather than the root cause. Regardless of their competence within their fields, their failure was pre-ordained simply because they failed to look sufficiently beyond their specialties to determine whether they (their specialties) were really the problem areas that needed solving in order to achieve the client's objective, namely to increase sales.

The Consultant Promises Too Much Too Soon. No one calls in a consultant unless he has a problem. This in itself generally creates a susceptibility to the consultant's expansive expression of confidence in his ability to solve the problem.

Many problem solutions look easy when discussed across a desk. The problem is often stated in such a way as to make the solution seem textbook. At this point, in the absence of specifics and problem nuances, it is often discussed in abstract terms. As a result, the consultant sometimes tends to tie his promise of success to the obvious simplicity of the solution. The client, often desperate, is eager to accept it. Thus, we have the elements of a potential explosion.

In actually addressing himself to the solution, however, the consultant often finds nuances that he hadn't expected — and the possibility of which he hadn't advised the client — perhaps elements of the problem that were not discussed at the interview because of the client's prejudicial point of view or because of his failure to attach significance to them. Perhaps the consultant finds other problems that flow into the main problem which gives it a different complexion from what he expected. As a result, he finds that the easy solution upon which he based his promises has changed along with his ability to deliver.

For example, a consultant was called to help reorganize a metal works company. The average age of the top 12 executives was 59. The president, 64, felt that the company's decline was due to the rigid thinking of his deeply patterned executives. He asked the consultant to run an executive evaluation of each department head and to recommend executive replacement where necessary. "I just can't get these people to move. The industry is passing us by and we just sit and look at each other. These people have been with me a long time. Too long perhaps."

Not an unusual situation, thought the consultant. Finding the weak sisters ought not to be too difficult, he assured the president. He'd soon have things turned around. The president was blissfully reassured. The consultant accepted the president's premise that the latter's dynamism was being sabotaged by the conservativeness of his key people. "It's like punching a balloon," complained the president. "My inputs just don't come out the other side when they're filtered through my key people."

The deeper the consultant probed, however, the more apparent it became that the problem lay principally with the president himself and the executive vice president — a presidential brother-in-law, a relationship which had not been explained at the interview. Both were in reality quite antagonistic to change ("I built this company, dammit, and I know what built it") and in a position to shift the responsibility of the company's resultant decline to the department heads.

Virtually every executive the consultant interviewed could pull program and ideas out of his desk that had been submitted and rejected. To the consultant, most of these made sense.

Final result? The consultant suggested that it might be a good idea if the president turned the reins over to someone else and went fishing. And while he was doing it, he might take his brother-in-law with him. The reaction, predictably, was explosive. Consulting had incurred another vocal enemy simply because the consultant promised expansively what he couldn't deliver. Even though he had the answer, it was not the one he had promised.

The Consultant Fails to Specify His Role. Often a consultant will accept an assignment and not indicate clearly to the client what form his help will take.

A consultant was hired by a large stereo equipment manufacturer to re-organize the company. The company felt it needed to regear itself to meet new changes in consumer buying habits and increased foreign-made competition. "Our organization functioned well during the growth years because we developed a good product line and the market was waiting for us. Now we're being hurt by a contracting market and not only is our domestic competition importing components from abroad but foreign competition itself is exporting to this country. We need to shift gears both organizationally to cut our costs and functionally to meet the shift in consumer buying habits."

The consultant agreed with the need. In came his associates with pencils and clipboards. Surveys were made, executives were evaluated, new production methods and techniques were developed. Two months later, the consultant submitted his report — all 104 pages of it single-spaced. He followed this up with his final bill.

The client hit the ceiling. "The report is fine," he said, "if I had the time to read it, digest it and could understand it. I thought the consultant would hold us by the hand during the reorganization and follow-up on it to make sure it worked — and to make adjustments where it didn't. By the time I got through reading this report, I could have done the job myself."

The report now reposes in the president's desk drawer. The company is out nearly $44,000 and the company's executives have very unkind things to say about consultants and consulting.

The Consultant Fails to Adapt to the Individuality of the Client's Problems. Consultants, as anyone else, often develop patterns of approaches based on their experiences. Often they view situations as they should be rather than as they are.

An "expert" on organization was called in by a growing conglomerate to help the company work in the newly acquired management teams it was absorbing. Coincidentally, he (the consultant) had just performed the same job for another conglomerate. The previous company had a strong operations-oriented management team. Its philosophy was to buy ailing companies at bargain prices and turn them around. With this company, the consultant had strengthened the bonds of corporate management and weakened the authority of the absorbed managements. It worked. The strong-willed competent corporate management made itself felt with success on the less competent absorbed managements.

The consultant was delighted. In his enthusiasm, he wrote an article on the subject based on his successful experience. Conglomerates, he concluded, should have strong central managements. With his previous success as a blueprint, he promptly proceeded to reorganize the latest client the same way. The result was chaos.

Theoretically, it should have worked and he would die, if necessary, defending his approach. After all, it had worked before. He had the experience to prove it. The client must be doing something wrong, he contended.

Unfortunately, although the circumstances appeared to be the same, obviously they were not. The top management of the latter client was financially oriented — not operationally oriented. Its philosophy was to buy moderately successful companies and infuse additional capital necessary to help them grow further. The absorbed managements were far more competent to operate their companies, to assess the risks, etc., than corporate management.

The company saved itself by reversing the consultant's blueprint and delegating more authority to the absorbed managements — the same managements that had built the successful subsidiaries in the first place and needed only the motivation of increased authority to make them continue to grow. The company's president made a vow never again to hire a consultant even if, at a later date, the firm faced disaster.

The consultant often fails to tailor his approach to the unique and different circumstances of his client. And every company is unique and different, with different people, different attitudes, operating under different pressures. The gap in communication so frequently complained about between the client's people and the consultant is most often due to the consultant's failure to adapt his approach to the specifics of the client-company.

The Consultant's Recommendations Are Not Feasible. There is a marked difference, obviously, between a good theoretical recommendation and a feasible practical one. And one consequential difference is a satisfied client and an unsatisfied one.

A medium-sized toy manufacturer had grown rapidly in the past few years. Its staff was located in three buildings in two different cities, 40 miles apart. Two of these buildings also housed its two factories. The third building housed only part of its staff. All three buildings were older types and low rental. Like Topsy, the company had just grown. It had concentrated its capital efforts in new equipment and product development to the point where it was skating on a thin edge of working capital.

It discovered that, as it grew, staff coordination became a problem. It called in an organization specialist to help solve the problem. He analyzed the communications break-down and concluded that the obvious and best solution was to house the staff in one building. This noble bit of intelligence cost the client $3100.

"I didn't need to spend $3100 for that answer," said the company president, not without heat. "If we had the money to build or lease a new headquarters we'd have already done it. We're not that stupid." Discarding the consultant report, the company, although disenchanted with consultants, was prevailed upon to hire a communications specialist. He promptly proceeded to set up a time-controlled system of interoffice, interplant communications.

Although it was not the optimum solution, everyone agreed, at least it "will help us grease the wheels to keep things moving until we can retrench our capitalization to the point where we can consolidate our staff into one building."

Optimum solutions, defensible on paper, are often not the "best" solutions for a particular time. When the consultant fails to distinguish this difference, the client–consultant relationship is doomed to failure.

The Consultant Lacks Competence. And here, reluctantly, we must include the "con man." Many consultants simply lack the expertise or temperament with which to solve a company's problem. The "con man" is the one who, despite this, attempts to sell his services — and, unfortunately, often does. He relies on glibness, rash promises, name-dropping, and often a working knowledge of the language used in his field of "expertise."

For example, the principle of a consulting firm visited a glove plant. He had never before been in one. Before going in he asked one of his senior consultants who had made the contact and who had toured the plant to name an operation. "Thumb setting." "How many do they do an hour?" "About 120."

When he too was given the tour, he stopped at the thumb-setting operation, turned to the company's vice president of manufacturing and noted, "Hmm, thumb setting. What do you run an hour, about 120?" This established him as an "expert" on manufacturing gloves.

Incompetence, of course, goes beyond the realm of deceit. A consultant may have worked for one or two companies, specializing in one area of operations. His successful experience, he feels, qualifies him to give counsel and advice. It may — and it may not. The problems he faced previously may not be the same problems, even within the same field of specialty, that the client-company faces. Or he may not be accountable in the same way as he was when he worked for an employer, and his solutions to problems may be more conservative or more radical than those he would have made when he was accountable.

Or his previous method of problem-solving may have been through trial and error — a luxury a client can ill afford if he's paying for outside expertise. Or his employment experience may have been such that he had had competent guidance — a factor that may be missing when he goes out on his own.

The reasons for incompetence are many and diverse and we need not dwell on them any further except to note in summary that consultants, as any other group of people, range from good to bad.

Some General Observations

Before getting into the client's contributions to the failure of a client–consultant relationship, we should make some observations. The reader will note that some of these contributions are so basic as to belong in an elementary primer on management. In substance, for example, we will point out that the client should exercise care in selecting a consultant and should know how the consultant will operate before he starts. Most readers, sophisticated and hard-headed, will smite their foreheads in anguish over the basic advice. "Come on, now," is apt to be the plea. "We didn't come this far only to be told this."

Unfortunately, between the smite and practice, something frequently happens. While admittedly many prospective clients are likely to establish the client–consultant relationship on some pretty firm ground, we are concerned here with the failure of these relationships, not the successes — and how these failures can be reduced.

With this in mind, let's look at why an experienced manager may commit a fundamental error which seems quite obvious when viewed in retrospect or when committed to paper.

Most consultants "sell" very well. They have to. They are selling an expensive intangible service to a very sophisticated market — top managements — and the cultivation of a good selling approach is a must. Virtually every consultant makes a good appearance. He generates an enthusiasm and climate of confidence that is often infectious — especially to a man who has lived with and brooded over a problem and who perhaps has reached the point where he's given up on it and recognizes the need for outside help. The consultant is almost always well-spoken with a glibness in the language of the trade. He is generally well-read and can cite the latest concepts in management technique that may or may not be applicable to the prospective client's problem — but which are impressive nonetheless.

He is often familiar with the problems of other companies (either through his experience, his reading, or his conversations with others) and how they did or did not solve their problems. This increases the client's receptivity to the consultant's "selling" because he is made to feel that the consultant knows a whole lot more about his problem than he (the prospective client) because the consultant either explicitly or implicitly indicates a familiarity with this type of problem.

Thus, what may appear to the prospective client a crisis problem oftens feeds back as just another easily soluble run-of-the-mill job for the consultant. The relief in being able to turn this over to the latter, to be able to turn his attention to other problems and opportunities with the feeling that the present problem is in capable, knowledgeable hands, can often make the prospective client a little careless in laying the proper groundwork for the resultant relationship.

The prospective client is often isolated from the specific problems of other companies and their company peculiarities. He recognizes the insularity produced by his company's in-bred attitudes and limited frames of reference. There is the feeling (and generally true) that the consultant because of his third-party perspective can bridge the gap between these attitudes and the rest of the industry "out there." Most companies' top executives harbor the subconscious feeling that someone else may be doing something better and they won't find out about it until it's too late.

The consultant's experience may criss-cross the industry and can provide this information — especially when the consultant drops the right tactical hints. This too tends to make some prospective clients, if caught at the right time, less prone to do their homework.

Many prospective clients don't delve as much as they should into how the consultant will operate. The reason is simple. They assume the consultant knows his business and they (prospective clients) are often results-oriented. Most top managements adhere pretty strongly to the principle of delegation, e.g. delegate responsibilities and evaluate results (even though in practice this principle is all too often ignored) and carry it over to the operation of a client–consultant relationship. This type of delegation is fine and desirable if the delegatee is an executive of the company building a career and risking this career constantly by his success or failure to achieve results. However, the consultant does not risk this. Obviously, he wants to succeed. But his relationship with the prospective client is not a career one. It may, and most likely will be, a one-time shot. Therefore, his mode of operation should become an important evaluative consideration to the client in determining whether to consummate the client–consultant relationship. All too often, unhappily, it is not.

With this background in mind, let's now look at the client's contributions to the failure of a client–consultant relationship and, more specifically, what he can do to reduce the incidence of failure.

Now, about the Client

As we stated previously, this coin has two sides. From the consultant's side of responsibility, we've covered some of the reasons why the client–consultant relationship doesn't work. We cannot leave the client out of this negative equation because he too may share the culpability. At the same time that we analyze his contribution to it, we will also note what steps he can take to insure that his experience with a consultant is both profitable and nonexplosive.

The Client Fails to Properly Screen a Prospective Consultant. Consultants come in all shapes and forms — from the one-man generalist to the one-man specialist, from the large firm with many consultants and many specialties to the moonlighting academician. Their specialties may vary from organization to data processing, from decision-making courses to fair employment practices, from labor relations to definition of management goals. The list is endless and if one probed deeply enough, one would even find consultants to consultants.

The prospective client, therefore, has a wide field to choose from. In selecting one, the client should exercise the same caution he uses in selecting a top executive. What is the consultant's experience? Whom did he work for and what did he accomplish? Does the consultant's field of expertise tie in with the client's needs? Is the consultant's personality such as to permit him to work with the company's people or will he generate negative-productive antagonism?

The client should check references and previous clients to verify the consultant's claims to success. Any consultant's refusal to cooperate in this background check should in itself raise a red flag of caution. Many consultants come to a client through one referral. Yet the new client's problems may not have the same mixture as the referral client's. Therefore, the former should, where possible, check beyond the one reference.

It has been a constant source of amazement to us how many hard-bitten, tough-minded, normally cynical executives accept at face value the man with whom they are ready to make a generally very expensive commitment — both in terms of fees and potential internal disruption.

The Client Does Not Seek Clarification of How the Consultant Will Operate. At the interview stage, a prospective client should have a clear-cut understanding of the approach the consultant intends to use and basically his method of operation.

These are the types of questions that should be asked: Will the consultant simply observe? Will he use a stopwatch? Will he be interviewing executives and/or employees? If so, which ones? How long will the job take? Will the consultant's services be intermittent or continuous until completion? What help will he need from the company? What records will have to be made available to him? Will he provide interim reports? Will he conduct expensive surveys that perhaps the company has already made? How many people will be assigned to the job? What are the potentials for disruption of the company's day-by-day operations? In short, the client should clearly understand what this comparative stranger will be doing around the company during his tenure.

The Client Fails to Seek Clarification of What His Money Will Buy. Here again, a clear-cut understanding should be reached at the interview stage. What exactly will the consultant do in terms of solving problems? Will he simply submit a report? Will he survey and do nothing more than re-define the problems from his perspective? Will he follow up on his recommendations? Will he provide interim reports, written or oral? Will he hold the client's hand and implement his recommendations? Will the client be doing business with the consultant or the consultant's staff? Does the consultant plan return visits to check on the implementation of his recommendations and adjust them where necessary?

If, for example, he finds a piece of equipment antiquated, will he simply note that fact or will he be specific in terms of suggesting a replacement by brand, cost, and anticipated results? How much will this service cost? If the consultant operates on a per diem basis, how many days should it take? And if the fee includes "expenses", just what do these expenses include?

Obvious? Seemingly so. Yet, surprisingly, many clients engage consultants without ever really knowing what final product they are buying until the very end of the consultant's tenure. By then, it's too late.

The Client Fails to Accurately Identify the Problem. We have already covered this facet from the point of view of the consultant. Let's look at it now from the client's. A small tool manufacturer found his costs were excessively high — as evidenced by the fact that while his prices were competitive, his competition was making money. High costs, he concluded, could only mean low productivity from equipment and/or personnel. His profit structure had been keeping pace with the rest of the industry up until a year ago. He called in a consulting firm heavily experienced in manufacturing.

After seven weeks of effort, the consulting firm, by re-vamping assembly lines, reduced manufacturing costs by 3¾%. Within his field of specialty, the consultant apparently did a competent job. The economics of the situation, however, were such that his bill, $11,000, absorbed the first 16 months of savings. The client was not ecstatic over the results, especially since the resultant savings did not really solve his problem.

Four months later, quite by accident, the client discovered that he had been buying a raw material alloy that was 12% higher in cost than what his competition was paying for a slightly different but equally functional material. Somewhere along the line the industry had changed alloys and he hadn't gotten the word. His purchasing department had been exposed to the new material but somehow between purchasing, engineering, and manufacturing, this exposure came to a

ARNULFO L. OLIVEIRA MEMORIAL LIBRARY

1825 MAY STREET

RROWNSVILLE TEXAS

dead end. As his company had a 58% material factor, a switch to the new material added almost 7% to his profits.

Identifying this type of problem is, of course, difficult. If it does elude identification or if there is any possibility that the problem itself lies elsewhere, then the client should enlist the aid of the consultant.

When interviewing the latter, the client should explain his definition of the problem and, if necessary, have the consultant spend a few days verifying it before committing both the client and consultant to a long-term expensive committment. In the above case, the client should have explained that his profits were about 2% of sales as opposed to about 9% for the rest of the industry. He should then have had the manufacturing consultant determine whether, after an analysis, he (the consultant) saw the possibility of saving enough by altering manufacturing procedure to increase the profitability of the company up to the industry average. And if so, how?

The Client Fails to Explain Its Resource Limitations. At the initial interview or shortly after the consultant has assessed the problem, the client should explain what resources the company has available for solving the problem plus any other limitations not at once apparent. The obvious purpose is to permit the consultant to either tailor his solutions to what is available or to very quickly assess whether he can indeed develop a useful product with these limitations.

For example, a consultant was called in by a medium-sized luggage manufacturer to reorganize its manufacturing plant. The plant was housed in an old building and its equipment reflected the age of the building. The consultant drew up a list of recommendations for the purchase of new equipment. With it, he recommended a new production flow line. "This will result," he reported proudly 3 weeks later, "in approximately $200,000 in labor savings per year. In addition, using the same space now being used, production output will increase 15–20%."

"How much will it cost?" asked a suspicious company president.

"The major pieces of equipment will run about $850,000 and ancillary equipment perhaps another $75,000."

"Beautiful!" said the president. "If we were General Motors, which we are not. We're up to our neck at the banks as it is. We thought if we went something less than first class, we could make a good start for something like $250,000 and then with the savings from that investment continue a program of modernization."

The consultant submitted his bill for $8500 and went off into the sunset mumbling something about "Why didn't someone tell me?" The president mumbled also. "That's the trouble with consultants. It's not their money. What do they care how they spend it?"

The Client Fails to Adequately Inform His Organization of the Consultant's Role and Goals. An electric appliance manufacturer projecting a substantial increase in his sales volume decided that his middle and lower levels of management needed to reorganize for this expansion. New responsibilities would have to be assigned; decision making at these levels would now have a greater impact as volume increased.

He called in an organizational specialist. "I've got good people. But I'm not sure we've delegated enough responsibility to make them maximally effective. I can visualize hiring more people as our sales increase but before I do, I want to make sure I'm using the people I've got to the fullest."

The client then passed the word along in memo form: "On Sept. 6th, Mr. _____ will, as an outside consultant, work with us in reorganizing our management structure. Your fullest cooperation is requested." Panic hit the ranks. There is a natural inclination to equate "reorganization" with "reductions in force." And an outside consultant is often considered a euphemism for "hatchet man."

Instead of getting cooperation, the consultant got inflated definitions of the responsibilities from the people he interviewed. Knives were sharpened as most of the executives attempted to defend their own jobs. It was every man for himself. The only unity was in mutual distrust of the consultant. The resistance fed on itself and reached the point where the consultant reported that his efforts were coming to nought. "They're pulling in one direction. I'm pulling in another. I can't get a straight story from anyone." The client blamed the consultant. "I can't hold your hand on this. Maybe it's the way you're going about it." The consultant's departure was imminent.

Fortunately, when the dust of recrimination cleared, the president issued a clarifying memo stressing that the reorganization would not result in reductions of force but rather would involve more individual responsibilities with greater personal opportunities through more visible efforts.

Failure to establish a cooperative climate for the consultant by top management is one of the chief reasons for the failure of the client–consultant relationship. It is often not recognized because the latter's natural tendency is to lay the blame for an antagonistic nonproductive climate on the consultant's techniques and personality.

The Client Fails to Adequately Try to Solve Its Own Problems. A medium-sized food processing company found its sales slipping. It called in a marketing specialist firm.

The consulting firm spent the first six weeks doing market surveys. It developed a very comprehensive picture of the company's marketing position, market potential, product acceptance, etc. Once it felt it had the tools with which to work, it went to work to try to solve the problem. During the course of its efforts, the senior consultant on the job lunched with the assistant manager. He posed the question, "What do you think is wrong?"

"I don't think. I know. Our salesmen were put on salary. They should be on commission. Our sales manager, my boss, is a driver. His idea of sales managing is to climb on his salesmen's backs. Their morale is shot and with little possibility of seeing their efforts more tangibly rewarded, their retaliation is to lay down on the job."

"Why haven't you told anyone?"

"I have. My boss. He told me that this is the way he did it with his previous company, not incidentally a food processing company, and this is the way we're going to do it here. I can't go over his head."

The consultant recommended that the salesmen be put on commission and that the sales manager be replaced. His fee for 7½ weeks of work including the surveys came to $38,000 — equivalent to slightly less than three years salary for the assistant sales manager. The company had the answer all the time. It just never looked for it, never probed deeply enough within its own organization for the answer. The company, therefore, had, in reality, no need for an outside consultant. When the story came out, it felt bilked. It hadn't been bilked. The consultant simply did what the company could have and should have done itself. This logic, however, had not abated its new-found antipathy toward consultants.

How Contacts Are Made

We should perhaps say a word about how contacts are made between client and consultant.

The Client Looks for a Consultant. This occurs when the prospective client recognizes the need for a consultant either to evaluate a course of action before it is taken, to solve a particular problem, or to evaluate a potential opportunity. Sources available to a prospective client to help him zero in on a consultant include friends, relatives, business acquaintances, trade associations, mailings from consultants, chance reading of a consultant's writings that touch a nerve, deans of graduate business schools (for moonlighting faculty members with generally very good in-depth skills), consultant's associations, etc. The list is endless. One might even find a consultant by cruising cocktail parties where someone is bound to be a "consultant." Finding a consultant is easy. One need, in fact, go no further than the yellow pages. Finding the right consultant is not so easy. Of the list above, trade associations, business acquaintances, and graduate business school deans probably represent the most reliable sources.

The Consultant Looks for a Client. Here again, we touch on mailings which generally include brochures and the inevitable copies of testimonials, etc. Mailings, however, are not generally productive to the prospective client unless the consultant is a specialist and his specialty hits a bull's-eye on a current or incipient problem with which a prospective client might be wrestling.

A second way is for the consultant to make a referral part of his deal with another client. "Mr. Smith, we do expect and hope that after we do a good job for you, you will perhaps call one or two business acquaintances and suggest that it might be useful if they see us." Sometimes they add, "It is this quid pro quo that reduces our selling costs and the savings, of course, are reflected in our fee schedule." This method can be useful if there is some relationship between the problem the referral had and the problem the prospective client has.

The third method is the cold call. This may be to sell a specific service (setting up a computerized bookkeeping system, for example) or a general service ("For a moderate fee, we'll send our people in to survey your business and make appropriate recommendations.") The latter consultant generally has a list of people that may be called for referrals. Unfortunately, the list of less-satisfied clients is generally larger, and of course, is tactfully omitted. This type of consultant, incidentally, is the most prone to make recommendations that are not feasible or which do not take into account the peculiarities of a particular business. At best, the prospective client would be taking pot luck.

Summary

Although most of the examples we've used relate to medium-sized companies, the principles apply also to small and large corporations. We believe the reader will share our conclusion that developing a higher rate of successful client-consultant relationships depends primarily on what safeguards the client takes initially. Despite the fact that the principle of caveat emptor applies in full force to this relationship, the company that feels the need for outside help ought not be deterred from seeking it.

A one-time expenditure to organize an on-going operation or a facet of management can be an extremely profitable investment. Nothing in this article should be inferred to discourage such investments. The inference, rather, is an exhortation to make them judiciously with a minimum of risk and a maximum of return. This judicious process starts with a recognition of the potential pitfalls.

Charles H. Ford is an author, lecturer, and consultant on organizational problems.

Chapter 2

Explorations in Consulting-Client Relationships

Chris Argyris

I should like to explore the role of the consultant based upon an analysis of two cases of a particular consultant group. Obviously one cannot generalize very much from such restricted data. This descriptive and exploratory report has as its objective the delineation of some issues and the generation of hypotheses. It marks the first stage of a long-range program whose ultimate goal is the development of appropriate models to understand the client-consultant relationship and its impact on organizational change and development.

The Nature of the Data Available

The consultants studied have had at least several years of experience as a team offering consulting advice to any unit within the corporation which requests it. Typically, they make notes of all their activities during each day in the field. These notes vary greatly in detail and scope. Although the policy followed is to record one's notes as soon as possible, there are times when there is a delay of several days.

I was given access to all the personal notes of all the consultants. Also, all the files were open for my use and study. According to my count, I read over three thousand pages of notes and research reports. I was given the freedom to interview anyone that I wished on the team or at the plants. Because of the exploratory nature of the study, I limited my interviews and discussions to the consultants. Although I had the complete cooperation of everyone, the nature of the data available does not permit us to reach any conclusions. The most that we can do is to raise questions for further research and indulge in some hypothesizing as to what might have happened if the consultants and the clients had behaved differently.

I have selected two cases from the files which I believe best illustrate the problems which I wish to discuss. The selection is, therefore, *not* a random one. It is specifically loaded in the direction of cases that illustrate the difficulties which consultants face. Consequently, the reader should not infer that the material accurately represents the competence, activities, and successes of the consultants.

Reproduced by permission of the Society for Applied Anthropology from *Human* Organization, Vol. 20, No. 3 (1961).

The Values of the Consultant Group

If we are to ascertain the effectiveness of the consultants, it is important to learn their objectives. What are they offering the client. Once having ascertained their objectives, then we may explore the degree to which they are able to achieve them. We may hypothesize that the consultants' effectiveness will tend to increase as the degree to which they achieve their objective increases.

The consultants studied offer professional assistance in the field of human relations. They view their overall objective as helping an organization solve its problems in such a way that it becomes more competent in solving the same or a similar class of problems without the continued help of the consultants. Thus we can ask at the end of the paper if the clients have resolved their problems in such a way that they no longer need the consultants.

There is another dimension along which insights can be obtained regarding the effectiveness of the consultants. They believe that there is a hierarchy of values whose fulfillment will tend to enhance the effectiveness of human relationships within organizations. These values are particularly relevant to our study. They may be outlined as follows:

1. Two important and interrelated components of administrative competence may be described as technical, intellective competence and interpersonal competence. Both levels of competence are important. If either or both is low, or if either is significantly higher than the other, administrative difficulties will tend to arise.*
2. Interpersonal competence, the consultants believe tends to increase as the executive:

   a. Becomes more aware of himself and of his impact upon others.
   b. Solves human problems in such a way that the same or a similar class of problems do not recur.

3. These two components of interpersonal competence will tend to increase as executives are able in their relationships to:

   a. Give and receive feedback about self and others so as to create minimal defensiveness in self and others.
   b. Own, and to help others own their feelings, values, and attitudes.

---

*Empirical research will be required to define the point at which interpersonal competence is low or the point where the gap between the two is too large.

    c. Remain open to new values and attitudes and help others to experience
      the same.
    d. Experiment with new values and attitudes and help others to do the
      same.[†]

From this we may hypothesize that the consultants will perceive that they are
achieving their objective as the clients begin to give and receive feedback with
minimal defensiveness to own their feelings, etc. But, as we shall see in a moment, in order for the consultants to be of help to the client along these dimensions they (the consultants) must behave according to these values. The consultants must behave *genuinely,* which we may define as behaving in accordance
with one's values.[‡] But to behave genuinely is not enough. It is important to behave genuinely in such a way that others (in this case the clients) have freedom to
behave genuinely. Whenever human relationships are established where genuineness is possible on the part of *both* parties, they may be defined as *authentic.* Individuals cannot be authentic; authenticity is a property of interpersonal
relationships. In our terms, the consultant hopes to influence his client to learn
to establish more authentic relationships within the firm. In order to accomplish
this, the consultant must also strive to establish authentic relationships in his relations with the client.

The Dilemma of the Consultant

Formal organizational strategy tends to reward communication, openness, experimentation on the rational level. It tends to penalize openness, leveling, and
experimentation on the interpersonal and emotional levels.[1] This, in turn, tends
to decrease the participants' interpersonal competence within the organization.[§]

[†]The major activities of the consultant group reside in the area of increasing interpersonal
effectiveness within the organization. Because the consultants focus in this area, it
should not be interpreted to mean that the consultants do not feel that there are other
areas which are as relevant to administrative competence and organizational development. The consultants recognize the importance of environmental and organizational
factors and do include these in their studies whenever they feel they are relevant to the
solution of the problem.

[‡]The concept of genuineness is, I believe, similar to and most certainly stimulated by Dr.
Carl Roger's concept of congruence.

[§]The degree to which each of these generalizations holds in real life is a matter of empirical study. I am predicting, however, that the overall trend would be in the direction implied in the propositions.

The emphasis upon rationality tends to create an organizational culture in which feelings are considered to be "bad," "immature," "irrational," and many times irrelevant. For example, in recent study of a top management group (N = 18), all but one reported that:

—Personal feelings should be kept out of group meetings.
—If people did become emotional it would be the leader's responsibility to bring them back to the facts being discussed.
—If the personal feelings continued the leader should call off the meeting and talk to the individuals involved separately.[2]

The point I am trying to make is that it is not possible for this type of consultant to help an organization deal with its interpersonal difficulties and with those organizational problems that have an interpersonal base without helping the clients to deal with feelings and emotions. Yet these are the very factors that the clients would tend to find painful, and which they have "learned" to consider as signs of "immaturity" and "incompetence."

A consultant therefore, who wishes to help an organization learn to solve its own interpersonal difficulties is faced with a serious dilemma. He believes that in order for him to be of help he may have to ask the client to consider values that are fundamentally different from those upon which the organization, its controls, and his leadership pattern are based. For example, instead of considering feelings and emotions as irrelevant in administration (as is the case of most of industry) he sees them as being central to the resolution of human problems and the enhancement of openness, accurate information flow, trust, and an attitude of experimentation and risk taking.[2]

As such, the consultant will probably be threatening to the members of the organization. Quite understandably, the members will tend to question seriously the necessity for the reduction of hostility, tension, interpersonal rivalries, etc. They may be even more skeptical about the consultant's assumption that openness, trust, feedback, experimentation, etc., if increased, will tend to alleviate significantly some of the problems that they have come to perceive as part of organizational life.

One of the best ways a client has to test the effectiveness of the consultant's ideas is to see if his "product" works. In most cases the client has to wait until the consultant is finished before he can make such a judgment. However, in the case of the consultant offering to increase the effectiveness of the human relationships, the client can actually begin to test the validity of the consultant's approach from the outset of the relationship. If the consultant's views of effective human relationship are valid and effective, the client reasons, I should be able to evaluate the consultant by seeing if he (the consultant) uses them while attempting to help the organization change and develop. If the consultant does not use his views to stimulate effective changes, why should the client adopt them in his relationships within the organization? Moreover, the client can increase the difficulty of the test which the consultant has to pass by simply increasing the forcefulness with which he apparently adheres to his ideas and "rejects" the consultant's. If, as the consultant attempts to help the client change, he does not behave consistently with his ideas and values then why should the client use these ideas and values?

The consultant is in a very difficult position. If he behaves according to his ideas and values, he stands a good chance of being a threat to the client. He could be asked to leave. If he decides to behave even temporarily in accordance with the client's values, he may be accepted but he runs a serious risk of failing to change and develop.

Case A

Let us begin with the consultants feeding back their results of a systematic interview-questionnaire diagnosis to the top management of plant A. The comments emphasized such findings as: (1) the employees report a barrier between themselves and the management, (2) the employees feel uninformed, and consequently (3) tend to feel confused and "left out" while at the same time, (4) they fear to communicate upward their feelings of mistrust. These findings were digested by the top management for several weeks before they invited the consultants to the plant for further consultations. A meeting was held where the results were again discussed.

Two of the consultants reported their impressions about the meeting:

Consultant A

This meeting was interesting in that the plant manager was neither outspoken nor defensive. We reviewed some of the highlights of the findings and certain members of the management committee discussed these in the meeting in his office. The meeting did not have too much spark until one of the young technical men started to express resentment in terms of being critical, partly of the accuracy of our findings, and partly of the fact that some of their employees were disloyal in the type of comments they made. Otherwise, most of the management committee seemed to be accepting the findings in the report, although admittedly they were not very vocal in expressing suggestions as to how to bring improvements.

Consultant B

At this meeting the newest department head was most angrily defensive about the report. His clear expression made it possible to focus the issues, openly face the fact that the report was a "hot potato," and also that necessity which fully justifies management actions could produce some unwanted results.

The meeting ended with the issue of what to do next up in the air. No one quite knew how the plant manager felt. There was an assumption that he would make a decision, but he did not make any.

The Consultants Do Not Behave According to Their Values

The consultants as well as many of the subordinates reported that they felt frustrated and had a sense of incompleteness as a result of the plant manager's silence. However, this frustration and concern was not communicated. They were not being open or leveling. Instead someone asked if the results should be fed back to the next lower level of management. The discussion was guarded and most looked toward the plant manager for his views. He decided, and the subordinates "agreed," that it would be best to give only a summary or "light" report of the findings.

This was done. The consultants attended the meeting where the data were fed back to the lower management in a summary form. They reported that,

. . . the reaction of the supervisors at this point is that the survey had not accomplished very much.

However, added the consultants, the supervisors were not too disappointed because,

. . . their expectations had not been too high that any public reporting of the data would be any more explicit than it was.

Here we see the consultants exposed to a situation where they chose not to behave according to their values. The plant manager, they reasoned, was not ready to discuss his feelings about the report, no less his interpersonal impact upon those at the meeting.

The Impact of the Consultants' Behavior

The immediate "pay off" for the consultants is that they are still in the "good graces" of the plant manager. But this is obtained at a cost. The first part of the cost is that the plant manager has living evidence that under stress the consultants do not tend to behave in accordance with their values. On the contrary, they use the values of the client-system. Why then should he change? A second part of the cost is that those present at the meeting also see that the consultants behave in accordance with the values of the client-system. Understandably, they may also have questions about the validity and practicality of the consultants' values.

Moreover, they can also interpret the consultants' actions as being submissive toward the plant manager. If this is the case, they may reason, the plant manager may have the consultants under his control. Perhaps they had best be careful in "leveling" with the consultants. Finally we note from the consultants' reports that the subordinates who viewed the feedback at a separate meeting concluded that "nothing had changed or would come of the research." Therefore, as some suggested later on, they concluded that the consultants might be "on the top management side" or at least certainly associated with the status quo.

To summarize, the costs for the consultants of going along with the client-system values seem to be fourfold. All the members of the client-system may begin to have decreased confidence in the consultants and especially in the values that they represent. Second, the subordinates may begin to view the consultants as agents of the plant manager. Third, the consultants, unknowingly let themselves and their research create an administrative situation in which the client-system values and the status quo are reinforced. Fourth, the clients may have learned that if enough pressure is placed upon the consultants, they can be manipulated to change their values. This conclusion may make the clients feel more secure in that they can "control" the consultants. However, this "control" can also act to increase deeper fears and insecurities, because it is not comforting to know that one's consultant can be as non-genuine as the client he is attempting to help.

Another alternative action for the consultants would have been to behave in accordance with their values. They could have told the plant manager during the meeting that they felt a sense of frustration and incompleteness. They might have asked the group if others felt as they did. Finally, they could have, again at the group meeting (or later in private if necessary) predicted for the plant manager some of the impacts outlined above. This could help him to see more clearly his impact upon the organization and prevent the reinforcement of the feelings of being left out, mistrusted, etc., reported in the diagnostic survey. More about this in the final section.

The Client-System Values Become Reinforced

Returning to the consultants, their notes suggest that they were aware of not behaving according to their values. However, they reported, this was necessary if they were to be asked to remain in the organization. They also reported that since they did not upset the plant manager they were in a better position to be of help to him.

The consultants held a meeting with the plant manager. They reported that they were able to convince the plant manager, "that a job lay ahead to develop the subordinates" especially in "leveling," "openness," "interpersonal impact," etc. Note that the plant manager was not told that he also may need such help. Moreover, the consultants suggested the establishment of a "steering committee" to help plan the laboratory.

The plant manager agreed. A Steering Committee was created whose task it was to examine the survey results to explore what ought to be done for organization improvement. As a result of the committee's meetings a decision was reached to hold a three-day workshop program where the survey results would be studied in detail by all the management to stimulate self-analysis.

The planning of the meetings was masterminded by one of the consultants. He wrote that he felt he had to engineer the programs since the committee lacked the concept of a "laboratory" program. He continued that he:

> . . . is able to move them in the direction of the laboratory design.

The consultant being quite secure and extremely competent also noted,

> . . . in this respect our meeting had been almost comic. I had insisted that the program was the Committee's or the management's and that my role was only to help them design it. However, I consistently felt that I should be designing the program since they didn't know how to. Of course, this eventually worked out into my doing so.

Thus we see that, in order to take some action, the consultants again had to behave in ways which reflect the values of the client system. They influenced the plant manager to approve training which he and few others in the client-system fully understood. Moreover, they created a Steering Committee to give the subordinates a greater feeling of participation. Yet they admittedly manipulated the members to go in the direction that they (the consultants) desired. All this was done in order "to get results."

This need, on the part of the consultants, to "get on with the job" is exactly what the clients desire. They can use it to manipulate the consultant to become responsible for planning and carrying out the change programs. The dependent relationship that the client has with the top management, he (the client) now creates with the consultant.

An example for the consultant's report that illustrates the points being made is:

> Members of the Steering Committee made it clear [to the consultant] they felt some pressure to get going, the pressure coming partly from their own feelings of frustration about lack of decision, and in part because they thought management was breathing down their necks with respect to some proposals. The comment was made in a joking manner that we'd better get something going in order to have something to submit to the manager. The time of the next committee meeting was set up at this time and I was invited to attend.

In this example, the committee tries to communicate their sense of frustration and urgency to the consultant. However, they also imply to the consultant that, along with them, *he* is now responsible for the success or failure of the project. If the consultant accepts the responsibility, he has unwittingly placed himself in a traditional leadership position within the group. Under these conditions, the consultant soon begins to feel that he *is* responsible for doing the creative thinking about what the committee ought to discuss during the next meeting.

Apparently this is what happens. The consultant, after listening to the above, develops an excellent list of questions:

—What is the plant manager's image of the desired direction which the company should go?
—How are the goals used by the people at headquarters to whom the plant manager reports, department heads and superintendents, operating management, and non-management?
—How much motivation is there to carry them out?
—How about people's skills for carrying them out effectively?
—What is required for movement toward these goals:
    By the management group?
    The work force?
    What obstacles can be anticipated?
—How to communicate the committee's report and recommendations to the manager?
—What is the first event in the improvement program?

These are important questions. However, in defining them as an agenda for the clients, the consultant becomes responsible for the group's diagnosis. In taking the initiative, the consultant again influences the clients to become dependent upon him. Such a requirement is congruent with the client's expectations and values, but not with the consultant's.

One wonders what would have happened if the consultant asked the group members why they were telling him about their failures and pressures. If, as he feels, this is an attempt by the clients to induce him to internalize their pressures and anxieties, he might profitably raise the issue. This would be an excellent opportunity for the committee to begin to become aware that they will seriously impair the consultant's potential contribution if they try to make him behave according to their values. If he is to be of help, he ought not be controlled by the very values which are the cause of their problems. Assuming these problems are worked through, then the consultant can help the group to develop its own list of questions. In doing so he places the emphasis upon the clients developing their own questions. He shows, by his actions, that he believes (1) clients can, through such activity, learn much about one another, their organizations, and the requirements of effective group problem solving, (2) that it is the group members who will have to take the action and thus should participate in the diagnosis,

(3) which, in turn, would begin the process of decreasing the clients' dependence upon the consultant.

Returning to our case, the consultants actually planned and held several different types of short laboratories. The attendees reported positive feelings about the programs. Generally they reported that they had been helped to understand one another's job, as well as to set the ground work for some concrete changes to be made in the practices as well as the organization of work. The data available suggested that some of these changes were carried out and other changes were planned and also carried out.

Although the men reported new and enlarged awareness about the difficulties of their fellow managers in getting the job done, the data suggested that this behavior did not change very much. Also, there was evidence that the enthusiasm for change was highest when the consultants were present. This sign of dependence of the clients upon the consultants did not disturb the plant manager. Indeed, he reported satisfaction that concrete tasks of important value to the plant were being accomplished.

The plant manager had no reason to be disappointed in the process by which these jobs were being done. It was the same one that he used in his relationships with the subordinates. The fact that the manager had established dependent relationships with the consultants did not displease him as long as actions were being taken. The consultants are now being perceived by the plant manager as resource people to be used by his subordinates in order to accomplish specific tasks. Little thought is being given to the original objective of helping the clients examine their basic values and interpersonal relationships. It is interesting to note that the consultants were lauded by the plant manager to their (the consultants') superior because:

> . . . they were not forcing themselves upon the plant and letting themselves be used as the plant members saw fit.

One of the consultants was not content with the compliment. He wrote:

> While this compliment sounds encouraging, I still have some feelings of uneasiness about the relationship. I think the main source of it now is that when I call the plant manager he is usually, in fact, almost always tied up at a meeting. Although I ask that he call me back he seldom does so. One day—I arranged an appointment with him to review how things were going. However, although I was there for a full half day, I was able to spend only approximately forty-five minutes with him, and this between telephone calls and other forms of interruption.

This is an excellent illustration of the human relationships which are typical of the client system. One possible reason is that the need for the consultant is now not as great. The plant manager may feel that he has received as much help as he can from the consultant. Another possibility is that, since the consultants have been incorporated and become so much a part of the client system, they no longer can put into use the skills and knowledge that they have regarding opening and facilitating effective change. Moreover, if the client can no longer see much difference between the consultants and the other members of the client system, there is no major reason to show any high interest in them. Finally, from research in clinical psychology and psychotherapy, we may hypothesize that a client can decrease his confidence in the consultant if he feels that he can manipulate the consultant to accept his (the client's) values and goals. A client, will probably not respect an individual who, in the face of stress, takes on the values and norms of the client culture. That is the very reason the client needs help.

We could continue to describe other events. They would primarily illustrate that the consultants had achieved great success in helping the organization accomplish certain specific tasks. However, the success does not seem as great in the area of interpersonal effectiveness. The consultants began their relationships with a strategy to behave according to the values of the client system until they had achieved acceptance by the top management and helped the clients to accomplish specific work tasks. This did indeed win compliments. However, it also created a chain reaction where the plant manager and the other clients induced the consultants to behave according to the client-system values. The consultants were never able to break away from this chain reaction. Although they were able to help some of the clients to explore their values, the impact was never very great. In short, they became "accepted" by becoming *a part of* the client system. They were not accepted as consultants with a set of different values whose effectiveness the client-system ought to explore seriously.

Case B

The second case begins with the consultants' explorations at a particular plant. Upon conducting a reconnaissance, the consultants concluded that, since the management group was relatively free of suspicion of consultants, the latter might be able to create a program which would help "to free" the clients (management and employees) in such a way as to release their potential. Moreover, because the organization was relatively small, they might be able to offer a two-pronged tailor-made program which could help achieve the management's objectives. The first prong was an

. . . emphasis on organization improvement rather than crisis or criticism.

The consultants believed that such an emphasis would steer away from the plant's history of difficult problems and relations thereby decreasing the clients' defensiveness and simultaneously emphasizing progress to be made in the future. In the opinion of the consultants such a strategy would lead to minimal client resistance. In the consultants' opinion this would make it easier for the clients to accept the idea of an organization improvement project.

The second prong was the consultants' desire to help the top management to:

1. Get [their] people to take a responsible lead in this work so that it is not just [top management's] program.

2. Prove that

   a. Their objective is a desirable change.
   b. They have confidence in the organization.
   c. They are not criticizing but are seeking consulting help to build for the future.
   d. They are not trying to import "any packaged program."

It is interesting to note a contradiction in the consultant's behavior. On the one hand, there is the consultants' desire to help the plant manager make this *his* program so that *his* people would, in time, make it *their* program. On the other hand is the fact that the consultants develop the prognosis with little or no participation from the clients. Assuming that the prognosis is valid, and assuming that it is accepted by the management, then one can predict that the plant manager will tend to develop a dependency relationship with the consultants. The plant manager will tend to feel that the program is not his but the consultant's, to the extent that he accepts what they tell him they think he ought to do. One may also hypothesize that, if this happens, it will decrease the probability that the subordinates will feel this is their program.

Another example of how the consultants tend to control the relationship with the client is when they decide unilaterally that the plant manager

. . . might consider improving upward communication; to signal ways he wants to operate.

Since the consultants believe the problems lay at the top, it would be necessary, they reason, to reassure the plant manager of his effectiveness and give him a chance to talk out his problems and ideas. Thus, once the top jobs are clarified as to scope and duties, it would be possible to reach out for new ideas.

If this strategy is valid, then the plant manager will be moved in the right direction *because of the consultants' prognostic* skills. But, the problem of the plant manager is to improve his own prognostic skills. A way for him to become more effective and simultaneously to decrease his need for the consultants would be for them to help him learn how to diagnose as effectively as they do.

The Projected Survey

The consultants recommended to the plant manager that a survey program be conducted to help the management people:

> . . . dig out and clarify their own goals and then find ways to attain them.

They also pointed out that:

> . . . the consultants would act as if they were outside consultants . . . All data would be for the local plant only. None would be communicated to higher authorities without clearance with the authorities at the local level.

The plant manager accepted the project. He suggested that the consultants explain it to Mr. Brown, an "old timer," who, according to the plant manager, feels hurt because he expected to become a plant manager but never made it. The plant manager also suggested that the projected survey be discussed with the top management committee (hereafter known as the committee). The consultants agreed.

Mr. Brown apparently resisted the consultants and their program. He questioned if the people would tell the truth. The consultants decided not to help Mr. Brown explore his fears toward them, research, and the past. Rather they attempted to allay his fears by pointing out that they were not interested in looking backward, in studying the mistakes of previous managers or in studying the plant's morale, but rather that the focus would be on the future.

One may question the effectiveness of asking Mr. Brown to forget fears which are related to the past by assuring him that the consultants will do so. The consultants note, among themselves:

> At the end of the meeting, Mr. Brown appeared to understand what the consultants were going to do from the point of view of the procedures involved in the survey. There is no evidence of support for the idea . . . the notion of organization improvement was not accepted or even understood by Mr. Brown.

Nor did they communicate to him their impression that in their opinion he is:

> . . . an incessant talker, oblivious to listener reaction, and very insensitive to his own needs and power.

This diagnosis may be correct. But is it not equally correct that one reason that the consultants did not "level" with Brown (a value which they hold) was because they were responding to their own needs. The consultants probably felt that it was best not to "level" with Mr. Brown lest this explode their projected survey.

The following day, the consultants held their meeting with the committee. They were introduced by the plant manager who told his subordinates: (1) that he wanted the consultants to be of help, (2) emphasized that he believes there is potential gain in having an outside group observe and lend assistance, and (3) by being particularly careful to say that, in his opinion, there was not necessarily anything wrong at the plant, but under the best of circumstances one can look for ways to do a better job.

How helpful is this introduction of the plant manager to the consultants and to the clients? How is this project going to become the subordinates' if they come to a meeting where (1) they are told to accept the consultants, (2) they sense the plant manager's defensiveness when he says that the consultants are not looking for anything to criticize, and (3) that they are told the organization is not doing an effective job? How helpful is this approach if everyone concerned feels that there *is* something wrong? If there are not weaknesses why hold the survey? Will not this approach be perceived by the subordinates as more of the top management "diplomatic talk that is always going on?" If so, what will be their view of the consultants if this management nonauthenticity is sanctioned by them? Is this not an opportunity to test the consultants to see if they really mean that "openness" is a good thing? If so, then the consultants tend to enhance the difficulties since they not only refrain from exploring the problem above but they sanction it by taking the same approach. They emphasize that they are not interested in the past, that they are not making a checkup of employee morale, and that they are interested in the future, and how the consultants might help the management better to achieve their goals for the future.

If the consultants want the subordinates to make this their project, then why do they not find out if the subordinates want the same? Moreover, how will they be perceived by the subordinates when the findings are released and the majority of them deal with their morale? Is the consultants' strategy more of a response to the plant manager's anxieties about getting the project accepted than a logically thought through plan which takes into account the total management group?

The consultants reported that the committee attitude appeared, on the surface, excellent, and that almost immediate joviality

. . . was used to mask feelings and keep conflict from becoming overt.

Here is an incisive hypothesis but the consultants do not explore its possible validity with the clients. The consultants also note that the committee does not function as a decision-making body. The consultants would not think of resisting the plant manager's proposal with the possible exception of Mr. Brown.

Why are these hypotheses not checked? One reason may be that the consultants want to refrain from doing anything which will upset the committee and doom the survey. Another may be that they believe that they ought not to begin to confront the committee until after the survey when the consultants will know much more about the clients. Finally, it may be that the consultants, temporarily acting as researchers, do not want to disturb the situation. However, subsequent data will show that the consultants continue this strategy after the survey is completed.

One interesting situation occurred during the survey. One manager reported to the plant manager that his people were worried over the possibility of holding a survey. Instead of helping the plant manager to resolve the issue, the consultants met with the reluctant group. They told them the same information that they gave the committee. Apparently (and we shall see later, only temporarily) the reluctant group "accepted" the survey. One wonders, for example, what might happen if, instead of doing the above, the consultant stated to the group:

> I am told that you are concerned about the survey. It makes us feel good that you raise these concerns openly. What kinds of information do you wish from me? How can I be of help to you?

The consultant might also ask if the group could help him understand the degree to which their concerns are shared by others, and what hunches they may have to deal with the problem.

The Results of the Survey

As in the previous case, a carefully planned systematic questionnaire and interview study was conducted. After feeding back the results to the plant manager the consultants suggested a series of courses of action that were indicated from the survey.

1. There is evidence of resignation if not a feeling of helplessness on the part of management.
2. Steps need to be taken to galvanize or stimulate the organization to new levels of spirit and enthusiasm.
3. Mr. Brown ought to be changed because the problems that his behavior causes could prevent the organization from carrying out any proposals that it evolves.
4. The number of levels of management need to be reexamined to see if they are all necessary.
5. To help the management look more creatively at what they can do both as individuals and as members of a team. Also to get them to feel that they *do* have the power, influence, and responsibility for getting it done.

In presenting the prognosis the consultants helped to focus the plant manager's attention on the steps that they felt were necessary if the organization was to improve. They were apparently most anxious to induce the plant manager to do something with Mr. Brown, who they felt was a thorn in the organization's as well as the consultants' side.

A meeting was then held with the committee to feed back the results. With the exception of Mr. Brown, the committee did not resist the results. Mr. Brown raised questions about the validity of the study and according to the consultant made a bit of a nuisance of himself. One of the consultants

. . . purposely took a seat next to Mr. Brown in order to restrain him from talking a great deal by putting his hand on Mr. Brown's arm or otherwise diverting his attention.

Although there was no overt disagreement by other committee members, the consultants left the meeting questioning the committee's probable degree of commitment to work through the results. Perhaps if the consultants had not viewed Mr. Brown's behavior as a thorn but as stemming from a person who is so anxious that he breaks the barriers of secrecy and tells the consultants how he (and perhaps others) feel, the consultants might have utilized his charges about the research to learn more about the other members' feelings. Such a step would also have helped the consultants begin to reach one of the objectives that they defined as crucial; namely, to help the committee work through their reluctance to be open.

Upon the return to the organization for further discussion with the committee the consultants explored plans which the plant manager might consider to cope with Mr. Brown. The plans became quite detailed to the point where the consultants considered suggesting a new organizational position for Mr. Brown; one which would, in effect, greatly decrease his power and control. From the consultants' viewpoint, this action was necessary if the plant was to progress.

Perhaps this was the case. However, if the plant manager accepted the plans, the consultants would make the plant manager more dependent upon them because one of the plant manager's basic problems was that he needed to become an effective diagnostician of such difficult situations. In filtering out the alternatives and presenting those with greatest merit, the consultants were preventing the plant manager from learning more about these crucial steps in the decision-making process. If the plant manager agreed with the consultants, then he would surely tend to increase his dependence upon them. Yet, the consultants believed that they must help the plant manager overcome his dependence upon them. Moreover, the consultants wished that the committee be less dependent on the plant manager. But, why should the committee believe the consultants' view that dependence is bad when they see that their boss is being made dependent upon the consultants?

Returning to Mr. Brown, the plant manager accepted the consultants' recommendations. As soon as Mr. Brown left for a vacation the plant manager announced to the management the realignment of duties which radically changed Mr. Brown's duties. Exactly why this decision was made after Mr. Brown left is not clear. One can only hypothesize that the plant manager must have felt quite uncomfortable in making the decision and thus waited until Mr. Brown left. Whatever the reason, it seems that the consultants should have helped the plant manager to explore the impact of the decision. To be sure, the survey results suggest that the management group is not particularly in favor of Mr. Brown. But to demote a man in this way is to provide living evidence to the management that the plant manager and the consultants are not able to be open when making difficult decisions. What guarantee do any of the managers have that their jobs might not be changed in the same way someday when they are on vacation?

As one might predict, upon his return to the plant Mr. Brown was astounded to hear the news of the change. He became depressed and hostile. From then on Mr. Brown evidenced increased hostility toward the plant manager. Mr. Brown became more withdrawn but made one final attempt to be open with his hostile feelings. He refused to listen and resisted. The consultants dealt with this defensiveness by suggesting if Mr. Brown did not cooperate, the consultants might be forced to leave the organization. Mr. Brown reacted with "violent hostility." No other comments exist about the meeting. The consultants noted, however, that since that meeting Mr. Brown promised the plant manager to cooperate until his retirement.

Thus Mr. Brown was neutralized and the consultants felt an important obstacle was removed.

The Decrease in Management Interest

However, it was not long before a new problem seemed to arise. The committees created to work through the survey results and suggest concrete action were, for the most part, ineffective. At the same time, the plant manager reported to the consultants that

. . . plant people are looking upon [them] as spies.

One employee even asked

. . . is it a good idea to have them around so much?

Apparently, the consultants did not take any action to explore these rumors. About a month later, the plant manager visited the consultants and reported "discouragement with the program." He said it has slowed down for various reasons: a main one being that less time was being spent by the consultants at the plant.

He stated that he was looking for some new ideas because of the loss of momentum in the program.

The consultants diagnosed the decrease in interest as

> . . caused by the fact that these [management] groups could not come up with any more problems and did not see any responsibility beyond problem definition.

The consultants apparently do not believe that they might be partially responsible for the lack of responsibility. After all, *they do* condone behavior on the part of the plant manager which is unilateral and punitive (Mr. Brown's case). Also, it *is* the consultants and the plant manager who want the study. Why should the shop feel responsible for something that they never really accepted?

According to the consultants, the few departments which needed help least were holding the more effective meetings. The poorer departments did not seem to be motivated to hold further meetings. After some visits by the consultants, the meetings were begun again. However, the consultants reported that there was not as much openness as they had hoped for.

After one meeting, a member told one of the consultants that the group wondered why he attended the meetings and wished they knew what they planned to do with his observations. They feared that he might report upwards. The consultant reported that he was

> . . . too confused after this meeting, because he was beginning to question whether his own behavior, as practiced in the meetings, was appropriate.

This is not an easy conclusion to contemplate, and it illustrates the internal security of the consultant. One wishes that he would have considered discussing his feelings with the management group. If he had been able to be open with them about their relationship, would not this have provided the clients with a rich living experience of how useful it is to explore one's inadequacies with a group of peers which provides a supportive climate? How is it possible for the consultants to expect the clients "to level" if they find it difficult to do so?

A New Change Program

Apparently, the consultants decided not to discuss their problems with their clients (e.g., being perceived as spies). Instead they decided that the next step should be a new workshop program.

In the meantime the plant manager again told the consultants that he was discouraged in the way the departmental meetings were dwindling. Perhaps, this would be an ideal moment for the consultants to invite the plant manager to become more aware of his dependency upon the consultants. It may also help the consultants to become more aware of their role in the problem. Moreover, if the plant manager experiences "the experts" raising questions about their effectiveness, he may begin to feel less anxiety about discussing his own difficulties.

Instead the consultants suggested that the plant manager might raise the question with the department heads as to whether or not they wished to continue. The plant manager replied that although he wished them to continue, he did not wish to legislate the group meetings.

The consultants reported that their impression was that the plant manager was attempting to get them to return to the plant and rejuvenate the program. For reasons not mentioned, the consultants do not use this ideal opportunity to explore their views of the plant manager's dependence upon them. Instead they suggest that they meet with some of the plant people to design a new program.

The consultants decided that a new training program might be useful because:

> The consultants after this meeting discussed between themselves the merits of continuing versus discontinuing the group meetings. It appeared that most groups were by now under a good deal of tension. They could not seem to see clearly any responsibility beyond problem definition and felt they had exhausted problem defining. If they could not move to the next phase of exploring solutions and taking action, it might be well to discontinue the meetings. After several days of consideration, the consultants decided that the two problems that were a contribution to the problem of group movement were: (1) Inadequate understanding of the objectives of the program (the objectives had been becoming clearer since the survey) and (2) Lack of skilled leadership in meetings (group functions were not being performed). The notion at this point was that if the groups could be helped to continue meeting, a number of desirable consequences could be achieved. First, plant problems would continue to get worked on a lower level; second, groups and individuals would get greater sensitivity to problems of group functioning, and third, the desire of top management, especially the manager, to move groups toward a better understanding of the goal of greater self-determination at lower levels would be pursued.

A program was evolved by the consultants with the overall objective of developing within the plant an atmosphere in which all members (1) feel a greater responsibility for influencing the future of the organization, and (2) feel they can influence this future constructively.

In a way the program is ironic. The employees are going to be induced to become more responsible, yet they are not really being offered an opportunity to develop a program to enhance their own feelings of self worth if they are given little opportunity to express their perceived need for the program or their ideas about the program and the kind of human experience it should be.

One can predict that if the program is composed of many experiences that involve the clients, and if these experiences are deeply meaningful to them, then they may increase their motivation. If this happens, one can predict further, however, that the "charge" given to them by the program will tend to wear off and a new program will be needed. If such is the case, then the consulting relationship has succeeded in shifting the dependence of the clients from their boss to the consultants.

Discussion and Conclusions

First, we must emphasize that the study is limited to those consulting relationships designed to increase the effectiveness of human interpersonal relationships within the organization. A consultant operating at this level tends to find himself in a major dilemma. It appears that if he tends to go along with the traditional values implicit in the formal organizational structure, he tends to set off a chain of events that have varying consequences. On the one hand, he does not tend to be very threatening to the client system. He is usually liked and accepted as "being one of the boys" and "part of the culture."

It also appears that the unintended consequences of this strategy are that the consultant soon finds that he has worked himself into the role of planning, creating, and implementing change. Moreover, he behaves toward the clients in the same way as the clients tend to behave toward their subordinates, i.e., in a directing, controlling manner. This relationship is usually well known by the subordinates. They, in fact, tend to use and go along with the consultant in this relationship because they can control him and protect themselves. For example, they gladly take on the reciprocal role of being dependent upon the consultant. This leads to the consultant becoming primarily responsible for change that may occur. Under these conditions changes *are* made in the organization. However, the quality and usefulness of these changes largely a result of the consultants' ingenuity. Thus, the organization has become dependent upon the consultants.

In traditional consulting practice, consultants who permitted themselves to get into such a position would probably be evaluated quite highly. After all, they have been able to get the organization to make progress in clearly defined and observable ways. Moreover, management acknowledges their value in helping to achieve certain crucial objectives. It may be argued that, given the realities of organizational life and the "human encounter" in which the consultants are immersed, this is probably as well as one can expect the consultants to perform. However, as we have seen, the success tends to be short lived and relegated primarily to certain non-human changes in interpersonal relationships and basic values which were originally planned never materialize.

The Marginal Role of the Consultants

In an attempt to help us to begin to understand the complexity of the consulting role it might be useful to explore it more systematically. What follows is an attempt to relate aspects of the consultative process to certain basic psycho-social concepts. However, appropriate examples will be used from the data available.

To the extent that the client's present value system is different from the one the consultant represents, the consultant places himself in a marginal position because he will work in a system whose values and norms are different form those of his own team. To make matters more difficult, most client systems are usually composed of two sub-systems. On the one hand, is the group which desires to see their organization change. In most cases this sub-system is composed of those in management who invited the consultants. On the other hand are all those who are either not aware of a necessity for change, disagree as to the proper direction for change, or resist any attempt at change. To the extent that any one or a combination of these factors exists, the consultant will find himself confronted with another set of factors that will tend to reinforce and magnify the role of a "marginal man."

From the research on the role of "marginal man" it is possible to infer that the consultant will tend to experience the following kinds of problems.

☐ Although he accepts the management's request to conduct diagnoses of the employees' world, the employees may choose not to inform him about the very problems he is supposed to help resolve.

In the cases just presented, no lower-level employees are included in the study. However, there are numerous examples where the lower-level supervisors tend to withhold information. For example, in case A the lower-level supervisors were not willing to discuss the difficulties which they felt with the leadership pattern of the top management echelons. They also resisted talking about the question, "How am I doing?" which was a question in which top management was most interested. Similarly, in Case B the supervisors had some serious questions about the role of the home office in the life of their organization. However, they did not feel free to discuss them openly with the top management. (They did discuss them, however, with the consultants.)

☐ Although the consultant is asked by management to help them, they may not inform him of their informal activities, especially those that they keep from one another. Usually, these are the activities that are the sources of many organizational problems.

It is difficult to cite examples of this condition because our raw data came primarily from the consultants' reports. However, there are a few examples that can be used where the top management withheld important information from the consultants. In Case A the management group met informally for four hours to discuss one of the consultants' questionnaires without inviting him to participate. Later the consultant learned that the management group never accepted phase X of his plan although for many months they acted as if they accepted it. In Case B the plant manager communicated confidential survey data about an employee to people outside the organization.

☐ The consultant could experience frustration and conflict if he is asked by members in either sub-culture to participate in activities that the other does not sanction. To the extent that he feels "required" to comply the consultant will tend to increase the probabilities of jeopardizing his position in the organization.

According to the consultants they experienced conflict numerous times when top management asked them to make evaluations of subordinates. They felt the subordinates would not approve these discussions. Equally conflicting, but not as numerous, were times when the subordinates attempted "to pump" the consultants as to what they were learning from the "top Brass."

☐ The consultant will tend to experience conflict and frustration to the extent that the two—sub—cultures fluctuate in their decisions, norms, etc. For example, he might feel that management ought to make up its mind on a particular policy so that he can provide consistent replies when asked by the employees. He may also feel that the employee attitudes about certain things do keep vacillating, and he is therefore unable to make a valid report to the management (which may be the employees' objective).

☐ The consultant will tend to experience conflict and frustration to the extent that his values are incongruent with the clients'.

The major portion of the paper is taken up with examples of the differences in values between the consultant and the clients. Whereas the former emphasizes openness, self-awareness, self-acceptance, and emotionality, the latter emphasizes diplomacy, subordination, dependence and rationality. These basic differences forced the consultant into continual conflict choice situations. In most cases, we have seen, the consultant's values were subordinated to the clients. The former became increasingly nonauthentic, which pleased the clients but prevented the consultant from providing the degree of help to which he was capable.

To summarize, the consulting relationship is influenced greatly by several complex factors. They are: (1) the discrepancy between the consultant's values and those of the clients, (2) the division of the organization into those who are aware of and/or wish, and those who are unaware of and/or do not wish, to bring about effective change, and (3) the division between those who invited the consultant "to straddle" a series of overlapping, conflicting, and at times antagonistic, sub-cultures.

This marginal status can lead to many difficulties for the consultant. If he attempts to behave simultaneously in accordance with the requirements of both sub-cultures, he will find himself in constant conflict since the demands are antagonistic. Moreover, he will tend to be perceived by those in the sub-culture, at best, as being ambivalent and unsure. At worst, the consultant will be perceived as a hypocrite and a man "playing both sides against one another." If he values one sub-culture over the other, then his behavior will be perceived as "management-dominated" or "employee-dominated," depending upon which sub-culture he values most and who is doing the judging.

Finally, each situation will tend to be new for the consultant. Consequently even with a high degree of training and experience his behavior will not tend to be efficient (e.g., follow the shortest path to the goal). There will be much exploratory, trial-and-error behavior. Errors and false steps will be made at the very time that he is being most cautious. Frustration and conflict will occur as well as feelings of ambivalence. These, in turn, will tend to lead the consultant to vacillate, to shift his ground, his strategy. He may be easily influenced and easily led especially by those representatives of the sub-culture that he values. His resistance to suggestion from the same group will tend to be low.[3]

The Emphasis Upon the Process of Development

The consultants upon whom we are focusing have an additional problem that confronts them continually. In many consulting relationships, the ends are considered more important than the means. If a marketing consultant comes up with a bright idea or an organization specialist suggests a more effective organizational structure, either not much attention is paid to the interpersonal processes involved in achieving these ends or strategies are developed and executed that "sell," "persuade," "pressure," "motivate" the employees to accept these changes.

A consultant who is interested in helping the organization achieve its needs in such a way that it can continue to do so with decreasing "outside" aid must give attention to the processes by which the new plans are developed, introduced, and made part of the organization. He will tend to invite a much greater degree of participation on the part of the clients in all the phases of the program. Such participation, if it is not to become bogged down, will have to be based on effective interpersonal and group relationships. At the core of such relationships are such factors as openness, the capacity to create minimal defensiveness in oneself and in others, listening with minimum distortion, etc. In order to succeed in their work these consultants must therefore be interested in the *processes* or means for development as well as the ends. For example, it is not very worthwhile to use covert or diplomatic approaches to get the clients to see that they are not open or that they are diplomatic in their relationships. It does not seem effective to help the clients become aware of their defenses if, in the process, the consultants behave defensively. Thus we find that the consultant strives to create a process for change which requires the very values that he is supposed to help the organization to overcome.

It is extremely difficult, however, for the consultant to be open when he is operating under the difficulties and ambiguities of a new situation compounded by being in a marginal role. All this is doubly compounded by the fact that his job depends upon not upsetting the clients whose basic problems are that they work in a system that sanctions non-authenticity and deplores authenticity. How is the consultant expected to behave according to his values and, at the same time, survive in a world in which these values may lead to failure? To make matters more difficult, he is on the client's payroll. Thus his job could be placed in jeopardy if he risks confronting the clients by questioning their values.

One implication is that management may need to learn to create a climate where the consultant can feel free and encouraged to express his beliefs, especially different ideas about the process of effective organizational change. Unless this is done, the consultant, quite understandably, out of fear of his own position and in need for acceptance, soon takes on the values already held by the organization that he is trying to help. At this point, he tends to lose the very qualities that would make him valuable to the organization.

Along with line management's helping to develop a climate where the consultants are helped to express their uniqueness, certain organizational changes might be considered organizationally to reinforce the consultants in their effective assistance. Specific recommendations for defining the nature of such a relationship go beyond the scope of this study. However, in other organizations, consultants have developed effective relationships where the following kinds of conditions existed. The consultants:

1. May never become part of line management.
2. Have their own professional salary scale as do medical directors.
3. May never be fired for focusing on such processes as openness and authenticity, but,
4. May be dismissed if they are judged by their professional colleagues to be incompetent, and
5. May be dismissed as part of the organization to the extent that it is coercing their behavior against their better judgment.

In addition, line management could optimize its return on the investment of the kind of consulting assistance discussed in this report if it would change its policy from asking for such assistance only when trouble is imminent or has already erupted to a more preventative philosophy of conducting their organizational diagnoses when the pressure "to put out a fire" is not at its peak. Under pressure of resolving a "hot issue," individuals tend to become more anxious, feel greater tension, see fewer alternatives, manifest less patience, and become less effective at problem solving. Their organizational defensiveness becomes more pronounced, and they demand more urgent solutions. Under these conditions it is difficult indeed to solve effectively important long-range organizational issues. One can imagine the difficulty if these issues are rooted in human relations, human actions, and human effectiveness. Under these conditions, the consultants, who would be the first to admit the infancy of their profession, cannot be expected to do the effective job the management desires.

At this point some readers have asked why it is dysfunctional for the consultant to accept temporarily the values of the client system. For example, is it not advisable for a consultant to suppress his feelings if he believes that the client is "not ready" to explore his interpersonal relationships? Why should not the consultant continue providing help to achieve the tasks with the hope that he will return to the interpersonal relationships later on? There are several reasons that might be worth exploring.

1. The two cases suggest that it is difficult for the consultants to help the clients to behave more openly if the consultants do not do so. The more the consultant is willing not to be open and to level, the more reason he gives the client to continue to lack genuineness. Every human interaction between client and consultant that is not authentic helps to build a norm of nonauthenticity. If most of the clients' interactions initially are nonauthentic, then the norm of the nonauthenticity (which already exists in the organization) becomes embedded in the client-consultant relationship. As these norms are reinforced it will tend to be difficult for the consultant to switch values and it will place the client in a strong conflict situation.

2. There are limits to the consultant's openness. If he believes that the members of the client system are psychologically too disturbed to deal with interpersonal relationship (and if some of the organization's problems are related to these interpersonal relationships), then the consultant may find it appropriate to recommend that the executives consider some form of therapy. If the client, after careful explanation and exploration, decides against therapy, the consultant may wish seriously to consider leaving. Otherwise, these interpersonal relationships will eventually embroil him, the executives, and others in the organization in great difficulties which he will be unable to cope with, since the client has said they were "off limits." If, however, the consultant believes that the client is not that defensive and that he can accept help in this area, even though at first it may be painful to the client, he should strive to provide help.

Some ask if the consultant does not run the risk of terminating the relationship if he upsets the client. The answer is yes he does run that risk. But, if he succumbs to this fear, then the client has control over the consultant. It is this fear of breaking off the relationship which probably makes the subordinates suppress their feelings. If the consultant can communicate that he does not fear terminating the relationship, then he helps the client to face up to his impact and responsibilities.

I do not, therefore, mean to imply that openness is an all-or-nothing phenomenon. Needless to say, the consultant will have to be cautious in his feedback until he ascertains the degree of receptivity of the client. I am suggesting, however, that, in an organization, the consultant may not have available to him as much time as he would wish to make a proper diagnosis, nor as much freedom to postpone being open. For example, in an individual therapeutic session, the therapist may be able to judge his openness primarily by the patient's response. In an organization, however, it is not so easy. If the key executive, for example, was more defensive and less aware than the subordinates, then the consultant's "patient waiting" for the opportune moment may be perceived by the subordinates as the executive controlling the consultant. The reader may recall that this is what occurred in Case A during the first feedback session.

In several instances where I have sensed that the defensiveness of the key executive is significantly greater than the others, I have found it helpful to work with him personally before the relationship expands to the remainder of the organization. Under these conditions, I was able to move more slowly without developing the problems discussed previously.

The defensiveness of the clients, however, is not the only relevant factor. The consultant's defensiveness is equally crucial. If he tends to be easily threatened by the hostility that understandably would flow from the confrontation of the client with his feelings, then he will not tend to see the appropriate moment for intervention, nor will he intervene in a way to optimize the possibilities for learning. He should strive to utilize his own values when he gives feedback. His feedback should be, as much as possible, descriptive of the situation as he sees it. He should minimize making evaluations. For example, the reader may recall that the consultants felt that Mr. Brown talked too much. There are several alternatives open to them for intervention. One is for the consultants to describe to Mr. Brown the impact he is having upon the group without evaluating it as good or bad. More important, however, they could hypothesize that Mr. Brown's talkativeness was not "too much." Rather they could view it diagnostically as Mr. Brown's attempt to deal with anxiousness about what the consultants were doing to him and to the others. If they could have raised this question (e.g., "Perhaps you feel we are meddling and not very helpful") this might have released the others to support that part of Mr. Brown's position which most of them felt was valid. The group support, might have influenced Mr. Brown to reduce the intensity of his need to fight the consultants.

In short, the appropriate time for the consultant to focus on interpersonal issues is when they become a problem. More specifically, the consultant should focus on interpersonal issues when he believes (1) that these are operating to block the client from achieving his stated objectives and (2) that the client by not being genuine is beginning to prevent the consultant from providing the skills and assistance for which he was hired.

It should be evident by now that there are many factors operating on the consultant, influencing him away from being effective. This leads to the final recommendation. Client systems may have to recognize that they have certain responsibilities which they must fulfill if the consultant is to optimize his—and therefore eventually help the client's—genuineness. A consultant is first a human being. Although he has much knowledge about human behavior he too can be influenced by pressures, conflicts, frustrations, and non-authenticity in an organization. This suggests that the clients should strive to minimize these or at least to encourage the consultant continually to raise the questions even though in doing so the clients should strive to minimize those situations where they are knowingly being nonauthentic with the consultant.

Typically many consultants hide these responsibilities from the clients. Indeed, some even prevent them from coming to the client's awareness. As long as the client (unknowingly or knowingly) turns over his responsibility to the consultant, then a strong dependency relationship is established between the client and the consultant. In my own experience, many consultants prefer the dependency relationship and not just for the increased "billing time." Less discussed, and perhaps equally important, is the consultant's deep anxiety to face himself and to see what he is *really* doing to the client system. Perhaps, the best sign of the strength in these consultants is their willingness to face themselves and their practice and to learn from this experience.

References

1. Argyris, Chris, *Personality and Organization,* New York: Harper Bros., 1957.
2. Argyris, Chris, "Toward a Theory of Authentic Relationships," mimeographed report, Yale University, Fall, 1960.
3. The analysis of the impact of a new situation on behavior is drawn from Roger Barker, Beatrice A. Wright, and Mollie R. Gonick, *Adjustment to Physical Handicap and Illness,* Social Science Research Council, Bulletin 55, 1946, pp. 1–44.

Chris Argyris is currently James Bryant Conant Professor of Education and Organizational Behavior at Harvard University.

Chapter 3

The Characteristics of a Helping Relationship

Carl R. Rogers

I have long had the strong conviction — some might say it was an obsession — that the therapeutic relationship is only a special instance of interpersonal relationships in general, and that the same lawfulness governs all such relationships. This was the theme I chose to work out for myself when I was asked to give an address to the convention of the American Personnel and Guidance Association at St. Louis, in 1958.

Evident in this article is the dichotomy between the objective and the subjective which has been such an important part of my experience during recent years. I find it very difficult to present an article which is either wholly objective or wholly subjective. I like to bring the two worlds into close juxtaposition, even if I cannot fully reconcile them.

My interest in psychotherapy has brought about in me an interest in every kind of helping relationship. By this term I mean a relationship in which at least one of the parties has the intent of promoting the growth, development, maturity, improved functioning, improved coping with life of the other. The other, in this sense, may be one individual or a group. To put it another way, a helping relationship might be defined as one in which one of the participants intends that there should come about, in one or both parties, more appreciation of, more expression of, more functional use of the latent inner resources of the individual.

Now it is obvious that such a definition covers a wide range of relationships which usually are intended to facilitate growth. It would certainly include the relationship between mother and child, father and child. It would include the relationship between the physician and his patient. The relationship between teacher and pupil would often come under this definition, though some teachers would not have the promotion of growth as their intent. It includes almost all counselor–client relationships, whether we are speaking of educational counseling, vocational counseling, or personal counseling. In this last-mentioned area it would include the wide range of relationships between the psychotherapist and the hospitalized psychotic, the therapist and the troubled or neurotic individual, and the relationship between the therapist and the increasing number of

Reprinted from *On Becoming a Person* by Carl R. Rogers, Copyright © 1961 by Carl R. Rogers. Used by permission of Houghton Mifflin Company.

so-called "normal" individuals who enter therapy to improve their own functioning or accelerate their personal growth.

These are largely one-to-one relationships. But we should also think of the large number of individual–group interactions which are intended as helping relationships. Some administrators intend that their relationship to their staff groups shall be of the sort which promotes growth, though other administrators would not have this purpose. The interaction between the group therapy leader and his group belongs here. So does the relationship of the community consultant to a community group. Increasingly the interaction between the industrial consultant and a management group is intended as a helping relationship. Perhaps this listing will point up the fact that a great many of the relationships in which we and others are involved fall within this category of interactions in which there is the purpose of promoting development and more mature and adequate functioning.

The Question

But what are the characteristics of those relationships which *do* help, which do facilitate growth? And at the other end of the scale is it possible to discern those characteristics which make a relationship unhelpful, even though it was the sincere intent to promote growth and development? It is to these questions, particularly the first, that I would like to take you with me over some of the paths I have explored, and to tell you where I am, as of now, in my thinking on these issues.

The Answers Given by Research

It is natural to ask first of all whether there is any empirical research which would give us an objective answer to these questions. There has not been a large amount of research in this area as yet, but what there is is stimulating and suggestive. I cannot report all of it, but I would like to make a somewhat extensive sampling of the studies which have been done and state very briefly some of the findings. In so doing, oversimplification is necessary, and I am quite aware that I am not doing full justice to the researches I am mentioning, but it may give you the feeling that factual advances are being made and pique your curiosity enough to examine the studies themselves, if you have not already done so.

Studies of Attitudes

Most of the studies throw light on the attitudes on the part of the helping person which make a relationship growth-promoting or growth-inhibiting. Let us look at some of these.

A careful study of parent–child relationships made some years ago by Baldwin and others[1] at the Fels Institute contains interesting evidence. Of the various clusters of parental attitudes toward children, the "acceptant-democratic" seemed most growth-facilitating. Children of these parents with their warm and equalitarian attitudes showed an accelerated intellectual development (an increasing I.Q.), more originality, more emotional security and control, and less excitability than children from other types of homes. Though somewhat slow initially in social development, they were, by the time they reached school age, popular, friendly, nonaggressive leaders.

Where parents' attitudes are classed as "actively rejectant," the children show a slightly decelerated intellectual development, relatively poor use of the abilities they do possess, and some lack of originality. They are emotionally unstable, rebellious, aggressive, and quarrelsome. The children of parents with other attitude syndromes tend in various respects to fall in-between these extremes.

I am sure that these findings do not surprise us as related to child development. I would like to suggest that they probably apply to other relationships as well and that the counselor or physician or administrator who is warmly emotional and expressive, respectful of the individuality of himself and of the other, and who exhibits a nonpossessive caring probably facilitates self-realization much as does a parent with these attitudes.

Let me turn to another careful study in a very different area. Whitehorn and Betz[2, 18] investigated the degree of success achieved by young resident physicians in working with schizophrenic patients on a psychiatric ward. They chose for special study the seven who had been outstandingly helpful, and seven whose patients had shown the least degree of improvement. Each group had treated about fifty patients. The investigators examined all the available evidence to discover in what ways the A group (the successful group) differed from the B group. Several significant differences were found. The physicians in the A group tended to see the schizophrenic in terms of the personal meaning which various behaviors had to the patient, rather than seeing him as a case history or a descriptive diagnosis. They also tended to work toward goals which were oriented to the personality of the patient, rather than such goals as reducing the symptoms or curing the disease. It was found that the helpful physicians, in their day-by-day interaction, primarily made use of active personal participation — a person-to-person relationship. They made less use of procedures which could be classed as "passive permissive." They were even less likely to use such procedures as interpretation, instruction or advice, or emphasis upon the practical care of the patient. Finally, they were much more likely than the B group to develop a relationship in which the patient felt trust and confidence in the physician.

Although the authors cautiously emphasize that these findings relate only to the treatment of schizophrenics, I am inclined to disagree. I suspect that similar facts would be found in a research study of almost any class of helping relationship.

Another interesting study focuses upon the way in which the person being helped perceives the relationship. Heine[11] studied individuals who had gone for psychotherapeutic help to psychoanalytic, client-centered, and Adlerian therapists. Regardless of the type of therapy, these clients report similar changes in themselves. But it is their perception of the relationship which is of particular interest to us here. When asked what accounted for the changes which had occurred, they expressed some differing explanations, depending on the orientation of the therapist. But their agreement on the major elements they had found helpful was even more significant. They indicated that these attitudinal elements in the relationship accounted for the changes which had taken place in themselves (the trust they had felt in the therapist; being understood by the therapist; the feeling of independence they had had in making choices and decisions). The therapist procedure which they had found most helpful was that the therapist clarified and openly stated feelings which the client had been approaching hazily and hesitantly.

There was also a high degree of agreement among these clients, regardless of the orientation of their therapists, as to what elements had been unhelpful in the relationship. Such therapist attitudes as lack of interest, remoteness or distance, and an over-degree of sympathy were perceived as unhelpful. As to procedures, they had found it unhelpful when therapists had given direct specific advice regarding decisions or had emphasized past history rather than present problems. Guiding suggestions mildly given were preceived in an intermediate range — neither clearly helpful nor unhelpful.

Fiedler, in a much quoted study,[7] found that expert therapists of differing orientations formed similar relationships with their clients. Less well known are the elements which characterized these relationships, differentiating them from the relationships formed by less expert therapists. These elements are: an ability to understand the client's meanings and feelings; a sensitivity to the client's attitudes; a warm interest without any emotional over-involvement.

A study by Quinn[14] throws light on what is involved in understanding the client's meanings and feelings. His study is surprising in that it shows that "understanding" of the client's meanings is essentially an attitude of *desiring* to understand. Quinn presented his judges only with recorded therapist statements taken from interviews. The raters had no knowledge of what the therapist was responding to or how the client reacted to his response. Yet it was found that the degree of understanding could be judged about as well from this material as from listening to the response in context. This seems rather conclusive evidence that it is an attitude of wanting to understand which is communicated.

As to the emotional quality of the relationship, Seeman[16] found that success in psychotherapy is closely associated with a strong and growing mutual liking and respect between client and therapist.

An interesting study by Dittes[4] indicates how delicate this relationship is. Using a physiological measure, the psychogalvanic reflex, to measure the anxious or threatened or alerted reactions of the client, Dittes correlated the deviations on this measure with judges' ratings of the degree of warm acceptance and permissiveness on the part of the therapist. It was found that whenever the therapist's attitudes changed even slightly in the direction of a lesser degree of acceptance, the number of abrupt GSR deviations significantly increased. Evidently when the relationship is experienced as less acceptant, the organism organizes against threat, even at the physiological level.

Without trying fully to integrate the findings from these various studies, it can at least be noted that a few things stand out. One is the fact that it is the attitudes and feelings of the therapist, rather than his theoretical orientation, which is important. His procedures and techniques are less important than his attitudes. It is also worth noting that it is the way in which his attitudes and procedures are *perceived* which makes a difference to the client, and that it is this perception which is crucial.

"Manufactured" Relationships

Let me turn to research of a very different sort, some of which you may find rather abhorrent, but which nevertheless has a bearing upon the nature of a facilitating relationship. These studies have to do with what we might think of as manufactured relationships.

Verplanck,[17] Greenspoon,[8] and others have shown that operant conditioning of verbal behavior is possible in a relationship. Very briefly, if the experimenter says "Mhm," or "Good," or nods his head after certain types of words or statements, those classes of words tend to increase because of being reinforced. It has been shown that using such procedures one can bring about increases in such diverse verbal categories as plural nouns, hostile words, and statements of opinion. The person is completely unaware that he is being influenced in any way by these reinforcers. The implication is that by such selective reinforcement we could bring it about that the other person in the relationship would be using whatever kinds of words and making whatever kinds of statements we had decided to reinforce.

Following still further the principles of operant conditioning as developed by Skinner and his group, Lindsley[12] has shown that a chronic schizophrenic can be placed in a "helping relationship" with a machine. The machine, somewhat like a vending machine, can be set to reward a variety of types of behaviors. Initially it simply rewards — with candy, a cigarette, or the display of a picture — the lever-pressing behavior of the patient. But it is possible to set it so that many pulls on the lever may supply a hungry kitten — visible in a separate enclosure — with a drop of milk. In this case the satisfaction is an altruistic one. Plans are being developed to reward similar social or altruistic behavior directed toward another patient, placed in the next room. The only limit to the kinds of behavior which might be rewarded lies in the degree of mechanical ingenuity of the experimenter.

Lindsley reports that in some patients there has been marked clinical improvement. Personally I cannot help but be impressed by the description of one patient who had gone from a deteriorated chronic state to being given free grounds privileges, this change being quite clearly associated with his interaction with the machine. Then the experimenter decided to study experimental extinction, which, put in more personal terms, means that no matter how many thousands of times the lever was pressed, no reward of any kind was forthcoming. The patient gradually regressed, grew untidy, uncommunicative, and his grounds privilege had to be revoked. This (to me) pathetic incident would seem to indicate that even in a relationship to a machine, trustworthiness is important if the relationship is to be helpful.

Still another interesting study of a manufactured relationship is being carried on by Harlow and his associates,[10] this time with monkeys. Infant monkeys, removed from their mothers almost immediately after birth, are, in one phase of the experiment, presented with two objects. One might be termed the "hard mother," a sloping cylinder of wire netting with a nipple from which the baby may feed. The other is a "soft mother," a similar cylinder made of foam rubber and terry cloth. Even when an infant gets all his food from the "hard mother" he clearly and increasingly prefers the "soft mother." Motion pictures show that he definitely "relates" to this object, playing with it, enjoying it, finding security in clinging to it when strange objects are near, and using that security as a home base for venturing into the frightening world. Of the many interesting and challenging implications of this study, one seems reasonably clear. It is that no amount of direct food reward can take the place of certain perceived qualities which the infant appears to need and desire.

Two Recent Studies

Let me close this wide-ranging — and perhaps perplexing — sampling of research studies with an account of two very recent investigations. The first is an experiment conducted by Ends and Page.[5] Working with hardened chronic hospitalized alcoholics who had been committed to a state hospital for sixty days, they tried three different methods of group psychotherapy. The method which they believed would be most effective was therapy based on a two-factor theory of learning; a client-centered approach was expected to be second; a psychoanalytically oriented approach was expected to be least efficient. Their results showed that the therapy based upon a learning theory was not only not helpful, but was somewhat deleterious. The outcomes were worse than those in the control group which had no therapy. The analytically oriented therapy produced some positive gain, and the client-centered group therapy was associated with the greatest amount of positive change. Follow-up data, extending over one and one-half years, confirmed the in-hospital findings, with the lasting improvement being greatest in the client-centered approach, next in the analytic, next the control group, and least in those handled by a learning theory approach.

As I have puzzled over this study, unusual in that the approach to which the authors were committed proved *least* effective, I find a clue, I believe, in the description of the therapy based on learning theory.[13] Essentially it consisted (a) of pointing out and labeling the behaviors which had proved unsatisfying, (b) of exploring objectively with the client the reasons behind these behaviors, and (c) of establishing through re-education more effective problem-solving habits. But in all of this interaction the aim, as they formulated it, was to be impersonal. The therapist "permits as little of his own personality to intrude as is humanly possible." The "therapist stresses personal anonymity in his activities, i.e., he must studiously avoid impressing the patient with his own (therapist's) individual personality characteristics." To me this seems the most likely clue to the failure of this approach, as I try to interpret the facts in the light of the other research studies. To withhold one's self as a person and to deal with the other person as an object does not have a high probability of being helpful.

The final study I wish to report is one just being completed by Halkides.[9] She started from a theoretical formulation of mine regarding the necessary and sufficient conditions for therapeutic change.[15] She hypothesized that there would be a significant relationship between the extent of constructive personality change in the client and four counselor variables: (a) the degree of emphatic understanding of the client manifested by the counselor; (b) the degree of positive affective attitude (unconditional positive regard) manifested by the counselor toward the client; (c) the extent to which the counselor is genuine, his words matching his own internal feeling; and (d) the extent to which the counselor's response matches the client's expression in the intensity of affective expression.

To investigate these hypotheses she first selected, by multiple objective criteria, a group of ten cases which could be classed as "most successful" and a group of ten "least successful" cases. She then took an early and late recorded interview from each of these cases. On a random basis she picked nine client–counselor interaction units — a client statement and a counselor response — from each of these interviews. She thus had nine early interactions and nine later interactions from each case. This gave her several hundred units which were now placed in random order. The units from an early interview of an unsuccessful case might be followed by the units from a late interview of a successful case, etc.

Three judges who did not know the cases or their degree of success, or the source of any given unit, now listened to this material four different times. They rated each unit on a seven-point scale, first as to the degree of empathy, second as to the counselor's positive attitude toward the client, third as to the counselor's congruence or genuineness, and fourth as to the degree to which the counselor's response matched the emotional intensity of the client's expression.

I think all of us who knew of the study regarded it as a very bold venture. Could judges listening to single units of interaction possibly make any reliable rating of such subtle qualities as I have mentioned? And even if suitable reliability could be obtained, could eighteen counselor–client interchanges from each case — a minute sampling of the hundreds or thousands of such interchanges which occurred in each case — possibly bear any relationship to the therapeutic outcome? The chance seemed slim.

The findings are surprising. It proved possible to achieve high reliability between the judges, most of the interjudge correlations being in the 0.80s or 0.90s, except on the last variable. It was found that a high degree of empathic understanding was significantly associated, at a .001 level, with the more successful cases. A high degree of unconditional positive regard was likewise associated with the more successful cases, at the .001 level. Even the rating of the counselor's genuineness or congruence — the extent to which his words matched his feelings — was associated with the successful outcome of the case, and again at the .001 level of significance. Only in the investigation of the matching intensity of affective expression were the results equivocal.

It is of interest too that high ratings of these variables were not associated more significantly with units from later interviews than with units from early interviews. This means that the counselor's attitudes were quite constant throughout the interviews. If he was highly empathic, he tended to be so from first to last. If he was lacking in genuineness, this tended to be true of both early and late interviews.

As with any study, this investigation has its limitations. It is concerned with a certain type of helping relationship, psychotherapy. It investigated only four variables thought to be significant. Perhaps there are many others. Nevertheless it represents a significant advance in the study of helping relationships. Let me try to state the findings in the simplest possible fashion. It seems to indicate that the quality of the counselor's interaction with a client can be satisfactorily judged on the basis of a very small sampling of his behavior. It also means that if the counselor is congruent or transparent, so that his words are in line with his feelings rather than the two being discrepant, if the counselor likes the client unconditionally, and if the counselor understands the essential feelings of the client as they seem to the client, then there is a strong probability that this will be an effective helping relationship.

Some Comments

These then are some of the studies which throw at least a measure of light on the nature of the helping relationship. They have investigated different facets of the problem. They have approached it from very different theoretical contexts. They have used different methods. They are not directly comparable. Yet they seem to me to point to several statements which may be made with some assurance. It seems clear that relationships which are helpful have different characteristics from relationships which are unhelpful. These differential characteristics have to do primarily with the attitudes of the helping person on the one hand and with the perception of the relationship by the "helpee" on the other. It is equally clear that the studies thus far made do not give us any final answers as to what is a helping relationship, nor how it is to be formed.

How Can I Create a Helping Relationship?

I believe each of us working in the field of human relationships has a similar problem in knowing how to use research knowledge. We cannot slavishly follow findings in a mechanical way or we destroy the personal qualities which these very studies show to be valuable. It seems to me that we have to use these studies, testing them against our own experience and forming new and further personal hypotheses to use and test in our own further personal relationships.

So, rather than try to tell you how you should view the findings, I should like to tell you the kind of questions which these studies and my own clinical experience raise for me, and some of the tentative and changing hypotheses which guide my behavior as I enter into what I hope may be helping relationships, whether with students, staff, family, or clients. Let me list a number of these questions and considerations.

1. Can I *be* in some way which will be perceived by the other person as trustworthy, as dependable or consistent in some deep sense? Both research and experience indicate that this is very important, and over the years I have found what I believe are deeper and better ways of answering this question. I used to feel that if I fulfilled all the outer conditions of trustworthiness — keeping appointments, respecting the confidential nature of the interviews, etc. — and if I acted consistently the same during the interviews, then this condition would be fulfilled. But experience drove home the fact that to act consistently acceptant (for example, if in fact I was feeling annoyed or skeptical or some other nonacceptant feeling) was certain in the long run to be perceived as inconsistent or untrustworthy. I have come to recognize that being trustworthy does not demand that I be rigidly consistent but that I can be dependably real. The term "congruent" is one I have used to describe the way I would like to be. By this I mean that whatever feeling or attitude I am experiencing would be matched by my awareness of that attitude. When this is true, then I am a unified or integrated person in that moment, and hence I can *be* whatever I deeply *am*. This is a reality which I find others experience as dependable.

2. A very closely related question is this: Can I be expressive enough as a person that what I am will be communicated unambiguously? I believe that most of my failures to achieve a helping relationship can be traced to unsatisfactory answers to these two questions. When I am experiencing an attitude of annoyance toward another person but am unaware of it, then my communication contains contradictory messages. My words are giving one message, but I am also in subtle ways communicating the annoyance I feel and this confuses the other person and makes him distrustful, though he too may be unaware of what is causing the difficulty. When as a parent or a therapist or a teacher or an administrator I fail to listen to what is going on in me, fail because of my own defensiveness to sense my own feelings, then this kind of failure seems to result. It has made it seem to me that the most basic learning for anyone who hopes to establish any kind of helping relationship is that it is safe to be transparently real. If in a given relationship I am reasonably congruent, if no feelings relevant to the relationship are hidden either to me or the other person, then I can be almost sure that the relationship will be a helpful one.

One way of putting this which may seem strange to you is that if I can form a helping relationship to myself — if I can be sensitively aware of and acceptant toward my own feelings — then the likelihood is great that I can form a helping relationship toward another.

Now, acceptantly to be what I am, in this sense, and to permit this to show through to the other person, is the most difficult task I know and one I never fully achieve. But to realize that this *is* my task has been most rewarding because it has helped me to find what has gone wrong with interpersonal relationships which have become snarled and to put them on a constructive track again. It has meant that if I am to facilitate the personal growth of others in relation to me, then I must grow, and while this is often painful it is also enriching.

3. A third question is: Can I let myself experience positive attitudes toward this other person — attitudes of warmth, caring, liking, interest, respect? It is not easy. I find in myself, and feel that I often see in others, a certain amount of fear of these feelings. We are afraid that if we let ourselves freely experience these positive feelings toward another, we may be trapped by them. They may lead to demands on us or we may be disappointed in our trust, and these outcomes we fear. So, as a reaction, we tend to build up distance between ourselves and others — aloofness, a "professional" attitude, an impersonal relationship.

I feel quite strongly that one of the important reasons for the professionalization of every field is that it helps to keep this distance. In the clinical areas, we develop elaborate diagnostic formulations, seeing the person as an object. In teaching and in administration we develop all kinds of evaluative procedures, so that again the person is perceived as an object. In these ways, I believe, we can keep ourselves from experiencing the caring which would exist if we recognized the relationship as one between two persons. It is a real achievement when we can learn, even in certain relationships or at certain times in those relationships, that it is safe to care, that it is safe to relate to the other as a person for whom we have positive feelings.

4. Another question the importance of which I have learned in my own experience is: Can I be strong enough as a person to be separate from the other? Can I be a sturdy respecter of my own feelings, my own needs, as well as his? Can I own and, if need be, express my own feelings as something belonging to me and separate from his feelings? Am I strong enough in my own separateness that I will not be downcast by his depression, frightened by his fear, nor engulfed by his dependency? Is my inner self hardy enough to realize that I am not destroyed by his anger, taken over by his need for dependence, nor enslaved by his love, but that I exist separate from him with feelings and rights of my own? When I can freely feel this strength of being a separate person, then I find that I can let myself go much more deeply in understanding and accepting him because I am not fearful of losing myself.

5. The next question is closely related. Am I sure enough within myself to permit him his separateness? Can I permit him to be what he is — honest or deceitful, infantile or adult, despairing or over-confident? Can I give him the freedom to be? Or do I feel that he should follow my advice, or remain somewhat dependent on me, or mold himself after me? In this connection I think of the interesting small study by Farson[6] which found that the less well-adjusted and

less-competent counselor tends to induce conformity to himself, to have clients who model themselves after him. On the other hand, the better-adjusted and more-competent counselor can interact with a client through many interviews without interfering with the freedom of the client to develop a personality quite separate from that of his therapist. I should prefer to be in this latter class whether as parent or supervisor or counselor.

6. Another question I ask myself is: Can I let myself enter fully into the world of his feelings and personal meanings and see these as he does? Can I step into his private world so completely that I lose all desire to evaluate or judge it? Can I enter it so sensitively that I can move about in it freely, without trampling on meanings which are precious to him? Can I sense it so accurately that I can catch not only the meanings of his experience which are obvious to him, but those meanings which are only implicit, which he sees only dimly or as confusion? Can I extend this understanding without limit? I think of the client who said, "Whenever I find someone who understands a *part* of me at the time, then it never fails that a point is reached where I know they're *not* understanding me again... What I've looked for so hard is for someone to understand."

For myself I find it easier to feel this kind of understanding and to communicate it to individual clients than to students in a class or staff members in a group in which I am involved. There is a strong temptation to set students "straight," or to point out to a staff member the errors in his thinking. Yet when I can permit myself to understand in these situations, it is mutually rewarding. And with clients in therapy, I am often impressed with the fact that even a minimal amount of empathic understanding — a bumbling and faulty attempt to catch the confused complexity of the client's meaning — is helpful, though there is no doubt that it is most helpful when I can see and formulate clearly the meanings in his experiencing which for him have been unclear and tangled.

7. Still another issue is whether I can be acceptant of each facet of this other person which he presents to me. Can I receive him as he is? Can I communicate this attitude? Or can I only receive him conditionally, acceptant of some aspects of his feelings and silently or openly disapproving of other aspects? It has been my experience that when my attitude is conditional, then he cannot change or grow in those respects in which I cannot fully receive him. And when — afterward and sometimes too late — I try to discover why I have been unable to accept him in every respect, I usually discover that it is because I have been frightened or threatened in myself by some aspect of his feelings. If I am to be more helpful, then I must myself grow and accept myself in these respects.

8. A very practical issue is raised by the question: Can I act with sufficient sensitivity in the relationship that my behavior will not be perceived as a threat? The work we are beginning to do in studying the physiological concomitants of psychotherapy confirms the research by Dittes in indicating how easily individuals are threatened at a physiological level. The psychogalvanic reflex — the measure of skin conductance — takes a sharp dip when the therapist responds with some word which is just a little stronger than the client's feelings. And to a phrase such

as, "My you *do* look upset," the needle swings almost off the paper. My desire to avoid even such minor threats is not due to a hypersensitivity about my client. It is simply due to the conviction based on experience that if I can free him as completely as possible from external threat, then he can begin to experience and to deal with the internal feelings and conflicts which he finds threatening within himself.

9. A specific aspect of the preceding question, but an important one, is: Can I free him from the threat of external evaluation? In almost every phase of our lives — at home, at school, at work — we find ourselves under the rewards and punishments of external judgements. "That's good"; "that's naughty." "That's worth an A"; "that's a failure." "That's good counseling"; "that's poor counseling." Such judgments are a part of our lives from infancy to old age. I believe they have a certain social usefulness to institutions and organizations such as schools and professions. Like everyone else I find myself all too often making such evaluations. But in my experience, they do not make for personal growth and hence I do not believe that they are a part of a helping relationship. Curiously enough, a positive evaluation is as threatening in the long run as a negative one, since to inform someone that he is good implies that you also have the right to tell him he is bad. So I have come to feel that the more I can keep a relationship free of judgment and evaluation, the more this will permit the other person to reach the point where he recognizes that the locus of evaluation, the center of responsibility, lies within himself. The meaning and value of his experience is in the last analysis something which is up to him, and no amount of external judgment can alter this. So I should like to work toward a relationship in which I am not, even in my own feelings, evaluating him. This I believe can set him free to be a self-responsible person.

10. One last question: Can I meet this other individual as a person who is in process of *becoming,* or will I be bound by his past and by my past? If, in my encounter with him, I am dealing with him as an immature child, an ignorant student, a neurotic personality, or a psychopath, each of these concepts of mine limits what he can be in the relationship. Martin Buber, the existentialist philosopher of the University of Jerusalem, has a phrase, "confirming the other," which has had meaning for me. He says, "Confirming means...accepting the whole potentiality of the other...I can recognize in him, the person he has been...*created* to become...I confirm him in myself, and then in him, in relation to this potentiality that...can now be developed, can evolve."[3] If I accept the other person as something fixed, already diagnosed and classified, already shaped by his past, then I am doing my part to confirm this limited hypothesis. If I accept him as a process of becoming, then I am doing what I can to confirm or make real his potentialities.

It is at this point that I see Verplanck, Lindsley, and Skinner, working in operant conditioning, coming together with Buber, the philosopher or mystic. At least they come together in principle, in an odd way. If I see a relationship as only an opportunity to reinforce certain types of words or opinions in the other, then I tend to confirm him as an object — a basically mechanical, manipulable object. And if I see this as his potentiality, he tends to act in ways which support this hypothesis. If, on the other hand, I see a relationship as an opportunity to "reinforce" *all* that he is, the person that he is with all his existent potentialities, then he tends to act in ways which support *this* hypothesis. I have then — to use Buber's term — confirmed him as a living person, capable of creative inner development. Personally I prefer this second type of hypothesis.

Conclusion

In the early portion of this article I reviewed some of the contributions which research is making to our knowledge *about* relationships. Endeavoring to keep that knowledge in mind, I then took up the kind of questions which arise from an inner and subjective point of view as I enter, as a person, into relationships. If I could, in myself, answer all the questions I have raised in the affirmative, then I believe that any relationships in which I was involved would be helping relationships, would involve growth. But I cannot give a positive answer to most of these questions. I can only work in the direction of the positive answer.

This has raised in my mind the strong suspicion that the optimal helping relationship is the kind of relationship created by a person who is psychologically mature. Or to put it in another way, the degree to which I can create relationships which facilitate the growth of others as separate persons is a measure of the growth I have achieved in myself. In some respects this is a disturbing thought, but it is also a promising or challenging one. It would indicate that if I am interested in creating helping relationships, I have a fascinating lifetime job ahead of me, stretching and developing my potentialities in the direction of growth.

I am left with the uncomfortable thought that what I have been working out for myself in this paper may have little relationship to your interests and your work. If so, I regret it. But I am at least partially comforted by the fact that all of us who are working in the field of human relationships and trying to understand the basic orderliness of that field are engaged in the most crucial enterprise in today's world. If we are thoughtfully trying to understand our tasks as administrators, teachers, educational counselors, vocational counselors, therapists, then we are working on the problem which will determine the future of this planet. For it is not upon the physical sciences that the future will depend. It is upon us who are trying to understand and deal with the interactions between human beings — who are trying to create helping relationships. So I hope that the questions I ask of myself will be of some use to you in gaining understanding and perspective as you endeavor, in your way, to facilitate growth in your relationships.

References

1. Baldwin, A. L., J. Kalhorn, and F. H. Breese, "Patterns of parent behavior," *Psychol. Monogr.* Vol. 58, No. 268 (1945), pp. – 75.
2. Betz, B. J., and J. C. Whitehorn, "The relationship of the therapist to the outcome of therapy in schizophrenia," *Psychiat. Research Reports #5. Research techniques*

in schizophrenia, Washington, D.C., American Psychiatric Association, 1956, pp. 89 – 117.

3. Buber, M., and C. Rogers, Transcription of dialogue held April 18, 1957, Ann Arbor, Mich. Unpublished manuscript.

4. Dittes, J. E., "Galvanic skin response as a measure of patient's reaction to therapist's permissiveness," *J. Abnorm. & Soc. Psychol.* Vol. 55 (1957), pp. 295 – 303.

5. Ends, E. J., and C. W. Page, "A study of three types of group psychotherapy with hospitalized male inebriates," *Quar. J. Stud. Alcohol.* Vol. 18 (1957), pp. 263 – 277.

6. Farson, R. E., Introjection in the psychotherapeutic relationship. Unpublished doctoral dissertation, University of Chicago, 1955.

7. Fiedler, F. E., "Quantitative studies on the role of therapists feelings toward their patients," In Mowrer, O. H. (Ed.), *Psychotherapy: Theory and Research,* New York: Ronald Press, 1953, Chap. 12.

8. Greenspoon, J., "The Reinforcing Effect of Two Spoken Sounds on the Frequency of Two Responses," *Amer. J. Psychol.,* Vol. 68 (1955), pp. 409 – 416.

9. Halkides, G., An Experimental Study of Four Conditions Necessary for Therapeutic Change. Unpublished doctoral dissertation, University of Chicago, 1958.

10. Harlow, H. F., "The Nature of Love," *Amer. Psychol.,* Vol. 13 (1958), pp. 673 – 685.

11. Heine, R. W., A Comparison of Patients' Reports on Psychotherapeutic experience with Psychoanalytic, Nondirective, and Adlerian Therapists. Unpublished doctoral dissertation, University of Chicago, 1950.

12. Lindsley, O. R., "Operant Conditioning Methods Applied to Research in Chronic Schizophrenia," *Psychiat. Research Reports #5. Research techniques in schizophrenia.* Washington, D.C.: American Psychiatric Association, 1956, pp. 118 – 153.

13. Page, C. W., and E. J. Ends, A Review and Synthesis of the Literature Suggesting a Psychotherapeutic Technique Based on Two-factor Learning Theory. Unpublished manuscript, loaned to the writer.

14. Quinn, R. D., Psychotherapists' Expressions As an Index to the Quality of Early Therapeutic Relationships. Unpublished doctoral dissertation, University of Chicago, 1950.

15. Rogers, C. R., "The Necessary and Sufficient Conditions of Psychotherapeutic Personality Change," *J. Consult. Psychol.,* Vol. 21 (1957), pp. 95-103.

16. Seeman, J., "Counselor Judgments of Therapeutic Process and Outcome," In C. R. Rogers, and R. F. Dymond (Eds.), *Psychotherapy and Personality Change,* University of Chicago Press, 1954 Chap. 7.

17. Verplanck, W. S., "The Control of the Content of Conversation: Reinforcement of Statements of Opinion," *J. Abnorm. & Soc. Psychol.* Vol. 51 (1955), pp. 668 – 676.

18. Whitehorn, J. C., and B. J. Betz, "A Study of Psychotherapeutic Relationships Between Physicians and Schizophrenic Patients," *Amer. J. Psychiat.,* Vol. 111 (1954), pp. 321 – 331.

Carl R. Rogers is a resident Fellow at the Center for Studies of the Person in La Jolla, California.

Part II

Client-Consultant Roles

Despite its apparent obviousness, the roles of the client and the consultant are often overlooked or glossed over in treatments of helping endeavors. Here "role" is used to mean those behaviors which are appropriate for individuals in a relationship. The roles characterize the relationship, with the client operating with certain expectations of the consultant, and vice versa.

Within the literature, there is a severe lack of material concerning the role of the client. A few articles can be found, but these typically are batterings on the "beware of the consultant" drum. Such tom-tom articles sound warnings to the prospective client, spelling out what to look for to avoid being taken by the consultant. Rarely do the writings emphasize the mutuality of the roles of consultant and client.

Further, there is lack of agreement regarding the roles of the consultant, as will be seen in the following article. There are, however, certain trends. One trend is a growing emergence of similarity in terminology. Not only is this a boon to communication, it leads to clarity in uncovering the obvious overlaps and redundancies. Another trend is the growing interest in consultative competencies, that is, identifying required skills and knowledge needed to effectively function in a specific consultant role.

An understanding of the roles in the client–consultant relationship is important in order to (1) aid both parties in the search, (2) specify mutual expectations and minimize confusion, and (3) help the consultant identify the skills and competencies associated with different roles.

Aid in the Search

Consultants are constantly seeking clients, for without clients there are no consultants! The client is enticed with repeated brochures, mailings, office visits, public seminars, and the offer of article reprints. The assessment of appropriate roles can aid the consultant in more effectively targeting his or her marketing to the most likely client-prospect, and can aid the client in selection of the appropriate helper.

Few consultants can function in all the roles that will be discussed in the following article. To maximize marketing efficiency and consultative effectiveness, a consultant should begin by identifying those roles in which he or she has had the most success. This success can be parlayed into positioning statements aimed at likely client markets. Consultant self-assessment requires objective self-awareness and the ability to articulate the findings in a client-oriented manner. For example, if the consultant has particular strength as a facilitator, he or she might be advised to project to prospects who need help in problem solving rather than those requiring an expert opinion.

For the client, the process must start with identifying the need or intention. When the client has some feel for the dimensions of the problem or need, it is easier to identify the kind of consulting roles which could be helpful. This facilitates the client's search for the appropriate helper.

Specify Mutual Expectations

The roles, when agreed upon by both parties, allow for a clarification of mutual expectations. A consultant can use role clarification as a way of communicating more effectively with the client. By surfacing the behaviors the client expects of the consultant, the problem and need can be more easily clarified and the end result can be more readily anticipated.

Both parties might begin role clarification by looking at expected behaviors and then labeling these behavioral roles. Clearly defined roles facilitate clear communication. If correctly employed, they enable the parties to resolve differences and negotiate agreements with mutuality and understanding.

Consultant Skills and Competencies

We can expect competent professionals to be constantly engaged in personal growth and development. The assumption that one has acquired all the useful skills and competencies is a reckless departure from the humility which leads to the maintenance of competence.

The need for a particular competency often surfaces when one is involved in a consulting relationship. The consultant may encounter an area of weakness (or even blindness) which requires work. Role clarification and perpetual reassessment enable the consultant to better forecast personal growth needs and plan required means of meeting those needs.

Roles are a way of helping the consultant identify needs before becoming involved in a client–consultant relationship. If a consultant recognizes the variety of roles which can be performed, he or she is better able to build the competencies which will facilitate successful performance in that role. Beyond identification, however, the consultant must take time for academic learning and personal growth experiences in order to remain current and prepared to deal with the future.

The past 20 years have brought massive changes in what has been required of consultants. With the changes, the use of consultants and the number of consultants have significantly increased. Some of the people new to the field have a much stronger theoretical and conceptual base than those who have been practicing successfully for many years. Obsolesence can catch up with even the most successful consultant who has not identified new material and trends in the field.

At this stage in the emergence of the field, there is continuing struggle with the appropriate roles and competencies. It has not yet been possible to provide the type of "laundry list" frequently sought by those wishing to grow. Some organizations have produced such lists for their members. On closer examination, these lists have turned out to be lists of cognitive areas rather than competencies.

The client competencies have not yet been identified to a point where they could be helpful. At best, we can only suggest some cautions. As we gain greater confidence in our understanding of consultation, it will become easier to spell out client competencies.

Consultants need to be clearer about their own roles and those they wish to perform. If the consultant intends to respond to the newer trends, it becomes more important to identify the competencies needed which the consultant does not have. It is not sufficient to do the "old wines in new goatskins" routine— taking existing competencies and giving them new names.

Internal vs. External Consultant Roles

One of the periodic disputes in the field takes place over the question of whether one can be a consultant to one's own organization. Usually none of the parties has bothered to define "internal" and "external." One way of looking at this is to recognize that the consultant may be either internal or external to the organization, but always is external to the problem or need. The consultant may be an employee of the organization, but not directly related to the unit, group, or individual seeking help.

Internal and external consultants in their ideal form are more alike than different. Both have no direct power or control over implementing the change needed but instead must depend on others. Both desire to be effective helpers.

There are differences. The external consultant typically has more freedom than his or her internal counterpart. The internal consultant is more likely to be politically astute regarding the culture of the client. The external consultant often has the power inherent in being an independent, "objective" influence, while the internal consultant may be a part of the problem.

Donald Swartz suggests the internal consultant can enhance the effectiveness of consultation by carefully clarifying consultant and client roles. Doing some external consulting can broaden the internal consultant's perspective and increase his or her personal confidence and organizational credibility.

For the external consultant, Swartz recommends never taking an assignment if the gut says "no." Collaboration with internal helpers is a suggestion the result of which not only improves the probability of success, but leaves the internal consultant with increased power.

Chapter 4
"The Consultant's Role in Organizational Change"
Neil G. Davey

The significance of this article is in its emphasis on the client–consultant relationship. Although Davey concentrates on organizational change, it is obvious that consultants do perform other tasks and other roles. It is suggested that if the characteristics of the client–consultant relationship could be clearly identified, they could provide clues to how the relationship could be made successful and rewarding for both parties.

Chapter 5
"The Trainer's Role as an Internal Consultant"
Gordon L. Lippitt

It is obvious to most consultant users that external consultants are on the increase. New directories and increased listings of external consultants are published each year. What about the internal consultant? Are organizations trapped in the mode of thinking that the only person who can help must be someone from the "outside"? Do organizations have internal resources they are neglecting? Gordon Lippitt sees an increasing role for the internal consultant. He relies on a roles approach to help the internal consultant and management identify their mutual expectations.

Chapter 6
"The Evolving Role of the Federal Training Consultant"
Neal E. Chalofsky

The evolution of the federal training consultant provides a sense of history that aids in preparing to move the field further. The Chalofsky article was written to give the reader this historical perspective as well as acquaintance with the skills and competence related to consultant roles. That acquaintance should foster better understanding on the part of client and consultant regarding how the consultant might function.

Chapter 4

The Consultant's Role in Organizational Change

Neil G. Davey

In meeting the challenges and demands of change, organizations frequently seek assistance from *external* agents to play some role in the process of need identification (diagnosis), program evaluation and planning, and the introduction or implementation of change programs. Substantial sums are spent annually by American organizations on the services of external consultants. Although on the whole they appear to be getting their money's worth, there is some evidence that the business clients are less than completely satisfied with the effectiveness of the help they receive in at least some instances.[1] Of even greater import, there is little or no evidence to explain the different levels of consultant effectiveness or organizational satisfaction with these relationships. Clearly, there is need for an empirical study of the relationship which develops between an organization and any consultant it retains.

The fundamental hypothesis underlying this study is that the effectiveness of consultant-assisted change efforts is a function of the relationship between an organization and the consultant it has retained. The question posed is whether an organization–consultant relationship which possesses some particular characteristics is typically associated with successful consultant-assisted change efforts, and whether a relationship with discernibly different characteristics is typically associated with unsuccessful or ineffective change efforts.

While it appears to have been little researched, the idea that the organization–consultant relationship is a vital factor in the effectiveness of consultant-assisted change efforts has appealed — either intuitively, logically, or experientially — to other authors.

W. G. Bennis suggests that

"Acceptance (of change) also depends on the relationship between the change agent and client system: the more profound and anxiety-producing the change, the more a collaborative and closer relationship is required. In

From *MSU Business Topics*, Spring, 1971, pp. 76–79. Reprinted by permission of the publisher, Division of Research, Graduate School of Business Administration, Michigan State University.

addition, we can predict that an anticipated change will be resisted to the degree that the client system possesses little or incorrect knowledge about the change, has relatively little trust in the source of change, and has relatively low influence in controlling the nature and direction of the change"[2]

R. Lippitt, J. Watson, and B. Westley, in their book *The Dynamics of Planned Change,* considered that the success of the change effort rests heavily on the quality and workability of the relationship between the change agent (consultant) and client system (organization) — and that many vital aspects of this relationship are established very early in the association. For example, a crucial feature is how the client system begins to think about the change agent.[3] A similar notion was employed by S. Tilles in suggesting that the determinants of the ultimate outcome of a client–consultant relationship are probably manifested much before the final stages of the relationship.[4]

Considerations Prior to Decision

The considerations of organization members which lead to the securing of consultant assistance will inevitably have an effect on the ensuing organization–consultant relationship. These prior considerations may have taken a variety of forms.

The board of directors or personnel of a parent company may decide on the engagement of a consultant and "impose" him on the organization. The organization's chief operating executive may make a decision to engage a consultant and proceed to do so, maintaining himself as the sole point of contact with the consultant, or "imposing" the consultant on other subordinate organization members. Then again, the decision may be made at a lower management level or could perhaps originate as a recommendation from a lower management level. A similar variety of possibilities exists with respect to the selection of a particular consultant and the process through which this is accomplished.

Whether only one consultant is asked to assist the organization, perhaps on the basis of a previously established personal relationship with an organization member, or for any reason, or whether a number of consultants are invited for preliminary discussions or to make preliminary diagnostic investigations could have an influence on the nature of the organization–consultant relationship which ultimately develops. Also, there will be variation in the timing at which consultant help is sought. An urgent appeal to assist with a dramatically serious situation, resulting from the ineffectiveness or inappropriateness of internally sponsored attempts, will likely produce a different type of relationship from one developed in a situation where the request for help is timely and made on more of a preventive basis.

Nature of Consulting Assignment

In addition to those preliminary considerations of seeking consultant help and the decisions actually relating to the consultant engagement, there are the questions which relate to the scope and nature of the intended consulting assignment. Relevant features here include:

— Whether the selected consultant is required by the organization to conduct preliminary diagnostic investigations and submit a proposed program for the organization's consideration and acceptance, or whether he is commissioned to proceed immediately with tasks designated by the organization;
— The scope of the consulting assignments as regards the phases of investigation, program development, recommendations, and implementation, and the manner in which this scope is determined;
— The extent to which the organization's expectations with respect to the required outcomes from the consulting assignment were identified, made explicit, and formalized in an agreement between the organization and consultant;
— The extent to which organization members were formally advised of the proposed introduction of the consultant and of the objectives of his assignment;
— the constraints or restrictions imposed on the consultant by the organization, with respect to areas in which the consultant should not work or to people or information to which he should not have access;
— The definition or shared understanding of the respective duties to be assumed by the consultant and organization members and their division of responsibilities; and
— The definition or shared understanding of the point at which the consultant's work would be regarded as complete.

Working Arrangements

There are many factors relating to the nature of the consultant's intervention or entry into the organization which will also influence the organization–consultant relationship. Proceeding beyond the consultant's period of entry, there are other features of the modus operandi which would appear to further influence the nature of this developing relationship. These concern the selection of an organization member as a point of contact and liaison with the consultant, the working methods and approach the consultant will be required to adopt, and the informing of organization members as to the intended introduction of the consultant into the organization. Whether such considerations are made prior to the establishment of contact with the consultant, or whether the consultant is made a party to such considerations (and in either case) the nature of the arrangements which do eventuate will all have an influence on the nature of the relationship.

More specifically, the relevant factors for this phase of development are:

1. The nature of the arrangements for collaboration, contact, and liaison between the organization and consultant during the working phases of the consultant's assignment;
2. The nature of the arrangements made for the consultant to report on his activities and progress during the consulting assignment and also at its completion;
3. The manner in which the consultant attempted to involve organization members in the assignment and secure their commitment to the programs he wanted recommended;
4. The consultant's relative emphasis on diagnosis and identification of the organization's problems;
5. The nature of any changes made in the scope, extent, objectives, or timing of the consulting assignment which were made during its progress on the recommendation of either the consultant or organization members; and
6. The extent to which the consultant participated in the implementation of any of the programs he recommended.

A Study of the Relationship

While there is an abundance of sources which emphasize the importance of the organization–consultant relationship, such references are almost exclusively homiletic and unsupported by significant empirical evidence which alone can confirm their veracity.

In this study the fundamental research hypothesis concerning the effectiveness of consultant-assisted change efforts and the organization–consultant relationship required: the identification of organizations which have used the services of external consultants; the means for distinguishing between different types or natures of organization–consultant relationships; and measures, or descriptions, of resulting effectiveness of the consultant-assisted change efforts.

Responses were received from the chief operating executives of 133 organizations, although only 91 of these described a consulting experience that took place during the preceding three-year survey period.[5] The research questionnaire sought information about the organizational arrangements before and during a consulting engagement, and also about its ultimate effectiveness as measured by subjective evaluations by key organization members on a scale ranging from *completely effective* to *no worthwhile results achieved.* In all of the analyses of the data, consultant assignments were judged as completely effective in less than 40 percent of all cases, and the recommendations made by consultants were completely accepted by the different levels of management in the responding organizations in less than 30 percent of all cases reported.

Prescriptions for Effectiveness

A review of the tentatively or "directionally" confirmed hypotheses indicates the following arrangements should be observed in order for consultant assistance to be most often judged as completely effective.

1. In considering consultant help, an organization should allow that some changes may be necessary and should reflect this by its identification and explication of specific objectives as bases for the engagement of a consultant.
2. An organization should regard a consultant as an expert resource, and a collaborating equal, and ensure his participation in the consideration of any changes which should be made in the assignment during its progress.
3. An organization should use a consultant-initiated suggestion that his services be retained as a basis for internal considerations which may lead to the identification of needs and explication of goals.
4. Rather than impose a possibly unwanted consultant on subordinate managers, a chief executive should encourage the initiation of pro-consultant discussions at this lower level and/or seek to secure consensus among subordinate managers before making a decision to engage a consultant.
5. Several management members of an organization should participate in pre-engagement discussions concerning consultant help, as well as in the decision that a consultant be retained.
6. Besides participating in the pro-consultant decisions, subordinate managers should participate with the chief executive in identifying and agreeing on the particular consultant to be appointed.
7. Before commencing a consulting assignment, an organization should identify and make explicit to the selected consultant its specific objectives and expectations with respect to the required outcomes from the assignment.
8. An organization should not closely direct a consultant's work, nor unreasonably constrain him by restricting personal contacts or access to organizational information.
9. Before commencing a consulting assignment, an organization should ensure that the respective duties to be undertaken by the consultant and by organization members are identified and understood. Such understanding should preferably be reached by mutual agreement between the parties, or otherwise through its clear explication by the chief executive.
10. A consultant should work closely and directly with members of the client organization and provide for their participation in the consulting assignment either by assignment to specific working roles, discussion of findings, or an opportunity to initiate proposals.
11. An organization should establish a specific point of contact and liaison for a consultant — either the assignment sponsor or other organization member — who can initiate other organization contacts and through whom the consultant can report.

12. An organization should select a consultant from among two or three who have been invited by the organization for preliminary discussions prior to a final appointment being made.

These prescriptions appear as a useful framework for the development of an organization–consultant relationship which will result in a high level of effectiveness of the ensuing collaborative effort.

References

1. Wilson Seney reported that 8% of his survey respondents indicated "unfavorable experiences" with consultants (Wilson, Seney, *Effective Use of Business Consultants* [New York: Financial Executives Research Foundation, Inc., 1963]). Fifty-three percent of C. L. Quittmeyer's sample were less than completely satisfied with their consultant experiences (C. L. Quittmeyer, "Management Looks at Consultants, " *Management Review* 50 [March 1961]). A study by R. F. Amon revealed that 30% of the business responding to that survey regarded the recommendations they had received from the external consultant as unsatisfactory or inadequate. (R. F. Amon et al., *Management Consulting* [Cambridge, Mass.: Harvard University Graduate School of Business, 1958]).

2. W. G. Bennis, *Changing Organizations* (New York: McGraw-Hill, 1966), p. 175.

3. R. Lippit, J. Watson, and B. Westley, *The Dynamics of Planned Change* (New York: Harcourt, Brace and World, Inc., 1958).

4. S. Tilles, "An Exploratory Study of the Relationship Between the Executives of Small Manufacturing Companies and Consultants," Ph.D. diss., Harvard University, 1960.

5. A random sample (from Dun and Bradstreet's *1968 Million Dollar Directory*) of 1,575 business organizations each having a reported net worth of $1 million or more and employing 100 or more people was collected, to which was added 120 federal government departments and agencies. The 133 responses were distributed among the principal categories as follows: industrial manufacturing, 44%; financial institutions, including banks and insurance, 19%; federal government agencies, 17%; merchandising and distribution, 9%. The small response reflects the lack of any, or any recent, consultant experience as well as disinterest in the inquiry.

Neil G. Davey was associated with P.A. Management Consultants Pty. Ltd., in Melbourne, Australia when this article was written.

Chapter 5

The Trainer's Role as an Internal Consultant

Gordon L. Lippitt

In an earlier article[1] I discussed four major roles performed by training and development departments or offices in modern organizations:

Role No. 1: As a *learning specialist* and instructor.
Role No. 2: As *administrator* of training and development staff and programs.
Role No. 3: As an *information co-ordinator.*
Role No. 4: As an *internal consultant* to the management of the organization.

It is my feeling that each of these four roles or functions requires different skills and abilities. In a small organization, the training director may perform all four functions, whereas in a larger organization the "head of a department" might well be the consultant to management for problem solving while those on his staff administer, design and conduct training and educational programs. In recent years it has been demonstrated that many management problems require for their solution a broader approach than that furnished by the usual training programs or methods.

An Increasing Role

The new challenge, then, for a training director and department is to develop their skills and role in the organization as *internal organizational consultants* on management problems, economic and social change, and organizational development. This "internal consultant" role of the training person is important for helping the changing organization and will require increased professionalization and skills of those in the training field.

The Training Director, in carrying out this internal consultant role, will not work from a power base, as is typical of a line manager, but as a staff specialist will use *influence power* that comes from four sources:

— influence by *competence*
— influence by *ideas*

Reprinted with permission, *Journal of European Training,* Vol. 4, No. 5, copyright © 1975, M.C.B. Publications, Ltd., Bradford, England.

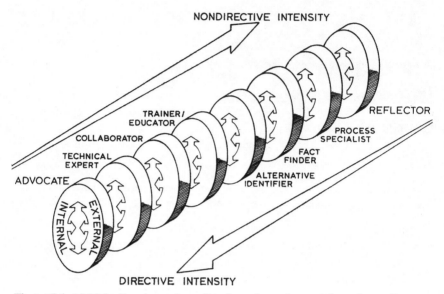

NONDIRECTIVE INTENSITY

REFLECTOR

TRAINER/
EDUCATOR

PROCESS
SPECIALIST

COLLABORATOR

FACT
FINDER

TECHNICAL
EXPERT

ALTERNATIVE
IDENTIFIER

ADVOCATE

EXTERNAL
INTERNAL

DIRECTIVE INTENSITY

Figure 5-1. Multiple directive and nondirective roles and approaches of consultants.

— influence by *acceptance*
— influence by *one's role* (legitimization)

These influence methods will have to be "earned" by the training professional. Influence power will not emerge without demonstrated skills and professionalism. As Beckhard put it,

> "The consultant (or person in a helping role) always enters such a relationship as a person with authority — achieved either through position or role in the organization or through the possession of specialized knowledge. To achieve an effective consultative relationship, it is essential that they understand the nature of this power and develop skills to use it in a way which will be viewed as helpful by the person receiving the help. A person entering a consulting or helping relationship must have the ability to diagnose the problem and goals of the person being helped, and be able to assess realistically their own motivations for giving the help. A consultant must also recognize the limits of their own resources to help in the particular situation."[2]

In carrying out a "helping" relationship to management, a training director will find himself operating along a continuum of consulting roles. In Figure 6-1 is illustrated some of these major helping relationships from directive to primarily nondirective consultations. By directive I refer to those behaviors where the consultant assumes a leadership position or initiates activity. In the nondirective role the consultant provides data for the client to use or not to use.

Situational Role Choices[3]

Situational roles are not mutually exclusive; they may manifest themselves in many ways in a particular client relationship. We see these roles as "spheres of expertise" rather than as a static continuum of isolated behavior.

Let us examine these different role choices in response to management need.

Advocate Role

In an advocate role, the consultant endeavors to influence the client. There are two quite different types of advocacy:

1. Positional or "content" advocacy is a role posture of trying to influence the client to choose particular goals or to accept particular values.
2. Methodological advocacy is a role posture of trying to influence the client to become active as a problem solver — and to use certain methods of problem solving — but being careful not to become an advocate, for any particular solution (which would be positional advocacy). In this role, the behavior of the consultant is derived from a "believer" or "valuer" stance about a content or methodological matter.

Technical Specialist

One of the roles of an internal consultant is that of technical specialist. The more traditional role of a consultant is that of a specialist who, through his special knowledge, skill, and professional experience is engaged, either through internal employment or under contract, to provide a unique service to an organization. Within this realm of augmenting client expertise, the client is mainly responsible for defining the problem and the objectives of the consultation. Thereafter, the consultant assumes a directive role until the client is comfortable with the particular approach selected. Later in the relationship, the consultant may act as a catalyst in implementing the recommendations he had made.

Either the internal or the external consultant may be a content specialist on the client's problem or a process specialist on *how* to cope with a problem. This particular role brings out the consultant's substantive knowledge.

Trainer/Educator

Innovative consultation frequently may require the use of periodic or continuous training and education within the client system. In this aspect of the helping relationship, the consultant can play a role in bringing to bear the learning process which best can be employed critically and creatively — depending upon the situation and the need. The consultant may be a designer of learning experiences or a direct teacher. In a sense, this role requires the consultant to have the skill of a learning methodologist and manager. A familiar role to most training specialists.

Collaborator in Problem-Solving

The helping role assumed by the consultant in the problem-solving mode utilizes a synergistic approach to complement and collaborate with the client in the perceptual, cognitive, and action-taking process needed to solve the problem. The consultant helps to maintain objectivity while stimulating conceptualization during the formalizing of the problem. Additionally, the consultant must help to isolate and define the "real" dependent and independent variables which influenced the problem's cause, and ultimately its solution. He also assists in weighing alternatives, aids in sorting out salient causal relationships which may affect alternatives, and synthesizes and develops a course of action for an effective resolution. The consultant in this role is involved in the decision making as a peer member.

Alternative Identifier

There are direct costs associated with decision making. While the value of a decision is dependent upon the attainment of a given set of objectives, in selecting an appropriate solution to a problem there normally can be proposed several identifiable alternatives, along with their attendant risks. The alternatives, either because of economics or other identifiable implications, should be discovered jointly with the client and the consultant. In this helping relationship the consultant must establish relevant criteria for assessing alternatives and develop cause–effect relationships for each alternative along with an appropriate set of strategies. In this particular situational role, however, the consultant is *not* a participant in the decision making itself, but a retriever of appropriate alternatives facing the problem-solver.

Fact Finder

Fact-finding is an integral part of the consulting process, whether it be for developing a data base or for resolving intricate client problems. It is perhaps the most critical area, and often the one that receives the least attention in actual problem solving and decision making. It first requires the development of criteria and guidelines to be used in the performance of the actual fact-finding process and related analysis. It ends when all available facts have been analyzed and synthesized. The result of this process is the obtaining or giving of information for problem solving by the client. Fact-finding can be as simple as listening or as complex as a formal survey utilizing a number of techniques. In this role, the consultant is functioning basically as a researcher.

Process Specialist

Here the consultant attempts to help the client to be more effective and responsive. The consultant must be specifically concerned with the work process itself as a way of achieving client adaptability.

As a process specialist, the consultant must sharpen all of his multiple role skills to help the client. The consultant works on developing joint client–consultant diagnostic skills for addressing specific and relevant problems in order to focus on *how* things are done rather than what tasks are performed. He helps the client to integrate interpersonal and group skills and events with task-oriented activities, and to observe the best match of relationships. In this role, the consultant functions as a "feedbacker."

Reflector

When operating in the mode of a reflector, the consultant stimulates the client to make decisions by asking reflective questions which may help to clarify, modify, or change a given situation. In utilizing this attribute, the consultant may be an arbitrator, an integrator, or an empathetic respondent who experiences along with his client those blocks which provided the structure and provoked the situation initially. In this role the consultant finds himself being an "overviewer" as well as a philosopher.

Skills and the Consulting Function

What kind of person is able to perform these multiple roles appropriately? For the staff person who carries the training and development portfolio, it will require the proper knowledges, skills and attitudes.

The effective development of the human resources of an organization is essential to its continued growth and viability. In most organizations someone with a training and development responsibility is expected to assist the organization in this respect.

What qualifications does this kind of person need to have? Must he be a behavioral scientist? Does he need to be an expert on communication systems? Does he have to be so courageous or personally active in initiating change, at a risk to his own job, that unusual psychological maturity is required?

Whoever is responsible for initiating human resource development will need to manifest *professional* behavior and leadership. Any list of the professional capabilities of a consultant is extensive. It looks like a combination of the Scout Laws, requirements for admission to heaven, the essential elements for securing tenure at a distinguished university.

It seems to me that the qualities a consultant needs fall into two broad categories. On the one hand such a person needs a number of distinctly intellectual abilities, and on the other he needs a number of distinctly personal attributes[4].

Dilemma Analysis Ability

Intellectually, the consultant needs what I call the ability to make a dilemma analysis, because an organization which uses a consultant is probably faced with a situation that appears insoluble. If the difficulty could be solved easily by the operating manager, a consultant would not be needed. The consultant must recognize that a dilemma, whether real or not, does exist in the minds of those within the organization. The consultant's role is to discover the nature of the dilemma and to determine the real causes of it, rather than what are thought to be the causes.

To accomplish this, the consultant must have a special type of diagnostic skill. He or she should approach a study of the organization's dilemma by means of an existential pragmatism[5] that takes into account the total organization setting and all situational variables. It is only through skillful examining of the organization's fabric that one can see the structural relationships between the various subsystems that comprise the total organization and the interdependent nature of its individuals, groups, substructures, and its environmental setting.

In order to make this kind of dilemma analysis, insight or perception and intuition are necessary. Insight or perception is vital because the problem and solution pertinent to almost any dilemma requiring outside assistance are going to be part of a very complex situation. The ability to penetrate the complexity and isolate the key situational variables is the toughest task. Unless the important factors can be sifted from the maze of detail and causes separated from symptoms, accurate diagnosis is impossible.

Sense of "Organizational Climate"

Intuition or "sensing" must be coupled with perception in order to assess the nature of power and politics in the organization. From my experience in bureaucratic structures, both public and private, these organizations are not just functional. Underlying and intermingled with the functional operations the organization performs are the crucial dynamics of internal power and politics. Invariably, people are vying with other people for organizational influence or for some internal political reason. Very often the consultant has been asked to help not just to provide needed assistance, but also as an instrument of a strategy designed to secure an influence objective.

Unless the consultant has the intuition to sense the organizational climate, he runs the risk of being nothing but a pawn in a game of organizational politics. If he has the ability to recognize and understand the dynamics of the internal power and political relationships, the consultant can masterfully utilize them in pursuit of whatever change objectives the client and consultant conclude are appropriate.

Apart from the diagnostic abilities, the consultant needs implementation skills. Obviously, he must have some basic knowledge of the behavioral sciences and the theories and methods of his own discipline. But more than these, the individual needs imagination and experimental flexibility. Dilemma-dissolving is essentially a creative enterprise. No real life situation is going to fit perfectly the mold suggested by typical techniques or textbook methods. Diversity and unique circumstances will almost always exist. The consultant must have imagination enough to innovate adaptations and tailor his concepts to meet real demands.

The consultant must be able to visualize the impact or ultimate outcome of the actions proposed or implemented[6]. But, like most things, this is as much a process of experimental trial and error as it is one of *a priori* solutions. The courage to experiment and the flexibility to try to discard as many approaches as needed to solve the problem are important ingredients in the practitioner's make-up.

Integrity Is Essential

The other major aspects involved are what I call the consultant's *personal attributes*. Above all, he must be a professional in attitude and behavior. To be successful, I think one must be as sincerely interested in helping the organization as any good doctor is interested in helping his patient. The consultant must not conceive of himself as, or portray the image of, being a huckster of patent medicines. The consulting role is no different from that of any other profession. If the training director's first concern as a consultant is to make an impression or build an "empire," and only secondarily to help the organization, the organization leaders will soon recognize the individual as a phoney and deal with him accordingly. People in top management generally are astute individuals. They can identify objectivity, honesty, and above all integrity.

When entering a client system, a strong tolerance for ambiguity is important. From my experience, the first acquaintance with an organizational problem is marked by a certain amount of bewilderment. It takes time to figure out the situation and during this time one is going to experience a certain amount of confusion. One must expect this to occur and not let it worry one.

Coupled to this type of tolerance must be patience and a high frustration level. Curing a client's ills is likely to be a long and trying experience. Quick results, full co-operation, and complete success are unlikely in the short run. Inevitably, attempts to change people's relationships and behavior patterns are going to be met with resistance, resentment, and obstructionism on the part of those who are, or who think they may be, adversely affected. It is important for the training professional as a consultant to have the kind of maturity and realism which recognizes that many of his actions and hopes for change are going to be frustrated. Such maturity is necessary to avoid the reaction of defeatism and withdrawal that commonly accompanies the frustration of a person's sincere efforts to help others.

Sense of Timing

Finally, the consulting practitioner should have a good sense of timing, a stable personality, and good interpersonal skills. Timing can be crucial. The best conceived and articulated plans for change can be destroyed if introduced at the wrong time. Timing is linked to a knowledge of power and political realities existing in the change situation and to the kind of patience that overrides the enthusiasm surrounding a newly conceived idea or training intervention that one can't wait to try out.

Obviously, consulting involves people dealing with people, more than people dealing with machines or mathematical solutions. The consultant must have good interpersonal skills. He must be able to communicate and deal with people in an atmosphere of tact, trust, politeness, friendliness and stability. This is important because the impact of the practitioner's personality must be minimized to keep it from becoming another variable in the existential setting and making a contribution to the existing complexity. Beyond this, his success will depend on the persuasiveness and tact he has in confronting the interpersonal contact on which the helping situation is based.

Professional Development of Consulting Skills

It is a prerequisite for effective consulting that those practicing such a role manifest professional behavior.

This cannot be merely an outgrowth of the acquisition of degrees. It must be a manifestation of appropriate knowledge, skills, and attitudes in our day-by-day work in and for organizations. In this sense, I have found the following guidelines helpful:

    a. Focus on the problem-solving approach to learning and change; use data, not just hunches.
    b. Develop interdependence with others, not dependency.
    c. Practice what we preach in the field of our specialized knowledges.
    d. Diagnose situations, rather than merely treat symptoms.
    e. Understand ourselves so thoroughly that we do not let our personal needs get in the way of helping people and organizations to develop.
    f. Communicate on a reality level in an "open" fashion.
    g. Admit mistakes and learn from failure.
    h. Develop interests and skills so as to be able to work with people in a noncontrolling manner.
    i. Be willing to experiment and innovate.
    j. Develop a personal philosophy about working and developing people and organizations.
    k. Be capable of saying, "I don't know."
    l. Be willing to learn and change.

These criteria may not be the most important or only criteria for professional behavior, but they are some I value highly. Unfortunately, I find I am unable to achieve these standards as consistently as I wish. Suffice it to say, that while we want to increase the professionalization of the field of training and development, the real goal is not some acquisition of certain areas of knowledge, but the professional styles of behavior each of us demonstrates in our human resource development responsibility.

In addition, I think we need to perform our task with a clear understanding of the ethical questions related to anyone who is involved in planned change through consulting.

The professional trainer is a person who has responsibility for initiating, designing, and implementing learning efforts that will hopefully change individual, group, organizational, or community performance and behavior. What right does the training and development professional have to try to make others grow, develop and change? On what grounds does he base his values as the professional training and development person?

Recognizing that many words have achieved evaluative weight, it might be well to divorce, for the moment, our necessary value judgments from the processes these words describe. Manipulate, for instance, means the arrangement of conditions so that change in a certain direction may or will take place. The training director who arranges his classroom setting, provides certain selected skill practice sessions, asks certain questions, demands certain self-directed learning experiences, and creates certain motivational drives. You are "manipulating," when you are teaching supervisory skills, technical expertise, or interpersonal effectiveness. From this point of view, each training professional, acting or refusing to act as a learning influence, is under judgment in accordance with his basic beliefs and, stemming from those beliefs, his ethical system.

If we accept this line of reasoning, if we recognize that our commitment to a specific training development responsibility in the organization often makes us potential renewal agents, then I submit that the question usually asked, "What right have I to try to make persons, groups and organizations different than they are?" must be reversed. The basic question which we cannot avoid is "What right have I to withhold myself, my skills and my convictions in a changing situation from helping that change to take place in a direction consistent with my convictions?"

In other words, the training and development professional should be *pro-active* and not just *re-active* in the way he demonstrates certain beliefs and values about the way people learn and change.

Most cultures are based upon a system of values which embrace both individual and social ethics. To apply these ethical standards in consulting with the organization, a group, or an individual is an essential undertaking. As I point out in the book, *Organization Renewal,* it is a challenge to relate these ethical values to individual and organization development. It is important, I think, to understand clearly that there are some underlying assumptions supporting the need for individual and organization renewal[7]:

"1. In today's organizations there are unavoidable human problems which involve varying degrees of interpersonal and intergroup tension and conflict that keep the organization from functioning most effectively.

2. It is better that such human problems be solved than remain unsolved.

3. Deliberate planning of solutions to these problems, which necessarily involve changes in the people, the groups, and institutions concerned, is necessary to a degree that it has not been in the past. Trial and error processes of historical accommodation are no longer adequate to the organizational needs of today.

4. The most promising source from which to derive principles of ethical control in the planning of the changes that we must make is in the system of democratic and scientific values. These values can be translated into norms or principles of *process* which can be used in the guidance and direction of the consulting process, of deciding what changes are needed, and in evaluating the changes that are produced."

Let me identify some ethical guidelines that I feel might be helpful to the training and development professional doing consultation.

The first guideline concerns motivation. A trainer-consultant can be motivated, in part, by such individual needs as status, security, and prestige. One's own awareness of these motivations may clearly demonstrate the professional aspect of his role. The approach to problem-solving consultation should be *task-oriented* rather than self-oriented. The essential concern should be that the new condition achieved is better than the first, not that the person initiating change should receive credit or have an enhanced standing in the eyes of others in the organization.

Secondly, the processes by which individual or organization development is planned should be collaborative; they should involve appropriately the persons affected by the change.

Thirdly, in order for training specialists to conform to democratic and scientific values, the methods of problem-solving should be *experimental.* An experimental approach means giving any reasonable but novel plan a try; it also means building into the consultation methods of evaluation which will reveal whether the altered practices approach the desired change goals.

Fourthly, the method used for consultation must be *educational and/or therapeutic* for the people involved, leaving them better able to face and control future situations. We are not trying only to solve present problems, but rather to know how better to deal with future problems as they arise. The idea is not to get away from problems, which is to get away from reality, but rather to help people to know how better to confront, diagnose, and solve problems.

Finally, it is my feeling that those of us who are initiating planned change must always be aware that we are *accountable*. In the first place, we are accountable to ourselves. The responsibility rests with us to examine our motivation, the results we desire and the methods we employ, and to see how consistently they correspond with the value response required of a professional. And we are accountable to those who are affected by our efforts. In this it is a help, and further guide, to accept the fact that the training and development specialist is always involved in and affected by the change he produces. We do not stand over and above — a little God who calls the shots and determines the destiny of others. We are involved and affected, whether as an outside consultant or a part of the organization system. We can never dissociate ourselves from the profoundly inextricable relationship we have with our consulting clients in the learning, training and development process.

If we have training professionals as internal consultants with these kinds of value, attitude, and belief we may yet re-institute a confidence in the training specialist as a valued human resource whose help derives from a process that provides mutual growth for both parties, and help to the organizational system in which he functions.

References

1. Lippitt, G., and L. Nadler, "Emerging Roles of Training Directors," *ASTD Journal*, August, 1967.
2. Beckhard, Richard, *Leader Looks at the Consultative Process*, Washington, D.C.: Leadership Resources, Inc., 1961, p. 3.
3. This section was formerly published as a portion of an article entitled "Consulting Process in Action" by Ronald and Gordon Lippitt, *ASTD Journal*, Madison, Wisconsin; May-June 1975.
4. The next section is adapted from a portion of an article by the author entitled "Criteria for Selecting, Evaluating, and Developing Consultants," *ASTD Journal*, August, 1972.
5. Lippitt, G., *Organization Renewal*, Englewood Cliffs, NJ: Prentice-Hall, p. 18.
6. Lippitt, Gordon L., *Visualising Change*, Fairfax, VA: NTL Learning Resources Corp., 1973.
7. Ibid, p. 170.

Gordon L. Lippitt is professor of behavioral science in the School of Business Administration, George Washington University.

Chapter 6

The Evolving Role of the Federal Training Consultant

Neal E. Chalofsky

It is no wonder government trainers feel a mixture of envy, cynicism, and fascination with the way federal managers perceive external consultants. The difference between management's oft-held perceptions of external consultants as part guru, part expert, and part confidant and their view of internal trainers as "paper processors" and course instructors has helped perpetuate the belief that trainers cannot function as consultants. I had the occasion to see this belief highlighted in my first government training position. A line-management official asked if I could help him complete the paperwork required for him to hire an outside consultant to facilitate a problem-solving session. He didn't ask me to assist him in their problem-solving session. He didn't ask me to advise him on what kind of consultant or who specifically I could recommend. He asked me to help him process the paperwork. This was a common view of the federal trainer's role as consultant.

Fortunately this view is changing — and for several reasons. First, when managers come to the training department and say they have a problem, get them a training course — trainers are no longer just shopping around for an appropriate training course. They are now starting to question whether training is the answer and whether performance or behavior is the problem. Secondly, trainers are beginning to take the initiative and go to managers, asking if they can be of service. Finally, trainers are slowly developing their consulting skills and increasing their knowledge of consulting theories, concepts, and resources.

Consulting as an Evolving Role

Initially, the federal trainer's primary role was instructing. This quickly expanded to designing and developing courses as well as instructing. At the same time, training began to evolve into a staff function within organizations, as opposed to just one part of a subject matter specialist's or personnelist's job.

The need for administrative and management support functions began to emerge. Training quickly became more than a one-man band. It became a visible organizational unit among the other staff functions such as financial management, procurement, and personnel management.

The early 1950s saw the emergence of the outside management consultant. As consulting became a respected and needed activity, organizations began to demand this type of "service" from their internal staffs.

Internal training staffs began being asked to assume the part of facilitator in problem-solving situations, advisor to line and top management, diagnostician in identifying performance deficiencies, and counselor in career development efforts.

The training client–consultant relationship can also be seen as an evolving series of interactions. Initially, the training consultant was concerned with assisting individual employees or groups of individual employees to improve their skills, to solve performance problems, or to increase interpersonal relationships.

The next level that emerged was to work with groups. The training consultant facilitated group process activities and was involved with intergroup relations.

Training consultants gradually became concerned with management's needs. They helped line management diagnose performance problems and advised on training strategies. As consultants developed more credibility, top management utilized them as advisors and resource persons. Finally, with the advent of the concept of organization development, they began to take a global view of the total organization.

At this point I need to stop the action and explain what may seem to be an obvious contradiction. On one hand I've said that the trainer is seen as a "paper pusher" by management and this perception is only now slowly changing. On the other hand, the evolution of the client–consultant relationship implies that trainers have been consulting for quite some time. Both statements are true. Many federal government trainers have never played the role of consultant, either because of lack of need or because of lack of capability, initiative, or authority. Yet, there are trainers who have proactively perceived one of their roles as an internal consultant, and there are now quite a significant number of practicing training consultants in the federal government. One question that has yet to be answered, however, is how consulting emerged as a viable role for federal trainers.

The Federal Training Consultant

The U.S. Civil Service Commission's Bureau of Training initially became interested in identifying the roles, tasks, and competencies of the federal trainer because of research which indicated that trainers were not meeting the needs of their organizations, especially in the area of consulting. A study designed to uncover the disincentives to effective employee development was conducted by the Bureau of Training.[7] One of the significant conclusions was "the employee development specialist (federal trainer) provides limited counseling and consulting services to the rest of the organization."

One of the data-collection activities was a literature review of the roles of the trainer. This review, based on Nadler's[6] three roles (learning specialist, administrator, and consultant) found that trainers felt they were performing as they thought they should, primarily as consultants and administrators. However, managers felt that trainers were spending too much time as administrators and not enough as consultants. Ackerman[1] discussed the ways in which trainers perceived their role and organizational location. In general, trainers perceived that their role should be:

"...one of providing assistance and advice, etc., to management on employee development and training, determining or aiding in the determination of training needs, administering the employee development program, and specific responsibilities such as evaluating training and arranging for training courses."[1]

The role of the trainer from the point of view of management was discussed in Epstein's study.[4] The purpose of this study was to determine line managers' perceptions and expectations of the operational functions of the trainer in a government research and development organization. Most managers surveyed in Epstein's study perceived the trainer as emphasizing his/her administrative function and as limiting his/her activities as a learning specialist and as an internal consultant.

Another data-collection technique in the Disincentives Study was in-depth case studies of three federal agencies. The three agencies selected represented varied missions, organizational structures, sizes, and occupations. In order to collect data from all levels in the organizations, several vertical slices were identified, each of which consisted of a major unit of the agency, one or more subordinate groups under it, several units under each of those, and so forth, until the employees under the first level supervisor were reached. Questionnaires and interviews were used to obtain individual perceptions. One finding directly related to the consultant role was:

"Employee Development Specialists (trainers) have minimal contact with others in the organization, providing next to nothing in the way of consulting services to top management, managers and supervisors, and individual employees..."[3]

Based on this conclusion, the report recommended that the Bureau of Training conduct a detailed examination of the performance requirements of the trainer in government and business. Furthermore, the Bureau should then develop performance requirements for government trainers.

In 1973, the Bureau of Training assembled a research team to examine the role of the trainer in the federal government.[3] The team developed a list of competencies and surveyed the manager of training in every federal agency. The results were clustered around four roles* and these lists of tasks and competencies were published in U.S. Civil Service Bulletin 410-85. "Improving the Effectiveness of Employee Development Specialists."[8]

The consultant was described as being concerned with research and development and providing management and employees with advice and assistance. The tasks of the consultant's role are to:

1. Counsel employees regarding training and developmental opportunities
2. Explain training policies and procedures to supervisors and employees
3. Counsel management on training implications related to anticipated organizational changes
4. Develop and conduct training needs surveys
5. Advise management of immediate and long-range training needs of individual employees as they relate to the organization
6. Explain training regulations, policies and procedures to management and help insure the execution of provisions of FPM Chapter 410 and appendices, as well as local regulations which apply to training and employee development
7. Assist management in analyzing performance problems
8. Measure indirect results of training based on post-training performance on the job to formulate and refine learning objectives
9. Assist employees in determining career development
10. Conduct manpower planning forecasts

Three of the ten tasks (1, 2, and 9) were clearly counseling activities. Yet, at this time, while career counseling activities were recognized as significant, they were lumped in with the consultant activities. Tasks 3, 5, and 6 represented the subrole of the consultant as advisor to management — the expert who described the potential benefits and problems related to training of a certain organizational change or the expert who explained whether a certain organizational policy was contrary to federal regulations concerning training. Tasks 4 and 10 were activities related to what we now refer to as front-end alyasis.

Task 8 is the most interesting. One activity that the consultant was expected to perform was to be "on the lookout" for unexpected results of a training experience while observing on-the-job performance. Once these unplanned-for behaviors were identified, the consultant was expected to feedback this data to the learning specialist so that he/she could build this information into the learning objectives of the training experience. Task 7 is the only task that directly relates to the consultant assisting in solving organizational problems.

---

*The study team based their role clustering on Nadler's three roles: learning specialist, administrator, and consultant. A fourth role, program manager, emerged during the study, to distinguish between administrative support functions and management functions.

The competency list also seemed to be a conglomeration of different abilities and knowledges that somehow related to the consultant tasks. The consultant must have the ability to:

— Establish rapport with people
— Apply a systematic approach to problem solving
— Predict training needs induced by organizational change and advise management of immediate and long-range training needs
— Assist management in analyzing performance problems
— Determing training needs based on job requirements and level of employee skill
— Explain complex procedures to others
— Apply counseling techniques
— Gauge effectiveness of consultation efforts
— Interface with people within the purview of the consultative strategy
— Conduct cost/benefit analysis

The consultant must have knowledge of:

— The workings and interrelationships of the related personnel functions such as staffing, position classification, salary and wage administration, job analysis, training, labor management relations, performance appraisal, and promotion
— The organization's mission, unit goals, objectives, and work processes
— The formal and informal organizational structure
— Counseling techniques

Some background is needed to provide the proper perspective for considering the above lists. First, this was the first attempt by the federal government (and, for that matter, any other major sector) to identify *specifically* what a trainer does and then categorize the information around certain roles. Secondly, the consultant role, being the newest and most vague of all the roles, was the last to be analyzed. Therefore, several of the tasks were literally "dumped" into this role because they did not fit anywhere else. Notice the mixture of client–consultant relationships. Finally, since this task list reflected more of what trainers actually did rather than what they should be doing, it demonstrated that trainers were not really fulfilling the expectations of management.

Management wanted trainers to operate like outside management consultants; consultants who would help in diagnosing problems, facilitating problem solving and applying consulting interventions aimed at increasing the effectiveness and efficiency of the organization. Trainers, on the other hand, seemed to be groping for the right combination of activities, and what this research captured was the federal training consultant role that was still evolving and had yet to really mature.

After completing Bulletin 410-85, the research team began the next phase of their long-term effort to increase the professionalism of federal trainers.[2] This project called for the development of a competency-based, nonacademic curriculum.[9] Since this curriculum was to be competency-based, a review of 410-85 as the foundation for such a curriculum seemed appropriate. But when the team attempted to match the competencies to their related tasks, it was like trying to put a square peg in a round hole. The competencies were developed separately from the tasks and were clustered around the roles, rather than the tasks.

The team opted to start from scratch in developing new lists, with each task matched with the competencies needed to perform that task. A new literature search was conducted, new data were gathered, and new task and competency lists developed. At this point a fifth role, career counselor, emerged, reflecting an increased emphasis on this set of activities. The team next developed behavioral objectives based on the tasks and competencies and organized these objectives into learning modules.

The consultant role retained the same definition and reduced from ten to eight tasks, but the content and approach totally changed. The consultant's tasks are to:

1. Negotiate with the client to determine the scope of consultation effort. The consultant must have:

   — Ability to determine consultative strategy
   — Conceptual understanding of the subroles of the consultant
   — Ability to construct a detailed plan for a job study specifying the scope and limits of the project, specific objectives, specific steps to meet objectives, time schedules, and staff and task assignments
   — Ability to clarify complex procedures
   — Knowledge of intervention, advisory, and persuasion techniques
   — Ability to apply a cost/benefit analysis
   — Ability to conduct meetings and interviews

2. Gather information on organizational goals, objectives, and work processes. The consultant must have:

   — Ability to learn a variety of specialized vocabularies
   — Ability to determine the formal/informal organizational structure
   — Ability to see the organization in terms of the interrelationships between the organization, its environment, and the groups and individuals composing the organization
   — Ability to gather information through interviews, observation, and research
   — Ability to plan and conduct reliability/validity studies

3. Conduct the data-gathering and problem-identification portions of a performance analysis. The consultant must have:

   — Ability to develop and use information-gathering techniques
   — Ability to determine and measure job performance requirements
   — Ability to determine and measure actual job performance

— Ability to use specialized vocabulary
— Knowledge of the formal/informal organizational structure
— Ability to identify the appropriate problem-finding techniques
— Ability to identify the appropriate problem-solving techniques
— Ability to collect problem indicators
— Ability to determine when to plan and conduct a reliability/validity analysis

4. Select, plan, and/or implement the solution(s) of a performance analysis. The consultant must have:

— Knowledge of training and other solutions
— Ability to apply a cost/benefit analysis

5. Evaluate results of a performance analysis. The consultant must have:

— Ability to determine the effectiveness of an implemented solution
— Ability to apply basic statistical techniques
— Ability to apply a cost/benefit analysis
— Ability to validate the process

6. Determine training implications of proposed changes in mission, technology, and organizational structure. The consultant must have:

— Ability to apply a cost/benefit analysis
— Ability to predict training needs induced by organizational change
— Ability to predict training needs given the plans and goals of the organization

7. Report results of a performance analysis. The consultant must have:

— Ability to advise management of immediate and long-range training needs
— Knowledge of appropriate agency reporting requirements

8. Guide agency personnel in the application of methods and techniques to facilitate the training and development process. The consultant must have:

— Ability to apply specific training methods and techniques to meet desired training and development objectives
— Ability to facilitate decision-making processes to help agency personnel to meet desired training and development objectives
— Ability to transfer to the client the problem-solving skills of the consultant

The tasks now represent a comprehensive role rather than a group of functions listed in a random and seemingly unrelated order. In addition, the competencies specifically relate to each task and are broader and stronger in scope. There is an emphasis on a process of negotiating a consultation effort, diagnosing the problem, developing solutions, evaluating results, and feeding back to the client. The tasks also clearly reflect a performance-based systems approach to consulting. In addition, the consultant is not just expected to gain expertise, but to transfer skills and knowledge to the client. This consultant role is much more proactive than the 410-85 role. It's important to note that this list of tasks and competencies has yet to be validated. Therefore, it is more representative of what trainers should be doing than what they actually are doing. But it is a vastly more mature, meaningful role than the 410-85 role. Hopefully, it will assist trainers in performing more effectively as consultants in their own organizations.

The Future

This new role description clearly implies a more ideal client–consultant relationship — one based on systematic problem solving, transfer of knowledge and skills from consultant to client, and an OD view of the consulting process.

The consultant role is certainly not static. It will continue to evolve and change. New consulting approaches, new techniques, and new interventions will precipitate changes in the tasks and competencies. Hopefully, the Bureau of Training will encourage periodic research efforts to update the consultant role, as well as the other roles.

The consultant role can help trainers to become involved in their organizations, thus increasing their credibility. Achieving and retaining credibility " . . . will more and more come to mean advising management, engaging in problem solving, facilitating organizational change, and aiding employees in their career growth."[5]

The consultant role, and the relationships it fosters between trainers and their clients, is one of the most significant stimulants to the professional growth of trainers in the federal government.

References

1. Ackerman, L., "A Study of Selected Employee Development Specialists in the Federal Government: Their Background and Perceptions of Their Role and Organizational Location," doctoral dissertation, The George Washington University, 1967.
2. Chalofsky, N.E., and J.A. Cerio, "Professional Development Program for Federal Government Trainers," *Training and Development Journal* (December 1975).
3. Employee Development Specialist Study Team, *Improving the Qualifications of Employee Development Specialists*. Washington, D.C.: Bureau of Training, January 31, 1975.
4. Epstein, J.H., "Line Managers Perceptions and Expectations of the Operational Functions of an Employee Development Specialist in a Federal Government Research and Development Organization," doctoral dissertation, The George Washington University, 1971.
5. Jorz, J.J., and L.M. Richards, "A Curriculum Plan to Develop Training Professionals," *Training and Development Journal* (October 1977).

6. Nadler, L., *Developing Human Resources,* Houston, TX: Gulf Publishing Company, 1970.
7. U.S. Civil Service Commission, Bureau of Training, *Disincentives to Effective Training and Employee Development,* Washington, D.C.: U.S. Civil Service Commission, 1973.
8. U.S. Civil Service Commission, *Improving the Effectiveness of Employee Development Specialists,* Bulletin 410-85, Washington, D.C.: U.S. Civil Service Commission, July 31, 1975.
9. U.S. Civil Service Commission, Bureau of Training, *The Employee Development Specialist Curriculum Plan: An Outline of Learning Experiences for the Employee Development Specialist.* Washington, D.C.: U.S. Civil Service Commission, November 1976.

Neal E. Chalofsky, formerly with the Bureau of Training, U.S. Civil Service Commission, is currently associate professor of education at Virginia Polytechnic Institute and State University.

Part III

Entry

A public speaker employs a joke or pleasantry at the beginning of a speech. The gaining of audience attention and interest is only part of the speaker's rationale. Similarly, the old Southern tradition of bringing homemade gifts when visiting a neighbor has more than friendship as its purpose. The white flag in a war zone, a warm-up exercise, and the "Could I get you a cup of coffee?" to an office visitor are other examples that, like the joke and the homemade gifts, might be termed "tools of entry."

Physical and psychological entry of one person into the life space of another carries unique ramifications. The tools of entry indicate that the parties involved are at a minimum intuitively sensitive to the relationship aspects of entry. Some students of behavior point to territoriality as the central variable. Others focus on the dissonance associated with a fear of the unknown. Perhaps the intuitive sensitivity is simply anxious behavior genetically linked to a prehistoric existence.

Whatever the reason, the tools tell the tale; the parties subtly recognize that entry is somehow distinctive from what occurs before and after entry. This distinctiveness resides in the relationship aspects of entry.

The entry phase of the client–consultant relationship generally begins when the client, feeling some need for help, contacts a consultant thought capable of providing that help. Less often, the phase begins when the consultant makes contact with a potential client during a search for new business. Even less frequent is the occasion of entry through a third party. Regardless of how the contact is initiated, the puncturing of one's life space by another surfaces relationship issues which impact the quality and the viability of the client–consultant relationship.

The primary goal of both client and consultant in the entry phase is to find sufficient clues to predict the profitability of the endeavor. Profitability can be defined in the eyes of the seeker; it may or may not be related to monetary gain. Improved performance, increased productivity, broader fame, larger fortune, and psychic satisfaction are but a few of the more popular profits pursued by clients and consultants. It is the search for predictability of profit that makes the entry phase glisten with intrigue and intuition.

Predictability is achieved in the minds of the parties when they have found enough clues to provide satisfactory answers to at least four major questions. The answers are drawn from the universe of information which batters between and around the potential client and potential consultant. While other questions can be fashioned which unlock clues to predictability, the four major questions represent giant steps toward a successful client–consultant relationship during the entry phase of consultation.

Why Am I Here?

Shared by both client and consultant, the "Why am I here?" question might be alternately stated, "What brings me to this moment in time?", "What is the impetus for our encounter and dialogue?" It is the struggle of the client to express the quality and quantity of need; it is the effort of the consultant to feel a kinship with that need and with its source.

A part of the client's attempt to adequately answer the "Why am I here?" question is the definition of the problem in such terms that there is an appropriate unsolved residue remaining. That unsolved residue is the parcel up for bargaining between the parties. Inherent in an adequate problem definition by the client is the justification of why a consultant is needed.

Tantamount to effective consultant assistance is the acceptance by both client and consultant that help is clearly needed. Help is not always helpful; intervention may be interference in sheepskin.

One definition of consultation is "the management of vibes between a helper and a helpee." Part of "vibe management" is a close assessment of the motives of the helper. He or she may seek to create indebtedness, stroke ego by demonstrating superiority, foster dependence, or prove rightness. Likewise, the consultant may want to improve performance, make the client happy, or simply facilitate client growth.

The motives of the helpee-client should likewise be scrutinized. A request for assistance can be a disguised search for a scapegoat. The helpee may be seeking help under duress, that is, pressured to obtain the aid of a consultant by a greater power. The helpee may be attempting to reduce personal guilt or satisfying a need for attention and recognition. Often the client, out of fear of the unknown, is self-induced into being sufficiently open to intrigue the consultant, yet sufficiently vague to maintain control.

The desire for control and the fear of exposure keeps the typical client at attention throughout entry. Most guard their clout and protect their flanks out of a duty both to their ego as well as their domain. The "Why am I here?" dimension of entry affords both parties an opportunity to unlock fears to enable trust to infiltrate the relationship.

The consultant's efforts to answer the "Why am I here?" question lies in determining whether consultant resources match client requests. The consultant is likewise concerned with the accuracy of problem definition by the client. While confidentiality is the badge of most consultants, cases in which the client withholds essential information can lead to dangerous results. Caveat emptor is applicable to both parties in consultation.

Who Are You?

The second question rumbling around in the heads of the potential client and consultant during entry is "Who are you?" The question is not one implying a "name-rank-serial number" answer. Rather, the "Who are you?" question is an inquiry into role definition.

Much has been written on the importance of the client finding the right consultant. Given the marketing side of consultancy, the client seeks to avoid buying the wrong resource. The client is interested in ample expertise, and, likewise, attempts to avoid consultant overkill. The client is interested in a cost–gain ratio that favors gain.

The consultant's first dilemma regarding the "Who are you?" question is to locate the client. The contact (the person asking for help) may not be the client (the person making the decisions about the consultation). Additionally, there may be a sponsor (the person or persons strongly interested in the outcome and who probably is paying the bill). Then there is the client system, the group directly involved in the effort.

For example, the board of directors (sponsor) instructs the president (contact) to find a consultant to help the operations group manager (client) find solutions for reducing turnover in the operations group (client system). Several roles can be played by a single person. The key dilemma for the consultant is "Who is the client?"

Another dilemma is whether the client identified has sufficient power and authority to effectuate the changes which come out of consultation. Too frequently, excellent advice and counsel have been for naught because the client lacked what it took to employ the product of the consultation. Not only is such an outcome frustrating to a results-oriented consultant, but it adversely impacts his or her reputation.

Tightly woven into the "Who are you?" fabric are threads of "Who am I?" The client contemplates self-role in the process to determine if its coupling with the consultant role will result in a complimentary union. Likewise, the consultant examines personal competencies against the demands for problem solution to assess his or her likelihood of effectiveness. Resources available to each are unveiled for inspection by the other.

What Is Likely to Happen?

The entry phase is the ground upon which expectations should be strewn for perusal by client and consultant. Once the problem and roles have been defined to the satisfaction of both parties, there must be clarification of the goal to be achieved and the means of expending energy toward that end.

The "What is likely to happen?" question is particularly pertinent to the client due to a fear of dependency on the consultant. Most client–consultant relationships begin with the client feeling one-down. The client is often fearful his or her momentary vulnerability will contaminate objectivity in consultant selection and contract negotiation. While the "he who pays the piper calls the tune" adage is at work in consultancy, the distance between an excellent piper and a poor tune caller is generally wide enough to make the "keeper of the purse" somewhat powerless.

Bargaining from a position of unequal strength can lead to pride-saving behavior on the part of the client. Such behavior may take the form of the client reporting situations in far more positive terms than really exist. Blaming others and rationalization are further attempts the client may use to ward off dependency on the consultant. Even when entry is around a positive situation (making a good situation better), the client will sometimes attempt to circumvent feelings of self-doubt or incompetence by deliberately or inadvertently altering the description of reality.

The consultant seeks an answer to the "What is likely to happen?" question to find the boundaries of the consultation. Only through boundary clarification can misperceptions be aptly avoided. The management of expectations requires front-end agreement on the norms and conditions of action. Planned renegotiation must be built into the agreement to allow for both reassessment and alterations as the relationship matures throughout the consultation.

Goal clarity and feedback are two crucial ingredients in the consultation contract. Only if expectations are acknowledged by both parties without the intrusion of ambiguity can there be a satisfactory meeting of the minds. A feedback system must be molded into the agreement to insure both client and consultant that consultation progress is on track and proceeding according to plan.

Minimizing organizational goal conflict is also of concern in the relationship. Too frequently, consultation follows the line akin to the familiar adage "the operation was successful but the patient died." It is imperative the goal be sufficiently congruent with other client system values to enhance long-term survival as well as short-run excellence.

What Will Be the Result?

The "What will be the result?" question might be labeled "toll clarification." The clues sought during entry provide the answer to the likely consequences resulting from the consultative effort. Both parties are interested in the toll they are required to pay and whether the relationship will end with a net gain. Unless both parties expect the relationship to result in a profit, they are not likely to invest their energies and time. Answers to the "What will be the result?" question help predict that profitability.

The client is obviously interested in getting the problem solved or the need met at the least cost. Like profit, cost has a broader definition than simply dollars and cents. The consultant is interested in achieving the greatest profit for services rendered.

The negotiation or bargaining between client and consultant typically results in a contract. There are generally two aspects to most contracts. The formal aspect covers time allocation, type and amount of payment, and services expected to be performed. The psychological aspect covers what each party hopes to gain from the relationship.

There are many words used for various types of contracts and fee arrangements. Per diem is a common method of fee setting. Retainer fee implies the client reserves a certain amount of the consultant's time. Cost plus fixed fee is a type of contract specifying that a fixed fee plus specified allowable additional costs will be paid. Cost reimbursable, on the other hand, is a contract issued on the basis of estimated costs; final payment is based on costs actually incurred.

Contract termination is an often overlooked aspect of toll clarification. The manner in which the contract will end holds emotional flavors which spice the relationship from the outset. The client is concerned with improving organizational results, enhancing individual growth, and increasing personal power. The consultant is guardian of much of these outcomes. For the client a challenge during entry is to time the relationship's duration at such a length that the desired outcomes will have occurred.

The consultant has a similar dilemma during entry vis a vis contract termination. Consultative success brings a sense of achievement and the feeling of satisfaction that an associate was made stronger by the relationship. Gauging the end to occur simultaneously with success requires effective planning, open communication, and ceaseless negotiation.

The degree to which the four key questions are answered to the satisfaction of client and consultant determines the success of the entry phase of consulting. Adequate answers increase predictability of profit and create a mental set of cooperation, trust, and openness. The goal is for both client and consultant to perpetually operate with what Chris Argyris calls "free, informed choice." That choices arises out of a cognitive map of where the parties involved wish to travel.

Chapter 7
"The Entry Problem in Consultation"
John C. Glidewell

John Glidewell was one of the first writers to address the predictability issue in the entry phase. His article is a classic in the field of behavioral science consulting. Even though it was written more than 20 years ago, it continues to be relevant and useful. The article is included because it provides an overview of the entry process. The issues raised are addressed in the articles that follow.

Central to the Glidewell focus is the necessity in entry to develop a client–consultant relationship which injects predictability into the perception of the parties. The greater the congruence of both parties in terms of need perception (Why am I here?), role expectations (Who are you?), feelings about control and values (What is likely to happen?), and resource and reward allocation (What will be the result?), the more likely the consultation will succeed.

Chapter 8
"Rate Yourself as a Client"
Antony Jay

The best assurance the client–consultant relationship will yield satisfactory results is for both client and consultant to exercise great care in selecting each other. Antony Jay's pithy article unfolds many pointers useful in choosing and using consultants. Most pointers are aimed at helping the client decide if help is needed and, once decided, how to be a good client.

Of particular use are the techniques identified to define the problem in a way that helps client and consultant come to grips with the "Why am I here?" question. As Jack Gibb, author of a subsequent chapter states, "Problem orientation...is the antithesis of persuasion. When a sender communicates a desire to collaborate in defining a problem...he tends to create the same problem orientation in the listener."

Chapter 9
"Client-Consultant Compatibility: The Client Perspective"
Fredric H. Margolis

The importance of good chemistry between client and consultant is in part a function of the type of consulting required. An engineering consultant sought to advise on correcting a structural flaw in a skyscraper might be viewed as first rate despite a crusty, abrasive personality. The capacity to influence would lie more in technical expert power than in personal (relationship) power.

This book focuses on behavioral science or human-system-type consulting. As such, the chemistry or compatibility is a crucial commodity in the effectiveness of the client-consultant relationship. Taken from his book *Consultants: A Buyer's Guide,* this article focuses on ways the client can select a consultant with a level of compatibility that fosters trust and confidence. Fred Margolis' vivid examples bring to life important issues rarely examined in consulting literature.

Chapter 10
"Contracting: A Tool for Client-Consultant Understanding"
Peter Block

Information is organized in our minds in very personal ways. When two people (client and consultant) decide to enter into a work relationship, certain vital information must be transmitted from each personally organized mind to create a "meeting of the minds"—data commonly understood and agreed upon. While a supportive climate and thoughtful questions are tools for accurate transmission of information, a contract is a tool for capturing such data and holding it for future review. Peter Block's highly acclaimed *Flawless Consulting* is a practical guidebook for the entire consulting process. We have taken his chapter on contracting from this book. It gives valuable techniques for collecting entry-related data and fashioning it into an agreement that supports understanding and mutuality.

Chapter 11
"Is Help Helpful?"
Jack R. Gibb

Jack Gibb's article slices through the presumption that because a person is in pain, they desire help. The article likewise surfaces the issue that not all help offered by a helper has the helpee's interests at heart. The cataloging of client–consultant orientations that both help and hinder the consultation is a useful tool for relationship clarification during entry.

Gibb's article provides hints on how client and consultant can manage expectations and boundaries. Armed with the proper orientations, the trust potential in the relationship is significantly increased and the likelihood of misuse of power is decreased.

Chapter 7

The Entry Problem in Consultation

John C. Glidewell

The aim of this article is to contribute to the definition of a complex problem — the problem faced by a consultant and a client when they first try to enter into a working relationship. It would be presumptuous to propose a solution to such a knotty problem. It seems more appropriate and realistic to limit this article to defining the problem.

The article is based upon the assumption that the entry of the consultant is a special case of a more general problem: the attachment of a new person to an existing social system.

Examples are legion. They might include the introduction into a family of a tutor for a child temporarily unable to attend school, the attachment of a social work consultant to an existing nursing staff, the assignment of a nursing consultant to a teaching staff, or the introduction of a human relations consultant to a corporation board. In each case the members of a functioning social system find that some operations are being initiated and performed by a new person. In this case, the new person, being a consultant, is presumably authoritative, and also, being new, he is relatively unpredictable. The problem is that some relationship to this new person must be developed. Some relationship must be developed so that his performance, and the responses of others to it, can be better predicted. Better prediction will make his performance more amenable to control in the interests of the goals of the system — both substantive achievement goals and affiliative human relations goals.

Limitations on the Problem

For the purposes at hand, a special and limited meaning will be given to the phrase "attachment to a social system." It will be used to refer to the process of development of relationships with a person who is to be only temporarily a member of the system. It will not be used to refer to the process of development of

Reprinted by permission from the *Journal of Social Issues,* Vol. 15, No. 2 (1959), pp. 51–59.

relationships with a person who is to be a permanent member of the system.* It is clearly true that the consultant role is often being established these days as a permanent one, but this permanence involves either the development of a new role and, therefore, a basic structural change, or it involves the socialization of a new person into an existing role. Both are more fundamental processes than can be explored here.

Accordingly, this article is limited to the exploration of the process of initiating a relationship between a client system and a temporary consultant. The consultation functions are to be performed temporarily either because the need is temporary or because the functions can be taken over — after a time — by existing roles.

Consultant vs. Consultant-Trainer

It is important to differentiate those functions which are expected to terminate at the expiration of a short-term need from those which are expected to be taken over and continued by existing roles. The first requires the application of objects, skills, ideas, or feelings which the client need never possess or control (like prescribing medication or greasing an auto). The second requires that the client acquire possession and control of the objects, skills, ideas, or feelings, and it therefore implies learning (like the improvement of a golf swing or the recognition of the proper consistency of a pancake batter). The first relationship involves a consultant role; the second, a consultant–trainer role. This article will be concerned with both roles. The distinction should be kept in mind, however, because the role of the consultant provokes less concern about demands for change in the system than does the consultant–trainer role.

Organizational Attachment and Predictability

It is proposed that a basic criterion of attachment to a social system is predictability. This is a special case of the general proposition that a basic criterion of the existence and nature of relationships is predictability. The statement of lawful relationships takes the form of predicting some aspect of one object or force from a knowledge of other objects or forces.

Any application of this proposition to social relations must take account of the notion that social systems develop ultimate values and immediate goals. For the members of the system, the significant predictability for social roles is the forecast

---

*The term "attachment to a social system" was borrowed from Jules Henry (1959) who uses it to refer to the state of being an integral part of a social system — in no way limited to temporary membership. For present purposes, however, "attachment" seems to carry the implication of a temporary arrangement as intended here. Perhaps the appropriate analogy is the military arrangement by which a person who is "attached" to an organization is only temporarily associated and entitled to only limited support from the organization.

of performance in relation to ultimate values and immediate goals. The kinds of relationships to be developed in the process of attachment to a social system are those which insure, not that one knows just what a member will do in a given situation, but that, whatever he does, it will contribute to ultimate values and immediate goals. If the people in the system set a great store by creativity and invention, it may be important that the exact nature of the performance be *unpredictable* — so long as its goal orientation is assured. To illustrate, it is not too important to predict just what sort of medicine a doctor will give you when you are sick. You may, in fact, feel that if he is a really good doctor, his treatment will be so clearly unique to the time, to you and your illness, that it would be impossible to predict from facts previously known to you. It is quite important, however, to insure that the physician contributes to the ultimate value of survival (that he doesn't kill you) and to the immediate goal of relief from distress and disability.

A Redefinition of the Problem

From the foregoing conceptions, limitations, and distinctions, the entry problem can be redefined as that of initiating the development of relationships to provide a basis for predicting the contribution to ultimate values and immediate goals of a set of functions having certain characteristics, namely:

— They are now needed by the system, although probably to a different degree by different members.
— They either are needed only temporarily or can be taken over by existing roles.
— They are not now available in the system.
— They can be performed expertly by the prospective consultant.

In summary the entry problem becomes more or less difficult, depending upon the goodness of fit between the consultant and the client system with respect to stabilities and change tendencies in terms of perception of need, assignment of values, role expectation, resource and reward allocation, and feelings about the control of dependency. Goodness of fit is intended to imply both congruence (as with values) and complementation (as with roles). The significant dimensions to be fitted can be outlined as follows:

1. Perception of need, in terms of the
   — extent of consensus in the total system that an immediate need exists, and
   — importance of the need as measured against the ultimate values of the total system.
2. Perception of appropriateness of role allocation by those empowered to allocate roles, in terms of the criteria that
   — the needed resources are not available in appropriate persons within the system, and
   — the needed resources are available in the prospective consultant.

3. Perception of the appropriateness of resource distribution by those empowered to distribute resources, in terms of the criteria that
   — the consultant will be available to the different members on an equitable basis, and
   — any new objects, ideas, skills, or feelings developed by the consultation process will be equitably distributed.
4. Perception of the appropriateness of reward distribution by those empowered to distribute rewards, in terms of the criteria that
   — the consultant's fee is appropriate to the need (relative to other needs), and of the quality and quantity of service proposed, and
   — any rewards (income to the system) accruing from the prospective need reduction will be equitably distributed among the members.
5. Perception of the appropriateness of the probable emotional interchange between the consultant and the members of the system, in terms of the criteria that
   — the members do not become so dependent that they will not be able to work without consultative support, and
   — the members do not become so hostile toward or frightened by the dependency involved in the consultation that the consultant cannot be constructively employed.

Each of the five dimensions carries its own dynamic for change. Need perceptions are never entirely satisfactory, and the search for the "real" needs is perpetual. Role allocation can never truly fit the individual differences among people and the ever-changing requirements of the tasks of the system. Both formal and informal role reallocation is continuous, although sometimes painfully slow. Resource distribution can never keep pace with changing needs nor reward distribution with the balance between needs and changing contributions.[15,16] Finally, the exchange of feeling can never be all-supportive. Interdependencies always yield fears of dependency. Deprivation — even relative deprivation — yields apathy or rebellion. Evaluation yields fight and flight. Even support can yield jealousy. Any situation into which the consultant intervenes has its own dynamic for constructive changes and restraints.[11] The task is to find and reduce the restraining forces — liberating the growth potential of the system.

Variations in Optimal Conditions for Entry

The foregoing outline of the significant conditions for entry were cast in terms of perceptions. It might be construed to mean that the optimal conditions for entry are those in which the perceptions of the consultant and those of the power centers of the system are in substantial agreement. Such a construction was not intended — and it seems unlikely that such a situation can ever be found. The entry of the consultant into the system implies more or less change in the system — due in part to success or failure in substantive problem solving and in part to the impact of the attachment of a new role to the old system of role, resource, and reward allocation. The question of optimal entry conditions involves estimates of the extent to which the consultant and the client system may hold congruent, complementary, or conflicting perceptions and change tendencies. Congruence implies almost no change; complementation, slow change; and conflict implies fast change or fast termination of the attachment. The possible combinations of conditions are tremendously large, but it seems likely that most of them have been met somewhere or other in the practice of the helping professions.

Consultation in Conflict. Sometimes a consultant finds himself motivated to attach himself to a social system which disagrees with him in all significant respects: about the existence of the need, about the internal availability of resources, about the consultant's resources, about the basis for role, resource, and reward allocation, and about the feelings appropriate in reaction to the consultant's efforts.

The great tradition of the reformer carries with it the theme of consultation in conflict. The theme has had many variations, but more often than not the reforming consultant and his client system have differed most sharply in their perception of the proper locus of power. For example, Poston's work has been stimulated by a gnawing dissatisfaction with power vested in central control of material resources.

"Human values were lost in a maze of punch cards and number systems which were devoid of flesh and blood. Neighborhood life in any meaningful sense, the environment which had nurtured initiatives, civic integrity, and social responsibility began to grow sterile. The control which men had once exercised over their own lives gradually slipped away into distant offices of a centralized and impersonal society."[18]

It was the intent of the consultant to alter the locus of power in the system, and consequently the distribution of roles, resources, and rewards. The success of the first foray of such a reform movement would appear to depend in part upon the direction of changes already under way in the system and in part upon the availability of a subsystem ready to promote the reform. Taylor's dream of a "third force" of efficiency experts independent of both labor and management lacked a power point of entry — until it sold its independence to either management or labor.[20] Poston[18] seeks his power point of entry in community organization of dormant leadership. His goal is to transfer power from existing "nondemocratic" organizations to the new democratic community organization.

Where resistance to consultation is involved, some consultants have been successful as methodologists who suggest and assist in the conduct of self-surveys or other interpretative appraisals by the client system. Attempts to provide interpretive consultation in conflict have produced some remarkable successes, as with the work of Jacques[9] and the Tavistock Institute, and Lindemann,[12] Klein,[10] and their associates at Wellesley.

One can ask, quite justifiably, whether such change agents as Poston or espe-cially Alinsky[1] were acting in the consultant's role. There is a broad and vague area which separates the consultant group from the assault force, but, differentiated or not, both must select carefully the point in the power structure at which they enter.

Entry in the Dark. As often as not, a consultant is called upon to enter the system without any information about the state of affairs within the system with respect to the dimensions significant to entry. He must gather data as he enters, and he must face the possibility that the need is not seen by the most powerful member (e.g., Poston in Montana); that there is no place for the consultant role in the correct perception of role, resource, and reward allocation; and that the typical emotional reaction to the prospect of the consultant role is one of hostility or fear or both. The entering consultant can assume that, in spite of manifest pleas for help, within the informal channels of communication in the client system, many mem-bers are committed — each to a different diagnosis, doctor, and treatment plan. Considering the amount of resistance that consultants regularly encounter, the fact that a consultant will enter in the dark is either a compliment to his courage, a comment on his conceit, or a manifestation of his masochism — or all three.

The Observation Phase. Is there a properly humble posture a prospective consultant can take? Perhaps. He can propose that a provisional relationship be established, enabling him to study the client system and enabling the system to study him. His "entry" is thus confined to the observer role. Observation is threatening to the system, to be sure, but less potent than the active consultant role. And the system is invited to make the observation a two-way activity, so that the consultant withholds no information from any members who could be affected by the problem (so far as he knows). If such a temporary arrangement can be made, data can be collected to provide an estimate of whether any active entry can be made at all, and, if so, at what time and place in the system. Where negative indications are found, a constructive withdrawal is presumably possible.

Congruent Need Perception. A consultant or a client may feel that a minimum requirement for entry is the mutual recognition of the need and its importance. Working on the congruence alone as a base for entry, he will undertake — after an observation phase — a trial period of active consultation. He will propose that the trial period will reveal, first, whether the needed resources are available within the system. If they are found, the relationship can be curtailed and gradually termi-nated. If they are not found, his own skills can be tested for quality. The distribu-tion of his services among the members of the system can be evaluated from time to time and modified to meet agreed upon requirements for equity. In a like manner the equity of the distribution of other resources and rewards can be insured, with particular attention to the separation of the consultant's and the executive's roles. Finally, the feelings of the members about the consultant's activities can be assessed and, when interpretation seems appropriate, interpreted to the members of the system.

This experimental period is much like the "pilot run" proposed by the Tavistock group,[9] but it differs in that it is seen as a more extensive period of experimentation. It runs through a series of phases, but never really ceases to maintain its experimental orientation, particularly where the consultant–trainer role is required.[21]

The crux of the experimental approach is the initial agreement between the consultant and the power figures of the system on the criteria and the rules of evidence by which the experimental results are to be evaluated. Such an agreement may or may not entail a congruence of ultimate values; it must entail agreement on methods and immediate goals.

In developing mental health consultant–trainer roles in public schools, the St. Louis County group began with observation, used a series of conferences to explore perceptions of needs and definition of roles, and to develop a provisional action plan, with a "built-in" evaluation technique. The results were a program with steady growth but a wide variation in need perception, consultant role definition, and action plans, including, in a few cases, the withdrawal of the consultant.[2, 5, 6]

Congruent Need and Role Perceptions. A less adventurous consultant will want not only an agreed-upon need, but also an authoritative establishment of the need for and acceptability of his role as consultant and the client's role as consultee. Resistance to consultation is often due to the feeling of the executive that he "ought to" be able to solve the problem without consultation. A successful solution by consultation is feared because, in the eyes of the executive, it would discredit his competence. The establishment and acceptance of the complementary consultation roles can neutralize such a source of resistance.

Given the agreement upon need and role allocation as a basis for entry (this assures the rate of the fee if not its cumulative amount), the consultant and the client system will try to agree upon a series of experiments with resources and reward distribution. Again, the necessary time investment must be made to reach initial agreement on experimental methods and evaluative critera.

Bases and Experimentation. A consultant may seek more and more congruence and leave less and less to experimentation, but at least two limits appear.

The consultant who expects fully to insure appropriate and realistic interchange of feelings between himself and the members is asking for some rather unusual advantages. He is asking for valid and reliable data about the feelings of persons, and this is hard to come by. He is also asking that both he and the client system resolve their conflicts about authority and dependency before he enters. Ten years of human relations training and research and experience by the National Training

Laboratories has reaffirmed the significance of dependency conflicts, but it has also established the difficulty of resolving them.[19]

A second limit is set by the strength of the value set upon progress and change. At least in western civilization (and certainly in modern India and China) the value set on progress is as strong as the resistance to change. The more the congruence of perception needed by the consultant as a basis for entry, the fewer are the opportunities for change. Most consultants seem to try to strike a balance between an assaultive consultation in conflict and a pedestrian consultation in comfort.

There are, of course, all sorts of possible combinations of agreement and experimentation. Role, resource, and reward distributions often get established before there is an agreement about the nature of the problem. Data collection follows. Sometimes constructive feeling interchanges emerge first and substantive experimentation follows. The situations are as varied as life.

The consultation is often admonished to enter "at the top" of the power structure, but, as has been pointed out[3] in complex organizations there may be many "tops" which will provide points of entry. The combinations and permutations of wholes and parts of a social system present infinite variety.

Experimentation is uncertain, costly in time and work, and provisional even in its outcome. Judgment about entry is a matter of calculated risk. Knowledge of the dimensions of the problem aid in the calculation.

Summary

In summary, it has been suggested that the entry problem can be defined in terms of the goodness of fit (in congruence, complementation, or conflict) between the consultant and the client social system with respect to three principal variables:

— Perception of need
— Perception of prospective equity of role, resource, and reward distribution
— Perception of prospective appropriateness of feeling interchange, with special concern about dependency and counterdependency

References

1. Alinsky, Saul D., *Reveille for Radicals,* Chicago: University of Chicago Press, 1946.
2. Buchmueller, A. D., and H. R. Domke, "The role of the public health department in preventive mental health service," *Children,* Vol 3 (1956), pp. 225–231.
3. Demerath, Nicholas J., "Initiating and maintaining research relations in a military organization," *Journal of Social Issues,* Vol. 8 (1952), pp. 11–23.
4. Festinger, Leon, and Harold H. Kelley, *Changing Attitudes through Social Contact,* Ann Arbor: Research Center for Group Dynamics, University of Michigan, 1951.
5. Gildea, Margaret C. L., "Community mental health research: findings after three years," *American Journal of Psychiatry* Vol. 114, No. 11 (1958), pp. 970–976.

6. Glidewell, John C., "An experimental mental health program in Webster Groves," In *Third Yearbook, American Association Public Schools,* New York: Columbia University, 1955.

7. Henry, Jules, Concepts of Social Structure and Personalization. Unpublished manuscript, Washington University, St. Louis, Mo., 1959.

8. Jacques, Elliott (Ed.) "Social therapy," *Journal of Social Issues,* Vol. 3, No. 2 (1947), pp. 1–66.

9. Jacques, Elliott, *The Changing Culture of a Factory,* New York: Dryden, 1952.

10. Klein, Donald C., and Ann Ross, "Kindergarten entry: a study of the role transition," In Morris Krugman (Ed.), *Orthopsychiatry and the School,* New York: American Orthopsychiatric Association, 1958.

11. Lewin, Kurt, "Frontiers in group dynamics," *Human Relations,* Vol. 1 (1947), pp. 5–41.

12. Lindemann, Elizabeth, Mental health in the classroom: the Wellesley experience. A paper presented at the annual meeting of the American Psychological Association, New York, 1957.

13. Lippitt, Ronald, Jeanne Watson, and Bruce Westley, *The Dynamics of Planned Change,* New York: Harcourt, Brace and Company, 1958.

14. Mann, Floyd C., and Ronald Lippitt, (Eds.), "Social skills in field research," *Journal of Social Issues,* Vol. 8, No. 3 (1952), pp. 1–58.

15. Parsons, Talcott, and Edward A. Shils, (Eds.), *Toward a General Theory of Action,* Cambridge: Harvard University Press, 1952.

16. Parsons, Talcott (Ed.), *Essays in Sociological Theory,* Glencoe, IL: The Free Press, 1954.

17. Poston, Richard W., *Small Town Renaissance,* New York: Harper, 1950.

18. Poston, Richard W., *Democracy is You,* New York: Harper, 1953.

19. Stock, Dorothy, and Herbert A. Thelen, *Emotional Dynamics and Group Culture,* Washington D.C.: National Training Laboratories, 1958.

20. Taylor, Frederick W., *The Principles of Scientific Management,* New York: Harper, 1911.

21. Thelen, Herbert A., *The Dynamics of Groups at Work,* Chicago: University of Chicago Press, 1954.

John C. Glidewell is a professor of psychology and director of the Corporate Learning Institute at Vanderbilt University.

Chapter 8

Rate Yourself as a Client

Antony Jay

It is over fifteen years now since I met my first really dumb multimillionaire, and it made quite an impression on me. Up till then I had thought that you needed brains to make money: I was used to being asked, "If you're so clever, why aren't you rich?" but this was the first I'd ever met someone to whom I could have said, "If you're so rich, why aren't you clever?" At least I myself could not have said it, because I do not have that kind of courage, but it would have been a fair question.

I say it made an impression on me, but what really made the impression was discovering the answer. I ought also to add that the passage of years and brief encounters with a few other millionaires now suggest to me that the original one may not have been quite so dumb as I took him to be: once you are a millionaire, certain social conventions are suspended and you do not have to take the trouble to appear intelligent, interested, alert, or even awake. And he had inherited some of the millions, though he had added many more by his own success. But even so, he was dumb. He had only one of the many qualities that top men are supposed to need, but he had developed it to such a degree of refinement that he did not need any of the others.

That quality almost amounted to genius — a genius for choosing and using professional advisers. Whatever his problem — computers, marketing, works of art, wine, long-range planning, long-range putting — he infallibly found the best man in the world to advise him on the subject and extracted the maximum possible value from the advice. I have since discovered that this skill is widely recognized at the top level, but because I am not a top-level person, it took me many years to make the discovery.

The skill was certainly recognized by one of the richest men in history — Andrew Carnegie's epitaph on himself was said to be, "Here lies a man who knew how to enlist into his service better men than himself." It also explains why the people who come out on top in school and college do not automatically rise to the top in industry and enterprise; the crucial qualification is not to *be* one of the brightest people but to know how to use them.

I came across the same truth from the other direction a few years later, when I was making a television program about the great modern Italian architect Luigi

Reprinted by permission from *"Harvard Business Review,* July-August, 1977, copyright © 1977 by the President and Fellows of Harvard College; all rights reserved.

Nervi. He attributed at least half the credit for one of his most successful buildings (the Pirelli building in Milan) to the fact that his client was as much of a master of the craft of being a client as Nervi himself was of the craft of being an architect.

Few of us, I suspect, have thought of ourselves in terms of how good we are as clients, though when we reflect on it we probably give ourselves pretty good marks. That's half the trouble — it's one of those private activities like selection interviewing or sexual intercourse which, since we never put them on public display or try them out in competition, we can always kid ourselves we're pretty good at. But unlike either of the other subjects, it has not been subjected to extensive and detailed scrutiny, nor has it generated a vast literature describing and analyzing the process and recommending the techniques that are most likely to achieve the desired result.

And yet, as professional skills multiply and the disciplines divide and subdivide, it becomes increasingly difficult for the executive or manager to acquire even the most basic knowledge himself. In addition, it has become increasingly expensive to keep on his payroll professionals of quality in all the disciplines that may at some time or other be relevant to his organization.

The solution, of course, is to hire professional advisers and consultants from outside, and it is a solution that more and more companies are finding, with results that fall fairly evenly along the spectrum from triumph to disaster. But how do you make sure that your own use of advisers and consultants puts you up at the triumphant end and not down with the disasters? Only by acquiring that one professional technique that you can never hire from outside: the technique of choosing and using advisers and consultants.

Twenty-Five Principles and Pitfalls

This technique is not, to be honest, one of the most fully developed in the world of government and management: there is no certificate or diploma, and no organized body of knowledge. But there are some master craftsmen, some directors and executives who over the years have discovered the principles and the pitfalls, and there are some top-class professional advisers who, after a lifetime of dealing with every kind of client, have come to identify very clearly the type of client attitude and behavior that leads to success, and those departures from it that lead to trouble, unhappiness, and failure.

It is the distillation of their wisdom that has led to this first formulation of the rules for the successful use of professional consultants and advisers:

1. Get the habit of asking yourself, whenever you are up against what appears to be a new kind of problem, whether it may not be in essence a problem lots of people have had before. If, for example, you are wondering whether there might not be a more economical way for your fleet of trucks to take the goods from your factories and deliver them to your warehouses or stores, it might occur to you that many others have asked themselves the same question in the past. But, until you learn to

ask yourself that kind of question, you may never even find out that there is something called transport optimization theory, linear programming, or even operations research. The surest way not to find the best professional advice is not to think of looking for it.

2. Before seeking professional advice, however, there is one vital question to which you owe yourself an honest answer: Have you the intention, the resources, and the will to implement the advice when you get it? There is no surer (or commoner) way of wasting money on consultants than by paying for surveys, reports, and recommendations and then doing nothing about them.

3. Once you have decided you need professional advice, give yourself time to choose the right person. Your choice of adviser is far and away the most important single determinant of success or failure, and the most frequent cause of failure is deciding too quickly that this is the person you want. And if there are others in your organization who will be working with him as much as you will, involve them in the selection process too. To foist your personal choice on colleagues or subordinates is asking for trouble.

4. Try to get someone else to make up your list of finalists. It is not just that the job may be tedious, with a lot of phone calls to discover, say, which marketing consultants have experience of international multilingual mailing campaigns, and what their previous and present clients have to say about them; it is also that the one indispensable qualification for success in the advisory field is the ability to impress potential clients and land the business, and you expose yourself to the risk of being charmed too quickly into picking a good person who is not the right person. A preselection by someone else at least ensures you against too grave an error.

5. You will obviously take advice from trusted friends and colleagues — especially those who seem to be experienced and successful with professional advice — but do not be content with client references alone. Clients can only judge part of a professional adviser's skill, and they do not often have a chance to make informed comparisons. A good extra source of advice is the body of people who work for and with many professional advisers: builders will tell you about architects, journalists about public relations companies, publishers about literary agents, insurance houses about brokers, and so forth; and they may give you very different facts and judgments from those of satisfied clients (so long as you don't ask for them in writing). You may also find a consultant network; for example, your lawyers who are accustomed to working with a particular firm of accountants may provide you with a pathway to the right person. Also, if you are going to ask consultants to work together, it helps a lot if they know each other already.

6. There is also the trade press — almost every profession has a journal, and a call to one of the editorial staff will be valuable if you ask the right sort of questions, namely objective and factual questions about the size of the group, how long they have been around, whether they are established or fast-growing, what subdivisions of their professional discipline they specialize in (tax consulting, investment planning, business systems) and what type of clients (government,

industrial, private) they most frequently work for. It is a good idea to avoid asking straight out for a direct assessment — good, mediocre, charlatan — unless you know your informant quite well.

7. It is also worth considering whether the professional advice you need necessarily has to come from a professional firm. If, for example, you want help in establishing a better staff appraisal system, you may find that another company has recently set up a very successful scheme and would be prepared to hire out to you, for two or three days a month, the executive who was responsible for its success. You might even find such skills somewhere within your own organization.

8. Pick someone your own size. An adviser who is in too small a business can be a dangerous risk on a big project — he has so much less at stake than you have. Equally, too large and grand a professional firm may well be unable or unwilling to give your small project the priority and high-level involvement that a smaller and hungrier group would devote to it. And it is also worth taking time to find an adviser who has already worked in your industry; apart from time saved on briefing and familiarization, he is also likely to have useful contacts and perhaps a refreshingly different point of view from yours.

9. Never take on an untried consultant for a project that could make or break the whole organization, or a significant part of it. It is much better to try the adviser out on a smaller and clearly defined project that will not be a great disaster if it fails. You can move on to more ambitious projects when you have discovered if you can work well together. And the experience and lessons of the pilot project will help ensure the success of the main one.

10. If you are personally impressed by a potential adviser, establish clearly, and, if possible, write into the contract how deep his personal involvement in the project is going to be. There was a famous London management consultant in the 1950s whose craggy face, bushy eyebrows, deep perception, and penetrating analysis were almost hypnotically irresistible to the boards of large corporations. But once the corporation was hooked, he was never seen again. For the next 18 months the offices were overrun with hordes of young, fresh-faced business graduates completing their management education at the corporation's expense. The corollary of this is that if the person you first meet admits he will not be doing the work himself, make sure that you meet the people who will be doing it before you decide to go ahead with them.

11. When you talk to potential advisers, get them as quickly as you can off the subject of their brilliant staff, their unrivaled resources, and their tremendous record of successful assignments, and on to the subject of your problem and your needs. Observe how well they listen and pay great attention to the questions they ask. If you are choosing from a list of finalists, ask each consultant to produce for you a brief analysis of your problem as he sees it and lines of approach that he would investigate if hired.

12. When you have appointed your expert, put his job in writing. Better still, get him to do so. He should set down the objectives you have asked him to achieve, the

division of responsibilities between him and you, any special instructions or constraints, the resources he will require from your organization, a provisional time schedule for the various stages and the review meetings, and all details of payment. He may want to add other things, too, but these are musts.

13. Always involve your advisers at the earliest possible stage. This is the single most important piece of advice for those who want value for money. It is an odd fact about large projects that the first few decisions are almost always both the most costly and the most arbitrary. It is at this stage that a good professional can save you millions. I once sat in with two of Britain's leading comedy writers who had been called in to advise on a comedy film that had been two-thirds shot. Their advice was very firm: on no account shoot the other third. But they would have made the same judgment six months earlier simply on the basis of the script, if anyone had shown it to them. Their fee would have been exactly the same, but the producers would have wasted only $800 instead of $80,000.

14. Tell your adviser the basic motivation for the project even if it is confidential or even slightly ignoble. If you have called in a production engineering consultant to give you ammunition for your battle against the board's decision to cut back the reequipment program, it is important that he should be aware of this from the start, even if you do not put it in writing or spell it out in so many words. Equally, it may take him a long time to discover that when you said, "Look at my organization structure," you only meant, "Find a polite way of moving Harry Green sideways."

15. Express the consultant's job in terms of the end result you want to achieve. If you tell the architect you want a three-story office building, that is what he will design for you. But if you explain to him the pressures of staff or the reorganization plan or the diversification policy that led you to the idea of the three-story building, he may see a better solution than you can. Without realizing it you have diagnosed your own complaint and written your own prescription before going to the doctor. So describe your need to your professional adviser in as much detail as possible, but leave it to him to work out the best means of satisfying it. Half the errors in the use of professional advisers spring from what is the equivalent of using a doctor as if he were a druggist.

16. Do not try to teach your adviser his own job — but do not ask him to do yours. The distinction between ends and means is at the heart of your relationship. You are the expert on ends; he is the expert on means. This is a barrier you cross at your peril, and the dangers of crossing it are greatest in areas where the client thinks he can understand what the adviser is doing. Marketing and advertising are minefields, and many a senior agency copywriter has felt his blood pressure rise to the threshold of cardiac arrest to see his granite-chiseled words "improved" by a trainee product-manager from the client company. Do not trespass on the areas of professional skill and professional judgment that you hired your advisers for.

17. An absurdly simple way of getting value from a professional, and one that is overlooked more often than you would believe, is to ask him a few really broad questions in the early stages. It is too easy to stick to limited and precise problems

and never ask him, "What is your view of the basic idea?" "Are we setting about this in the wrong way?" "Can you think of anything else we ought to be doing as well?" "Is any of this unnecessary or extravagant?"

If you do not ask these broad, general questions, he may not feel it is his place to volunteer his view. The higher powered the adviser, the greater his value in these wide, general areas, and it may be worth paying for two or three expensive days of a really top person's time to range over the problem and perhaps guide you toward the right adviser when the proper approach has been identified. One such conversation proved to a senior executive that he did not in fact want a foremen's training program at all, though that was why he sought advice: the fault was in selection of foremen, and it was the selection procedures that needed the urgent attention.

18. Never pretend to understand something out of reluctance to reveal the depth of your ignorance. All professionals slip from time to time into jargon or, even worse, a specialized use of a general term. It is much better to start from the basis that you are slow-witted and ignorant, and that he has to make everything crystal clear. It is nice if you really are well informed, but honest ignorance is a hundred times better than simulated understanding. You and your consultant have to learn to communicate with each other very accurately, which means spending some time in your early meetings constructing a vocabulary; so never hesitate to ask for clarification by example, definition, or synonym.

19. Learn as much as you can about what your expert's skills and abilities are and how his job works. This can be grasped in outline by half an hour's reading but is best filled in over a drink or a lunch. You may discover he is equipped to do many more things than you have required of him. You may find that some things you have kept away from because you thought they were too expensive are in fact very cheap. You may find a simple change in your operation could greatly ease and simplify his work and reduce your costs. But you will never find any of this out unless you talk about his business in a general way as well as talking about the project in a specific way.

20. Try to integrate your adviser into the team working on the project. This is much better than having the professional person bring in his own team, not only because of the problems of teaching a lot of outsiders about your business and its needs, and the dangers of communications difficulties, rivalries, and resentments, but also because he will be spending his skill and knowhow among your people and giving them a short course in his discipline. And at the end of it you have not just a completed project or system but also an educated team. If you do not integrate him, his presence at your side may stimulate suspicion and resistance. And obviously you are heading for disaster if ever you find yourself playing off your outside adviser and internal staff against each other.

21. Never abdicate. This would be too obvious to be worth stating were it not that it has happened so often. The classic years were the 1950s and early 1960s, when every computer horror story turned out to be the story of an abdication by an executive or director to a consultant. Abdication is never the result of any action; it is always a consequence of inaction. The moment you are tempted to leave an

executive decision to your adviser or rubber-stamp his recommendations because the facts and arguments are too complicated for you to follow, you are on the edge of abdication.

You absolutely must stay in firm control of your professional so that you always know what he is doing, why, when it will be done, what its implications for, and repercussions on, the rest of the organization will be, and how much it is going to cost. How he is doing it is another matter. You can expect to understand that only in very broad terms. You are in greater danger of abdication if you have not got absolutely clear in your own mind from the start precisely what the project is intended to achieve, and if you have not built the review points into it from Day 1.

22. One of the reasons for abdication is that the client gets drawn into the adviser's jargon, and then into his assumptions and his world. You have to keep clear to yourself what you are doing in your own words and in your own terms. A good discipline is to imagine you have received a strong memo from your chief executive saying that he has heard you are wasting everyone's time and money on a pointless and self-indulgent exercise: the discipline is to draft your reply, even if only in your own mind. As you work out in clear, straightforward English the reasoned justification of your project, you find yourself redefining your adviser's objectives in a most valuable way.

23. Be enthusiastic if you are pleased. Advisers and consultants (like most other people) blossom in a warm climate, and if they really enjoy the project and feel they are being appreciated, they give much better value. A professional's reputation is like the share price of a company. If he feels that the job he's doing is raising it, he is increasing his market valuation even if he is not actually getting a bigger dividend. The corollary is to tell him clearly and early if you are unhappy with the ways things are going.

24. There is sometimes (especially in England) a certain embarrassment about discussing fees with professional people. The problem is that they are social equals, and in the conventions of polite society money does not change hands between gentlemen except in the payment of gambling debts. To pay someone money for goods or services is to demote him to the category of tradesman or servant, and to argue with him about it is even worse — that reduces him to the status of a stallholder in an Eastern bazaar.

One consequence of this embarrassment has been the monstrosity known as the fee scale, whereby the professional is paid according to a long-established percentage of the total cost of the job. It is a monstrosity because it does not necessarily reflect either the amount of work or the value of the work he does, and because it gives him a pecuniary incentive to inflate the total cost of the work to increase his own fee.

It can often make a great deal of sense to agree to pay the full scale fee and then involve your professional adviser in a cost-cutting exercise that reduces the overall cost of the operation while leaving his personal recompense intact. Other professionals simply charge by the hours they work, and in this case it becomes extremely important to know which activities consume a lot of their time and which do not. Alternatively, you can tell your prospective consultants the budget at the start, and ask them how much they will be able to do for the money.

But whatever method you use, there is no alternative to bringing the question up and laying it on the table. Both the method of payment and the amount have to be got clear and straight before any work begins. If the fee seems too large, you simply have to ask the adviser if you are playing out of your league and ought to go to someone less august and respected, or whether there are ways the project can be modified to reduce the fee to manageable proportions. While there could, of course, never be any question of a professional and a gentleman trying it on in the matter of money, it is sometimes surprising how much the fee can be reduced without any visible diminution of service, so long as there is no direct confrontation with overcharging and exploiting a social relationship for commercial advantage. But whatever else you do, fix an overall sum. Never hand the man a taximeter.

25. Finally, when the project is complete, ask for a report. Not a report on the project, which you presumably will be getting if it is that sort of project, but a report that reviews how the adviser–client relationship worked in practice and what should be avoided or repeated next time. Were there any misunderstandings? Was there information on either side that was not discovered by the other until too late? Did either side cause the other a lot of work or expense that could have been avoided? Were any shortcuts missed? Was the initial formulation of the objective too broad, or too narrow, or too vague?

All these questions have implications for future projects, even if with other advisers and other clients, and putting them on paper helps to focus the mind and activate the memory. You may also want to add an implementation review, perhaps even as much as two years later, to see how it finally worked out in practice and what can be learned from it. A good relationship with a professional adviser improves all the time as you get to know more about each other. Every family doctor or family lawyer knows how much better a job he does through knowing the family over the years and indeed the generations, but the family, too, gets to know how to use the doctor or lawyer. Your professional adviser can therefore do more than complete your project successfully — he can help you to become a more sophisticated client as well.

This then is a first formulation of the rules for using advisers and consultants for your own advantage rather than theirs.

The Seven Deadly Sins of Advisers and Clients

From discussions with a dozen or so top executives and leading professional advisers, one point emerges very clearly: although it takes time to become expert in the use of experts, many of the most serious mistakes can be eliminated as soon as you become aware that you are making them. So, perhaps it is best to end with the seven deadly sins on each side.

Those of the advisers are:

1. Applying tired formulas and book solutions instead of studying the problem with an open mind: adapting the client's problem to fit their expertise instead of adapting their expertise to fit the client's problem.

2. Using a high-powered front man to sell the service and then handing the job over to inexperienced people, inadequately supervised.

3. Using the client's name without permission.

4. Overcommitting themselves, from an emotional inability to turn down offers of work even if accepting means that they will be dangerously overstretched.

5. Privately criticizing and disparaging the client's staff when talking to top executives, and criticizing top executives to the staff.

6. Doing work on fees for the client that could be done just as well, and less expensively, by the client's own staff.

7. Concealing the fact that another company whose products or services they are recommending is giving them a commission or paying them a retainer.

The clients' sins are:

1. Failure to define their requirements clearly to themselves and effectively asking the consultant to find the problem as well as the solution.

2. Changing their minds and altering their decisions on the basis of casual and ill-informed criticism from colleagues or friends.

3. Reacting to criticism from superiors by putting all the blame on the adviser, even though they have approved what the adviser is doing.

4. Not bringing real worries and criticisms out into the open and confronting the adviser with them: terminating the consultant's services without warning, or not having the courage to terminate when they should.

5. Interfering and second-guessing on matters that lie within the adviser's expertise and are outside their own.

6. Blurring responsibility for the consultant's work, so that all those involved try to arrange it so that they take the credit if it succeeds and avoid the blame if it fails.

7. Freeloading, that is, employing an adviser on a small, well-defined project and then trying to milk him "informally" for free advice over a wide range of other, unrelated problems.

Antony Jay is chairman of Video Arts, Ltd., a British film production and distribution company.

Chapter 9

Client-Consultant Compatibility: The Client Perspective

Fredric H. Margolis

A critical part of the client-consultant relationship not often talked about is the personality mix. The consultant's personality may irritate you or conflict with the organization's norms and expectations. On the other hand, the consultant may feel uncomfortable and distracted by you (as sponsor) or the tone of the client organization as a whole.

There are other less easily measured personal characteristics that can have an even more profound effect on the success of the consultation. These include the consultant's belief system, source of motivation, personal ethics, objectivity, forthrightness, and capacity for loyalty. It is important these qualities be assessed early in the relationship.

The Consultant's Compatibility with the Organization

There are two legitimate reasons for seeking a client-consultant relationship with good "chemistry." The first is your personal satisfaction. As sponsor, you are going to be spending time with the consultant so naturally you will want the relationship to be enjoyable as well as productive. The second is the impact of personality on the success of a consultation. To some extent, the importance of this factor varies with the situation. When you need expert technical skills for a limited task, you clearly will want someone whose skill and knowledge you respect. You may or may not like this person. A patient in need of open heart surgery, for instance, will find the *best* surgeon possible, rarely fussing if this surgeon happens to wear flashy clothes and espouse strange political views.

A comfortable personality fit, however, is essential if the consultant is to work closely with people in organization development activities. Participants must be able to talk as openly to the consultant as they would to a personal physician or other trusted advisor. Without this kind of confidence, clients will not be willing to disclose painful information or take risks often necessary to resolve a problem. A certain degree of personality fit is a prerequisite.

Adapted with permission from *Consultants: A Buyer's Guide* by Fredric H. Margolis and Larry N. Davis, Austin: Learning Concepts (in press).

The judging of compatibility and integrity is more difficult. You have to act intuitively on information often highly subjective; every situation is different. It's up to you to decide the crucial ingredients for good chemistry in your unique situation. To assist you, this chapter offers guidelines and raises questions for consideration in some of the important areas. You and the other people who will be working closely with the consultant must identify the criteria you will use in making a decision.

Recognizing the Consultant's Belief System

You are buying a system of beliefs when you contract with a consultant. It is important you find out what it is and estimate how well it will fit your situation and organization. One obvious way to determine a consultant's belief is to ask some direct questions like: "What is your view of organization development?" "What do you think the role of the consultant should be?" "Describe how people best learn?" or "What are the crucial ingredients for organizational improvement?"

The trouble with direct questions is that you may hear the "official" belief system, not necessarily the *operating* belief system of the consultant you are interviewing. The consultant may say one thing in the interview and later do something entirely different. Operating belief systems can be inferred to some extent by listening carefully and drawing out the consultant about his or her approach to your problem. Reference checks also can help get an accurate picture. You will never know for sure, however, until you actually are well into the consultation.

Clues can be provided by the consultant's emphasis and use of language. Some consultants may emphasize formal data collection and analysis methods and use the vocabulary of technical and business specialties. Another may talk about systems. Others may talk about analyzing the contingencies of reinforcement and setting up an effective positive reinforcement program. The focus may be on shaping the working environment. Still another consultant may emphasize development of individual people and groups and talk about growth, motivation, group process, trust levels, and team building. If you hear terminology unfamiliar to you, find out where it comes from and ask for references to basic literature on the subject.

Other clues come from the way the prospective consultant relates to you during the exploratory meeting. Does he or she appear to be outside or inside the consulting relationship? Listen for the kind of data the consultant requests and the way the consultant talks about the relationship with you. When requesting data, some consultants will want "just the facts, Ma'am"—the hard data. Another may want to know the objective facts, but also will ask questions like, "What is your *impression* of the situation?" "What is your *hunch* about the causes of the problem?" and "How do you *feel* about what is going on?" This person will probably point out any inconsistencies between the objective and subjective data. For example, there may be lack of agreement about whether a problem really exists, or there may be a more fundamental problem under the one presented by the client.

After interviewing the consultant, ask yourself these questions: What are my and my organization's beliefs about change? What do we believe is the best way to motivate people? To learn new skills and knowledge? To manage the organization? Do people agree about these beliefs for the most part, or is there serious conflict? What are the beliefs of the people who will ultimately hire the consultant? Who will receive the consultant's help? What are the end user's beliefs? Is the consultant's belief system compatible with my organization's philosophy and practices?

The stability and climate of your organization should be taken into account when choosing a consultant. Avoid hiring a consultant whose belief system contradicts your organization's philosophy, unless you want to consider *changing* your organization's beliefs.

Personality Fit

Personality elements that can have an impact on the consultation include dress and appearance, language, background and interests, interaction style, and character traits. Some of these, like appearance and background, are important only when they interfere seriously with the work the consultant was hired to do. The consultant's personality becomes a problem when people are offended to the extent that they cannot concentrate on a task or they reject an entire intervention effort. This doesn't mean, however, that in order to be effective the consultant's way of dressing, talking, and thinking *has* to conform to your organization's image. As an outsider, a consultant can say and do things not allowed normally. In fact, it can be an advantage to hire a consultant who isn't a carbon copy of people in your organization. A different perspective and viewpoint can help you understand your own organization better—its unique qualities and strengths, and its hidden assumptions.

When sizing up the acceptability of dress, appearance, language, or any other personality variable, remember the consultant is not an extension of your organization's image or management style. As a group, consultants are staunchly independent. Their role is to provide new ideas and fresh perspective, not to endorse the status quo. The real issue is whether a consultant and a client organization can accommodate each other. Can you respect the consultant's difference? Is the consultant willing to compromise to some extent with your organization's ways? As a rule of thumb, viva la difference—until consultants step over the line from *doing* their thing to *flaunting* it. As sponsor, you have to judge where that line is by knowing the tolerance limits of the organization.

A consultant was hired by a firm that had a dress code for men. They could wear a jacket of any color provided it was the same color as their pants! The consultant disliked business suits and preferred to dress in sport shirts and casual pants. He compromised by wearing a conservative sport jacket, tie, and contrasting pants. Had he shown up in an open shirt with no jacket, he would have been flaunting his difference.

Another case illustrates the stress that can result when organizations lack tolerance for differing standards of dress.

An organization that makes sporting goods hired a consulting firm whose dress code called for vested suits. The client requested that representatives of the consulting firm dress in casual slacks and shirts when visiting company headquarters. The consultant was obliged to carry two outfits, one casual and the other formal, when shuttling back and forth from the consulting firm and client headquarters. He felt like Superman having to undergo a quick change in the men's washroom.

A consultant whose background and interests are very different from those of participants sometimes may be unable to get past this barrier to a productive working relationship.

A consultant was hired to train first and second level supervisors in an Appalachian coal company. It was deer season and conversation was dominated by hunting stories. The consultant had grown up in New York City and had no knowledge of hunting. Worse yet, the client's world of interests and values was so different that even to ask questions was to draw attention to his ignorance. He could neither share his experience nor understand theirs. For their part, the supervisors liked their "us versus the world" feelings and were not willing to let the consultant into their life. He was unable to work successfully with that client.

While such a contrast can inhibit the working relationship, it can sometimes help by fostering new perspectives, ideas, and views. You must judge if the gap becomes unproductive conflict instead of useful contrast.

Once appearance and other visible personality factors are accepted, other aspects of personality—sense of presence, interaction style, and character traits—become more important to the success of the consultation. To assess self-assurance, observe whether the consultant's manner is relaxed, confident, well-organized, and responsive to the here-and-now situation. Do you have the sense that he or she is speaking rehearsed lines or responding to what is happening right now? To assess personal *interaction style,* notice how the consultant treats you. A deferential manner probably means this style could be expected toward others with authority. An aggressive approach is an indication that participants or end users might receive the same treatment. Notice also whether the consultant can state an opinion or viewpoint with confidence and still listen to your position without becoming defensive.

During the interview, you can form an impression of the consultant's character. The ideal consultant might sound like a cross between an Eagle Scout and Superman. But, there are only a few traits that are really critical—a stable personality, a mature sense of realism about what can and cannot be accomplished, a high frustration threshold, and a tolerance for ambiguous situations. Translated: Good consultants know themselves, know what they can do well, but don't have the illusion they can work wonders. Trust is also very important. You will have a better sense of whether you can trust the prospective consultant when you know something both about what motivates that person to work as well as his or her personal ethics.

The Consultant's Motivations

Everyone, including consultants, works for certain payoffs. These may include money, challenge, status in a consulting firm, recognition from professional colleagues, satisfaction in helping others, and advancement of professional beliefs or social causes. Any combination of payoffs is fine so long as it doesn't get in the way of the consultant's working for your best interests. You are not likely to find out directly what a person's motivations are. You can, however, pick up certain useful clues which help in drawing a tentative conclusion.

A consultant who is working solely for money or status is likely to be either a yes-man or a super salesman. In the first instance, the consultant may have an ingratiating manner calculated to flatter you. In the second instance, the consultant will oversell his wares by painting a rosy picture of the proposed problem solution and assuring you it will work in your situation. But there may be some reluctance to fully explain the rationale for the methods or to discuss the potential problems. The following scenario is an example.

> *Client:* My managers are having trouble getting along with each other. They're always bickering and undermining each other's efforts. What should I do?
> *Consultant:* What they need is a transactional analysis workshop. I have designed a training package that works in your kind of setting.
> *Client:* What's transactional analysis?
> *Consultant:* You haven't heard of TA? It's a proven way of analyzing structures of personality, interpersonal transactions, games, and scripts.
> *Client:* Oh. (Looks puzzled.) Sounds like some kind of therapy.
> *Consultant:* (Smiles) You might say that.
> *Client:* You want to run a TA workshop. What will happen if some of my managers don't want to be analyzed in that way?
> *Consultant:* Believe me, that will never happen.

The consultant has not been willing to explain transactional analysis so the client can understand what it is about. Like a salesman, the consultant has also devalued the client's concern about manager acceptance of a TA workshop.

During an exploratory meeting, insist on getting clear answers to your questions about a consultant's principles or strategies. Notice whether you are feeling put down for asking questions or if your concerns are being ignored. If you are saying "bull" to yourself very often, something is seriously wrong. It's time to terminate the conversation and seek another consultant.

Beware also of the consultant with a *cause* to champion, whether it be affirmative action, ecology, participative management, or changing the corporate culture! Of course, every consultant has personal and professional biases. However, there is a difference between persuading others and badgering them into dealing with an issue. The best consultants do not seek out difficulties which are unresolvable for you, your staff, your customers, or your clients. They share their biases, but do not make issues of them. If a consultant is opposed in principle to the objectives or proposed methods of a consultation and the client organization is unwilling to change these, the consultant should decline to work with that client and explain the reason.

A consultant who values one particular cause above an organization's development will be impatient about using noncoercive ways of bringing about readiness to deal with that issue. In the 1960s, a number of organizations were injured by well-meaning consultants committed to civil rights. The same situation is happening in this decade over issues like affirmative action. Such a consultant doesn't hesitate to keep an axe close to the vest while being hired and to bring it out to grind on the job. Besides wasting people's money and creating unproductive conflict, the consultant with a cause can also drain material resources from an organization. To illustrate:

A consultant was hired to head a task force charged with improving the working climate of an organization. This consultant was a radical feminist. At the first meeting, she challenged the membership of the task force because it did not have a balanced representation of men and women. She overlooked the fact that the task force had been appointed by management, had no say in its composition, but was genuinely interested in bringing about improvements. At the next meeting, the consultant used every opportunity to focus the discussion exclusively on women's issues and to criticize sexist attitudes of task force members. There were indeed a number of issues affecting women, but these were not the exclusive focus of the task force. Her tactics served to divide the task force prematurely into factions and to make productive work impossible. After the third meeting, this group was disbanded.

Look for a consultant who is dedicated to the HRD profession, who believes in the work you need done, and who cares about what happens to you and the participants or end user group. Among the signs of genuine interest are:

—The consultant is willing to spend time and energy to learn about your organization and your need or problem.
—The consultant doesn't demand a long-term commitment from you at the beginning, but is willing to start with a limited task.

—The consultant is interested in how much involvement you want in the project and shows willingness to include you at the appropriate points.

—During the exploratory discussion, concern is shown for the impact of a change effort on the organization. The consultant may express interest in (1) assessing readiness before starting the project, (2) field testing a product or system before instilling it systemwide, and (3) helping to alleviate anxiety about anticipated changes.

—The consultant doesn't try to make you dependent on his or her expertise, but works to transfer it to the client organization.

Consultants' Ethics

Every consultant abides by a set of ethical do's and don'ts. These have evolved from professional beliefs, personal motivations, and experiences with the pitfalls of consulting. Certain ethical standards have become widely accepted in the consulting field. They include objectivity, honesty, loyalty, and confidentiality. However, consultants don't always interpret these in the same way or apply them consistently in specific situations. It is important to learn enough about a consultant's ethical views and track record to decide if that person is trustworthy in potential problem situations.

You can't very well ask a consultant direct questions like "Will you be loyal to me?" "Honest?" "Objective?" However, while discussing the consultant's past experiences and potential approach to your problems, you can listen for the presence or absence of ethical sensitivity. You can ask "What if" questions about possible consulting situations that involve ethical dilemmas. You can also question previous clients about the consultant's ethical behavior.

Objectivity

Beware of a consultant with an investment in his initial conception of a problem and optimum solution. Someone who immediately says, "I have just the program you need," may be jumping the gun. A consultant must be willing to work with you to understand the situation fully, so you can both agree on what has to be done.

Look for a consultant who will listen carefully, absorb data, ask questions, and be open-minded all the way to the end. If you try to get an instant answer, the consultant will resist:

> *Client:* We've been having problems here: sickness, absenteeism, lateness, longer coffee breaks, people disappearing at lunch. What should we do?
> *Consultant:* I don't know what the problem is. What do you think it is?
> *Client:* Some kind of morale problem.
> *Consultant:* What do you think is causing the problem?

Client: Well, I'm not really sure. I thought you might have the answer.

Consultant: No I don't, but maybe I can help you get it. You have mentioned some symptoms. There could be several causes: salary problems, supervisory problems. One way to find out is to . . .

When a tentative diagnosis is made, some reservations will be offered:

Consultant: I think your problem is that your selection system is inadequate. But there is a possibility that this and this and this is also true. We can try modifying the selection system, see what happens, and back up if we have to.

Look for a consultant who will level with you rather than try to please you or to sell a particular solution. An ethical consultant who suspects you have a more serious problem or a different problem than you are aware of will be candid about what he or she thinks, even if it's something you don't want to hear. The consultant will also inform you of any circumstances that might influence judgment or objectivity. An example is the consultant who is being paid a retainer or commission by a company whose products or services he is recommending to you.

Honesty About One's Capabilities

Beware of consultants who say they can do anything. Honest consultants accept only those assignments they are qualified to perform and which they believe will provide real benefit to your organization. They represent their skills and experience accurately. There are several signs of honesty. For example, the consultant can say "no" to a job not in his or her areas of competence.

A consultant was asked to provide training to managers in communication skills and organizational planning. She replied that she had experience in the area of communication skills but not in planning. "To be very frank with you, that is not my area. I would have to go to the library and put something together. I could do a passable job. But you need somebody with knowledge and experience in planning. So I will not accept the offer."

When selecting a "full-service" management consulting firm, check the extent to which the scope of available services matches your needs. A firm may claim capability of staffing all phases of a consulting project but be unable to deliver the goods on one or more tasks. Some firms don't want to identify a problem it can't entirely solve and be obliged to refer the client to other resources. One way to check capability is to assess the track record of every individual who will be working on the project, just as you would for an independent consultant. You can also question the seller or prospective project director about staff capabilities. If this person is willing to be honest with you about the weaknesses as well as strengths of the firm's consultant, you can be reasonably assured of a good job. To get maximum protection, contract for a problem diagnosis separately from a problem solution. Once you have an accurate assessment of the problem, you can decide whether the firm meets your needs or whether you should seek help elsewhere.

Another sign of honesty is willingness to disclose past failures as well as successes. Naturally, a consultant is selling knowledge and experience and will refer to successful projects. To assess honesty, ask the consultant how previous clients would assess his or her strengths and weaknesses. Ask also if you may quote these statements when talking to these former clients. Comparing these statements allows you to check the honesty and accuracy of both consultant and previous client. It is also a good way to get around the reticence of a former client to divulge negative information. Ask the open-ended question first: "What are the consultant's strengths and weaknesses?" Then report what the consultant said and get the client's reaction.

Perhaps an even tougher test is to ask the consultant for a description of a consultation that did not go well. Ask what the consultant learned from the experience. Notice whether consultation with minor problems or a real disaster is described. Has the consultant thought about past mistakes and learned from them?

Other signs of honesty are: clear communication during initial meetings about fees and the conditions under which the consultant is willing to work, willingness to have his services evaluated, and corroboration from former clients about past consulting engagements.

Loyalty, Confidentiality, and Disclosure

Personal and organizational change involves taking risks to gain new advantages. People need a relatively safe environment in which to make mistakes, work out conflicts, and learn new skills. One of the consultant's functions is to create such a climate. For this reason, a consultant is obligated to use great care in withholding or disclosing inside information about a consultation. In general, the consultant has an obligation to enhance and not harm the client organization. Specifically, the consultant has an ethical obligation to the sponsor and to the end user.

The consultant's primary loyalty is to the sponsor. Occasionally the sponsor may be a top manager when the task involves systemwide issues and functions. Usually, however, the consultant reports to a lower echelon manager in charge of the unit where the problem or opportunity is located. A consultant should not betray the sponsor's confidence by leapfrogging to higher authorities. If the scope of the consultation expands and communication with top management is needed, the lower echelon manager can still be kept informed and involved. The consultant should always get permission before repeating confidential information.

Not all consultants are scrupulous about maintaining confidential relationships with parties in conflict. When you are hiring someone to deal with interpersonal problems or conflicts, try to check former clients or others who could give you a reading in this area. You can also ask "what if" questions about possible situations that could arise. Are there some points that seem threatening to you? Ask what the consultant will do to be responsible and supportive to you. For example:

> *Manager:* This project could create some anxiety for me. I know some of my subordinates don't much like my ways of running the department. What if they start bad-mouthing me during team-building sessions? What will you do?
> *Consultant:* I'll listen to what they say. I won't necessarily agree. But I will listen, and then I'll check out whether in my observation there's any validity to what they are saying. If there is, I will come to you and tell you what I'm seeing. You and I will decide together where to go from there.

An ethical consultant is also careful not to use inside information for personal benefit or to help another client at the expense of your organization. Obviously, knowledge of a company's plans will not be used to tip off his relatives to good investment opportunities! When describing specific past consulting experiences, the identity of other clients will not be revealed. (Of course, references for previous work should be given.) The consultant who is doing an executive search for another organization won't steal your personnel. If invited to work for a competitor, you will be consulted if knowledge of your organization could directly benefit the other client. Consultants must be careful to use their knowledge to benefit and not harm clients.

Fredric H. Margolis is an independent consultant in Washington, D.C., specializing in the application of adult learning principles to technical-professional areas.

Chapter 10

Contracting: A Tool for Client-Consultant Understanding

Peter Block

At the beginning of every workshop I conduct on consulting skills, I ask people what they want to learn about consulting. The first wave of answers is very reasonable and task oriented.

—How do you set up a project?
—How do you measure consulting effectiveness?
—Can you act as an umpire and helper at the same time?
—What do you do to elicit client expectations?
—How do you get in the door when you are not welcome?
—How do you establish trust?
—What are consulting skills anyhow?
—When do we break for lunch?
   . . . and on and on.

As we get into the workshop, it is easy to see the real desires that underlie these wishes. What do consultants want to learn about consulting? We want to learn how to have *power over our clients!* How do we influence them, get them to do what we want, manage in our own image? And while we are doing all of this to them, how do we keep their respect and appreciation?

The phrase "power over our clients" is a distortion of the more promising expectation to have power *with* our clients. If we want to control our clients, it puts us on a pedestal and them on the ground floor. This is a very unstable arrangement because clients soon realize we want to control them and are able to topple us with ease. Why shouldn't they be able to topple us, managers get rewarded for keeping control and have to have political smarts or they wouldn't be managers. So the desire to have power *over* the client is a no-win position for the consultant. The realistic alternative is to have power *with* the client. To have direct and constructive impact while standing on the same level.

Excerpted from *Flawless Consulting: A Guide to Getting Your Expertise Used* by Peter Block, Austin: Learning Concepts, 1981. Distributed by University Associates, San Diego.

I believe the point of maximum leverage for the consultant is probably during the contracting phase of the project. There are possibilities for impact that may be lost for the life of the project if they are not pursued in contracting. The contract sets the tone for the project, and it is much easier to negotiate a new, initial contract than to renegotiate an old one. Anyone who has been married more than a year understands this.

Contracting—The Concept and the Skill

The kind of contract I am talking about here is really a social contract. A contract is simply an explicit agreement of what the consultant and client expect from each other and how they are going to work together. It is usually verbal, sometimes in writing. Contracts with external consultants are more often in writing because external consultants are trusted less than internal consultants, especially when it comes to money. Some internal consultants always like to have a written document describing the project they are working on. This is probably a good idea, even if it is in the form of a letter. But essentially a contract between an internal or external consultant and a line manager is a social contract. It is designed not so much for enforcement, but for clear communication about what is going to happen on a project.

The Word *Contract*

"We are not lawyers," people say. "A contract is a legal document that is written in formal language, it is binding and in writing, and it is stiff and formal. Why not call it a working agreement?" The word *contract* is useful in two ways. Because we are not accustomed to thinking of social or work relationships in contractual terms, the word calls attention to the need for specific expectations in the consulting relationship. Also, some of the legal connotations of the word *contract* are applicable to consulting relationships.

Legal contracts contain two basic elements that apply to consulting relationships—mutual consent and valid consideration.

Mutual Consent

Both sides enter the agreement freely and by their own choosing. The concept of mutual consent directly addresses the issue of how motivated the staff person and the line manager are to engage in a project together. There are many forces in organizations that tend to coerce people into working together. For example, the fact that everybody is doing it is often a pressure on managers. They don't really want to do a survey of their employees, but that is the thing to do, and so it leads them into a conversation with a staff consultant about doing a survey. Internalized "shoulds" or the fad of the day can become powerful coercive forces. The staff person also operates under many "shoulds." "A staff person should never say no to a line manager" is a belief that can lead to beginning a project that a staff person does not believe in.

The coercion can also be very direct.

When some variation of this dialogue occurs, the client and the consultant have an agreement about work to be done, but they are not working with a solid or valid contract. The consultant is operating under coercion and has not freely entered the agreement. It is often not possible to negotiate a valid contract. That's OK. The key is that when a manager is eventually dissatisfied with the results of the new appraisal form, the problem should be defined as the imbalance of the original contract, not the elegance of the form.

Key Concept: Valid consideration must be given *both* parties for a solid contract to exist.

Valid Consideration

For our purposes, *consideration* is the exchange of something of value between the consultant and the client. Internal consultants are especially accustomed to focusing on the consideration given to the client. The initial impetus behind a discussion between a line and staff person is to discuss services to be provided to the line person. This service—or consideration—takes the form of advice, analysis, or just reflection. For a valid contract to exist, however, the staff person needs to receive something of value in return. It is this side of the equation that is often undervalued, ignored, or assumed without discussion.

Staff people will often say that all they really need is appreciation, some knowledge that they have made a contribution. On an emotional level that may be true, but there are some more tangible items that consultants need that should be a part of the original contract.

—Operational partnership in the venture. This means having influence on what happens, finding out about significant events, maintaining respect for the unique contribution you bring.
—Access to people and information in the line organization. Freedom of movement to pursue issues and data that seem relevant to you.
—Time of people in the line organization. The major cost to most improvement projects, even where heavy equipment is involved, is the time of people in the line organization to plan and incorporate changes into their operation. Many times the consultant is given an assignment with the proviso not to take up too much of the time of the line people because "they" don't want to interrupt production. This is a warning signal that the contract is inequitable and needs to be renegotiated.
—Opportunity to be innovative. Consultants generally want to try something different. You have the right to ask for this opportunity directly and not have to bootleg it.

What's important to remember here is that you only undermine your leverage if you underplay your own needs and wants at the beginning. The contract needs balanced consideration to be strong.

Contracting Skills

To contract flawlessly is to—

1. Behave authentically, and
2. Complete the business of the contracting phase.

The business of the contracting phase is to negotiate wants, cope with mixed motivation, surface concerns about exposure and loss of control, clarify all parties to the contract. Before getting into the actual steps in a contracting meeting, here is a list of the consulting competencies required to complete the business of contracting.

You should be able to:

—Ask direct questions about who the client is and who the less visible parties to the contract are.
—Elicit the client's expectations of you.
—Clearly and simply state what you want from the client.
—Say no or postpone a project that in your judgment has less than a 50/50 chance of success.
—Probe directly for the client's underlying concerns about losing control.
—Probe directly for the client's underlying concerns about exposure and vulnerability.
—Give direct verbal support to the client.
—When the contracting meeting is not going well, discuss directly with the client why this contracting meeting is not going well.

The prior list contains the very crucial ones, the ones that many of us have a hard time doing. The hard time we have is not really with the action itself, but with valuing the importance of these actions. Having direct discussions with the client—about control, vulnerability, your wants, the chance of success, and how the discussion is going—make the difference between an average contracting meeting and an excellent one. The problem is that it is possible to have a contracting meeting where none of these subjects are discussed directly. When this happens, the consultant and client are actually colluding with each other in not bringing up certain touchy subjects. The rationalization we use is, "Well, I'll deal with these areas if it becomes necessary." *It is always necessary to talk about control, vulnerability, your wants, chances of success.* If you are thinking as you read this that *you* always confront these areas with your clients, then you should feel good—you may be operating more flawlessly than you think.

Elements of a Contract

Up to this point we have focused on the process of developing a contract. This section offers some suggestions about what the content of the contract should include. But first, a word about form.

People always ask whether the contract should be in writing. If you have the energy and the time, the answer is yes. The reason for putting it in writing is for clarity, not enforcement. If it is in writing and the client changes his or her mind about the services wanted from you, you are going to have to renegotiate a new contract or stop the project. Having the original agreement in writing isn't going to change that. If you are investing out-of-pocket dollars or billable time in the project, then a written contract will help your claim to be paid for the money and time invested should the project be terminated. For most internal consultants, the real value of a written contract is to clarify the understanding with the line manager before the project begins. It is a good test of whether you have a solid contract. Writing down the agreement forces you to be more explicit about what you are going to do.

The form of the written document should be brief, direct, and almost conversational. The purpose is to communicate, not to protect yourself in court.

The following elements should be covered in most of your contracts, especially when the contract signals the beginning of a significant project.

The Boundaries of Your Analysis

Begin with a statement of what problem you are going to focus on. If it was discussed in the contracting meeting, you can include a statement of what you are not going to get involved in.

Examples. "The study will deal with the Brogan Reactor Furnace and its peripheral supporting network. We will get into the problems existing in Power Plant B."

"We will assess the effectiveness of the current Marketing organization structure and its interface with the Sales department."

Objectives of the Project. This identifies the organizational improvements you expect if your consultation is successful. This is your best guess on the benefits the client can expect. Sometimes this statement is to help the client be realistic about the limitations of the project. You are not a magician and need to keep reminding the client of this.

There are three general areas where you can expect to help the client. You should be clear in the beginning which of these are part of your contract.

To Solve a Particular Technical/Business Problem. The client is willing to talk to you because there is some pain somewhere in the client's organization. The immediate goal is to reduce the pain, whether the pain is from currently unsatisfactory results or the fact that opportunities to improve a situation are not being exploited.

To Teach the Client How to Solve the Problem for Themselves Next Time. It is possible for you to develop a solution and merely hand it to the client. If there is the expectation that the client can do it alone when the problem occurs again, be clear about it. This will require a lot more involvement from the client during the life of the project if the problem-solving process you are using is going to be transferred to the client.

To Improve How the Organization Manages Its Resources, Uses Its Systems, and Works Internally. Every business or technical problem has a component where the problem being managed is part of the problem. This is sometimes called the "politics" of the situation. Many internal consultants are reluctant to get into this area. The more you can include this as an objective of the project, the more long range help you are likely to be.

Examples: Business Objectives. "The objective of the study is to increase operating efficiencies of the furnace by 4%."

"Our goal is to increase the responsiveness of the Marketing department to shifting consumer demand. We particularly expect to develop ways to reduce the time it takes to introduce a new product by 6 weeks."

Learning Objectives. "A second objective is to teach the plant engineering group how to perform this kind of reactor analysis."

Organizational Development Objectives. "The Marketing staff should become more effective in assessing its own market responsiveness and restructuring itself in the future."

"This project will help the plant manager develop ways to better manage the interface between plant engineering and plant operations."

"A goal of the project is to increase cooperation between the market research group and the product directors."

The Kind of Information You Seek

Access to people and information are the key wants of the consultant. The major ambivalence of the line organization is how far to let you into the bowels of their organization. They want to tell you what is really going on and at the same time are afraid of telling you what is really going on. Come close, but not too close. Despite what the line manager says to you, there is always some desire for confirmation that the organization is doing the best that can be done under the circumstances. This desire at times can be stronger than the desire to solve the problem. One way to hedge against this ambivalence is to be very explicit at the beginning what kind of information you need.

Some of the kinds of information you may want to specify in the contract are technical data, figures, work flow; attitudes of people toward the problem; and roles and responsibilities.

Examples: Technical Data, Figures, Work Flow. "To complete the project, we will require daily output figures for the equipment and the operating temperatures and pressures for the furnace."

"Your part in the project will require providing a list of procedures for reconciling daily ledgers and the turnover figures for the group."

"We will want to see the planned and actual schedules for the last six product improvement introductions after we get into the project."

Attitudes of People. "We want to interview at least fifteen people to identify how they currently view the marketing function."

"We want to talk with the operators of the furnace to identify the kind of training they feel they need and to uncover their perceptions of the way the supervisory group rewards good and poor performance. We also plan to ask the same questions of the supervisors."

Roles and Responsibilities. "The marketing organization will provide a definition of who is responsible for major decisions on new products at each stage of the process."

"We will obtain information from all supervisors on their view of their jobs and the authority they have to manage their sections of the operation."

Your Role in the Project

This is the place to state *how you want to work* with the client. If you want a collaborative relationship, this is the place to state it. Make it a statement of intent and spirit. It doesn't pay to spell out all the ways you are going to work together. It is hard to predict at the beginning what is going to come up. You can make some statements about the desire for a 50/50 sharing of responsibility for identifying problems, interpreting the findings, and developing recommendations and action plans.

Example. "Our primary role is to give you a clear and understandable picture of how your plant is currently operating and maintaining the reactor furnace. While we have expertise on the design of the equipment, your group has a great deal of knowledge of day-to-day operations. We would expect to present our analysis of the efficiency problems and then jointly develop recommendations with you on what changes should be made. A major part of our role is to help you solve this problem for yourself next time. This requires that the plant supervisors have some involvement at each step of the study. We are committed to both develop specific solutions to the present concerns and to play an important educational role with you and your supervisors."

The Product You Will Deliver

Here it is important to be very specific about what you are offering. Will your feedback be an oral or written report? How long will it be and how much detail will the client get? Is the report likely to be five pages or fifty pages? How far into specific recommendations will you get? Will you give some general suggestions about how to improve things or will you give a list of steps that can be implemented right away? Will you present actual solutions or steps that can be taken that will eventually lead to solutions?

Of course you can't predict all of these in the beginning, but you do know from your own experience how specific you will be. This dimension of a consulting relationship—specificity and nature of recommendations—is a major cause of client disappointment in the consulting services they have received. This doesn't mean that recommendations should always be specific or should always be general, that depends on the task the consultant is engaged in. It does mean there ought to be a clear understanding with the client on what your product will look like.

Example: A Promise for Specific Recommendations. "The outcome of this project will be a detailed written description of our findings running somewhere between 15 and 40 pages. For each major finding, we will offer specific recommendations that you can act on."

Example: A Promise for General Recommendations. "The outcome of these interviews will be roughly a one-page outline of our major conclusions. These will only identify the critical areas to be considered. Actual recommendations will be developed jointly with you after the outline of issues has been discussed. These recommendations will be developed in the half-day feedback meeting we have scheduled at the end of the project."

In promising results to the client, remember that you will be turning the action over to the client at some point. It is the client who is going to actually deliver continuing results, not you. You *can* guarantee a solution to a problem, but you *can't* guarantee that the solution will be followed. To take the solution totally on your shoulders may feel comfortable to you, but it can deprive clients of responsibility for the solution that is rightfully theirs.

What Support and Involvement You Need from the Client

This section is the heart of the contract for the consultant. This is where you specify what you want from the client to make this project successful. This list is what the client is offering to you. Include here particularly those wants that were the subject of some discussion in the verbal contracting meeting. Writing down your wants is to ensure communication and if there was a sensitive point discussed, put it down to make sure it was resolved.

Example. "You (line manager) have agreed to communicate the existence and need for this project to your organization. We have also agreed to meet with the division vice president to get his view on the problem and to include him in the second feedback meeting. (An example of what might have been a sensitive topic of discussion.) In addition, two people from your staff will be made available to us for a maximum of seven days each to help with the data analysis and summary."

Time Schedule

Include starting time, any intermediate mileposts, and completion date. If you want to give interim reports to the client before you tie the ribbon on the package, schedule them at the beginning. It is always easier to cancel a meeting than to set one up at the last minute.

Example. "We can begin this work in six weeks and plan to complete it ten weeks from when we start."

Confidentiality

Since you are almost always dealing with a political situation as well as a technical one, who gets what report is a constant concern. I tend to be quite conservative on this and prefer to give the client control on the people they want to share the findings with. This is a luxury of being an outside consultant. As an inside consultant, you may not have any choice but to send a technical study or an audit report up the line. All you can do is to acknowledge to the client who you are required to give copies of your report to. This gives clients a choice about how to protect themselves, if necessary.

Example: Easy Case. "The results of this study will be given to the director of engineering (the client). Any further reporting will be up to the director. Should the internal consultants be required to report any results to the larger organization, the director will be informed and invited to attend any meetings held on the subject."

Example: Hard Case. "The results of the audit will be reported to the Management Audit Committee. Before the report is released, the division controller (the client) will be able to review and comment on the audit findings and recommendations. The intent (and the common practice) is that the audit report goes to the committee with the support of both the division controller and the audit team. The final report also includes the list of corrective actions that the division plans to take."

Feedback to You Later

An optional element to the contract is to ask the client to let you know the results of your intervention six months after you leave. If you want to know, but usually don't find out, ask for it.

Example. "About six months after the project is completed, the consultant will contact the client for feedback on the impact of the project. This might take the form of having people complete a questionnaire, respond over the phone, or send some recent operating data to the consultant."

Analyzing One of Your Contracts

Pick a complicated contract that you have negotiated. Write up the elements of that contract using the following headings.

1. The Boundaries of Your Analysis
2. Objectives of the Project
3. The Kind of Information You Seek
4. Your Role in the Project
5. The Product You Will Deliver
6. What Support and Involvement You Need from the Client
7. Time Schedule
8. Confidentiality
9. Feedback to You, Later

Ground Rules for Contracting

Underlying the model for a contracting meeting is a set of ground rules for contracting, which have come primarily from my exposure to Gestalt psychology.[1]

1. The responsibility for every relationship is 50/50. There are two sides to every story. There must be symmetry or the relationship will collapse. The contract has to be 50/50.
2. The contract should be freely entered.
3. You can't get something for nothing. There must be consideration from both sides. Even in a boss-subordinate relationship.
4. All wants are legitimate. To want is a birthright. You can't say, "You shouldn't want that."
5. You can say no to what others want from you. Even clients.

6. You don't always get what you want. And you'll still keep breathing. You will still survive, you will still have more clients in the future.

7. You can contract for behavior, you can't contract for the other person to change his or her feelings.

8. You can't ask for something the other person doesn't have.

9. You can't promise something you don't have to deliver.

10. You can't contract with someone who's not in the room, such as clients' bosses and subordinates. You have to meet with them directly to know you have an agreement with them.

11. Write down contracts when you can. Most are broken out of neglect, not intent.

12. Social contracts are always renegotiable. If someone wants to renegotiate a contract in midstream, be grateful that they are telling you and not just doing it without a word.

13. Contracts require specific time deadlines or duration.

14. Good contracts require good faith and often accidental good fortune.

Reference

1. I attended a workshop run by Claire and Mike Reiker in which they presented these ground rules in such a clear and powerful way that I have used them ever since.

Peter Block is a principal in the training firm of Block Petrella Weisbord/Designed Learning, Inc., located in Plainfield, New Jersey.

Chapter 11

Is Help Helpful?

Jack R. Gibb

People in the service professions often see themselves as primarily engaged in the job of helping others. Helping becomes both the personal style of life and a core activity that gives meaning and purpose to the life of the professional. The youth worker, the camp director, the counselor, the consultant, the therapist, the teacher, the lawyer — each is a helper.

Helping is a central social process. The den mother, the committee chairman, the parent, the personal friend, the board member, the dance sponsor — each is a helper.

Help, however, is not always helpful. The recipient of the proffered help may not see it as useful. The offering may not lead to greater satisfaction or to better performance. Even less often does the helping process meet a more rigorous criterion — lead to continued growth on the part of the participants.

To begin with, a person may have varied motivations for offering help. He may wish to improve performance of a subordinate, reduce his own guilt, obtain gratitude, make someone happy, or give meaning to his own life. He may wish to demonstrate his superior skill or knowledge, induce indebtedness, control others, establish dependency, punish others, or simply meet a job prescription. These conscious or partially conscious motivations are so intermingled in any act of help that it is impossible for either the helper or the recipient to sort them out.

Depending upon his own needs and upon the way he sees the motives of the helper, the recipient will have varied reactions. He may feel gratitude, resentment, or admiration. He may feel helpless and dependent, or jealous of the helper who has the strength or resources to be in the helper role. He may feel indebted, or pressured to conform to the perceived demands or beliefs of the helper.

We have all noticed that in certain cases the recipient of the help becomes more helpless and dependent, less able to make his own decisions or initiate his own actions, less self-sufficient, more apathetic and passive, less willing to take risks, more concerned about propriety and conformity, and less creative and venture-

---

Reprinted by permission from the February 1964 issue of the *Forum,* Journal of the Association of Professional Directors of YMCA's in the United States.

Table 11-1
The Helping Relationship

Orientations that help
1. Reciprocal trust (confidence, warmth, acceptance)
2. Cooperative learning (inquiry, exploration, quest)
3. Mutual growth (becoming, actualizing, fulfilling)
4. Reciprocal openness (spontaneity, candor, honesty)
5. Shared problem solving (defining, producing alternatives, testing)
6. Autonomy (freedom, interdependence, equality)
7. Experimentation (play, innovation, provisional try)

Orientations that hinder
1. Distrust (fear, punitiveness, defensiveness)
2. Teaching (training, advice giving, indoctrinating)
3. Evaluating (fixing, correcting, providing a remedy)
4. Strategy (planning *for,* maneuvering, gamesmanship)
5. Modeling (demonstation, information giving, guiding)
6. Coaching (molding, steering, controlling)
7. Patterning (standard, static, fixed)

---

some. We have also seen circumstances in which, following help, recipients become more creative, less dependent upon helpers, more willing to make risk decisions, more highly motivated to tackle tough problems, less concerned about conformity, and more effective at working independently or interdependently. Help may or may not lead to personal growth and organizational health.

Under certain conditions both the giver and the receiver grow and develop. In general, people tend to grow when there is reciprocal dependence —*inter*dependence, joint determination of goals, real communication in depth, and reciprocal trust. To the degree that these conditions are absent, people fail to grow.

Orientations That Help or Hinder

From the standpoint of the organization, help must meet two criteria: the job or program must be done more effectively, and the individual members must grow and develop. These two criteria tend to merge. The program and the organization are effective only as the participants grow. The same conditions that lead to organizational health lead to personal growth. Table 11-1 presents a theory of the helping relationship. Seven parallel sets of orientations are presented. One set of conditions maximize help and a parallel set of conditions minimize help.

Reciprocal Trust. People accept help from those they trust. When the relationship is one of acceptance and trust, offers of help are appreciated, listened to, seen as potentially helpful, and often acted upon. The receiver accepts help from one whose perceived motives are congenial to him. He tends to reject offers from people whose offering is seen as a guise for attempts to control, punish, correct, or gain power. "Help" is most helpful when given in an atmosphere in which people have reciprocal feelings of confidence, warmth, and acceptance. When one feels that his worth as a person is valued, he is able to place himself in psychological readiness to receive aid.

Distrust. When people fear and distrust each other, even well-intended help is resisted, resented, or seen as unhelpful. Offers of help are sometimes given in service of motivations that are unacceptable to the receiver. That is, one offers help in order to place the other person in a dependent position, elicit expressions of gratitude, assert one's superiority, or punish him. In distrust the recipient's guard is up. He is likely to project his distrusts onto the helper and to resist or resent the help.

One often gives help to camouflage or assuage his desire to change another person — change his character, habits, or misconceptions. The desire to change another person is essentially hostile. At a deep level, one who genuinely accepts another person does not wish to change him. A person who is accepted is allowed to be, become, determine his own goals, and follow them at his own pace. The person who genuinely wishes to help offers the help that the recipient wishes. Genuine help is not foisted upon the receiver. Neither the punisher nor the child really believes that the punishment is given "for the good of the child."

Punishment or censure may be given with a conscious desire to help but usually is accompanied by a deep component of retaliation or by a desire to hurt, control, or assert superiority. The giver often speaks of his act as "helpful" in order to rationalize to himself and to the receiver acts that are done for other motivations.

Cooperative Learning. People are helpful to each other when they are engaged in a cooperative quest for learning. The learning atmosphere is one of joint inquiry and exploration. Needs for help and impulses to give help arise out of the demands of the common cooperative task. Help is thus reciprocal. The helper and helpee roles are interchangeable. Each participant has the intent to learn and feels he can learn from the partners and from the common task. The boss and the subordinate, the teacher and the student, the professional worker and the youth — all are most helpful when each member of the pair sees the relationship as a quest with potential learning for each. An effective project team is guided by the task and not by the teacher. It is motivated by the shared potential for learning.

Teaching. When one participant in a project sets out to teach, train, advise, persuade, or indoctrinate the other members or is seen as wanting to do so, the learning of each member is reduced. People cannot be taught. People must learn. People cannot be trained. They grow and develop. The most deeply helpful relationship is one of common inquiry and quest, a relationship between co-learners and co-managers in which each is equally dependent upon the other for significant help and in which each sees and accepts this relationship.

Mutual Growth. The most permanent and significant help occurs in a relationship in which both members are continually growing, becoming, and seeking fulfillment. Each member participates in a mutual assessment of progress, accepts this reality of growth, and participates in a way that will maximize the growth of both participants. In a fundamental sense one can only help himself. The helper can only participate with another in an effort to create a climate in which growth can occur.

Evaluating. Growth is often hindered when one member of the helping team sets out to appraise or remedy the defects in the other member. Help is most effective when it is seen as a force moving toward growth rather than as an effort to remove gaps, remedy defects, or bring another person up to a standard criterion. The limits of growth of any person are extremely difficult to foresee or to assess. The potential for growth is consistently under-estimated by both participants in the helping relationship.

Reciprocal Openness. One of the essential conditions for effective human learning is the opportunity for feedback or knowledge of progress. Feedback is essential in acquiring skills, knowledge, and attitudes. In the areas where professional help is most commonly sought or given, the essential progress in learning and growth is blocked most often by the failure to obtain adequate data on people's feelings and perceptions of each other. In order to do effective work one must know how others feel and how they see things. In the usual situations in which professional helpers find themselves, there are many pressures which camouflage or distort the relevant data necessary for efficient work and best learning. Many factors reduce the availability of the relevant data: differential status, differential perceived power, and fears that one can hurt or be hurt.

Strategy. When some part of the helping process is closed or unavailable to all participants, people are likely to become anxious, resentful, or resistant. Neither participant in the helping process can "use" the other for his own needs. The helping process is most effective when one plans with another, not for another. One is not helped when he is maneuvered into some action which he does not understand. Gamesmanship and gimmicks are antithetical to the helping process.

Shared Problem Solving. The productive helping relationship focuses upon the problem to be solved. Problem solving involves a joint determination of the problem, continual redefinition of the problem as successive insights are gained, joint focus upon possible alternative solutions, joint exploration of the data, and continual reality testing of the alternatives. The expertness and resources of each person are shared. The aspect of the behavior about which help is given is seen as a shared problem — not as a defect to be remedied or as something to be solved by the helper as consultant.

Modeling. A common image of the helping relationship is one where the helper offers a model for the advisee to follow. The expert gives a demonstration of how the recipient may solve his problems. The problem is defined by the expert. Diagnosis is made by the expert. The expert is challenged to offer additional alternatives to the solution of the problem and perhaps even to test the solutions. The process is unidirectional. The limitations of modeling are many. Dependency is increased. The pupil seldom gets better than the model. The worker tries to conform to the image of the supervisor. Growth is limited.

Autonomy. The ideal relationship for helping is an interdependent one in which each person sees the other as both helper and recipient in an exchange among equals. It is essential that each participant preserve his freedom and maintain his autonomous responsibility for guiding himself toward his own learnings, growth, and problem solving. The helper must work himself out of the helping job. The supervisor, youth worker, and counselor must become decreasingly necessary to the people being helped. Psychological weaning, however painful to both helper and recipient, must continue if help is to be truly helpful.

Coaching. The coach molds, steers, or controls the behavior of the recipient, much as a tennis coach or physical education director molds the behavior of the athlete or skill-directed recipient of help. This is another unidirectional process in which the coach is assumed to have special diagnostic and observational powers which he applies in a skilled way to the behavior of the recipient, who puts himself in the hands of the coach. The recipient of help is encouraged to maintain respectful dependency upon the coach, to not challenge his authority or expertness, to put implicit trust in his abilities and powers, and to receive from the coach motivational or inspirational guidance. Both coach and pupil suffer under this pattern. Each may gain in skill. Neither grows as a person.

Experimentation. Tentativeness and innovative experimentation are characteristic of the most productive helping relationship. There is a sense of play, excitement, and fun in the common exploratory quest for new solutions to continually changing problems. The helping process is viewed as a series of provisional trials. Each participant joins in the game and adds to the general excitement. Errors can be made — and are perhaps expected. Help is a search. Finding creative solutions to newly defined problems is a game — full of zest and intrinsic drives that keep the game going.

Patterning. Help is limited when the process is seen as an attempt on the part of one person to help another meet a prescribed standard, come up to a criterion, or reach a goal specified in advance. Helping is a creative synthesis of growth and a continual search for new forms.

"Help" is not always helpful — but it can be. Both the helper and the recipient can grow and learn when help is given in a relationship of trust, joint inquiry, openness, and interdependence. Growth-centered helping processes lead to healthy groups and effective organizations.

Jack R. Gibb is an organizational psychologist, consultant, and president of Omicron in La Jolla, California.

Part IV

Diagnosis

"On the morrow Moses sat to judge the people, and the people stood about Moses from morning till evening. When Moses' father-in-law saw all that he was doing for the people, he said, 'What is this that you are doing for the people? Why do you sit alone, and all the people stand about you from morning till evening?' And Moses said, 'Because they come to me to inquire of God; when they have a dispute, they come to me and I decide between a man and his neighbor.' ...Moses' father-in-law said to him, 'You and the people with you will wear yourselves out, for the thing is too heavy for you; you are not able to perform it alone. Listen now to my voice; I will give you counsel.' "

Exodus 18: 13–19

Moses' working relationship with his father-in-law, Jethro, represents one of the earliest references to consultation. The "what" and "why" type inquiry employed by Jethro provided the diagnostic framework for his advising Moses to select competent leaders ("Choose able men who are trustworthy..."), provide training ("...teach them the statues and the decisions..."), and provide an organization structure ("...place such men over the people as rulers of thousands, of hundreds, of fifties, and of tens...").

The power of accurate diagnosis cannot be overstated. As the platform for action, its essence pervades the remaining acts of the consultative drama. The precise beginning and ending of the diagnosis phase is blurred and elusive. While still in entry, the consultant is gathering data which will form a part of diagnosis. At the other end of the diagnosis phase, the data-gathering action is itself a response in that it intervenes into the client culture and precipitates some change. Ask me a question and I am instantly altered by my contemplation of an answer.

What is the relational nature of diagnosis? It is at the outset a bargaining of perceptions — a kind of collusion of reality and truth. There *is* reality and truth. However, the consultant's perception of reality coupled with the consultant's perception of the client's perception is the stuff of which diagnoses are generally made.

The bargaining of perceptions is borne out of client–consultant trust, the greater their trust, the better the bargain for both. "Betterness" for the consultant entails such disclosure on the part of the client that sufficient, quality information is made available. "Betterness" for the client occurs when the consultant gains enough information to intervene usefully, causing minimal pain and disruption in the process.

Client–consultant trust is fostered by joint goal setting, empowering the client and managing client resistance. All three efforts involve consultant initiative; only one involves client initiative. This underscores the fact that diagnosis is primarily consultant lead.

Joint Goal Setting

Diagnosis can be humbling, painful, and humiliating for the client. It can reveal unpleasantries lined with hurt and disappointment. Even on the most positive end of potential outcomes, it is cloaked with the mystery and uncertainty of the unknown.

The first time one of the authors had a physical examination which included use of a proctoscope, the new physician assumed previous experience with the humbling inspection. Needless to say, cooperation was less than enthusiastic. Some explanation of what was to happen and why no doubt would have resulted in a somewhat more trusting subject.

Apprehension can be reduced by actively involving the client in establishing the goals for diagnosis. These goals would include the determination of the type of data required, the manner in which it will be obtained, the persons to be involved, target dates for completion, etc. It is likewise imperative the client play an equal role in ascertaining how the data will be used after accumulation.

The formation and maintenance of a client–consultant trust relationship is enhanced significantly by active client involvement in the joint goal setting process. By-products of the effort include commitment and ownership. Their existence will bolster the relationship and aid the client in functioning as an ally to the undertaking.

Empowering the Client

It goes without saying that part of the end result of consultation is some improvement in the client system. However, in order for that improvement to be maintained, the client must learn from the experience. A major key to a trusting client–consultant relationship occurs by the consultant helping the client to use the consultative experience for personal growth.

Growth comes through undertaking activities one has not perfected. Engaging in such imperfected activities carries risk of embarrassment and decreased power. It is the responsibility of the consultant to provide sufficient emotional support to the client for experimentation to occur despite the risk. Ultimately, increased client growth brings decreased dependency on the consultant.

Diagnosis can be used to empower the client by making data gathering a learning experience. The type and sequence of information can precipitate not only client discovery regarding the content but enhanced skill regarding the process. For instance, joint review of a questionnaire before use and subsequent study of the information generated by the questionnaire can significantly upgrade the diagnostic and problem-solving skills of a client.

Managing Client Resistance

There are activities in diagnosis that are nonreactive or unobtrusive in their impact on the client or client system. Such activities enable the gathering of data without fostering client resistance. Historical data (memos, charts, reports), external data (conversations with suppliers, major stockholders, customers), and observational data exemplify unobtrusive diagnostic activities.

Reactive or obtrusive activities (interviews, surveys, questionnaires) are of such a nature that the potential runs high for the client or client system to exercise some resistance. The potential for pain inherent in the inspection of the unknown necessitates special precautions to anticipate client resistance and take measures to counteract their occurrence.

Resistance management is a highly intuitive skill few consultants completely master. In essence, it involves the consultant disassociating self from actions to assume the self of the client. Much of the time, resistance is due to issues related to the relationship (e.g., telling another what to do) rather than the substance of the diagnosis or action itself.

Central to managing resistance is the consultant's playing his or her role in a manner which gives the client little to resist. By causing the client to experience psychological kinship with the consultant, the need to resist will be reduced.

Diagnosis relates to the acquisition of knowledge, and knowledge is a source of power. The client–consultant relationship can be made productive and positive for all concerned only through the parties managing it with equality of power as a criterion.

Chapter 12
"Diagnosis: Frameworks for Consultants and Clients"
Chip R. Bell

Many consultants have been summoned by a client to assess an organization and provide recommendations for improvement only to have those recommendations shunned, side-stepped, or shelved. While the causes for such resistance are varied, a part of it lies in the mystery of diagnostic methods used by the consultant.

The Bell chapter presents a variety of diagnostic frameworks with the task of eliminating some of the mystery. Part of the goal of successful consulting is to help an organization solve problems in such a way that it becomes more competent in solving similar problems without help from the consultant. The diagnostic frameworks may promote richer client-consultant understanding and greater client-consultant problem-solving competence.

Chapter 13
"The Organization as a Micro-Culture"
Leonard Nadler

The vantage point of a cultural anthropologist is a useful perspective for the diagnostician. The anthropological perspective reflects an attempt on the part of those involved in diagnosis (a consultant and/or client) to perceive reality and trust with maximum precision and minimum prejudice. While a value-free inspection of anything "life-ful" is improbable, one moves closer to an egoless inspection as one attempts to acquire the skill of the anthropologist.

The Nadler article provides some of the landmarks along the path to an anthropological perspective. While such dimensions as structure, relationships, communication, and technical-operating systems are typically included in the domains to be perused, the diagnostician less frequently includes time, space, language, and gender in the elements that make up a thorough diagnosis. As Harry Levinson states in his mammoth text *Organization Diagnosis,* "Any fool can tell that a river flows. Only he who understands its cross-currents, its eddies, the variations in its speed, the hidden rocks, and its action in drought and flood is the master of its functioning."

Chapter 14
"Consultants and Detectives"
Fritz Steele

There is editorial danger in lifting a chapter out of a book and presenting it as a separate article. It is somewhat like playing singularly the viola part of a concerto; while it may sound complete as a solo, it misses the breadth of the larger score.

The point of "Consultants and Detectives" is sufficiently provocative to risk losing some of the book's larger message. Taken from his book *Consulting for Organizational Change,* the chapter compares the consultant's diagnosis with the detective's investigation. The persistent forcing of the direct analogy unleashes creative insights into this phase of consulting process. Of particular importance to the client-consultant relationship is the acquisition of credibility without permanent closeness.

Chapter 15
"Managing Resistance"
Anthony O. Putman

"You can lead a horse to water, but you can't make him drink." So the familiar adage goes, but one famous consultant has added, " . . . no matter how vital the water to the horse's health nor how vividly you describe the desert conditions on the journey ahead!"

Resistance is a predictable barrier to overcome in most client-consultant relationships. Tony Putman offers excellent insight into the reasons for most resistance and gives pragmatic approaches to recognizing, managing, and preventing resistance.

Chapter 16
"Surviving as a Messenger: The Client-Consultant Relationship During Diagnosis"
Richard M. Furr

The space between entry and diagnosis is one not known for preciseness. Given that, the Furr article offers us transition by focusing on the use of power as an ingredient required during diagnosis. While some readers may find the recommendations disquieting, we feel they offer a fresh way of looking at the relational aspects of diagnosis. Unlike other areas of consultation, little has been written about the client-consultant relationship. This is particularly true of the diagnosis phase.

Chapter 12

Diagnosis: Frameworks for Consultants and Clients

Chip R. Bell

Diagnosis or assessment can be one of the most sensitive areas of the consulting process. The consultant, in a quest to be helpful and "justify his or her presence" seeks errors, gaps, weaknesses, and problems. Rarely does one hear of the consultant reporting to the client, "Contrary to what you are feeling, I give your organization a clean bill of health."

The client, despite initial recognition of a problem (rarely are consultants called in for just a checkup), is typically apprehensive about the potential skeletons which may be found. It's an "I don't want to know but I need to know," approach-avoidance apprehension in many cases. Just as the doctor's bedside manner contributes to greater mental comfort during examination, the consultant bears the greater responsibility in minimizing client discomfort during diagnosis.

One major method for managing the client-consultant relationship during diagnosis is to share with the client the frameworks (perspectives) employed in conducting a diagnosis. As the doctor jointly studies x-rays with the patient or invites perusal of a slide under a microscope, openness and candor can eliminate the lion's share of client anxiety. What follows are a series of frameworks on diagnosis which can be useful to consultant and client.

Frameworks are essentially roadmaps to enable those traveling on the path to effectiveness to anticipate special vistas along the way. Frameworks also allow us to notice time without being a victim of time. They provide a structure which facilitates the release of insight and creativity.

A framework provides a recipe, in my way of thinking. I use the recipe analogy deliberately because a recipe frees the cook from having to remember all the ingredients and allows innovation around how those ingredients are used. In other words, a person adapts the recipe—the model or framework—to his or her own taste. Also, as blueprints of the possible, recipes enable the user to readily identify gaps and problems that need to be addressed. A famous chef once said,

Adapted from *Influencing: Marketing the Ideas that Matter* by Chip R. Bell, Austin: Learning Concepts, 1982. Distributed by University Associates, San Diego.

"If you didn't have a recipe, you probably wouldn't know you were out of vanilla."

There are assorted ways of "seeing" organizations. Getting a "feel of the workplace," as Fritz Steele calls it, entails feeling/experiencing/sensing a work environment from a number of perspectives. It is as though you had a collection of glasses, each with different-colored lenses. Wearing a particular set of lenses (using a particular perspective) reveals the culture—issues, problems, and opportunities not visible with another pair. Part of the assessment process requires facility with lenses. Only by multiplying perspectives can you attain sufficient perceptual scope and depth for resolving issues.

This chapter will connect you and your skills at "seeing." Not all the lenses will be unveiled—I by no means know them all. Starting down the path of assessment, however, will begin a momentum in you, freeing you to discover which lenses you need to be useful to consulting and the client-consultant relationship.

An accurate assessment of an organization requires appropriate frameworks, models for understanding. You cannot walk into an organization and begin by saying, "Hey, I'm Studs Terkel—tell me about work." If you have models or frameworks for your assessment work, then your questions can be more focused and the discrepancy between reality and ideals can be more apparent.

You need to experience the organization in a variety of ways so that the total effect has depth and meaning. It is not just a long look—it is a measured, complete look. Carl Sagan looked at the cosmos. Edward Hall looked at proxemics. Margaret Mead looked at the Mindugomores in New Zealand. Jay Bronowski looked at science. Peter Drucker looked at the concept of the corporation. As the old adage states: "Before I wore shoes, I had never known of leather. Now that I have shoes, the world is covered in leather." If you have a model from which to pattern your impressions, your whole perception is enriched.

Gap Identification

Once upon a time, there was a cobbler who had the well-deserved reputation of being the best shoemaker in the area. People came from far away to buy shoes from him. The demand quickly exceeded his ability to supply shoes, and he asked another good cobbler to join him. Life was busy but manageable. Communications were informal and disputes settled swiftly. Records were kept in a ledger book, supplies were readily obtained from the local tanner, and marketing was done by the word-of-mouth advertising of satisfied customers.

You may have already figured out where this story is going. Success bred success, and many more cobblers were hired. Machines increased output, word-of-mouth advertising was amplified by salespeople in the field, and supplies and raw materials were purchased from various distributors all over the country. The simple ledger gave way to computers and CPAs. Communication occurred primarily through formal reporting relationships, and disputes were settled through complicated rules and procedures. The cobbler's business evolved into an "organization."

Organizations generally evolve as in the cobbler's story. Often they get bigger; then they get better. They grow faster quantitatively than qualitatively.

The cobbler had no difficulty when one person maintained the accounting system with a spindle for tickets filled out. At the end of the day, so many tickets could be checked off. "We've done these. I've delivered those. I haven't paid for this. That's Mrs. Smith—she won't pay until the end of the month, but she always pays." The system was easy to keep track of.

The *form*—that is, the process by which individual orders were kept on the spindle, checked off, entered into the ledger—was in synchronization with the *substance,* which is what was required in the situation. As the organization grew larger, the old form no longer fit the new substance. Increases in substance—in the size, character, complexity, or nature of the work—require a similar shift in the form for managing that substance. When substance and form are out of sync, gaps exist. The purpose of examining gaps is to gain greater sensitivity to the *perceived* needs of the organization versus the *actual* needs.

All organizations need certain forms in order to operate. For instance, there needs to be a system for some sort of planning. For the cobbler, that system might simply be asking himself, "What am I going to do? What materials will I need for the work I'll probably have next week?" As an organization gets larger, the complexity, design, and character of its plan—the *form* of the plan—must match the changing *substance.*

Another form all organizations need is a definition of purpose. Another is some type of organizational infrastructure—the way in which people, materials, and systems operate together for the organization to achieve its purpose. Organizations need some access to their marketplace. There need to be tasks, objectives, performance standards, and so on, linked to financial objectives. There needs to be a management information system of some kind. All are forms to manage substance.

When Substance Outpaces Form

A fundamental characteristic of the growth of any organization is the occurrence of gaps between what exists and what is required. For example, adolescents experience a gap between their physical development and emotional development. Much frustration and anxiety are then centered around that distortion. An example of a common organizational form-substance gap is the proliferation of hard data within the organization on the one hand and the organization's inability to make meaningful decisions using that data on the other. It is far easier for a manager to get more data (via computers, research studies, reports) than it is for the members of the organization to achieve the wisdom needed to fully comprehend and rationally use the available data.

The point of all this is that a certain form is appropriate to each organization, whether it is one entrepreneur or a huge, complex corporation. The task in assessing the client organization is to determine where gaps or distortions occur. In what areas are the form which exists and the substance which is required out of sync?

The list of questions in Figure 12-1 provides several cues to aid in identifying areas in the organization in which the substance has outpaced the form needed to manage that substance. Examine the list and check the appropriate block for each item. For any item you give a "yes" to, rate its effectiveness in the right-hand column, with "1" being totally ineffective, and "10" being extremely effective.

The goal of the Form-Substance Checklist is to identify gaps. All "no's" and any "yes's" rated less than 10 point to potential gaps between what is and what should be. The "don't know's" signify areas you need to explore more fully, until you are satisfied the information either does not exist or you cannot gain access to it.

Bruce Fritch[1] states that one of the important means of assessing organizations through gap identification is to look at form-substance dichotomies. One type of form-substance dichotomy is the variance between language used and actions employed. An example of this type of dichotomy is the organization that claims commitment to affirmative action practices but, when reality is examined, not only tolerates racial imbalance but fails to institute consequences for managers who perform well or poorly in affirmative action efforts.

The disparity between form and substance that occurs when the organization's needs outpace the means to meet those needs might be pictured as in Figure 12-2. The farther apart the circles are (that is, the wider the gap), the greater the anxiety, frustration, and discord are likely to be within the organization.

Another time form and substance get out of sync is when people in the organization have one foot so planted in the outside world that they uncritically embrace the latest bell and whistle. The danger is the bells and whistles have a way of constantly pressuring the organization to keep up with the Joneses, whether it fits what the organization requires or not. The president of a company with an overly aggressive data processing manager might lament, "We have a Rolls Royce computer, and we're still just a Ford."

There is merit, of course, in an organization's staying up with or leading its competitors. Acquiring or creating a new form well ahead of what the organization actually requires can be an effective way of encouraging growth and planning for advancement. The problem comes when the gap becomes so wide that it creates undue anxiety and needless disruption.

Understanding how the client organization tends to get form and substance out of whack can aid in learning the organizational culture. You can identify these gaps by staying attuned to the top concerns among key decision makers. Antici-

	Yes	No	Don't Know	Rating of Effectiveness
1. Is there a well-defined, widely communicated statement of organizational mission or purpose?	☐	☐	☐	_____
2. Do employees have clear work goals (or objectives) and an effective system for their being motivated?	☐	☐	☐	_____
3. Is there an organizational structure which provides for:				
a. Adequate span of control?	☐	☐	☐	_____
b. Balanced allocation of resources?	☐	☐	☐	_____
c. Sufficient interdependence between units?	☐	☐	☐	_____
4. Are there training activities that provide employees the competencies needed for accomplishment of their work objectives?	☐	☐	☐	_____
5. Is there a process for ensuring the right people are in the right work roles?	☐	☐	☐	_____
6. Does the organization have effective ways of ensuring employees get performance feedback which:				
a. Is timely?	☐	☐	☐	_____
b. Is communicated clearly?	☐	☐	☐	_____
c. Is usable in improving performance?	☐	☐	☐	_____
7. Do employees have a way of determining the priority of their work objectives to enable them to put the greatest energy on the most important tasks?	☐	☐	☐	_____
8. Is there a method for communicating management information needed to achieve work objectives?	☐	☐	☐	_____

Figure 12-1. A form-substance checklist.

	Yes	No	Don't Know	Rating of Effectiveness
9. Does the organization have a process that allows employees to contribute to the development of work objectives?	☐	☐	☐	_____
10. Are there methods for employees to be appropriately rewarded for their contribution?	☐	☐	☐	_____
11. Do employees have the tools and aids they need to perform their work?	☐	☐	☐	_____
12. Is there a process that ensures employees have the freedom they need to perform their work effectively?	☐	☐	☐	_____
13. Are job descriptions:				
a. Existent?	☐	☐	☐	_____
b. Up to date?	☐	☐	☐	_____
c. Communicated to employees?	☐	☐	☐	_____
d. Used by manager *and* employee?	☐	☐	☐	_____
14. In the space below, add your own areas for consideration.				
_____	☐	☐	☐	_____
_____	☐	☐	☐	_____
_____	☐	☐	☐	_____
_____	☐	☐	☐	_____
_____	☐	☐	☐	_____

Figure 12-1. Continued.

Ideal

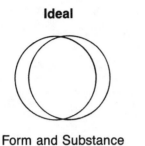

Form and Substance
Overlap

Normal

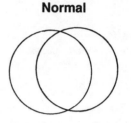

Form   Substance
(Some Gap)

Major Problems

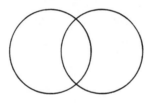

Form   Substance
(Large Gap)

Figure 12-2. Diagrams showing form-substance disparity.

pate the emphasis. Will there be a short-term shift in objectives, markets, products, services, or people? Such short-term shifts are often due to the pinches
created by gaps between what is and what needs to be.

Inspecting What's to Come

Another perspective helpful in your comprehensive assessment of the client
organization is to consider where the organization hopes to be in the future.
Think of what the next two years hold for your organization. What are the
chances there will be a major change in any of the areas listed in Figure 12-3?
Check the appropriate box for each item. This can be an important framework in
which to actively involve the client.

	Small Chance	Some Chance	Good Chance	I Need To Find Out
• Organization structure	☐	☐	☐	☐
• Organization's perception of its purpose or mission	☐	☐	☐	☐
• Products or services that the organization provides to its customers	☐	☐	☐	☐
• Markets or areas in which the organization operates	☐	☐	☐	☐
• Legal and regulatory environment	☐	☐	☐	☐
• Customers' perception of the organization	☐	☐	☐	☐
• People who are key decision makers in the organization	☐	☐	☐	☐

Figure 12-3. Long term assessment exercise.

Assessment of the Organizational Culture

So far, we have examined two frameworks for assessing the client organization—identifying gaps and looking at what's to come over the long-term. A third perspective is to examine the culture of the organization. Culture includes the norms, values, myths, beliefs, and philosophies that make the organization unique. Part history and part present practices, culture is the context within which the organization meshes people, systems, and resources to achieve a mission in the marketplace.

Few anthropologists have achieved the stature and popularity of Margaret Mead. Not only was she a brilliant scientist, but her work has also been useful to our own culture in better understanding. Central to Margaret Mead's way of looking at the world was her unique ability to couple a cold objectivity with a warm compassion. The synergy of these two faculties enabled her not only to "see" a culture, but to feel it as well. She possessed the ability to combine a "separate from" position with a "kindred with" position, a detached objectivity with a human empathy. Her way of looking at the world coupled realness with reality.

You have the capacity to assess the organization like a competent cultural anthropologist. Four perspectives will be presented for your use. The first is assessment through analogies. You begin by symbolically going up 50,000 feet, to view the organization with a kind of detached objectivity. Consider each perspective carefully, jotting down your thoughts as you go.

. . . through Analogies

The use of sports, seasonal, or literary analogies can help spark new views of your organization, fresh perspectives for understanding the unique culture that is the organization.

If the organization were a sport or game, what would it be? Chess, rugby, roulette, bridge, tennis, hang gliding? What season of the year? What novel or play best characterizes the drama played out in the organization? *The Old Man and the Sea? The World According to Garp? War and Peace? Stop the World, I Want to Get Off?* What kind of music? A slow waltz, hard rock, progressive jazz?

. . . through Norms

The second technique useful in diagnosing the organization's culture is to scrutinize its norms. List four norms of behavior—unwritten but accepted "rules"—that exist in the organization. Examples might be how one is expected to address senior managers, dress codes, how one acts in a meeting, topics not to be discussed outside one's department. Again, the participation of the client in this process can pay rich dividends in a trusting relationship.

. . . through Life Stages

Part of a cultural assessment of an organization takes its life stage into account. Figure 12-4 is a model developed by Gordon Lippitt in his work on organizational effectiveness. It aids in understanding the different concerns and key issues organizations face as they progress through three developmental stages—birth, youth, and maturity.

STAGE	CRITICAL CONCERN	KEY ISSUE	CONSEQUENCES IF CONCERN IS NOT MET
B I R T H	1. To create a new organization 2. To survive as a viable system	What to risk What to sacrifice	• Frustration and inaction • Death of organization
Y O U T H	3. To gain stability 4. To gain reputation and develop pride	How to organize How to review and evaluate	• Reactive, crisis-dominated organization • Opportunistic rather than self-directing attitudes and policies • Difficulty in attracting good personnel and clients • Innappropriate, overly aggressive, and distorted image-building
M A T U R I T Y	5. To achieve uniqueness and adaptability 6. To contribute to society	Whether and how to change Whether and how to share	• Unnecessarily defensive or competitive attitudes; diffusion of energy • Loss of most creative people • Possible lack of public respect and appreciation • Bankruptcy or profit loss

Note: Reprinted by permission of the *Harvard Business Review.* An exhibit from "Crises in a Developing Organization" by Gordon L. Lippitt and Warren H. Schmidt, *Harvard Business Review,* November/December 1967, p. 103. Copyright © 1967 by the President and Fellows of Harvard College; all rights reserved.

Figure 12-4. Stages of Organizational Development.

. . . through Growth Phases

The fourth and final technique to aid you in your assessment of the organization is based on a model developed by Larry Greiner at Harvard.[2]

Greiner holds that growing organizations move through five very distinguishable phases of development, each containing relatively calm periods of growth which end with some type of management crisis (Figure 12-5). Since each phase

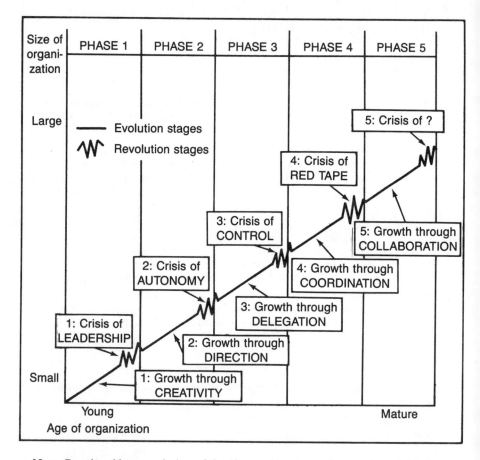

Note: Reprinted by permission of the *Harvard Business Review.* An exhibit from "Evolution and Revolution as Organizations Grow" by Larry E. Greiner, *Harvard Business Review,* July/August 1972, p. 41. Copyright © 1972 by the President and Fellows of Harvard College; all rights reserved.

Figure 12-5. The Five Phases of Growth

is so strongly influenced by the previous one, your sense of the organization's place in its history can anticipate the next development crisis so that your consulting goal could help bridge the gap.

Greiner refers to *evolution stages* as being periods of growth where no major upheaval occurs in organization practices. *Revolution stages* occur when there is a great deal of turmoil in the organization. The amount of time between stages is a function of several factors. The greatest seems to be whether the organization is in a high growth, medium growth, or low growth industry. The higher the rate of growth, the more quickly the stages occur.

Organizations in the first phase of growth, *creativity,* are characterized by informal structure and a highly individualistic and entrepreneurial style of leadership, with a "make-and sell" management focus. Rewards come largely through ownership. The creativity that got the organization started must now be replaced by strong business management.

The second phase, *direction,* is characterized by centralized and functional structure, more directive leadership, and development of explicit standards, with rewards occurring largely through salary and merit increases—the focus is on efficiency. Centralized leadership leads to demands by lower level managers for greater autonomy.

The third phase, *delegation,* generally gives rise to a more decentralized or geographically dispersed structure, with a delegative leadership style at the top. Cost centers become profit centers, and the reward system shifts toward greater use of individual bonuses. The focus is on expansion, new product development, and acquisitions. Delegation is then carried too far, and top management seeks to regain control from autonomous field managers running their own shows.

Organizations in the fourth phase, *coordination,* typically treat line-staff and product-service groups as investment centers. Consolidation becomes the focus, as top management assumes a watchdog style. Rewards gravitate more toward profit sharing and stock options, as the entire planning process becomes more formal and closely monitored. Expanding coordination systems and programs soon overstep their usefulness, resulting in excessive red tape and resentment of staff by the line.

The fifth phase of growth, *collaboration,* has the organization's focus shifting to innovation and problem solving. Leadership becomes more participative; task forces and matrix arrangements dominate as the characteristic organizational structures. Rewards gravitate toward the form of team bonuses; mutual goal setting occurs as managers are trained in teamwork and conflict resolution.

Greiner labels the fifth-place crisis stage with a question mark because no organization has yet reached that point. He anticipates the fifth-phase revolution will center around the "psychological saturation" of employees who become emotionally exhausted by the intensity of teamwork and pressure for innovation.

There are many perspectives helpful in conducting a comprehensive assessment of the needs of the organization. I hope the perspectives presented here have enriched your understanding and sharpened your focus on the client organization.

Several vantage points have been laid on the table for your perusal and use. We started with identifying gaps between form and substance, examined long-term needs, and concluded with a cultural assessment using four techniques— analogies, norms, life stages, and growth phases. All organizations contain the three dimensions we have explored—current reality, a future perspective, and a cultural milieu of norms, values, and beliefs.

As anxiety-producing as diagnosis can be to a client, you can minimize potential pain and increase client commitment to needed change by sharing perspectives and securing their participation in the process. Many clients are intrigued by what appears to be magic. They may never be able to fill your shoes; yet, the closer they come to appreciating your vantage point, the more kinship will be present in the relationship.

References

1. Appreciation is expressed to Bruce W. Fritch of Fritch-Butterfield Company in Charlotte, North Carolina for assistance on many of the concepts in this chapter, particularly gap identification as a method of diagnosis.

2. Larry E. Greiner, "Evolution and Revolution as Organizations Grow," *Harvard Business Review,* (July/August 1972), pp. 37–46.

Chip R. Bell is an independent consultant in Charlotte, North Carolina.

Chapter 13

The Organization as a Micro-Culture

Leonard Nadler

We have all walked into a room where there are people who are dressed differently. We recognize there are differences and adjust our behavior accordingly. When we look at people who might be the same as we are, but who then begin talking a different language, we receive a signal that they are different and we therefore modify our behavior. In both cases we have experienced obvious differences which are cultural. The different language and the different dress are automatic signals.

In our daily life we often see signals from different cultures but since they may not be highlighted by dress or an obviously different language, we are sometimes unable to see or hear the signals and therefore behave inappropriately. If this is so, is it possible that there are aspects of our behavior within our work organizations which are likewise the result of a cultural orientation? It is possible that some of the training activities for which we have responsibility — particularly organizational development — should give adequate recognition to the various cultures which we embrace.

One of the more obvious examples of people crossing cultures is seen in the waves of migration which came to our shores during the nineteenth and early twentieth century.* This gave rise to a concept of the United States as a melting pot. It was thought that through a process of assimilation and acculturation all the children of the immigrants would now be the same. History has since taught us that the result was not the melting pot but a pluralistic society in which each cultural group has retained some of its own habits and customs.†

Volumes have been written on the organization man in his many aspects. Still, we notice differences within organizations and we wonder if a large organization is not more likely to be a pluralistic society rather than a melting pot. Each organiza-

---

*In his book *The Uprooted*, Oscar Handlin explores the cultural implications of the great migrations, New York: Grosset & Dunlap, 1951.

†In a follow-up volume entitled *Children of the Uprooted*, Oscar Handlin has brought together a book of the writings of the second generation which indicates that they did not become one indistinguishable mass, New York: George Braziller, 1966.

Reprinted with permission from *Personnel Journal*, copyright © December 1969.

tion has a culture of its own which is unique, and within a large organization it is possible to identify more than one culture as we move from one unit to another.

In the above paragraphs, the word "culture" has been used many times without definition. It could be wasteful to engage in a long discourse on the appropriate definition of this provocative word. Rather, let us look at two definitions which are offered by writers in the field and which will satisfy our needs. One definition is "common and more or less standardized ideas, attitudes, and habits which have evolved with respect to man's recurrent and continuous needs."*

Another way to look at culture is to see it as "the cumulative ways of mankind, of the capacities the human animal has developed to tame or cope with the world of nature and the world of his own kind."†

A definition I have evolved and found useful in introducing this topic to managers is "culture can be viewed as the habits and customs that people develop to cope with changing conditions." This definition, which is not seen as being in conflict with most of the accepted definitions of the word, is the one which will be used in this article.

"Habits and customs" are usually based on tradition, which is sometimes defined as "anything that has been done twice!" It is amazing how rapidly traditions develop.**

Habits and customs, for purposes of studying culture, do not include those which have been codified by law or regulations, for once a habit or custom is written, it is no longer cultural behavior but legal behavior. This does not mean that everybody obeys it, but at least it is written and identified and available for everybody to see. We are more concerned with those habits and customs which "everybody knows," yet nobody can point to a written or common source which can be used as the basis for everybody knowing it.

A second part of the definition is "people develop." Cultural behavior is constantly developing. It is what people do to themselves rather than something that is imposed from the outside. There have been times in history when a conqueror has tried to impose a new cultural behavior, and in the world of business we see similar practices as acquisitions have become part of our current economic behavior. Basically, no matter what the conqueror or parent organization does, the people affected will develop their own cultural pattern to deal with the situation. It is usually not planned behavior, but behavior which develops and evolves.

The third part of the definition is to "cope with changing conditions." Conditions are constantly changing and, therefore, to cope effectively it becomes

---

Sociology by Kimball Young, New York: American Book Co., 1942, p. 35.

†*Personality and Social Life* by Robert Endelman, New York: Random House, 1967, p. 4.

**Where do traditions come from? In the hit play, "Fiddler on the Roof," one of the opening songs is about tradition. The actor steps to the front of the stage to explain to the audience how tradition gets started. He looks at the audience, shrugs his shoulders, and says, "I don't know."

necessary for people to change their habits and customs. We are concerned here with those changes which are not planned, but which merely develop as people try to cope with the changing world around them. Sometimes, a change in a law or regulation induces a cultural change so that people can cope with the new legal behavior which is expected of them.

Micro-Culture

The common term that is used to identify a culture which is part of something larger is the term "subculture." However, I have found that there appears to be an implication in using the prefix "sub." From the viewpoint of an exact definition one would probably find that the use of this prefix is perfectly in order. But in terms of the reactions of various groups and individuals, the experience has been that the term "sub" connotes something which is less than or under. It contains the implication that it is not as good as something else. Therefore, in order to avoid any value judgments let us use the term "micro-culture." There are instances of others concerned with this area who have also begun to use the term to mean one of the many cultures to which all of us belong.

In behavioral science terms it has frequently been said that we hold membership cards in many organizations. Likewise, we hold membership in many micro-cultural groups. For each of us, these will be different and might include the company we work for, the community in which we live, the religious group to which we belong, the kind of recreation we seek, and our racial group. The list could be much longer. By reviewing the various micro-cultures to which we belong, it can be seen that as we move from one micro-cultural group to another, we modify our behavior accordingly. The habits and customs we practice in a religious institution are different from those we use in our work organization.

This does not address itself to ethical values but to the specific form of behavior such as the appropriate dress for each situation. However, if we were to change our religious affiliation, we might find that some new forms of behavior would be required beyond that which is contained in the ritual of the new religious group. We would find this modification of behavior equally valid as a move from one job to another, from one business organization to another. Might not the new organization have cultural patterns which are unknown to us and a source of difficulty until we have been able to identify them? Bell has commented on "the tendency of employees reared in a given culture to carry values consistent with that culture into other organizations and occupations in which they participate."*

We are constantly seeking to identify the behavior that a particular micro-culture expects of us so that we can behave in the accepted ways. Even those who believe they are in revolt against the existing cultural patterns (by being part of the hippie

---

Organization and Human Behavior, edited by Gerald D. Bell. Englewood Cliffs: Prentice-Hall, 1967, p. 11.

movement, for example) find that they, too, must accept the norms of that particular new micro-culture or risk being expelled.

Why Look at Culture?

In our early years we go through a constant process of acculturation in order to make us more effective members of a particular group.† Sometimes, this behavior is fairly obvious and we come to it almost spontaneously. At other times we need additional help in understanding the behavior expected of us in a particular micro-culture. Then training becomes not only appropriate but mandatory.

Knowing the accepted culturally directed behavior can be extremely helpful. It can help us avoid making mistakes (i.e., coming into conflict with the accepted cultural behavior). It can signal ways in which we can make the most effective use of human resources in a particular micro-cultural group. If we violate the expectations within our particular micro-cultural group, we may find ourselves ignored, pushed outside the group, and blocked for reasons which we have been unable to identify. Those of our population whom we now classify as the subemployed** are faced with just this problem of not knowing the cultural signals of the system they have been trying to enter. They have not been able to learn the appropriate cultural behavior to give them entry, acceptance, and success in the micro-cultures of business and industry.

Each of us carries with him his own cultural baggage. It is not necessary to describe the baggage as we move from one micro-culture to another in the course of a day, but it is necessary to understand what behavior is appropriate for each of the micro-cultures. It is amazing how rapidly we are able to modify our behavior as we receive cultural signals.

Our own cultural baggage can impose limits on our creativity. Too strong an identification with a particular micro-culture may deny us the possibility of changes which new experiences in new cultures can demand. Cultural baggage of which we are not aware may produce tunnel vision, which prevents us from seeing the world except through a very narrow peephole.

The behavior of individuals within any micro-culture can be identified in many dimensions. For purposes of this article, only four of these will be discussed. They are space, time, language, and gender. There is no implication that these are the only manifestations of micro-culture behavior, nor are they necessarily the most significant. However, in the years that I have been using this topic in training sessions, I have found that these four areas are the ones which have proven the most

---

†Endelman, *op. cit.* See chapter 2 ("Socialization: the Family and Its Alternatives") and Chapter 3 ("Socialization: Some Problems in Large-scale Societies.").

**For more on the sub-employed see "The Concept of the Sub-employed" in *Manpower Report of the President,* Washington, D.C.: U.S. Government Printing Office, 1968, p. 34.

recognizable to the trainees and most easily identifiable within their own organizations. If we can deal effectively with at least these four, we may be on the way to
understanding much more of our own behavior which is culturally biased.

Space

There are many aspects to the use of space. One of these is the concept known as
the "territorial imperative."* In one sense this tells us that certain functions are
performed in specific places by particular groups and that it is helpful to learn
which functions are performed where. The child is taught one aspect of cultural
behavior in his early years and we call it toilet training. For the adult in the work
situation we assume that toilet training is no problem, but we do give keys to the
Executive Washroom to some and not to others. Presumably, certain space can
only be used by selected individuals, although they perform like functions.

In how many places do we have Executive Dining Rooms? Sometimes it is
specifically stated as to who can or cannot eat in the Executive Dining Room, but in
other situations the actual break in the executive line, as to who can eat in the
Executive Dining Room and who must eat in the general cafeteria, may not be
clearly stated as much as generally understood. It then becomes a manifestation of
cultural behavior for that organization.

Another concept related to space is that of the "space bubble."† This says that
each of us has a need for a certain amount of space around us. At certain points we
feel we are being crowded or invaded and respond accordingly. Hall's work in
measuring this space should be of importance to those who are engaged in
international operations.** Its implications should not be overlooked, however,
for those working within the United States or even within a single organization.
How is individual space allocated in your organization?

It is also possible that this use of space must be considered when selecting
training techniques. Today, we are offered the possibilities of individual study
carrells with individual space clearly defined. At the other end of the spectrum is
the new work being done in the body-contact training programs where individual
space is purposely invaded. Might it not be desirable for us to have some research
or at least some sophisticated exploration of the implications of each of these
training techniques as they relate to cultural behavior?

The Territorial Imperative by Robert Ardrey, New York: Atheneum, 1966. The reader
should be alert that the book is based on research with animals, not with people.

†A brief version of the concept can be found in William Kolman, "E.T. Hall and the
Human Space Bubble," *Horizon*, Autumn, 1967, pp. 42-47.

**See Edward T. Hall, *The Hidden Dimension*. (New York: Doubleday and Co., 1966),
pages 118-119 for an interesting table listing some of the distance involved between
people.

The use of space within organizations raises some questions such as, where should meetings be held? Sometimes it is fairly obvious, since a conference room may be specifically designated for this activity. There are some kinds of training which, by their very nature, indicate the particular space which is required. This may not be directly related to the quality of the physical facility as much as how it is viewed within the organization as being a status or nonstatus site for training. The use of "off-the-ranch" training facilities with certain status implications is an example of culturally identified space. Even our use of the words "cultural island" for certain kinds of training indicated our desire to create a different use of space and a new culture with its attendant culturally oriented behavior.

What about performance appraisal? Does it make any difference whether the appraisal is held in the supervisor's office, at the employee's work station, or at some neutral territory?

Time

There are those of us who see time as being something which is broken into small segments, or the instrument which is used to mark off the segments. If you are engaged in international operations, you have experienced the concept of time which varies from one country to another. In some countries it is absolutely necessary to keep an appointment at the specific time designated; whereas in others, when a meeting is called for a definite time, it will not start for at least one hour after the time agreed on. It is almost impossible to find these time perceptions written down, although occasionally a sensitive social scientist will be able to reduce some of this to writing.*

How else can time be conceptualized? The examples are endless, yet we seem to deal with time as if everybody knows its dimensions and expressions.† For those who have not developed a sensitivity to cross-cultural implications there may be difficulty in appreciating the wide divergence in the cultural use of time when it occurs quite close to home. For example, the subemployed probably have a different concept of time and deferred gratification in their micro-cultural behavior than the cultural norm required in business and industry.

You and I have not had this difficulty. If we had, I probably would not be writing this article and you probably would not be reading it. We have absorbed the cultural

---

*One description tells of a dinner invitation for 8:00 p.m. Those who have accepted because they want the food will arrive at the exact time, and never earlier. The more courteous guest will arrive anytime between 9:00 and 11:00 p.m. (In Cultural Patterns in Ethiopia as employees of the Agency for International Development, 1959, p. 5.)

†Very few books have dealt with this aspect of cultural behavior as well as Edward T. Hall in *The Silent Language*, Garden City, NY: Doubleday, 1959. See particularly Chapter 9 ("Time Talks: American Accents").

concept which signifies that there are many kinds of activities which need not produce any immediate results, but are engaged in for their long-range contribution to our growth and welfare. Some of our citizens have difficulty with this, for there is little in their previous experience to indicate that building for the future produces any rewards.

Within organizations time can vary from unit to unit as easily as from organization to organization. For example, what is the length of the work day? Where there is union agreement, a management directive, a time clock, or some physical manifestation, the length of the day as well as the starting and stopping time may be fairly exact. But what happens where the micro-cultural practices have not been agreed upon or reduced to writing? The experience of organizations with "washup time" has provided the basis for many a grievance hearing.

What constitutes coming in late? If there is no directive, then culturally directed behavior becomes the norm. In your organization, what is "late"? Is it one minute after some agreed upon starting time? Is it ten minutes, or is it half an hour? In some organizations there is no regulation and yet the standards have evolved within that particular micro-culture. A new person entering the organization will not be privy to this information with the result that his/her standards may appear to not conform to the accepted practices. In such a situation, we usually penalize the newcomer until somehow he learns the appropriate cultural behavior or leaves the organization.

One of the more obvious conflicts in time occurs in the use of time for coffee breaks. It appears that many organizations try to avoid the legitimization of the coffee break by not specifying the behavioral rules involved. Other organizations have identified periods of time, but in still others there are some implied agreements such as a ten-minute limit. In the latter situation it is not unknown for the coffee break to go to thirty minutes! The length of break for the individual or a unit may be related to status within the organization or some other cultural component which an outsider may have difficulty identifying.

Even where the time has been specified by some directive, it does not mean that all will adhere to it. A mutual unwritten understanding as to how it will be interpreted for different units within the same organization may arise, and then it once again becomes micro-cultural behavior.

The same cultural conflicts can apply to the length of the work day, rest periods, lunch period, and other activities where time is a factor. It may include practices such as the appropriate time to utilize certain services of the organization which are based on cultural understandings rather than specific planning and directives.

In the field of training and development, what is the appropriate length of a training session? Is there still the tendency to design a two hour session? Historically, we conducted sessions for two hours a day for fifteen weeks. This was probably related to the source of our instructors, in those days college professors, who had organized themselves in the typical college pattern of the two 1-hour-15-minute session which made a semester of learning.

With the advent of programmed instruction and the movement towards some kind of individual learning, we had hoped to see some breakdown in traditions. As we would expect, however, cultural practices have rapidly evolved and now we find teaching machines being scheduled in half hour blocks of time. There is little in the way of research to reinforce this practice, but a folklore has evolved and crystallized into cultural behavior. I have observed organizations using teaching machines where there is an actual schedule established in thirty-minute blocks. This is institutionalization of cultural behavior, and change becomes difficult. Notice how rapidly cultural behavior can become institutionalized. The very element which was introduced to bring about change becomes an element which blocks change.

Language

Language as cultural behavior should be easy to identify but we use so much of it we do not remain sufficiently sensitive. The sociologists tell us that language is a manifestation of culture. Language is one mechanism whereby we transmit our cultural behavior to others. If a particular practice does not exist in our micro-culture, we will not have words to express the practice for we have no need for such words.

An example of language manifesting culture may be found in the word "snow." In most parts of the northern United States the word snow is fairly obvious and communicates to the listener who has had similar cultural experiences. To the person from the tropics, snow is a meaningless term until it is described to him and even then he can only surmise what it is and may not be able to identify it when presented with the real thing. It is doubtful if his language will even have a word for this natural phenomenon if it is not part of the changing conditions with which he must cope.

For the Eskimo, the snow is so significant that it is estimated that there are more than twenty different words to describe this aspect of his changing conditions. There is no one word which can adequately describe the condition. To survive, the Eskimo must know a great deal about snow, so his language has words which tell when it fell, its thickness, quality, tendency to drift, etc. To those of us living in the temperate zone these distinctions are meaningless and we cannot include them in our cultural behavior. To an Eskimo, either he learns this extensive vocabulary concerning snow or he does not survive.

Within organizations in business and industry, language may not be a matter of life and death, but the result of not knowing the culturally oriented language can mean the difference between effective utilization of manpower or the waste of this valuable resource. Each of our organizations has specialized language which an outsider cannot possibly understand. The more physically oriented the work, the more likely it is that a specialized kind of vocabulary or speech pattern may emerge. Frequently, there is no glossary which is formally written to capture these micro-cultural differences, but some nationwide organizations have found it necessary to develop such a glossary.

Given the number of new plant startups in which many of our organizations are involved, it would seem that this problem of language becomes acute. People from different sections of the country, even if part of the same national organization, may be using different language to describe different functions or products within the organization. Until these culturally variant vocabularies have been reconciled, communication may be difficult.

In most countries of the world, social status is significant and different vocabularies and speech patterns emerge as part of the cultural behavior. The child may not be taught the differences in any organized way, but he learns them as he grows up and moves from one micro-cultural group to another.

In the United States we have prided ourselves on being a classless society. Yet, do we use exactly the same language to the person who is below us in the hierarchy as to the person above? It is not a question of being polite — it is something more and very difficult to define and identify. It is culturally oriented behavior. Taking just one example, when is a first name used or when is a title used within the particular organization with which you are familiar?

Our movie films have captured this for us in innumerable pictures about the military. Custom says (and it may even be written down somewhere) that military personnel usually address each other by rank. When the individuals involved use their respective first names, it is a signal that a comradeship had developed which supersedes the regulations. As the movie proceeds to the climax the actors reach an emotional point when they are in conflict and then each reverts to using the rank in addressing his colleague. What has happened? In our cultural framework the audience now knows that they are signalling a new aspect of their previous relationship. Culturally, through the use of language, the film has communicated much more to us than the spoken word.

Gender

The drive towards equal opportunity has highlighted discrimination based on gender in our society. Some of this is based on the realities (how real?) of the nature of the jobs to be performed and the need for the worker to have certain physical attributes. Some jobs, then, are classified as either male or female—or at least they have become culturally classified.

In the course of business a phone call is made and a female voice responds on the other end of the line. The immediate assumption is that this is the secretary. How embarrassing it becomes when one discovers that the "C.T. Jones" who left a call-back message is not Charlie but Carolyn! And, Carolyn is not a secretary but an executive!

As our practices change is it possible that the male voice on the phone is the secretary and his boss (female) is the executive? At this moment in our cultural evolvement, this could be extremely disquieting and yet there is little that keeps this state of affairs from becoming reality. The prevalent cultural practice is not having a man work for a woman, not having a woman executive, not having a male secretary — yet all of these are perfectly acceptable and do happen in some micro-cultures all around us.

Cultural behavior which discriminates against gender prevents us from using many of those in our population who have positive contributions to offer. The shortage of nurses in our hospitals might be alleviated if our traditional picture of the female nurse could be changed. The cultural bias might then be altered to an affirmative one for the male nurse, allowing and encouraging many more men to enter this noble and short-staffed profession.

Conclusion

This article has endeavored to look at the influence of micro-cultural behavior on organizations and individuals. Only four of the many dimensions were identified, namely time, space, language, and gender. Much more profitable work could be done in exploring these four elements as they relate to organizational development, organizational renewal, career development, and other aspects of our efforts to more effectively utilize our human resources.

Cultural behavior can be changed if this is necessary and desirable. There will always be culturally determined behavior. The need is to explore how behavior, which is the result of a particular micro-culture, might be adapted without doing an injustice to the individual and the culture involved.

At the outset, cultural behavior must be identified and recognized. It must be differentiated from behavior which is organizationally determined and directed by rules and regulations. Next is the recognition that culturally determined behavior cannot be eliminated. There will always remain the need for individuals and groups to develop new habits and customs as conditions change.

When the need exists, a new cultural behavior will rapidly emerge if the micro-cultural group is not thrown into chaos. In the process of forming new cultural behavior, it is possible for the sensitive behavioral scientist and the trained manager to recognize those areas in which the group is to be allowed to develop their own customs, as contrasted with those areas in which the organization must exert some influence through rules and regulations. To the degree the group-induced behavior does not correspond with the organizationally-directed behavior, we produce cultural conflict within our own organizations.

Each of us carries his own cultural baggage. We must not presume that the cultural baggage we carry is similar to that of other members of our organization. Each man belongs to many micro-cultural groups and he carries some behavior from one group to another.

It is hoped that we can begin doing much more work in identifying micro-cultural behavior. This does not relate only to the introduction of the hard-core unemployed into our organizations, where the cultural conflicts may be obvious, but also to the cross-cultural problems created by new plant startup, acquisitions, the recruitment of large numbers of college graduates, and similar situations where micro-cultural groups can be expected to impact.

Today, there is a healthy movement towards organization development and renewal. Such activities can be expected to disturb the cultural practices which crept into our organization and training program which have therefore inhibited our tendency to explore change and new behavior.

The exploration and identification of micro-cultural behavior can prove exciting and rewarding to the trainer. He may need to seek out his own areas of competence in recognizing such behavior, or he may need to identify those competencies which he must further develop as he serves his organization.

Leonard Nadler is a professor of human resource development and adult education in the School of Education and Human Development at George Washington University.

Chapter 14

Consultants and Detectives

Fritz Steele

After years of avidly reading the British detective novels of such authors as Dorothy Sayers, Margery Allingham, Michael Innes, and the like, it occurred to me that the same personal characteristics which draw me to consulting work may determine the form taken by my flight-relaxation behavior. This in turn suggested to me that we may, by examining activities other than those connected with consulting per se, be able to discover some of the more subtle attributes and dilemmas connected with the consultant's role.

In this chapter, I demonstrate this process by comparison of the similarities in the roles of the consultant and the classic British detective. Although I have chosen to focus attention on my interest in British detectives, there are obviously many other attributes which might be looked at: preferences for social gatherings and interpersonal encounters of one sort or another, interest in various sports, activities in the arts, and so on. Many of these might be worth exploring for the same kinds of analogies which will be discussed here.

Comparing the Two Roles

The format will be a rather basic listing and discussion of some of the major similarities which I see between the role of the organizational consultant and the role of the British detective. I should emphasize here a fundamental point: there are obviously many different styles and kinds of organizational consultants, and the analogies I will be making will depend to a great extent on my own personal view of what a consultant does. Also, when I use the term *consultant* here, I am referring to those consultants who are specifically oriented toward changing the structure or behavior of the client system through application of behavioral science knowledge. I do not consider specifically other types of consultants, such as market research firms, which provide services related to the actual tasks of the organization itself.

Reprinted by permission from *Consulting for Organizational Change,* copyright © 1975 by the University of Massachusetts Press.

The Focus on Evidence

Clearly, one of the major activities of the detective is an extensive search for clues and evidence as to what has occurred in a specific situation. Quite often this evidence is fleeting and must be gathered as it passes, as in the following example from Marsh.

> "Alleyn moved forward. He noticed as he did so that Peregrine stationed himself beside Miss Emily Dunne, that there was a glint of fanaticism in the devouring stare that Jeremy Jones bent upon the glove, that Winter Meyer expanded as if he had some proprietary rights over it and that Emily Dunne appeared to unfold a little at the approach of Peregrine."[7]

The detective's reason for wanting evidence may be described as falling into two major categories: one need is to gather clues to help him to *understand* what has occurred in a given criminal situation, and a second need concerns using that understanding to search out more adequate evidence in order to *prove to others* what has occurred and make a case which can stand up in court. Both of these seems to me to be of vital importance to the consultant as well. A consultant who focuses attention on active intervention in an organization must be continually seeking to understand the data with which he comes into contact. And it is of great value to collect and organize these data in such a way as to provide clear, straightforward evidence to the client system supporting the points which he will use in trying to bring about change in the system.

It has been my experience that this building up of a pool of evidence which is clear and can be seen in a relatively undistorted way by the client system is a very important focal point for the consultant who wishes to guide an organization in the direction of greater acceptance of reality. In other words, just *telling* a client system where it ought to go because of a theory which one has about how organizations ought to operate is not really enough. The consultant must be able to present a very good case for where the organization is, what the consequences of its present position are, and some of the major factors which keep it in that particular position. He should also strive to build *within* the client system the capacity and inclination to *continually* collect evidence of what is going on so they can make cases to themselves.

Considering this focus on evidence apart from questions of effective performance, I also recognize in myself a strong emotional attachment to the process of trying to solve challenging puzzles. This is probably one of the clearest of the common attributes which draw me to both the detective novel and the consulting process. I obviously share this love of puzzles with Dickenson's Sir Henry Merrivale:

> "Sudden inspiration seemed to distend H.M.'s cheeks, like an ogre in a pantomime. Breaking open the magazine, which showed the ends of cartridge cases, he plucked out one bullet. He scrutinized it carefully, also weighing it

in his hand. He did this, while Cy's nerves ached, with every bullet in the magazine; and shut it up again.

"So!" he repeated, dropping the revolver on the floor with an echoing clatter of marble. "Don't you see what this place means now?"[5]

As I will discuss below, the love of puzzles for their own sake can at times be a diversion for the consultant from the needs of the client, especially when the consultant gets wrapped up in demonstrating his ability to unravel the puzzle.

Temporary Involvement

Another characteristic of the British detective is his temporary involvement in a system or group of people. He establishes a network of relationships for the duration of the case. He may be quite central to several of these relationships, and they may be very important at the time, but then he generally moves on to a new set. The network of relationships in the detective story implies a sense of impermanence and some psychological distance. The detective acquires a kind of credibility without permanent closeness.* Here is Allingham's Albert Campion settling into a new scene for the first time, a place which will be the locus of a number of startling events.

"Mr. Campion appeared to have been forgotten, and he sat in a little recess in a corner of the hall and looked through the open doorway at the quivering leaves and dancing water without. The old house seemed very quiet after the hullabaloo. It was really amazingly attractive. Like all very old houses it had a certain drowsy elegance that was soothing and comforting in a madly gyrating world."[1]

Campion is at the same time establishing a relationship with the family who lives in the house, and for the duration of the mystery, they and the house are his world.

I find myself strongly drawn toward this temporary kind of involvement with a group of people, and I gather from my contacts with other consultants that many of them do also. This seems to be a seductive characteristic which often intrigues the client system members as well, and they often speak longingly of the consultants' chances to use a variety of settings and engage is a variety of activities day to day. However, this orientation can also have some costs. It may serve as flight from necessary deep involvement in and working through a particular problem, and this may either reduce the clients' willingness to provide important data or impair the consultant's ability to understand the situation. I am sure that there are moments for both the detective and the consultant when each would like to take the earliest opportunity to get out of the system, because things are getting too close or unmanageable. However, as I see it, each has a certain innate basic curiosity or

---

*This is similar to the notion of temporary structures which Bennis sees as being a central characteristic of organizations of the future.[3]

desire to be competent which leads him generally to stay with a particular case or problem or to terminate the relationship because of a prediction of little likelihood of further change (rather than termination simply because of a need to move on).

Another side of the question of involvement concerns the power which a system has over someone who is trying to change it. In the case of a detective the system generally has little or no power over him, including the decision whether he is to be there or not. In the case of the consultant the system has only limited power, chiefly in that area of decisions related to whether the consultant should continue in a relationship with the client (a power which the consultant shares). In this sense, then, a consultant is intermediate (in terms of freedom of action) between the detective and internal members of a system, such as internal agents of change. This in turn suggests that serving as an internal consultant carries with it a need for some important assumptions, such as a willingness to test the degrees of freedom one has, or a willingness to try to increase those degrees of freedom.

Incorporation into the System

One of the forces which is often at work on the British detective is related to his relative independence of a given group. There is usually a series of attempts by the persons with whom he is involved to incorporate him into the group. He is a real threat to that particular group of people, and they attempt to neutralize his threat to them by drawing him inside their boundaries as best they can. Here is another example from Allingham, where Campion's protagonist is attempting to win him over.

> "As he sat down again he [Campion] noticed that the other had undergone a complete change of mood. His bullying vanished and seemed to have decided to become hearty.
>
> 'Well, my boy,' he said, 'So you've come about the papers. Rather good that eh? It sounded interesting. Didn't give anything away. Now, I've been hearing a good deal about you, one way and another, and I've sent for you because I think I can put something your way that may interest you.'
>
> Mr. Campion peered round the corner of his handkerchief.
>
> 'Very nice of you, as long as it isn't a spoke in my wheel,' he murmured idiotically."[1]

The point is that I have had more than one very similar conversation with a company executive at about the time during a project that it began to look as though real change might occur. I believe that the consultant is subject to the same kinds of forces and for the same reasons: he represents a certain threat to the client system, possibly one that has not even been consciously considered by the individuals involved. However, their way of dealing with the threat which he raises is to try to swallow him, if a figurative sense, by making him a permanent part of the system and thereby increasing the system's power over him. Almost every consultant with whom I am associated can call to mind numerous instances of the client system's attempt to incorporate him and make him a permanent resident of that system. One reason for this may relate to his perceived competence and his abilities, which could be of great value for a long term to the group; but I am convinced that at least a large part of this need stems from the threat, which may be unnamed, to the clients themselves. In sociological terms, this is similar to the process of attempted "co-optation" into a system.

Intuition

The British detective often uses intuition as a mode of operation. He generates hypotheses from within, which he then attempts to test by either gathering new data or by sifting through the old data again. He often does not know for a considerable length of time why he is looking at a particular corner of the data pile, but his intuition keeps him there until the connections get made. Consider this description of Gideon from Marric.

> " 'Just tell me what it's all about and I'll tell you what I can.' Gideon did not know why he evaded the question as he did; there was something of a sixth sense in his move, that sense which made him so much more able than most detectives. He knew that Abbott would not interrupt or give him away, and he said: 'She's been missing since Wednesday evening.' "[6]

I think that the intuitive mode is also a very important one for consultants. I find that sometimes I almost stop trying to control *where* I focus my attention and let natural awareness lead me in whatever direction it will. In a sense, I try to stop staring (looking hard without really seeing) at the data and allow the figure and ground relationships to shift around and take on new meanings or new potencies for me. I do not believe that a consultant can do this without some intuition, some way to generate contextual notions so that he can understand what it is he sees as he lets his eye and mind roam over the situation.

One bit of evidence for intuition as an important process for consultants is presented in a study I made.[8] I found that laboratory trainers had a high mean score on the sensation-intuition of the Myers-Briggs Type Indicator. The trainer's mean was 135, compared with 98.7 for a sample from middle management; the higher the score on this scale, the stronger the indication of preference for intuition as a means of becoming aware of things, that is, for generating possibilities from within as well as using data obtained through the senses.

By stressing intuition here, I am not suggesting that the detective and the consultant do not put a very large amount of energy into purposeful plans, logically aimed thinking, or follow-up, but only that a too-quick focusing in on what are "obviously" the major elements in the case or the problem situation may lead to staring. This in turn can create an inability to see new relationships which may, in fact, be more important than the first ones that come to mind.

A Sense of the Dramatic

The British detective likes to be at center stage and to control the timing of events. He often works very carefully to choose just the right time for certain actions, sometimes as much for effect and his own personal centrality as for any other reason connected with accomplishing the case. Agatha Christie's Hercule Poirot is a good example, as are those two rotund rooters-out of crime, Sir Henry Merrivale:

"H.M., as usual, was basking in the spotlight. In response to the cheers he first bowed, then he lifted both hands above his head and shook hands with himself, like a prize fighter entering the ring."[5]

and Dr. Gideon Fell:

"Now, then, excuse the old charlatan a moment. I am going to make some telephone calls. Not under torture would I reveal what I intend to do, or where's the fun of mystifying you, hey? Hey! There's no pleasure like mystification, my boy, if you can pull it off..."[4]

I know I can sense within myself at times this same wish to be in the center of an unfolding drama. I suspect that I make more choices to create this situation than I like to think I do. There are times in group settings where I think I do something dramatic, and it is for at least two reasons: one is the perception on my part that confrontation at a particular moment will help to shake up the situation and bring a bit more data to the surface, and the other is that I like the image of myself as one who confronts. I think I like to engage in some behaviors which are seen by the clients as beyond the bounds of what they would do but still within their definition of what is dramatic, unusual, and exciting, with a certain flair.

I am calling attention to this need to be dramatic, because I think there are times when it can get in the way of effective consultation if it is not tested for its value as an intervention. The more dazzling the footwork of the actor, the less the members of the audience are aware of themselves. In consultation, the focus of attention on the consultant may block the clients' awareness of how central *they* must be in the drama of unfolding organizational change, and it may actually decrease self-awareness instead of increase it. It can also lead the clients to a definition of the situation such that most of the responsibility for change, innovation, and creation of excitement lies in the consultant rather than in themselves.

The Expert

Just as the detective–consultant's dramatic *actions* may cause the client's attention to focus too completely on the consultant, the same effect may also be brought about by idealized perceptions of the consultant's *knowledge* in a particular problematical situation. The detective has a tendency to unfold little of his reasoning prior to the climax of a case, and the more he does this, the more likely he is to appear omniscient in the end if he gets the pieces together (for either the right or the wrong reasons). This is another of Sir Henry's favorite tricks:

> " 'Look here,' said Cy, and drank a cup of cold coffee. 'Why in blazes can't you just tell us?...Yes, yes, I know!' he added hastily, as H.M. began to draw himself up, 'you're the old man! We understand that. All the same, can't you give us an idea?'
> 'I told you last night,' H.M. pointed out, 'that Manning's trick was based on the same principle I used myself when I hocussed the subway turnstiles.'
> 'And that tells me a hell of a lot, doesn't it?' "[5]

I think the role of "expert" is a quite seductive one for the consultant; all the more so in behavioral science, since the variables and their relationships are often very fuzzy and complex. It can be quite personally gratifying to have others see me as someone who really "knows" what is going on or what should be done in a given situation. Besides personal gratification on the part of the consultant, another factor pushes him toward the stance of expert: the client's wish to see himself safely in the hands of an expert who is wise and able, so that anxiety over present or future difficulties can be reduced.

Both the consultant's and the client's needs, then, may propel the consultant toward exclusive occupancy of the role of expert in their relationship. This may have some benefits, such as making it more likely that the consultant will be listened to, but it also has some costs. One that is usually mentioned is the potential price in terms of increased dependency of the client on the consultant, a dependency which may keep the client from developing his own strengths and competencies for the diagnosis and solving of problems. A second cost, one which is less often considered, is that a reliance on the consultant as the exclusive expert may often lead to inadequate decisions. The client often has great wisdom (intuitive if not systematic) about many aspects of his own situation, and an overweighting of the value placed on the consultant's knowledge may indeed cause poorer choices to be made than if there was a more balanced view of what each can contribute to the situation.†

Who Are the Suspects?

Another characteristic of the detective's role is the necessity of his considering all possibilities regarding those whom he should suspect in a given case. This means that he tends to consider all people as possible culprits, including both those who seem to be the most innocent and those who seem to be the most guilty. The former category may often include the very people who call the detective onto the

---

†This view of the price paid by ignoring the innate wisdom of the client was clarified for me in a conversation with Edgar Schein.

case in the beginning. Consider this reaction from the member of a theater company being interviewed by Inspector Alleyn after a murder:

> " 'Who's going to pitch into me next?' he asked. 'I ought to be getting hospital attention, the shock I've had, and not subjected to what'd bring about an inquiry if I made complaints. I ought to be home in bed getting looked after.'
> 'So you shall be,' Alleyn said. 'We'll send you home in style when you've just told me quietly what happened.'
> 'I have told. I've told them others'
> 'All right. I know you're feeling rotten and it's a damn shame to keep you but you see you're the chap we're looking to for help.'
> 'Don't you use that yarn to me. I know what the police mean when they talk about help. Next thing it'll be the Usual Bloody Warning.' "[7]

Imagine how much help Alleyn will get from him in his present mood of mistrust. But his feeling is well founded, for at the moment Alleyn needs his help and simultaneously must consider the possibility that he actually is the guilty person masquerading behind his hurt feelings.

In a very similar manner, the consultant must stay open to all possibilities in terms of who may be the "culprits" in a given problem. This means that he considers suspect even those persons who originally invited him into the system. By "suspects," in this instance, I mean people who may contribute in some significant way to difficulties or problem situations. Interestingly enough, the members of the client organization often seem to feel very similiar to the suspects in a detective case, particularly if they do not know exactly what line of thought the consultant is taking. They have a fear of being "caught," even when they do not know at *what* they may be "caught." The analogue in the organization to a crime in the detective novel seems to be being ineffective or doing something which is not seen by the consultant or persons in positions of power as leading to productivity or success in the organization. Using this definition, it has been my experience that almost everyone in a client system seems to feel that the consultant may uncover some "crime" which he has committed in the past or is committing at present. It is no surprise, then, that members of a client system often exhibit many of the same characteristics of uneasiness or mistrust toward a consultant that suspects in a detective case exhibit toward the investigator.

One of the consequences of this mistrust or uneasiness is the withholding or distortion of information which is vital to an understanding of the problem situation. This obviously makes the task of understanding and changing a system just that much more difficult and, at times, impossible. This implies that a key task of the consultant would be to help people stop defining themselves as culprits, that is, to change their view of less-than-perfectly-effective behavior from criminal to human and to redefine change as a continuing process of improvement, rather than a weeding out of antisocial elements.

This redefinition should probably start with the consultant's view of his own process. I think it is all too easy for a consultant to emotionally respond to members of the client system as if they, based on their willingness to change, were two distinct groups, the Goodies and the Baddies, and to treat them so that the Baddies *do* get the impression that they are criminals to be hunted down. This can be very self-defeating behavior on our part if the guilt we induce in the Baddies cannot be dealt with and resolved, and it may also create in the Goodies a sense of having "succeeded" to the point of closing them to an awareness of needed changes in their behavior. In addition, even the Goodies are not outside the limitations of the crime-and-punishment set of assumptions; when a consultant does confront them with some data he feels they should consider, they often feel that a "surprise arrest" has been made when they least expected it, and this can make their resistance to considering the possibility of change just as high as that of the so-called Baddies.

Action Intervention

One characteristic of the style of a number of fictional detectives with whom I am familiar is a precipitation of specific planned events which the detective predicts will produce an imbalance in the situation. This imbalance then causes someone to react, to take further action, which then provides more information about the total situation which the detective is trying to understand. This reaction helps the detective in diagnosing what the major forces are in the problem situation, helps him to understand better the orientations of the other individuals involved, and creates forces for change in the situation. Here for example, is another instance of Albert Campion stirring the pot:

> "But consider, my dear old flag-wagger, how on earth do you imagine this beautiful soul down here [a crook] ever heard about the oak? He heard about it because little Albert sent him a note with 'Look what I've found in the mill loft, Ducky', or words to that effect, neatly written above my usual signature.' "

In this instance, Campion sensed that the best way to find out what the man wanted was to hold out some opportunity for him to get it.

This action–reaction process is very similar to Lewin's suggestion that if you want to understand something, a good approach is to try to change it. It seems to me that one of the reasons why I intervene in a system (such as in confronting someone), as well as affecting that system in some way which I think may be positive, is also just to find out more about the system. In the same way that the detective may obtain some expected or unexpected results from his intervention, I often think that the consultant may gather a large portion of his data by actually doing things: by acting in the system itself. For me, it is this orientation toward action which makes the temporary involvement which I mentioned earlier a palatable one, and this may be true for other consultants as well.

There is another side to this question of action, however. As I thought about it, it dawned on me why I am using British detectives, and not American, as my role comparison. It is because there is less action for action's sake alone in the British detective stories. Rather, there is a mixture of contemplation, detection, and action which I find more appealing than the more violent American novels. The parallel to consulting is clear here: I am suggesting that at times it may be quite important that the consultant *not* engage in action for action's sake, particularly since this often seems to be one part of the clients' value system which is getting them into some of their difficulties. As Argyris[2] has pointed out, engaging in some behavior simply because it fits the clients' expectation or value system may in fact limit the usefulness of the consultant to the client.

Self-Consciousness

A very important characteristic related to taking action in a system is self-consciousness about one's action. This is reflected in the detective's attempts to really step outside himself and look at himself as if he were someone else observing him in action. Here is Alleyn in a "processing session" with himself:

> "He could have kicked himself from Whitehall to Blankside. Why, why, why, hadn't he put his foot down about the safe and its silly window and bloody futile combination lock? Why hadn't he said that he would on no account recommend it? He reminded himself that he had given sundry warnings but snapped back at himself that he should have gone further."[7]

The tendency toward self-examination obviously varies with the detectives involved, but I think that it sheds a great light on a key demand of the consultant role.** To me, this self-consciousness needs to be a central characteristic of the consultant's functioning, similar to its importance for the psychoanalyst and psychotherapist. This is because the consultant is serving as a data-gathering instrument (mainly trying to become aware of the data in the situation but also trying to understand how he is "calibrated"), and he himself is also one of the major inputs, causing reactions in the system as he is diagnosing, intervening, et cetera. As such, he must be able to have a sense of who and what he is, what he represents to the client system, what actions he is taking, and whether he can accept them or not.

I find this to be one of the most interesting, most compelling, and most difficult aspects of the role. It requires a great deal of discipline to keep one's self from throwing away three-quarters of the relevant data. By this I mean that so many of the important things having to do with the consultant's own process in a given

---

**The most notable examples with which I am familiar are Tey's Inspector Grant, Simenon's Maigret, and Marric's Commander Gideon.

situation are so close to him and so much a part of him that it is very difficult for him to see them. He therefore has to be willing to take a look at himself in terms of dimensions which he may consider to be almost self-evident, such as the ways he feels when he is about to contact the client, or the method he chooses when he does it. Many of these kinds of data may have important implications for the consultant–client relationship and for needed changes in the consultant's behavior.

Collaboration

Perhaps the above considerations are some of the reasons why most of the British detectives seem to have some sort of partner with whom they can talk, get new ideas and energy, relieve tension, or just speak the same language.†† They are generally people who have worked with the detective in the past, and they often refer to other cases and their similarities to the present one. This may serve as a good advertising mechanism for the author, but in terms of the relationship between the detective and his sidekick, it also seems to signal to each other that they speak a common language, that they understand each other and think along the same dimensions, and that they thereby share a closeness which is lacking in the detective's relationships with others in the case.

It is very important to have an associate in the organizational consulting process. It seems to me that there is a clear need on the part of someone who is dealing with ambiguous data, difficut emotional issues, and a relatively new field, to have someone who speaks his language so that he can discuss problems, issues, and just general feelings of frustration, anxiety, and elation. I know this is true for me, and I also have some sense that this is true for others. For T-group trainers, one major benefit gained from conducting a laboratory is having intensive contact with other trainers. As another example, I served for some time as a consultant to an internal consultant in a company, and one of my major functions was simply to be an available professional who spoke his language. I provided someone to whom he could let off steam and talk about things in a relatively unguarded way that would be understood. In essence, I am saying here that it really is very difficult for a consultant to try to go the whole route alone; he could probably go just so far without some chance to connect with others who are concerned with similar issues in the field or organizational change.

The mirror image of this process is also important: the conflict and competition which can develop between detectives (and consultants) who interact for mainly collaborative purposes. When collaboration occurs under the stress of a crisis situation, whether it be a crime or an interpersonal crisis within the organization, the outside professionals involved are also likely to experience a rise in their own

---

††For instance, Sherlock Holmes has Watson, Sir Henry Merrivale has Inspector Masters, and Roderick Alleyn has Inspector Fox.

emotionality, and hence the likelihood that they may create difficulties for each other. Here is an example of Commander Gideon with a colleague:

> "The manner in which the words were uttered annoyed Gideon, and for the first time, he thought: *I'm going to have to watch him.* He stared into Cox's very bright dark-blue eyes, and read the defiance in them. If he used the wrong tactics now he might make co-operation extremely difficult, and he had plenty to do without adding a kind of departmental feud."[6]

Consultants are likely to create similar problems for one another, particularly when feelings run high, and it is difficult to know whether or not you are being truly effective with the client. A consulting colleague offers an easier, safer target for pent-up feelings. This release can be useful *if* there is enough open processing to keep it manageable, as noted in chapter six.

Sequential and Parallel Cases

One final dimension of the detective and consulting roles was suggested to me by the *differences* among detectives rather than by a basic pattern common to all of them. This is the question of whether the detective works on cases one at a time; in sequence; or on several cases at once, in parallel. Most of the detectives whom I have read about tend to work on the sequential model, but J. J. Marric's George Gideon is a notable exception to this rule. In fact, one of the main attractions of his books to me is the number of different cases in which he is involved at once, and the ways in which his thinking about one case produces ideas or new directions for another which is continuing at the same time.

I think this same variation exists in terms of the consultant's process. Working on several cases in parallel can lead to many conflicts in terms of time and energy and in terms of emotional commitment to several systems. On the other hand, I seem to be drawn toward these kinds of conflicts, and I apparently like having to make those kinds of choices. I find that working on several cases in parallel leads to getting more ideas about each than I would if I were working in one client system at a time. My experiences in one setting seem to trigger off new ideas or new ways of looking at the experiences that I am having in another, and I feel that they build upon each other in a way that they couldn't if they were taken over more extended periods or separated times.

It is not clear to me that there is really a "best" position for a consultant on this particular dimension. I can also see advantages to working in sequence, because it does cut down on the demands in terms of output of conflicting time and inputs of energy, and also because it provides one with a chance to stop and think a bit about the previous case before moving on to another. This may lead to better planning than would have occurred if both were happening at the same time. The choice of sequential versus parallel cases should probably depend on several factors, such as the personality and stage of development of the consultant, the needs of a particular phase in a client system, and other demands which life makes on the consultant.

Conclusions

At this point, I should like to summarize very briefly what has been written and sketch out one or two patterns which seem to emerge. I have looked at the attributes of the role of the fictional British detectives and tried articulate points where it seemed to me to be analogous to that of the behavioral science oriented organizational change consultant. One major theme was that both roles seemed to have several attributes which I find to be emotionally satisfying and which I am guessing may also be a positive force on other consultants: the temporary nature of involvement in a system, the concentration on gathering evidence and trying to solve the puzzles which it represents, the potential for "dramatics," the potential for action and the excitement it contains, the stance of "expert" in behavioral science, and the stimulation of working on several cases at once. It was suggested that each of these satisfactions, while important, carried potential dangers in terms of making it more difficult to reach the major task goal of the consulting process, which is to improve the capabilities and functioning of the client system. Several other demands of the consultant role were described, and these might be seen as ways of keeping the above satisfactions from getting out of hand: promoting consciousness of self; avoiding incorporation into the client system; arranging for some collaborator or sounding board with whom to check perceptions, ideas, and feelings; using intuition as one means of generating ways to understand the situation; and being wary of the tendency to lump people into the over-simplified categories of "good" and "bad."

There are also two general questions relating to consulting which seemed to come up again and again as I thought about the above categories. The first one is well known: How does a consultant facilitate the obtaining of *informational inputs* to his "detection" process? How does he get valid information from the organization and its members, ideas they may have about problem solutions, useful ideas from behavioral science in general, outside views of his own operation, and new ways of his own for looking at the situation? Several means have been suggested, such as an intuitive stance, parallel cases, action intervention, a focus on evidence, self-consciousness, and collaboration (both with clients and with external professionals). One implication of this chapter is that there are some tensions among these various means of getting inputs. For instance, an active step (such as immediate feedback to a working group) which is too threatening may lead to the clients defining themselves as "suspects" and consequently cause them to eliminate or distort the information they communicate to the consultant. This suggests the obvious point that the degree of *trust* between the client and the consultant will be an important determinant of the consultant's success at being able to accurately perceive reality in a given consulting situation.§

Less obvious, perhaps, is the notion that the consultant's trust of *himself* is also a factor in this search for useful definitions of the situation. He needs this trust in order to be willing to look at the data which his own self-consciousness will generate. He also needs it in order that his own anxiety about getting a viable view of the situation not block him from obtaining new views through following events wherever they lead, that is, to look at the client system for some period with an intuitive stance requires some confidence on the consultant's part that something *will* come out of this free period, that a total blank will not be drawn. This may seem like an unnecessary elaboration of a simple point, but I think that this lack of trust in self may be at least part of the reason why some consultants tend to go into an organization with a relatively solidified view of what they will find; a view which sometimes proves not to be very useful but can be held to very tenaciously.

This brings me to the second general question which is relevant here: How does the consultant balance his professional needs with his other personal needs? For example, how does he get satisfaction in terms of feeling competent, being active, being central, being held in high esteem by the clients, et cetera, without blocking or overshadowing the clients' view of themselves and thereby limiting possibilities for growth in the client system? I have suggested that the consultant can strive for self-awareness and getting data from others as ways of testing why he is doing something at a given moment. This does not mean that he should discard some behavior just because it is personally gratifying to him; that would be removing many of the very reasons why the consultant has chosen to play this particular role. Rather, it suggests trying to choose based on a view of integrating both the professional and the personal, a process that I think is quite possible given the high motivation toward professional competence of many of the consultants with whom I am acquainted.

Finally, there is an interesting similarity in role structure between detective and consultant which the writing of this chapter has clarified for me. Expressed simply, the detective (consultant) is able to develop a certain amount of credibility and connectedness with those involved in a mystery (the particular members of an organizational unit) because of his structural position. At least for the amateur detectives, they represent some general societal values, such as truth and justice (effectiveness, organizational and individual health) without being an official member of the governmental hierarchy, for example, the police department (or the

---

§I had originally assumed that the question of trust was a point (like many others not discussed in this article due to limitation of space) where the analogy between the detective and the consultant was not relevant. It became clear, however, that although the detective often starts out operating on a model of *mistrust,* the costs to him are the same as to the consultant: it becomes much more difficult to get accurate data from participants in the situation or help in solving the mystery.

top management of the organization.) Both the detective and the consultant then, tend to be seen as not having a particular vested interest to uphold other than getting at the truth of a situation. When this disinterest is doubted, each has a much more difficult task, usually because of interference from those most concerned.§§

In terms of the process of this chapter, I would also like to repeat my beginning suggestion: as a part of the continuing search for better understanding of the organizational change consultant and his process, one useful strategy seems to me to look at the interests and peripheral characteristics of those who are drawn to consulting. Not, as in the case of much of the early leadership literature, only to see what makes a "good" consultant, but rather to discover and articulate new dimensions of the consultant's role.

References

1. Allingham, M., *Sweet Danger,* Harmondsworth, Middlesex, England: Penguin, 1950.
2. Argyris, C., "Explorations in Consulting-Client Relationships," *Human Organization,* Vol. 20 (1961), pp. 121–133.
3. Bennis, W., *Changing Organizations,* New York: McGraw-Hill, 1966.
4. Carr, J.D.., *The Blind Barber,* New York: Collier, 1962.
5. Dickson, C., *A Graveyard to Let,* New York: William Morrow, 1951.
6. Marric, J.J., *Gideon's March,* New York: Berkeley, 1963.
7. Marsh, N., *Killer Dolphin,* London: Ngaio Marsh, 1966.
8. Steele, F., "Personality and the Laboratory Style," *Journal of Applied Behavioral Science,* Vol. 4 (1968), pp. 25–45.

Fritz Steel, formerly a professor at Yale University, is a consultant in Boston, Massachusetts and a partner in Portsmith Consulting Group (PCG) in Portsmith, New Hampshire.

---

§§The vested interests of the police are partly created by the government agency most concerned about public opinion, while the stockholders' opinion is the threat in many organizations. Both these groups of people are usually very far removed from the actual facts of a case and therefore call for mainly image projection rather than effectiveness.

Chapter 15

Managing Resistance

Anthony O. Putman

Consultants are rarely eager to talk about their failures. Unlike fishermen, we seldom look for opportunities to tell tales of "the big one that got away." Like surgeons and actors, we prefer to be seen as having an unbroken string of stirring successes.

But when we do take the risk of actually talking to each other about what went wrong, the conversation often goes something like this:

"This has been one of the most frustrating clients I've ever had. It's perfectly clear to all of us what needs to be done, but the client just won't bite the bullet."

"What happened?"

"I don't really know, that's what's so frustrating! We were very careful to make sure that the contract was right, and I would defend our data-gathering methods and analysis to anybody. The recommendations were realistic, are a good fit for the corporate culture and everybody agrees that they are right on target! But all they're getting is a lot of lip service; nobody is doing anything about them."

The listener smiles, nods knowingly, sympathetically, and utters the magic word: "Resistance."

Resistance. The very word sounds cautionary, warning us of hidden forces acting to undo our plans, mysterious and implacable. For many consultants it is the X factor in our calculations; a seemingly senseless aberration in human nature that causes otherwise sensible people to refuse to do what they know they should. Others of us think of resistance as a natural force accompanying any change, the socio-cultural equivalent of friction. Without friction, every well-designed engine is a perpetual motion machine; without resistance, clients act on a good consultant's recommendations.

If we accept any of these views of resistance, we find ourselves in a basically untenable position: to be successful as consultants, we must manage, or work around a mysterious oppositional force of nature that is essentially outside of our control.

I would like to suggest that the difficulty here lies not in our skill or intentions as consultants, but rather in our basic understanding of resistance and where it comes from. Really effective consultants are rarely waylaid by resistance: they prevent it whenever possible, handle it when necessary, and utilize it to the benefit of the organization as the occasion demands.

Implicit in their strategies is a stance of taking responsibility for resistance. I suggest that an effective consultant, instead of blaming resistance on "them" or "the way things are" sees resistance as a direct result of the way the consultant treats the client. Elaborating this view of resistance—what it is, how to prevent it, how to handle it when it arises—is the aim of this chapter.

What Is Resistance?

Resistance is not just another word for "opposition." People within a client system oppose a consultant's interventions for many reasons; if your recommendation includes eliminating three branch offices, chances are good the managers of those offices will oppose the plan. When the basis for opposition is clear and straightforward we are not inclined to use the word "resistance." Indeed, we reserve "resistance" precisely for those times when on the face of it there is no good ground for opposition: logically the "resister" really ought not to oppose the plan.

A graduate school wit once said, "If it's not logical, it must be psychological." Resistance is a psychological force, which I define as "a motivation to *not* do what someone is trying to get you to do." The "someone" in that definition is central; while the resistance may be focused on a particular course of action, the person advocating the action is also being resisted. Like all other motivations, people will act on resistance unless they have strong enough reason not to.

But where does this motivation to *not* do come from? The words resistance and change have been so closely coupled that they have merged into a stock phrase "resistance to change." Indeed the most common view of resistance among consultants links it to change like the old song linked love and marriage: "You can't have one without the other." But I suggest that it is precisely this misconception that lies at the root of our difficulties with resistance. Further, I would suggest that common everyday experience gives us daily lessons on how change occurs without resistance.

This was brought home to me vividly some years ago in a very ordinary personal incidence. My father, who was born and reared in Texas, had a long-standing habit of doing auto-mechanic work while wearing cowboy boots. Despite the predictable lower-back pain and muscle strain this practice induced, he had no inclination to change it; cowboy boots were what he wore to work in and that was that.

One day he went with me to a sporting goods store where I was buying a new pair of running shoes. Intrigued by the waffle tread on the soles and the lightness of the shoes, he tried a pair on. After walking around in them in the store for a few minutes, he took out his wallet and bought them on the spot. The cowboy boots were stowed behind the driver's seat of his pickup for use on muddy road calls, and he hasn't worked in anything but running shoes since.

As I reflected later on this startling change of a lifelong habit, what struck me most strongly was that it occurred with no discernible resistance. My dad saw what he wanted, realized that it was better than what he had, and changed on the spot. If I chose to I could construct an explanation that postulated some "readiness to change" factor, but I would have just been making it up—there was no evidence for it. As I reflected a little further I realized the most instructive thing about this incident was its very ordinariness. I noticed that in day-to-day life change is a common and frequent occurrence and that it typically occurs without observable resistance. It seems to me that resistance to change in ordinary life is the exception rather than the rule—which may account for why it is so striking when it does occur.

If resistance is not an automatic reaction to change then, what is it? I examined that question intensely a little over ten years ago as part of a personal process of wrapping up the loose ends of graduate school. As part of my doctoral training, I studied closely the methods of three great psychotherapists: Milton Erickson, Peter Ossorio, and Fritz Perls. The specific methods of these three were as different from one another as one could conceive, but they had one key characteristic in common: all had a masterful understanding of and skill at utilizing resistance. To help myself account for how these three achieved their masterful results, I formulated what I somewhat facetiously labelled "The Third Law of Psychodynamics," (making playful reference to Newton's famous Third Law: "Every action has an equal and opposite reaction.") It states: *Coercion elicits resistance.*

By coercion here I mean the situation in which one person illegitimately or inappropriately limits the behavioral options of another person. To be less exact and more clear, coercion is a case of pushing somebody around. This "law," then, is saying explicitly that resistance is nothing more nor less than a reaction to being pushed around.

At this juncture most self-respecting consultants are likely to respond with some more or less polite version of: "Nonsense, I don't push people around." I whole-heartedly agree; very few consultants intentionally set out to coerce their clients (and those few who do typically know exactly what they are up to and do it, as did Erickson and Perls, deliberately to achieve specific outcomes). But before dismissing this idea out of hand, consider the following explicit points:

—*Resistance is a psychological reaction to a perception.* Coercion, like beauty, is in the eye of the beholder. No matter how well-intentioned I actually am, if you *perceive* me as coercing you, your resistance will be elicited. Preventing resistance, then is a fairly simple matter: Avoid creating in your client the feeling or perception of being coerced. Simple this may sound, but easy it is not. Many seemingly straightforward moves in the consulting game are easily perceived by the client as coercive (we will look at some of the more common of these and how to avoid them later). And it is clear that some people have a kind of resistance allergy: they perceive coercion in the simplest and most straightforward move. A few tips for managing these coercion-sensitive clients will also be offered.

Resistance is fundamentally a relationship issue. "I need that report by Friday." Consider three different situations in which you might hear that statement: from a paying client, from your boss, or from a clerk conducting an audit of your expense account. In the first case you almost certainly will not see this statement as coercive; you are in the business of meeting the customers' needs, and it is completely appropriate for them to inform you of their deadlines. In the case of the boss, most (although certainly not all) people will experience little resistance; although setting a Friday deadline is a restriction on your behavioral options, most people will consider it a legitimate one unless it seems arbitrary or high-handed. In the third case almost everyone will feel coerced—who do those auditors think they are, anyway?—and will experience resistance (although most of us out of either fear or prudence will choose not to act directly on it). The "same" statement, three different responses—the differences are due to the different relationships.

The example of the audit clerk contains a subtle but important point. Even if I were to see the Friday deadline as reasonable and not arbitrary, chances are good I will nonetheless feel coerced by it. In this case, coercion is virtually built into the relationship that exists between us. Thus almost anything the audit clerk says is likely to elicit my resistance. What is true of audit clerks is also true of consultants. Once someone in a client system experiences a consultant as coercing, anything the consultant does from that point on is likely to be seen in that light.

Preventing resistance boils down to non-coercive consulting. Conduct your consultations so your client does not feel coerced by you; take care to establish and maintain a relationship with your clients so that what you say and do is perceived as both legitimate and appropriate by them. Let us look at a few simple principles and strategies for acting on this general policy.

How to Prevent Resistance

Respect and Reflect the Other Person's Viewpoint. A good friend of mine (let's call him Jack), in the mid-seventies seemed to have everything going for him to be a world-class consultant. He was bright, well-spoken, and competent with an unrivalled ability to deal with complexity; he cared intensely about his client's well-being and worked harder than anyone to promote it. His methods and recommendations were always insightful and on target, occasionally brilliant, and unfailingly practical.

He also had an unbroken record of getting booted out by clients before his recommendations were implemented.

As a friend and colleague I helped Jack sort out what was going on with his consulting. A distinct pattern emerged: at first Jack joined with the client in identifying problems and targets of opportunity. Jack's enthusiasm and obvious competence at this stage were a great plus; clients would become stimulated and excited about the benefits they perceived from his consultation.

Working with the client, Jack would gather data, pull together plans and points of view, and start to shape a strategy. At this point things would start going subtly wrong. Jack would continue to be enthusiastic and competent, but these energies would become more and more directed toward the emerging plan rather than the client relationship. Jack would begin campaigning for the plan, using his considerable persuasive skills and interpersonal power to line up support and get people on board. Whenever he encountered less than enthusiastic support he treated it as a problem to be solved and brought to bear the full power of his intelligence and persuasion on the problem.

In other words, many people in the client system began to feel more and more backed into a corner by Jack. Jack was creating resistance, and being a powerful individual, he created powerful resistance. Eventually, an opportunity would present itself, and one of the "resistors" would seize the opportunity to get rid of Jack.

Jack's fatal error lay in his management of the relationship dynamics with the client: he forced the client to be wrong. This is a common trap in the consulting business and an easy one to fall into. It reflects what I believe to be a fundamental misconception of why clients hire consultants and what success in consulting really is.

Look at the consulting relationship from the client's point of view for a moment. Jack's clients hired him because they already knew that they didn't have all the answers (or at least they wanted a second opinion), and they had reason to believe that Jack could help them. In short the client hired Jack to help them change their own view of what needed doing in the organization and how to do it. Jack's success or failure as a consultant depends directly on the extent he actually brings about the needed changes in the *client's* way of viewing things. No matter how brilliant or on-target the program, if the client does not come to see it and choose it as what is needed, the consultation has been a fundamental failure.

The business of changing someone's view of things is considerably more challenging and subtle than the business of coming up with a good set of recommendations. If the consultant is careful or lucky enough to make only those recommendations that the client is predisposed to hear and act on, there is little difficulty—but how often does that happen in real life? The hard work of consulting starts precisely when we need to influence the client to change things they are not already predisposed to change, and in my experience that requires the consultant to straightforwardly *respect* and *reflect* the client's point of view.

This is more than just good manners or an ethical issue. It is a pragmatic necessity. Influence must be earned; it does not come along with the consultant's contract. If your task is to change my view of things, you must first become eligible in my eyes to do that. Since the way I already see things makes sense to me, saying or implying that it doesn't make sense is coercion. What you have to do first is *demonstrate* to me that you understand the way I see things, and appreciate the way in which it makes sense. Only then am I likely to give you the eligibility to help me change my view of things.

So what does all this mean to us as consultants? Jack evolved a useful rule of thumb for himself; whenever a client seems obviously wrong or wrong-headed, the *consultant* has gotten off target. Jack finds it necessary to work hard at ensuring that he understands the client's point of view and at communicating that understanding in a way that conveys his respect for it. So long as he keeps his focus on changing the client instead of promoting his program, he finds that resistance is rarely a problem.

He must be doing something right; today Jack is one of the busiest consultants I know—and he almost never loses clients.

"Take the Cash and Let the Credit Go." This line in the Rubiayat of Omar Khayyam struck me as a good candidate for inclusion in the consultant's credo. It's also a good prescription for avoiding one of the most subtle and pervasive forms of coercion. Here is how it looks in action:

Ralph thinks and talks about twice as fast as anyone else. He enjoys brainstorming and problem-solving; his insights and ideas come out like a machinegun, and many of them are quite good and interesting. But even when he slows down to normal human pace, Ralph has discovered a frustrating fact: people usually either ignore or argue with even his best ideas. As he himself puts it, "I can toss in an idea and nobody responds. Three minutes later Bob comes up with exactly the same idea, and everyone thinks it's great. For some reason people resist my ideas and they don't resist Bob's."

Ralph's dilemma stems from not being able to choose between two desirable but sometimes contradictory goals: influence and acknowledgment. Ralph really wants people to acknowledge how smart or competent or creative he is, and how good his ideas are. He ruefully admits that a part of him is working hard to get a response of open-mouthed amazement at his insight; instead he gets ignored or attacked. The very energy and conviction with which he presents his ideas coerces people into considering them. Most people, lacking good reason not to, act on the resistance Ralph's coercion elicits.

It is an ironic dilemma: Ralph can get the acknowledgment and credit that he craves only if his ideas actually influence people, but he only becomes influential with people when he stops trying to get acknowledgment.

The solution to Ralph's dilemma is to recognize that *you* cannot act on *my* idea. Even if I originate the idea, before you can do anything with it you have to make it your own. If I am trying to be effective in influencing you, I will make it as easy as possible for you to do that: I will present the idea clearly and straightforwardly as something to be considered rather than saluted and not intrude into the private ground of your mind. Let your ideas become orphans; if they are in fact good ones, they will find plenty of adoptive parents. Consultants who want to prevent resistance must learn when to take the "cash" of effective influence and let the "credit" for the ideas go.

Legitimize Ambivalence. Life, as a great comic-strip philosopher once said, is a trade-off. It is rare in my experience for clients to greet substantial recommendations with immediate wholehearted acceptance (fortunately it is even more rare to encounter complete wholehearted rejection). Over time objections, doubts, and concerns are talked out, worked through, and resolved for most people. But virtually everyone initially reacts to a consultant's recommendations with some degree of ambivalence, and typically some people in the client system will remain ambivalent. Consultants who fail to acknowledge and accept that fact are very likely to push some of the people in their client system into resistance.

Ambivalence, the experience of reacting to something with two opposed and contradictory feelings, is a common experience that has puzzled the human race throughout history. An ancient Roman poet expressed it succinctly: "I hate and love at the same time, for heaven's sake, Cattulus, how?" While hate and love are a bit strong for describing how most clients respond to a consultant's recommendations, resolving that kind of polar response in an individual is a necessary part of helping clients to change.

The psychodynamics of ambivalence are very powerful and very tricky. So long as I remain ambivalent, any attempt to strengthen one pole of my ambivalence has the unintended effect of strengthening the opposite pole in reaction. If the executive vice president likes my recommendations but has doubts and misgivings about them, my attempt to sell her on the merits of the program will almost certainly strengthen her feelings of doubt and misgiving. Even worse, my attempts to persuade her are a way of treating her ambivalence as illegitimate; I am attempting to coerce her into being not ambivalent and am likely creating resistance. The end result is that I am very likely to drive a potential supporter into opposition and resistance.

The potential for coercion (and therefore resistance) is enormous here. Masterful psychotherapists such as Milton Erickson and Fritz Perls deliberately use coercion to help their clients resolve ambivalence; they appropriately see working with their ambivalence as dynamite which can help break up a long-standing log-jam. Ambivalence is dynamite, and a consultant would be well-advised not to play with it. Instead, I would recommend the strategy used by another group of masterful therapists such as Peter Ossorio, who help the client clarify and legitimize their own ambivalence and support the client in resolving their ambivalence—or not, as the client chooses.

The key move is to legitimize ambivalence. Start with yourself. So long as it is *not* OK with you for people to be ambivalent about your proposal, you are explicitly setting yourself in opposition to them. Recognize that ambivalence is a natural and desirable response in the early stages, which if handled properly will have one of two outcomes: (1) The client moves from ambivalence to support, or (2) you learn in what important way your proposal was off target so you can revise it. Give yourself and the client room to find out which of these is the case. If your recommendations are in fact what the client needs, with your support they will come to recognize that.

Do not expect everyone to jump on board the bandwagon, however. Ron Lippitt, who legitimizes ambivalence in his clients as well as anyone I know, likes to point out that agricultural agents never expect farmers to all adopt new methods at the same rate. They typically find three groups: the pioneers, who are the first to try any new method; the second wave, who watch carefully the experience of the pioneers and immediately adopt any method that the pioneers prove out; and the conservatives who will watch this innovation from a distance, if allowed to, but will take their own time about adopting it, if they ever do. Consultants sometimes need to have conservatives become pioneers—but treating their ambivalence as illegitimate is not the way to succeed at it.

Handling Resistance

Even the editor of *Prevention Magazine* gets occasional colds; even the most non-coercive consultant will encounter resistance from time to time. How can a consultant handle resistance most effectively when it arises? Two slogans stand me in good stead in this task:

Join with the client. Margaret is one of my favorite people in the world. She is a caring, no-nonsense, level-headed consultant in her fifties who is both fearless and utterly lacking in pretension. She also has one of the most severe allergies to coercion I've ever encountered. If I were to say, "Everyone knows the sun will rise tomorrow," I can rely on her to respond, "Oh yeah? Says who?"—and mean it.

Everytime I run into resistance with Margaret, I notice that it stems from my failing to remain joined with her in a mutual enterprise. Whenever I begin to do *my* thing instead of *our* thing with Margaret she feels coerced. This has provided a wonderful laboratory for me to refine techniques for handling resistance, which I find apply across the board to any client.

I have found that I can be a powerful advocate with Margaret so long as I am careful to get her explicit sanction for doing so. For instance, I once told her straightforwardly, "Margaret I want to influence you in this area." She looked intrigued, said, "Okay," and listened while I laid out exactly how I felt she should change her approach and why. When I had finished, I said, "End of sermon. What do you think?" thereby rejoining her to our mutual task of exploring what to do. She took the "advice" without a flicker of resistance.

With some clients where I judge that resistance is in the picture, I have been careful to *perform* my advocacy speeches rather than delivering them. Here's how that looks:

"Look, there's an idea here I want to try to nail down. Help me out here; bear with me for a few minutes while I play devil's advocate and see if I can work out the logic of this position." After everyone has nodded agreement, I move to a different location in the room, adopt a deliberately more impassioned, definitive manner of speaking and perform a straightforward advocacy speech with high energy and intensity. When I have finished I physically adopt a more relaxed posture, move back to where I started from in the room, and in a very matter of fact voice say, "Okay, now let's look at that. Does any of it make sense?" Often this kind of move has the desired result: persuasion without coercion.

You can't win them all. This is my second slogan, which I use to keep me grounded in the consultant's reality. No matter how non-coercive I am, no matter how skillful I am at handling resistance, some people simply will not buy the program. If that person is a key decision-maker I will take my best shot at persuasion; otherwise I am willing to let the person remain unconvinced. Rarely does any important change occur in an organization without some opposition; my task as a consultant is to help it occur without resistance.

Anthony O. Putman is a human systems consultant in Ann Arbor, Michigan.

Chapter 16

Surviving as a Messenger: The Client-Consultant Relationship During Diagnosis

Richard M. Furr

The relationship aspects of the client–consultant engagement are complicated, exciting, and rewarding. A key mechanism for shaping change, the relationship is in fact part of the intervention rather than separate from it.

This article focuses upon the relationship dimensions of the consulting engagement, particularly in the diagnostic stage.

The first part of this article is designed to provide background from which to view the relationship aspects of diagnosis. The components of the relationship and the steps in accomplishing the purposes of diagnosis will then be examined.

The Diagnostic Stage

The diagnostic stage of a consulting engagement is important to both the consultant and the client. To the consultant it is important as a means of learning what he needs to know in order to shape an appropriate response strategy. The diagnostic stage is used as a means for establishing initial awareness and growth in the client as well as influencing the client to feel responsible for ensuring a successful outcome. Change starts with the diagnosis, not after it.

Likewise, the diagnostic stage is important to the client. Here he learns what he needs to understand to achieve the results he wants. It allows the client opportunities to name the game and define how he wants it played in his organization and in the relationship with the consultant.

Perspectives on Diagnosis

There are several perspectives about the diagnostic stage of consultation which warrant attention by the consultant. One simple perspective might be labeled *Multiple Purpose Thinking* and suggests that the consultant proceed with a flexible agenda. This perspective is illustrated by the consultant's thinking, "Given that we are going to do an assessment of some kind, how else can we use it to benefit the client?" Frequently, subpurposes, which can be included efficiently, will become evident.

A second perspective might be called *Evolving Diagnosis*. Such a perspective presumes that diagnosis is not a discrete stage of the engagement but is rather a nearly perpetual enterprise, beginning with the initial client contact and lasting throughout the entire engagement. Everything the consultant does is viewed and managed to further refine the Evolving Diagnosis. Running a seminar at a later stage of the engagement, for example, can be done in a way which allows additional input into the diagnosis.

One further perspective is the distinction between "doing a diagnosis" and *Creating Awareness* or causing the client to arrive at a diagnosis. In the "doing a diagnosis" view the consultant executes the diagnosis and brings the client the results. In the latter view the consultant starts thinking about how to cause the client and key players in the system to see what they need to see in order to achieve the result they want. The key difference is that the consultant focuses on the process of creating awareness rather than the tactic of "doing a diagnosis." This "management of the process" approach tends to keep the client actively and responsibly involved and fosters less client resistance because the consultant is not laying it on him. When performed most effectively, the client may discover things he had never seen before.

Purpose of Diagnostics

As the consultant proceeds through the engagement, his usefulness will be largely a function of energy focused for effectiveness. Rather than energetically charging-up the client and zealously pursuing truth, the consultant must maintain focus assiduously. Focus is manifested in the consultant's commitment and purposefulness. While the former is dependent upon the personal psychological needs of the consultant, the purpose can be defined here.

Concentrating upon the diagnostic stage, we can identify six interrelated aspects of the purpose of diagnosis. The first is to precipitate change itself. Secondly, the diagnosis should provide an assessment of the variables relevant to the change goal. Thirdly, the diagnosis can create an expanded awareness and growth in the client. Fourth, and very specific to the relationship, it should create in the client a personal value out of the relationship separate from his objective organizational purpose. The fifth aspect is to energize momentum toward the change. The sixth is to focus the client's attention on the variables necessary to create the change and to achieve his goal.

The purposefulness of diagnosis is a key relationship consideration. Next, we will look at a relationship model which focuses upon four key operating components.

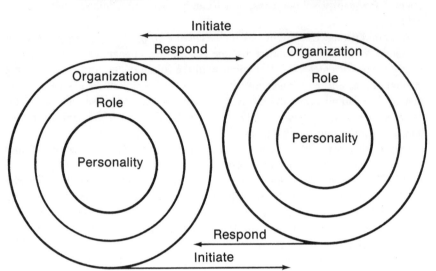

Figure 12-1. The components shaping the behavior of the client and the consultant.

Components of the Relationship

The client–consultant relationship has four components operating simultaneously to shape the behavior of the client *and* the consultant and, ultimately, the
outcome of the relationship. As reflected in Figure 12-1, both the client and the
consultant are substantially influenced by their own personality dynamics, their
perception of their roles, and their experience of the demands of the organization.
The fourth component surrounding, integrating, and interfering with these three is
the nature of the communications between the client and consultant. The four
components are illustrated below.

Each individual's personality dynamics include their personal needs, self-
image, beliefs, feeling, games, and resulting behavior patterns. Compounding
these variables, the personal make-up of one individual may be affected by the
personal make-up of the other. The client, for example, may be a shy person who is
personally intimidated by a consultant who acts very self-assured and assertive.

The second component of the client–consultant relationship is each individual's
perception of his own role and the role of the other person. Each individual will
most appropriately relate to the other person in a way that conveys respect for role.
For instance, the consultant should establish himself as at least a professional peer
in the eyes of the client. However, when the client is aloof and generally inaccessi-

ble to the consultant, he is probably not being viewed by the client as a professional peer. The result is a consultant having limited access to the power of the client's role.

The third key component is founded in one's experience of the organization — a result of the values, traditions, and norms inherent in the formal organization and the informal organization. From these organizational predispositions, each individual acquires certain expectations. For example, frequently an experience occurs as a result of an institutionalized anticonsultant bias throughout the client's firm. In such cases, the client may perceive that he risks reproach and reprisal from colleagues and as a result may be resistant to taking highly visible and risky actions stemming from the consultation.

The fourth component of the client–consultant relationship is the nature of the communications between them. Like a rapid-fire tennis match, the action–reaction communication sequences shape the perceptions and reactions in each individual. Each person attempts to influence the other by what he initiates as well as by how he responds to what the other communicator initiates. The resulting dialogue shapes the foundation and fabric of the relationship.

With the preceding model of the components of the client–consultant relationship as background, a key to the consulting process becomes the posture or stance the consultant takes in that relationship. A proper consultant stance implies that the consultant functions in a fashion unencumbered by personal dynamics, role influence, organizational influence, or the manipulation attempts of the client. While this describes an idealized stance, the more it can be approximated, the less judgment and action will be influenced by circumstances unrelated to the client situation.

Toward Achievement of the Relationship Objective

While the preceding information is intended to provide a stage, what follows approximates the play. The client–consultant relationship during diagnosis can be viewed as a play with three acts: the shaping of client–consultant agreements necessary to manage the change throughout the diagnosis; the empowering of the client to perform to his fullest capacity; and the handling of resistance.

Shaping Agreements

In shaping the agreements necessary to achieve certain changes, some of the following guidelines and techniques may become appropriate:

— It is important for the client and the consultant to clearly agree on the intention of the diagnosis as it relates to achieving the client's objective. If it becomes necessary for the consultant to be the active agent in obtaining the diagnostic data, the consultant needs to create enough latitude to be able to get the information required. For example, in solving a quality problem it may be important for the consultant to establish broad freedom and trust within the relationship to be able to assess effectively the impact of the leader's behavior on the quality problem.

— The client and consultant need to agree on how the diagnostic information will be handled to meet the client's purpose and to satisfy all ethics criteria.

— The consultant may need to establish a contract with the client regarding the client's implied obligations which may arise as a result of the diagnosis. This is particularly important when a diagnosis involving some of the client's employees raises their hopefulness that something will happen as a result. The client needs to be aware of such expectations and to be committed to taking serious, reasonable steps to follow-up on the implication of the diagnostic results. This also, very positively, reduces resistance at later stages in the consultation.

— Often, it is beneficial for the client to collect his own data. This can be accomplished through a carefully designed process in which the client hears the truth but which provides the necessary protection of others involved. Agreements are formed which establish the respondents' requirements for confidentiality.

— Often, when the consultant must be the one to collect the data, it is very desirable to get the client to ask for it from the followers directly. This practice can speed the data collection and increase the chance of the client learning by direct experience. The client's communication should establish the purpose of the study, the methodology, the ethics, the use to be made of the results, and the value the leader places upon honesty and candor.

Empowering the Client

The second key step in accomplishing the purpose of the consulting engagement through the diagnostic stage is empowering the client. The empowering of the client means helping the client to perform his function to the fullest extent of his ability *and* facilitating his growth as a person in areas which go beyond work.

This is a crucial result of successfully handling the relationship dimensions of the diagnosis and can substantially increase the consultant's value to the client. Likewise, it can enable the client to execute his role in the response phase of consultation. The two issues of empowering — will be addressed separately, though they are clearly interrelated.

Empowering the client to perform excellently involves the consultant looking at those conditions likely to increase the client's *ability,* his *motivation* to act appropriately, and the *organizational* conditions within which the client operates. To increase ability, the consultant will need to work with the client in a manner which increases the client's awareness of what needs to be done *and* increases his own capacity to do it. Additionally, the consultant may need to help the client acquire the necessary skills to do what is required, and the diagnostic process can be one vehicle for doing this.

Increasing the client's motivation to act requires that the consultant arrange positive rewards for acting and entails reducing the self-restraints in the personal make-up of the client. In order to increase motivation positively, the consultant must learn the client's personal needs and arrange positive rewards for taking appropriate steps. The consultant might then arrange feedback to the client from the client system so that the hoped-for reward occurs. An example of empowering the client motivationally occurred when a consultant accurately assessed the client as a person with a need to be seen as progressive and important. The consultant then helped the client view the recommended course of action as progressive and an enhancement to the client's self-esteem.

In addition to empowering the client by causing him to see valued reward from taking action, another technique for empowering the client is to cause the client to see and work through his own immobilizing behavior. What occurs then is a reduction of self-restraints. For example, upon getting the client to see how his decision aversiveness or crippling attention to detail is contributing to the very problem he is trying to solve, an uncomfortable internal conflict is established which the client is motivated to reduce. The consultant can get the client to see the unsolved problem as a risk of even greater proportion which he can avoid by being more decisive and less compulsive about detail.

The third class of conditions which may need to be managed to empower the client is the organizational system. The client may have the ability, vision, skill, and motivation to perform to his fullest capacity, but the organizational variables may be limiting. While these are often used as cop outs which allow the client to disown responsibility, at times the conditions are, in reality, barriers. For example, when roles, goals, and reward systems are in conflict or unclear, they have a limiting effect on the performance of otherwise well-motivated, talented people. One way of empowering the client is for the consultant to assume the role of stimulator, helping the client reduce the drag of these barriers on performance, by clarifying roles, goals, and reward systems. The very process of helping him to act to remove the barriers himself is empowering in the sense of the two earlier conditions. Each success experience builds power.

Handling Resistance

The third key step in accomplishing the purpose of the client engagement through the diagnostic stage is the process of preventing and handling resistance. A major consideration is "Who can resist what?" The resistors could be the client, the client's followers, or the consultant himself. The client or his followers can resist dealing with their beliefs and fears and can resist changing the way they perform their roles. They can also resist changes in the demands the organization makes on them, and can resist the consultant altogether. As for the consultant, we will assume at this point that he is aware of and can manage his own resistance.

A few basic perspectives about resistance may be helpful. One is that resistance is always a motivated behavior on the part of the client, and it makes perfectly good sense to that person to resist. This resistance is often tied to an avoidance of imagined, threatening conditions — a very strong motivation. In such a case it is useful to consider, "What could this person be fearing; what is he attempting to avoid by resisting?"

A second perspective about resistance is that the consultant is far better off proactively managing the relationship to *prevent* or minimize resistance than assuming it will happen and reacting to it after it has built to a peak. From the client's view, the client will typically have many reasons to resent and devalue the consultant who is reactive at this point.

A third perspective about resistance is that the consultant should not play his role in a way that gives the client anything to resist. This is comparable to judo in that the consultant should employ the energy and momentum of the client. Here, a strategy of dominance holds little usefulness since it gives the client much to resist. The key perspective is to operate from the "plain of effectiveness" rather than the "plain of right or wrong."

A fourth perspective in reducing resistance is based on the consultant building a "hopefulness for change" perception and a "seriousness of intent" perception. Both perceptions must be real, with no intent to deceive. In effect the follower's resistance to the diagnosis will be reduced to the extent he (a) feels hopeful that management really wants the truth, and (b) believes management will use the diagnosis responsively.

As in judo, general strategy for managing resistance is to include their purpose in yours rather than argue for your own purpose or against theirs. For example, the president of a company may want his leaders to take the initiative, when they have traditionally avoided doing so. They have already staked themselves out in the position that not taking the initiative is the best way to play the game. On the other hand, they are frustrated by problems which affect their department, and a valued purpose of theirs is to see them solved. If they viewed the consultant's purpose as primarily to get them to take initiative, they may be inclined to resist. However, by incorporating their purpose in his, the consultant can relate what he is doing to something they want done, thus gaining support by providing support.

Several techniques are available for handling the client's or follower's resistance which arises during the diagnostic stage of the engagement. Some are based on the preceding perspectives. Resistance from the client might be managed in the following ways:

— Self-image maintenance is one technique for minimizing resistance. To do this, the consultant learns how the client wants to be viewed by superiors, peers, and followers. The consultant then positions what needs to be done as a means of maintaining or increasing the likelihood the client will be seen that particular way. For example, if a leader wants to be seen as assertive, the consultant might wish to position his recommendations so as to indicate that their implementation clearly demonstrates assertiveness by the client. As the program unfolds, the consultant might arrange honest feedback from superiors, peers, or followers that indicate the perception of assertiveness.

— Another technique which may assist in reducing the client's resistance is creating conformity pressure. In this instance the consultant arranges feedback to the client which results in that client perceiving that the other people he values (those with power, status, popularity, etc.) are doing what the consultant wants the client to do. In order to be identified with them the client will likely want to do it, too.

— Creating a kind of "what if" anxiety is an additional technique. A client who perpetually worries about something going on that he doesn't know about or have under control can be approached from the angle that he would be better off finding out and managing it than remaining in the dark. Or the consultant can arrange a tidbit of feedback that all is not well. The diagnosis in these instances would be positioned as a means for the client to learn what is going on and to re-establish control.

— Another tactic deals with resistance to accepting feedback which indicates that conditions are not what the client expected. Before the data comes in, the consultant needs to establish the perspective with the client that good managers can accept and handle feedback which is not what they thought it would be. This establishes the return of the data as an opportunity for the client to prove his competency.

— When the time or cost of the diagnosis or its potential response is a primary source of resistance, the consultant can bring up awareness of time and money consequences for *not solving* the problem. This awareness can extend to the nonfinancial costs of not solving the problem, such as frustration, tension, and loss of good people. The consultant might also establish the perception in the client that he gets what he pays for.

As mentioned earlier, the views of the client's followers are sometimes sought in the diagnostic process. Their resistance to participating openly and honestly often arises from several sources. These include the fear of repercussions from leaders who might be angered by the data, the expectation that there will not be any response, the reluctance to involve their leader in any kind of trouble, and fear of rejection by peers for participating truthfully.

Techniques for handling the resistance of followers are largely based on the perspectives for handling resistance mentioned earlier. In general, the followers often face a conflict between wanting to tell the complete truth about how they see things and wanting to be sure they remain safe and protected.

— One of the techniques for minimizing follower resistance was alluded to in the discussion about agreements. That is, when there is to be a questioning of followers by the client, by the consultant or through some sort of questionnaire, the consultant should get the leader to state the purpose of the diagnosis, the methodology, how the data will be used, the ethics and the value of their candor. This reduces resistance resulting from some of their uncertainty and it reduces their concern about someone being out to get their leader, since he is indicating he wants their honest views at the outset.

— Clear assurance to the followers that they will be informed of the outcome of the diagnosis is often useful in reducing resistance. This informs followers of management's open and constructive attitude. In reality, the followers do not want to be faced later with data which they know is not representative of the truth, so their inclination is to be honest.

— Follower resistance sometimes occurs due to fear of exposure. Confidentiality and anonymity are frequently key issues. A set of techniques to deal with this would include the consultant emphasizing the value he and the client place on participation, while at the same time making it clear that nonparticipation is okay. In additon, the consultant can waylay some anxiety by visibly putting the interviewee in control of what data goes into the formal study (e.g., "Shall I include that or not?" or "How do you want me to say it?"). The follower, realizing that the consultant is willing to go to some length to protect the anonymity of each respondent, usually decides it must be safe enough to participate openly.

— One kind of follower resistance is the depth of perception. One way the consultant can manage the level of openness is by giving the respondent a bench mark as to what his peers must be saying. For example, having heard about problem X from other sources, or even rumor, the consultant can say "Tell me about X" or "I hear that X...What is your view?" This usually causes the respondent to think to himself, "Oh, people are being *that* open;, well, okay..."

Conclusion

The basic process for managing the client–consultant relationship through diagnosis is that of influence. The responsible consultant must execute those influence attempts which will move the client and followers toward achieving the client's purpose. In reality, the basis of the influence process is that of manipulation. However, all the manipulations are guided by the position of professional ethics and responsibility in accordance with the goal of the engagement. Ultimately, the consultant uses the manipulation process to manage the relationship dynamics so that the client sees what needs to be done, assumes the appropriate responsibility, and is empowered to progress. The client's resistance to doing the appropriate thing at the appropriate time is reduced, and if the consultant has done his job effectively, the client will generally be rewarded by achievement of his goal.

In the days of kings and kingdoms, it was often the case that the messenger who brought bad news to the king was executed. As a consultant, our survival as a messenger, especially during the diagnostic stage of the engagement, is as important to the client's well-being as it is to our own. Our facility in handling the client–consultant relationship during diagnosis is a crucial aspect of our effectiveness and is the foundation on which the total relationship is built.

Richard M. Furr is a principal with LEAD Associates, Inc., a management consulting firm headquartered in Charlotte, North Carolina.

Part V

Response

The response phase of the consulting process is often seen as the most crucial. Peter Block refers to response as "the main event." Relying heavily on what has come before, it represents the focal point or main event of consultation. It is in response that the most obvious action takes place. Variously termed "intervention" or "strategic and tactical planning," response is the time when both client and consultant begin to see the possibility of successfully completing their relationship and meeting their mutual expectations.

The response phase must be girded by the diagnosis phase. At the end of diagnosis, the consultant is typically in a position to present the client with a variety of alternatives which the client may have helped to generate. The alternative ultimately selected may be a hybrid alternative produced either by combining alternatives or creating one out of the substance of the discussions. This collaborative process can be enormously beneficial. Synergistic client–consultant relationships enhance creative action planning.

The range of possible responses appears to be endless. Some writers have even developed helpful systems to categorize the input and indicate the appropriate answer. Response in a can! The listing can be misleading for it implies comprehensiveness when we are continually evolving new interventions. There is likewise a temptation, particularly for new consultants, to look for the kind of list which indicates that for Diagnosis A one should use Response B. The field has yet to reach such a level of research and practice which precipitates clean choices of action.

Among consultants there exists a wide range of expertise, despite the use of the label identifying an individual with a specific background and experience. This imposes limits on the response phase: the consultant can legitimately focus on those responses which are clearly within the realm of personal expertise. If the consultant lacks the knowledge and skills for a particular response alternative, it may be time to secure the assistance of another consultant or terminate the existing client–consultant relationship.

This conflict often arises when the consultant uses "training" as a response. (In this context, training is defined as a learning experience, usually in a group situation.) When a person designs and conducts a learning experience, he or she is assumed to have competencies as a learning specialist. While it is likely there are consultants who can function as learning specialists, it is doubtful all consultants have such ability. Therefore, while training can be an appropriate response alternative, it is not one every consultant can employ without obtaining additional assistance.

Similarly, not every learning specialist can function as a consultant. Learning specialist and consultant entail specific kinds of behavior requiring different skills, knowledge, and experience.

If the chosen response is a plan, the consultant should devise a plan which the *client* can successfully implement. If additional resources are needed to implement the plan, the consultant should be certain these are carefully and clearly specified.

A common error among clients and consultants is to view the response phase as the only action phase and to proceed with desperate vigor for a "win." Organization development efforts are commonly burdened with this distortion — inappropriately amplifying the consultant's importance. If the consultant becomes too directly involved in carrying out the plan, it is easy for the consultant to become the change manager. Here, the consultant's role will have been altered so significantly that the usual consultant behaviors are no longer effective. The consultant and client should recognize that if this happens, the former can no longer effectively function as a consultant but has in reality become a part of the system. This role change can also occur when the consultant has a retainer arrangement and therefore can be called upon readily and frequently. The consultant can easily cross the line to become a part of the client system, thus diminishing consultative effectiveness.

An ethical consideration arises when the plan calls for the use of an external resource and the consultant appears to fill that requirement. While there are times this is unquestionably logical and appropriate, there are other situations where the consultant-produced plan specified that only that consultant can bring the effort to a successful conclusion. For example, in the U.S. government an initial, small contract is often given for consulting. The end product is to be a plan arrived at through a feasibility study or by actually producing a plan of action. The contractor is then awarded a "sole source" contract, or the original contract gets an "add on." There are times when such action by the contracting and/or project officer is clearly in the best interests of the government. There are other times, however, when the contractor knows this process beforehand and takes the initial consulting contract at a ridiculously low fee knowing the pay-out will come in the subsequent contract to implement the plan.

In the private sector this occurs less frequently. Consultants have, however, assumed contracts which would produce a plan, knowing full well the plan will be something which only that consultant can carry out, or which will definitely require the consultant's help. The client has some responsibility for being familiar enough with the consultant and the plan to avoid such ethical dilemmas. An important consideration is the timing and the response. It is obviously desirable to bring the client and consultant's time expectations to the surface as early as possible. Developing a plan as a response can usually be completed in a short period of time. It is unusual, but possible, for this to extend over a period of several months. An action response — actually conducting those activities which will result in a desired change — can easily extend from several months to several years.

Organizations and people generally change slowly, and in the process new factors may arise to modify the situation. There are times when the client is given the impression that a particular response by the consultant will cause the desired change to occur with lightning speed, followed by a thunderous clap of the door closing as the client exits with finality. Instead, the relationship is extended over a longer period and the solution process is prolonged. Gaps in expectations about timing can cause the relationship to terminate prematurely, ultimately because insufficient funds will have been provided for the long-range relationship needed to implement the action.

By the end of the response phase, it will be possible for the client and the consultant to see how the objectives of their relationship will be met. Some formative evaluation (i.e., during the consultation) is usually built into the relationship, making it possible to determine if the objectives can be met by successfully concluding the response phase. The final evaluation usually takes place in a later phase.

Chapter 17
"Choosing the Depth of Organizational Intervention"
Roger Harrison

Harrison makes an important point in his article which might too easily be by-passed. He says, " ...an intervention strategy can focus on instrumentality or it can focus on interpersonal relationships, and that there are important consequences of this difference in depth of intervention."

He defines instrumentality as "change work behavior and working relationships" but sees interpersonal relationships as a deeper level where " ...the focus is on feelings, attitudes, and perceptions which organization members have about each other." He helps focus on the need for relating the interventions to the appropriate need. The selection of strategies is value laden — the values of the client as well as the values of the consultant must be considered.

Chapter 18
"Managing the Response: A Client Perspective"
Fredric H. Margolis

As Roger Harrison examined response from the consultant view, Fred Margolis looks at the phase from the client perspective. All the energy expended in entry and diagnosis is done for response (or intervention)—the main event. After examining client and consultant roles during response, he describes useful steps the client should take to ensure a positive, productive relationship.

Chapter 19
"Client-Consultant Relationship in Organizational Transition"
Leonard Nadler and Zeace Nadler

Consultancy is almost synonymous with change. In a merry-go-round world in which figure *and* ground are moving, the helping process becomes uniquely challenging. Len and Zeace Nadler speak from extensive, world-wide experience as they reveal new perspectives on managing the relational tensions during organizational transition. Tools, resources, roles, and plans are presented along with beneficial cautions associated with the phases of transition.

Chapter 20
"The Consultant's Role with Entrepreneur-Owners"
C. William Webb

Economic improvement has spawned a resurgence in the number of new businesses started annually. The entrepreneur-owners at the genesis of such ventures are more likely to seek the assistance of consultants than their boot-strap predecessors of even a decade ago. Central to the successful client-consultant relationship in an entrepreneurial environment is the consultant's sensitivity to characteristics often unique to the client.

Bill Webb draws from his years both as a successful entrepreneur and as a consultant to small- to medium-sized closely held-business owners to outline traits frequently found in entrepreneur owners. He succinctly spells out tips for managing such a relationship. While provocative, his ideas provide fertile ground for fresh thinking.

Chapter 21
"Managing the Consultant"
Marie S. Nock and Alex L. Moore

There is a paucity of literature about consulting written by clients. Marie Nock and Alex Moore each have extensive experience managing external consultants. Their "lessons learned" address the entire consulting effort (entry to closure), but principally zero in on response or implementation. Assembled around five common pitfalls, their message is important to clients *and* consultants.

Chapter 17

Choosing the Depth
of Organizational Intervention*

Roger Harrison

Since World War II there has been a great proliferation of behavioral science-based methods by which consultants seek to facilitate growth and change in individuals, groups, and organizations. The methods range from operations analysis and manipulation of the organization chart, through the use of Grid Laboratories, T Groups, and nonverbal techniques. As was true in the development of clinical psychology and psychotherapy, the early stages of this developmental process tend to be accompanied by considerable competition, criticism, and argument about the relative merits of various approaches. It is my conviction that controversy over the relative goodness or badness, effectiveness or ineffectiveness, of various change strategies really accomplishes very little in the way of increased knowledge or unification of behavioral science. As long as we are arguing about what method is better than another, we tend to learn very little about how various approaches fit together or complement one another, and we certainly make more difficult and ambiguous the task of bringing these competing points of view within one overarching system of knowledge about human processes.

As our knowledge increases, it begins to be apparent that these competing change strategies are not really different ways of doing the same thing — some more effective and some less effective — but rather that they are different ways of doing *different* things. They touch the individual, the group, or the organization in different aspects of their functioning. They require differing kinds and amounts of commitment on the part of the client for them to be successful, and they demand different varieties and levels of skills, and abilities on the part of the practitioner.

I believe that there is a real need for conceptual models which differentiate intervention strategies from one another in a way which permits rational matching

---

*A revised version of a paper presented at the International Congress of Group Psychotherapy, Vienna, Austria, September 16, 1968.

Reproduced by special permission from *The Journal of Applied Behavioral Science*. Vol. 6, No. 2, pp 181–202. Copyrighted by NTL Institute, 1970.

of strategies to organizational change problems. The purpose of this article is to present a modest beginning which I have made toward a conceptualization of strategies, and to derive from this conceptualization some criteria for choosing appropriate methods of intervention in particular applications.

The point of view of this article is that the depth of individual emotional involvement in the change process can be a central concept for differentiating change strategies. In focusing on this dimension, we are concerned with the extent to which core areas of the personality or self are the focus of the change attempt. Strategies which touch the more deep, personal, private, and central aspects of the individual or his relationships with others fall toward the deeper end of this continuum. Strategies which deal with more external aspects of the individual and which focus upon the more formal and public aspects of role behavior tend to fall toward the surface end of the depth dimension. This dimension has the advantage that it is relatively easy to rank change strategies upon it and to get fairly close consensus as to the ranking. It is a widely discussed dimension of difference which has meaning and relevance to practitioners and their clients. I hope in this article to promote greater flexibility and rationality in choosing appropriate depths of intervention. I shall approach this task by examining the effects of interventions at various depths. I shall also explore the ways in which two important organizational processes tend to make demands and to set limits upon the depth of intervention which can produce effective change in organizational functioning. These two processes are the autonomy of organization members and their own perception of their needs for help.

Before illustrating the concept by ranking five common intervention strategies along the dimension of depth, I should like to define the dimension somewhat more precisely. We are concerned essentially with how private, individual, and hidden are the issues and processes about which the consultant attempts directly to obtain information and which he seeks to influence. If the consultant seeks information about relatively public and observable aspects of behavior and relationship and if he tries to influence directly only these relatively surface characteristics and processes, we would then categorize his intervention strategy as being closer to the surface. If, on the other hand, the consultant seeks information about very deep and private perceptions, attitudes, or feelings and if he intervenes in a way which directly affects these processes, then we would classify his intervention strategy as one of considerable depth. To illustrate the surface end of the dimension, let us look first at operations research or operations analysis. This strategy is concerned with the roles and functions to be performed within the organization, generally with little regard to the individual characteristics of persons occupying the roles. The change strategy is to manipulate role relationships; in other words, to redistribute the tasks, the resources, and the relative power attached to various roles in the organization. This is essentially a process of rational analysis in which the tasks which need to be performed are determined and specified and then sliced up into role definitions for persons and groups in the organization. The operations analyst does not ordinarily need to know much about particular people. Indeed, his function is to design the organization in such a way that its successful operation does not depend too heavily upon any uniquely individual skills, abilities, values, or attitudes of persons in various roles. He may perform this function adequately without knowing in advance who the people are who will fill these slots. Persons are assumed to be moderately interchangeable, and in order to make this approach work it is necessary to design the organization so that the capacities, needs, and values of the individual which are relevant to role performance are relatively public and observable, and are possessed by a fairly large proportion of the population from which organization members are drawn. The approach is certainly one of very modest depth.

Somewhat deeper are those strategies which are based upon evaluating individual performance and attempting to manipulate it directly. Included in this approach is much of the industrial psychologist's work in selection, placement, appraisal, and counseling of employees. The intervener is concerned with what the individual is able and likely to do and achieve rather than with processes internal to the individual. Direct attempts to influence performance may be made through the application of rewards and punishments such as promotions, salary increases, or transfers within the organization. An excellent illustration of this focus on end results is the practice of management by objectives. The intervention process is focused on establishing mutually agreed-upon goals for performance between the individual and his supervisor. The practice is considered to be particularly advantageous because it permits the supervisor to avoid a focus on personal characteristics of the subordinate, particularly those deeper, more central characteristics which managers generally have difficulty in discussing with those who work under their supervision. The process is designed to limit information exchange to that which is public and observable, such as the setting of performance goals and the success or failure of the individual in attaining them.

Because of its focus on end results, rather than on the process by which those results are achieved, management by objectives must be considered less deep than the broad area of concern with work style which I shall term instrumental process analysis. We are concerned here not only with performance but with the processes by which that performance is achieved. However, we are primarily concerned with styles and processes of work rather than with the processes of interpersonal relationships which I would classify as being deeper on the basic dimension.

In instrumental process analysis we are concerned with how a person likes to organize and conduct his work and with the impact which this style of work has on others in the organization. Principally, we are concerned with how a person perceives his role, what he values and disvalues in it, and with what he works hard on and what he chooses to ignore. We are also interested in the instrumental acts which the individual directs toward others: delegating authority or reserving decisions to himself, communicating or withholding information, collaborating or competing with others on work-related issues. The focus on instrumentality means that we are interested in the person primarily as a doer of work or a performer of functions related to the goals of the organization. We are interested in what facilitates or inhibits his effective task performance.

We are not interested per se in whether his relationships with others are happy or unhappy, whether they perceive him as too warm or too cold, too authoritarian or too laissez faire, or any other of the many interpersonal relationships which arise as people associate in organizations. However, I do not mean to imply that the line between instrumental relationships and interpersonal ones is an easy one to draw in action and practice, or even that it is desirable that this be done.

What I am saying is that an intervention strategy can focus on instrumentality or it can focus on interpersonal relationships, and that there are important conse- quences of this difference in depth of intervention.

When we intervene at the level of instrumentality, it is to change work behavior and working relationships. Frequently this involves the process of bargaining or negotiation between groups and individuals. Diagnoses are made of the satisfac- tions or dissatisfactions of organization members with one another's work behavior. Reciprocal adjustments, bargains, and trade-offs can then be arranged in which each party gets some modification in the behavior of the other at the cost to him or some reciprocal accommodation. Much of the intervention strategy which has been developed around Blake's concept of the Managerial Grid is at this level and involves bargaining and negotiation of role behavior as an important change process.

At the deeper level of interpersonal relationships the focus is on feelings, attitudes, and perceptions which organization members have about others. At this level we are concerned with the quality of human relationships within the organiza- tion, with warmth and coldness of members to one another, and with the experi- ences of acceptance and rejection, love and hate, trust and suspicion among groups and individuals. At this level the consultant probes for normally hidden feelings, attitudes, and perceptions. He works to create relationships of openness about feelings and to help members to develop mutual understanding of one another as persons. Interventions are directed toward helping organization members to be more comfortable in being authentically themselves with one another, and the degree of mutual caring and concern is expected to increase. Sensitivity training using T Groups is a basic intervention strategy at this level. T-Group educators emphasize increased personalization of relationships, the development of trust and openness, and the exchange of feelings. Interventions at this level deal directly and intensively with interpersonal emotionality. This is the first intervention strategy we have examined which is at a depth were the feelings of organization members about one another as persons are a direct focus of the intervention strategy. At the other levels, such feelings certainly exist and may be expressed, but they are not a direct concern of the intervention. The transition from the task orientation of instrumental process analysis to the feeling orientation of interpersonal process analysis seems, as I shall suggest later, to be a critical one for many organization members.

The deepest level of intervention which will be considered in this article is that of intrapersonal analysis. Here the consultant used a variety of methods to reveal the individual's deeper attitudes, values, and conflicts regarding his own functioning, identity, and existence. The focus is generally on increasing the range of experiences which the individual can bring into awareness and cope with. The material may be dealt with at the fantasy or symbolic level, and the intervention strategies include many which are noninterpersonal and nonverbal. Some examples of this approach are the use of marathon T-Group sessions, the creative risk-taking laboratory approach of Byrd,[1] and some aspects of the task group therapy approach of Clark.[2] These approaches all tend to bring into focus very deep and intense feelings about one's own identity and one's relationships with significant others.

Although I have characterized deeper interventions as dealing increasingly with the individual's affective life, I do not imply that issues at less deep levels may not be emotionally charged. Issues of role differentiation, reward distribution, ability and performance evaluation, for example, are frequently invested with strong feelings. The concept of depth is concerned more with the *accessibility* and *individuality* of attitudes, values, and perceptions than it is with their strength. This narrowing of the common usage of the term "depth" is necessary to avoid the contradictions which occur when strength and inaccessibility are confused. For instance, passionate value confrontation and bitter conflict have frequently occurred between labor and managment over economic issues which are surely toward the surface end of my concept of depth.

In order to understand the importance of the concept of depth for choosing interventions in organizations, let us consider the effects upon organization members of working at different levels.

The first of the important concomitants of depth is the degree of dependence of the client on the special competence of the change agent. At the surface end of the depth dimension, the methods of intervention are easily communicated and made public. The client may reasonably expect to learn something of the change agent's skills to improve his own practice. At the deeper levels, such as interpersonal and intrapersonal process analyses, it is more difficult for the client to understand the methods of intervention. The change agent is more likely to be seen as a person of special and unusual powers not found in ordinary men. Skills of intervention and change are less frequently learned by organization members, and the change process may tend to become personalized around the change agent as leader. Programs of change which are so dependent upon personal relationships and individual expertise are difficult to institutionalize. When the change agent leaves the system, he may not only take his expertise with him but the entire change process as well.

A second aspect of the change process which varies with depth is the extent to which the benefits of an intervention are transferable to members of the organization not originally participating in the change process. At surface levels of operations analysis and performance evaluation, the effects are institutionalized in the form of procedures, policies, and practices of the organization which may have considerable permanence beyond the tenure of individuals. At the level of instrumental behavior, the continuing effects of intervention are more likely to reside in the informal norms of groups within the organization regarding such matters as delegation, communication, decision making, competition and collaboration, and conflict resolution.

At the deepest levels of intervention, the target of change is the individual's inner life; and if the intervention is successful, the permanence of individual change should be greatest. There are indeed dramatic reports of cases in which persons have changed their careers and life goals as a result of such interventions, and the persistence of such change appears to be relatively high.

One consequence, then, of the level of intervention is that with greater depth of focus the individual increasingly becomes both the target and the carrier of change. In the light of this analysis, it is not surprising to observe that deeper levels of intervention are increasingly being used at higher organizational levels and in scientific and service organizations where the contribution of the individual has greatest impact.

An important concomitant of depth is that as the level of intervention becomes deeper, the information needed to intervene effectively becomes less available. At the less personal level of operations analysis, the information is often a matter of record. At the level of performance evaluation, it is a matter of observation. On the other hand, reactions of others to a person's work style are less likely to be discussed freely, and the more personal responses to his interpersonal style are even less likely to be readily given. At the deepest levels, important information may not be available to the individual himself. Thus, as we go deeper the consultant must use more of his time and skill uncovering information which is ordinarily private and hidden. This is one reason for the greater cost of interventions at deeper levels of focus.

Another aspect of the change process which varies with the depth of intervention is the personal risk and unpredictability of outcome for the individual. At deeper levels we deal with aspects of the individual's view of himself and his relationships with others which are relatively untested by exposure to the evaluations and emotional reactions of others. If in the change process the individual's self-perceptions are strongly disconfirmed, the resulting imbalance in internal forces may produce sudden changes in behavior, attitudes, and personality integration.

Because of the private and hidden nature of the processes into which we intervene at deeper levels, it is difficult to predict the individual impact of the change process in advance. The need for clinical sensitivity and skill on the part of the practitioner thus increases, since he must be prepared to diagnose and deal with developing situations involving considerable stress upon individuals.

The foregoing analysis suggests a criterion by which to match intervention strategies to particular organizational problems. It is *to intervene at a level no deeper than that required to produce enduring solutions to the problems at hand.* This criterion derives directly from the observations above. The cost, skill demands, client dependency, and variability of outcome all increase with depth of intervention. Further, as the depth of intervention increases, the effects tend to locate more in the individual and less in the organization. The danger of losing the organization's investment in the change with the departure of the individual becomes a significant consideration.

While this general criterion is simple and straightforward, its application is not. In particular, although the criterion should operate in the direction of less depth of intervention, there is a general trend in modern organizational life which tends to push the intervention level ever deeper. This trend is toward increased self-direction of organization members and increased independence of external pressures and incentives. I believe that there is a direct relationship between the autonomy of individuals and the depth of intervention needed to effect organizational change.

Before going on to discuss this relationship, I shall acknowledge freely that I cannot prove the existence of a trend toward a general increase in freedom of individuals within organizations. I intend only to assert the great importance of the degree of individual autonomy in determining the level of intervention which will be effective.

In order to understand the relationship between autonomy and depth of intervention, it is necessary to conceptualize a dimension which parallels and is implied by the depth dimension we have been discussing. This is the dimension of predictability and variability among persons in their responses to the different kinds of incentives which may be used to influence behavior in the organization. The key assumption in this analysis is that the more unpredictable and unique is the individual's response to the particular kinds of controls and incentives one can bring to bear upon him, the more one must know about that person in order to influence his behavior.

Most predictable and least individual is the response of the person to economic and bureaucratic controls when his needs for economic income and security are high. It is not necessary to delve very deeply into a person's inner processes in order to influence his behavior if we know that he badly needs his income and his position and if we are in a position to control his access to these rewards. Responses to economic and bureaucratic controls tend to be relatively simple and on the surface.

If for any reason organization members become relatively uninfluenceable through the manipulation of their income and economic security, the management of performance becomes strikingly more complex; and the need for more personal information about the individual increases. Except very generally, we do not know automatically or in advance what styles of instrumental or interpersonal interaction will be responded to as negative or positive incentives by the individual. One person may appreciate close supervision and direction; another may value independence of direction. One may prefer to work alone; another may function best when he is in close communication with others. One may thrive in close, intimate, personal interaction, while others are made uncomfortable by any but cool and distant relationships with colleagues.

What I am saying is that when bureaucratic and economic incentives lose their force for whatever reason, the improvement of performance *must* involve linking organizational goals to the individual's attempts to meet his own needs for satisfying instrumental activities and interpersonal relationships. It is for this reason that I make the assertion that increases in personal autonomy dictate change interventions at deeper and more personal levels. In order to obtain the information necessary to link organizational needs to individual goals, one must probe fairly deeply into the attitudes, values, and emotions of the organization members.

If the need for deeper personal information becomes great when we intervene at the instrumental and interpersonal levels, it becomes even greater when one is dealing with organization members who are motivated less through their transactions with the environment and more in response to internal values and standards. An example is the researcher, engineer, or technical specialist whose work behavior may be influenced more by his own values and standards of creativity or professional excellence than by his relationships with others. The deepest organizational interventions at the intrapersonal level may be required in order to effect change when working with persons who are highly self-directed.

Let me summarize my position about the relationship among autonomy, influence, and level of intervention. As the individual becomes less subject to economic and bureaucratic pressures, he tends to seek more intangible rewards in the organization which come from both the instrumental and interpersonal aspects of the system. I view this as a shift from greater external to more internal control and as an increase in autonomy. Further shifts in this direction may involve increased independence of rewards and punishments mediated by others, in favor of operation in accordance with internal values and standards.

I view organizations as systems of reciprocal influence. Achievement of organization goals is facilitated when individuals can seek their own satisfactions through activity which promotes the goals of the organization. As the satisfactions which are of most value to the individual change, so must the reciprocal influence systems, if the organization goals are to continue to be met.

If the individual changes are in the direction of increased independence of external incentives, then the influence systems must change to provide opportunities for individuals to achieve more intangible, self-determined satisfactions in their work. However, people are more differentiated, complex, and unique in their intangible goals and values than in their economic needs. In order to create systems which offer a wide variety of intangible satisfactions, much more private information about individuals is needed than is required to create and maintain systems based chiefly on economic and bureaucratic controls. For this reason, deeper interventions are called for when the system which they would attempt to change contains a high proportion of relatively autonomous individuals.

There are a number of factors promoting autonomy, all tending to free the individual from dependence upon economic and bureaucratic controls, which I have observed in my work with organizations. Wherever a number of these factors obtain, it is probably an indication that deeper levels of intervention are required to effect lasting improvements in organizational functioning. I shall simply list these indicators briefly in categories to show what kinds of things might signify to the practitioner that deeper levels of intervention may be appropriate.

The first category includes anything which makes the evaluation of individual performance difficult:

— A long time span between the individual's actions and the results by which effectiveness of performance is to be judged.
— Nonrepetitive, unique tasks which cannot be evaluated by reference to the performance of others on similar tasks.
— Specialized skills and abilities possessed by an individual which cannot be evaluated by a supervisor who does not possess the skills or knowledge himself.

The second category concerns economic conditions:

— Arrangements which secure the job tenure and/or income of the individual.
— A market permitting easy transfer from one organization to another (e.g., engineers in the United States aerospace industry).
— Unique skills and knowledge of the individual which make him difficult to replace.

The third category includes characteristics of the system or its environment which lead to independence of the parts of the organization and decentralization of authority such as:

— An organization which works on a project basis instead of producing a standard line of products.
— An organization in which subparts must be given latitude to deal rapidly and flexibly with frequent environmental change.

I should like to conclude the discussion of this criterion for depth of intervention with a brief reference to the ethics of intervention, a problem which merits considerably more thorough treatment than I can give it here.

There is considerable concern in the United States about invasion of privacy by behavioral scientists. I would agree that such invasion of privacy is an actual as well as a fantasied concomitant of the use of organizational change strategies of greater depth. The recourse by organizations to such strategies has been widely viewed as an indication of greater organizational control over the most personal and private aspects of the lives of the members. The present analysis suggests, however, that recourse to these deeper interventions actually reflects the greater *freedom* of organization members from traditionally crude and impersonal means of organizational control. There is no reason to be concerned about man's attitudes or values or interpersonal relationships when his job performance can be controlled by brute force, by economic coercion, or by bureaucratic rules and regulations. The "invasion of privacy" becomes worth the cost, bother, and uncertainty of outcome only when the individual has achieved relative independence from control by other means. Put another way, it makes organizational sense to try to get a man to *want* to do something only if you cannot *make* him do it. And regardless of what intervention strategy is used, the individual still retains considerably greater control over his own behavior than he had when he could be manipulated more crudely. As long as we can maintain a high degree of voluntarism regarding the nature and extent of an individual's participation in the deeper organizational change strategies, these strategies can work toward adapting the organization to the individual quite as much as they work the other way around. Only when an individual's participation in one of the deeper change strategies is coerced by economic or bureaucratic pressures do I feel that the ethics of the intervention clearly run counter to the values of a democratic society.

So far our attention to the choice of level of intervention has focused upon locating the depth at which the information exists which must be exchanged to facilitate system improvement. Unfortunately, the choice of an intervention strategy cannot practically be made with reference to this criterion alone. Even if a correct diagnosis is made of the level at which the relevant information lies, we may not be able to work effectively at the desired depth because of client norms, values, resistances, and fears.

In an attempt to develop a second criterion for depth of intervention which takes such dispositions on the part of the client into account, I have considered two approaches which represent polarized orientations to the problem. One approach is based upon analyzing and overcoming client resistance; the other is based upon discovering and joining forces with the self-articulated wants or "felt needs" of the client.

There are several ways of characterizing these approaches. To me, the simplest is to point out that when the change agent is resistance-oriented he tends to lead or influence the client to work at a depth greater than that at which the latter feels comfortable. When resistance-oriented, the change agent tends to mistrust the client's statement of his problems and of the areas where he wants help. He suspects the client's presentation of being a smoke screen or defense against admission of his "real" problems and needs. The consultant works to expose the underlying processes and concerns and to influence the client to work at a deeper level. The resistance-oriented approach grows out of the work of clinicians and psychotherapists, and it characterizes much of the work of organizational consultants who specialize in sensitivity training and deeper intervention strategies.

On the other hand, change agents may be oriented to the self-articulated needs of clients. When so oriented, the consultant tends more to follow and facilitate the client in working at whatever level the latter sets for himself. He may assist the client in defining problems and needs and in working on solutions, but he is inclined to try to anchor his work in the norms, values, and accepted standards of behavior of the organization.

I believe that there is a tendency for change agents working at the interpersonal and deeper levels to adopt a rather consistent resistance-oriented approach. Consultants so oriented seem to take a certain quixotic pride in dramatically and self-consciously violating organizational norms. Various techniques have been developed for pressuring or seducing organization members into departing from organizational norms in the service of change. The "marathon" T Group is a case in point, where the increased irritability and fatigue of prolonged contact and lack of sleep move participants to deal with one another more emotionally, personally, and spontaneously than they would normally be willing to do.

I suspect that unless such norm-violating intervention efforts actually succeed in changing organizational norms, their effects are relatively short-lived, because the social structures and interpersonal linkages have not been created which can utilize for day-to-day problem solving the deeper information produced by the intervention. It is true that the consultant may succeed in producing information, but he is less likely to succeed in creating social structures which can continue to work in his absence. The problem is directly analogous to that of the community developer who succeeds by virtue of his personal influence in getting villagers to build a school or a community center which falls into disuse as soon as he leaves because of the lack of any integration of these achievements into the social structure and day-to-day needs and desires of the community. Community developers have had to learn through bitter failure and frustration that ignoring or subverting the standards and norms of a social system often results in temporary success followed by a reactionary increase in resistance to the influence of the change agent. On the other hand, felt needs embody those problems, issues, and difficulties which have a high conscious priority on the part of community or organization members. We can expect individuals and groups to be ready to invest time, energy, and resources in dealing with their felt needs, while they will be relatively passive or even resistant toward those who attempt to help them with externally defined needs. Community developers have found that attempts to help with felt needs are met with greater receptivity, support, and integration within the structure and life of the community than are intervention attempts which rely primarily upon the developer's value system for setting need priorities.

The emphasis of many organizational change agents on confronting and working through resistances was developed originally in the practice of individual psychoanalysis and psychotherapy, and it is also a central concept in the conduct of therapy groups and sensitivity training laboratories. In all of these situations, the change agent has a high degree of environmental control and is at least temporarily in a high status position with respect to the client. To a degree that is frequently underestimated by practitioners, we manage to create a situation in which it is more unpleasant for the client to leave than it is to stay and submit to the pressure to confront and work through resistances. I believe that the tendency is for behavioral scientists to overplay their hands when they move from the clinical and training situations where they have environmental control to the organizational consulting situation, where their control is sharply attenuated.

This attenuation derives only partially from the relative ease with which the client can terminate the relationship. Even if this most drastic step is not taken, the consultant can be tolerated, misled, and deceived in ways which are relatively difficult in the therapeutic or human relations training situations. He can also be openly defied and blocked if he runs afoul of strongly shared group norms; whereas when the consultant is dealing with a group of strangers, he can often utilize differences among the members to overcome this kind of resistance. I suspect that, in general, behavioral scientists underestimate their power in working with individuals and groups of strangers, and overestimate it when working with individuals and groups in organizations. I emphasize this point because I believe that a good many potentially fruitful and mutually satisfying consulting relationships are terminated early because of the consultant's taking the role of overcomer of resistance to change rather than that of collaborator in the client's attempts at solving his problems. It is these considerations which lead me to suggest my second criterion for the choice of organization intervention strategy: *to intervene at a level no deeper than that at which the energy and resources of the client can be committed to problem solving and to change*. These energies and resources can be mobilized through obtaining legitmation for the intervention in the norms of the organization and through devising intervention strategies which have clear relevance to consciously felt needs on the part of the organization members.

Unfortunately, it is doubtless true that the forces which influence the conditions we desire to change often exist at deeper levels than can be dealt with by adhering to the criterion of working within organization norms and meeting felt needs. The level at which an individual or group is willing and ready to invest energy and resources is probably always determined partly by a realistic assessment of the problems and partly by a defensive need to avoid confrontation and significant change. It is thus not likely that our two criteria for selection of intervention depth will result in the same decisions when practically applied. It is not the same to intervene at the level where behavior-determining forces are most potent as it is to work on felt needs as they are articulated by the client. This, it seems to me, is the consultant's dilemma. It always has been. We are continually faced with the choice between leading the client into areas which are threatening, unfamiliar, and dependency-provoking for him (and where our own expertise shows up to best advantage) or, on the other hand, being guided by the client's own understanding of his problems and his willingness to invest resources in particular kinds of relatively familiar and nonthreatening strategies.

When time permits, this dilemma is ideally dealt with by intervening first at a level where there is good support from the norms, power structure, and felt needs of organizational members. The consultant can then, over a period of time, develop trust, sophistication, and support within the organization to explore deeper levels at which particularly important forces may be operating. This would probably be agreed to, at least in principle, by most organizational consultants. The point at which I feel I differ from a significant number of workers in this field is that I would advocate that interventions should *always* be limited to the depth of the client's felt needs and readiness to legitimize intervention. I believe we should always avoid moving deeper at a pace which outstrips a client system's willingness to subject itself to exposure, dependency, and threat. What I am saying is that if the dominant response of organization members indicates that an intervention violates system norms regarding exposure, privacy, and confrontation, then one has intervened too deeply and should pull back to a level at which organization members are more ready to invest their own energy in the change process. This point of view is thus in opposition to that which sees negative reactions primarily as indications of resistances which are to be brought out into the open, confronted, and worked through as a central part of the intervention process. I believe that behavioral scientists acting as organizational consultants have tended to place overmuch emphasis on the overcoming of resistance to change and have underemphasized the importance of enlisting in the service of change the energies and resources which the client can consciously direct and willingly devote to problem solving.

What is advocated here is that we in general accept the client's felt needs or the problems he presents as real and that we work on them at a level at which he can serve as a competent and willing collaborator. This position is in opposition to one which sees the presenting problem as more or less a smoke screen or barrier. I am not advocating this point of view because I value the right to privacy of organization members more highly than I value their growth and development or the solution of organizational problems. (This is an issue which concerns me, but it is enormously more complex than the ones with which I am dealing in this article.) Rather, I place first priority on collaboration with the client, because I do not think we are frequently successful consultants without it.

In my own practice I have observed that the change in client response is frequently quite striking when I move from a resistance-oriented approach to an acceptance of the client's norms and definitions of his own needs. With quite a few organizational clients in the United States, the line of legitimacy seems to lie somewhere between interventions at the instrumental level and those focused on interpersonal relationships. Members who exhibit hostility, passivity, and dependence when I initiate intervention at the interpersonal level may become dramatically more active, collaborative, and involved when I shift the focus to the instrumental level.

If I intervene directly at the level of interpersonal relationships, I can be sure that at least some members, and often the whole group, will react with anxiety, passive resistance, and low or negative commitment to the change process. Furthermore, they express their resistance in terms of norms and values regarding the appropriateness or legitimacy of dealing at this level. They say things like, "It isn't right to force people's feelings about one another out into the open"; "I don't see what this has to do with improving organizational effectiveness"; "People are being encouraged to say things which are better left unsaid."

If I then switch to a strategy which focuses on decision making, delegation of authority, information exchange, and other instrumental questions, these complaints about illegitimacy and the inappropriateness of the intervention are usually sharply reduced. This does not mean that the clients are necessarily comfortable or free from anxiety in the discussions, nor does it mean that strong feelings may not be expressed about one another's behavior. What is different is that the clients are more likely to *work with* instead of *against* me, to feel and express some sense of ownership in the change process, and to see many more possibilities for carrying it on among themselves in the absence of the consultant.

What I have found is that when I am resistance-oriented in my approach to the client, I am apt to feel rather uncomfortable in "letting sleeping dogs lie." When, on the other hand, I orient myself to the client's own assessment of his needs, I am uncomfortable when I feel I am leading or pushing the client to operate very far outside the shared norms of the organization. I have tried to indicate why I believe the latter orientation is more appropriate. I realize of course that many highly sophisticated and talented practitioners will not agree with me.

In summary, I have tried to show in this article that the dimension of depth should be central to the conceptualization of intervention strategies. I have presented what I believe are the major consequences of intervening at greater or lesser depths, and from these consequences I have suggested two criteria for choosing the appropriate depth of intervention: first, *to intervene at a level no deeper than that required to produce enduring solutions to the problems at hand;* and second, *to intervene at a level no deeper than that at which the energy and resources of the client can be committed to problem solving and to change.*

I have analyzed the tendency for increases in individual autonomy in organizations to push the appropriate level of intervention deeper when the first criterion is followed. Opposed to this is the countervailing influence of the second criterion to work closer to the surface in order to enlist the energy and support of organization members in the change process. Arguments have been presented for resolving this dilemma in favor of the second.

The dilemma remains, of course. The continuing tension under which the change agent works is between the desire to lead and push, or to collaborate and follow. The middle ground is never very stable, and I suspect we show our values and preferences by which criterion we choose to maximize when we are under the stress of difficult and ambiguous client-consultant relationships.

References

1. Byrd, R. E., "Training in a Non-group," *Journal of Humanistic Psychology,* Vol. 7, No. 1 (1967), pp. 18–27.
2. Clark, J. V., Task group therapy. Unpublished manuscript, University of California, Los Angeles, 1966.

Roger Harrison is a principal with Harrison Associates, Inc., in Berkeley, California.

Chapter 18

Managing the Response: A Client Perspective

Fredric H. Margolis

Response. The consultant can do parts of it for you. The two of you can do some tasks together, and some tasks you, as sponsor, can do on your own. But regardless of the arrangements, it's *your* show. *You* make it happen and *you* live with the results. Many times people say to the consultant, "Hell, we've tried everything we can. We're going to turn it over to you completely." Sorry, but the client is *never* off the hook. The sponsor who wants the project to succeed must stay involved to the end.

This chapter is about the process of managing a consultation. It covers the consultant's roles and responsibilities and the sponsor's roles and responsibilities. It also looks at what you should do when problems arise.

The Hazards of Implementing the Consultation

Response (or implementation) is the point at which many a promising consultation fizzles out. No matter how effective the data-gathering and diagnosis have been, there is in the end no substitute for management decision and action. The following story is typical of many a sad ending.

> The president of a company hired a consultant to find out what training was needed in his manufacturing plants. He asked the consultant to submit a report. The consultant wanted to make sure that the members of the manufacturing division management were involved in the study so they would accept and use the results, so he made a counter proposal. He suggested that he work with an in-house management task force. The consultant would ask the task force for guidance on what data to gather, conduct the study, and present the data during a four-hour meeting with the task force. He would serve as a resource person and facilitator during the task force's deliberations, and then the task force would prepare the report. His proposal was accepted and the work went off without a hitch. During the final review session, both consultant and task force said that the work had been done well. The task force was to prepare a written report and submit copies to the consultant and the president. But, nothing happened. Nine months later, the report was languishing on the bottom of a stack of papers somewhere in one of the task force member's office.

Adapted with permission from *Consultants: A Buyer's Guide* by Fredric H. Margolis and Larry N. Davis, Austin, Texas: Learning Concepts.

Don't let your critical thinking and managerial initiative become paralyzed by the fact that you have an expert working for you. You're the expert on your organization and you're in charge.

What the Consultant Can Do

The consultant can function in many different ways in the response phase. The consultant may function as an advisor, counselor, educator, analyst, leader, or facilitator. The following case exemplifies the variety of tasks a consultant may perform.

> A team of consultants from a nearby medical center was hired to assist a Headstart program. During the first six weeks of school, teachers spent time observing children in the classroom and assessing their special needs. They met with the consultants to discuss their observations. The consultants did follow-up evaluations of selected students. During the second phase of the engagement, the consultants worked directly with selected students, trained teachers in skills of working with certain handicaps, and assisted in the development of curriculum units. During the third phase, the consultants counseled with parents. Teacher skills improved visibly and staff members were able to meet most of their objectives in working with the children.

There is one function the consultant should never be asked to assume—that of decision-maker or manager. At that point, he or she ceases to be a consultant in the true sense of the word and becomes a staff person. In the Headstart program, consultants were asked to help teachers interpret their observations, but were not permitted to make instructional decisions for teachers. In certain situations, a consultant may easily turn into a manager. When this happens, be *aware* that you have acquired an employee, not a consultant. The following story illustrates what can happen.

> A division vice president of a company was having serious problems in the management of production. He hired a consultant he had worked with previously to conduct a needs diagnosis. The consultant's analysis corroborated what the vice president had suspected. He decided the manufacturing manager must go, and asked the consultant to step in and run the operation. For eight months, the consultant managed manufacturing while she and the vice president looked for a replacement manager. During that time, the consultant was successful in getting people from engineering, manufacturing, and support services to communicate and work together. After a new manager came on board, the vice president removed the consultant from that job and gave her other assignments. She did troubleshooting in other management areas, developed special studies, and assisted with long-range planning. Although the consultant continued to be paid as an outside consultant, she had really become a trusted staff assistant to the vice president and was perceived by people in the organization as an employee.

Consultants may advise you and perform certain tasks for you, but they should not make management decisions. They should not even be asked to give professional advice about a decision that involves information or assumptions they have not checked out independently. When a consultant becomes a manager replacing in-house personnel, morale problems can result, and the consultant can lose his or her status as a detached outsider.

What You Can Do

As sponsor, you have four responsibilities: to coordinate or direct project activities, to provide encouragement and support to people in the project, to monitor and evaluate the progress of the work, and to decide what to do if the project gets off track.

Coordinating or Directing Activities

Managing a consultation requires a balance between controlling and giving freedom. Controlling means knowing at all times what the consultant is doing, why it is being done, when it will be done, what it will cost, and the profitable results of the work. If asked by your boss or executive board, you can say in your own words (not the consultant's words) what the project is about and what is being accomplished. Giving freedom means that you allow the consultant to exercise professional judgment in recommending courses of action and choosing methods. You can set some boundaries on objectives and acceptable methods, but not dictate how the job should be done.

Controlling also means you make sure the client organization is giving the cooperation and support necessary. You make specific definite assignments to project staff and make sure they are doing them. The consultant lacks the organizational authority to supervise your staff. You provide office help and technical assistance as needed and make sure that people are available and prepared at prescheduled activities. On the other hand, you do not attempt to control all aspects of the end users' relationship with the consultant. They must establish their own relationship and ground rules. The group may challenge and test the consultant, as the following story illustrates.

The training director of a school district hired an external consultant to function as a trainer by developing and conducting a course that would train school administrators to communicate effectively in crisis situations with students, teachers, and parents. The consultant put together a five-day experiential course using case studies and role play around typical school situations. This was the first time that administrators in the district had ever been asked to be away from their desks for an extended period of time to do training. Some of them had difficulty giving themselves permission, as training was not perceived as part of their job. So they were invited, not required, to come.

On the first day, certain administrators challenged the credentials of the consultant: "We're spending our valuable time. What makes you think you have anything to share with us?" He replied, "I don't know if what I have prepared will be useful to you. I can say that I have these experiences (he rattled them off) and I think I have these skills to offer (he described them). Beyond that, you're just going to have to sit back and listen, and try out the activities. If you feel this isn't appropriate for you by the end of the day, then you need to go to the training director and ask him to do something else for you." His answer satisfied the challengers. He presented various techniques and got participants involved in role playing to give them practice. He did a careful debriefing after each exercise to see what was going on and why it evolved as it did. The participants stuck with the course and feedback was positive afterwards. The training director began to get requests for a repeat workshop.

Ultimately, good management of the consultation means setting up systems or mechanisms to institutionalize the work of the consultant. The consultation should be consistent with what is happening in the organization, and not peripheral. The sponsor's role includes working with the consultant to transfer the consultant's skills to staff members. When they value and understand the consultant's work, it has a better chance of continuing.

Providing Encouragement and Support

Encouraging others means giving them the courage to accomplish a task. To give courage, you must have it. As sponsor or top authority, you must have the confidence to allow people to take risks in making a change. When they are deciding to make a change, they need to be able to think out loud and try out new ideas without having to go on record or to justify themselves immediately to outside pressure groups. When they are trying out alternative methods or new behavior, they need room and time to experiment. After a new system or behavior has become accepted, it takes time to become established. People must practice, master, and institutionalize the change before they can become accountable for its operation. Provide encouragement and protected conditions for people to work through these stages.

Your consultant also needs encouragement and consistent support. Give it with your behavior as well as your words. A discrepancy between what you say and what you do can undermine the consultant's credibility with the staff as the following story illustrates.

A manager brought in a consultant to help develop participatory management in her organization. In the past, the manager had used an authoritarian style. After much exploratory discussion, the consultant decided the manager was serious about wanting to make the change. The work was clicking along until the third session. The consultant sensed something was wrong. There was anger and resistance. He found out that the previous week the manager had behaved in a defensive, authoritarian way, not allowing input from her people and putting them down for making suggestions. The consultant was left in a vulnerable position by this action. The manager's problem was a lack of congruency between her professed values and her actual behavior. Eventually, she was able to take the risk of learning and practicing new behavior.

If you are contemplating a change that requires you to change your behavior, talk over the risks with your consultant. Figure out what you can do if you backslide.

When the consultant is going to do something risky that may affect your standing in the organization, talk it out as much as you can in advance. Provide all the information needed. Do as much contingency planning as you can, and then stick by your consultant through the difficult time. You selected this person carefully, and now you've got to trust him or her to do the job. If your personal risk is considerable, agree in advance that you will dissociate yourself publicly from the proceedings. Get a gunfighter from out of town for this kind of job! The consultant will take the flack, and can leave without being hurt if it bombs. You can pretend surprise at what happened and say you'll never hire him or her again.

Supporting the consultant also means that you don't change the plan in the middle of the project without a mutually agreed upon and sound reason. You expect the consultant to keep within the defined purpose and scope of the project and you must do the same. You don't drag in other concerns in order to get free advice from the consultant. You don't change your mind in the middle because the project is being criticized by colleagues or friends. You should have checked out probable reactions before you started and now you should be prepared to stand firm. You also take responsibility for consultant actions you have approved. If the boss criticizes an action, you don't pass the buck and blame the consultant, unless you have a prior agreement with the consultant to protect your flanks. Violating this principle means you will not get the best work from the consultant and you will probably lose respect.

Don't switch the rules of the project in the middle either. For example, if you have agreed that certain information will be confidential, don't ask the consultant to divulge it. The following story shows what can happen.

Two consultants were hired by a school system to train a group of educators in team teaching. The educators were to go through a series of exercises to learn new behaviors. The contract agreement was that they would not be evaluated for salary promotions. At the beginning of the second week, the assistant principal asked the consultants to review the personnel recommendations he was making on the educators. He said that an evaluation was required by law. The consultants refused. When the administrator insisted, the consultants said they would agree to evaluate, but they would no longer create situations where the educators had to take risks to try new behavior. The administrator finally backed down.

Treat the consultation as a learning opportunity and pay the compliment of learning as much as you can from the consultant. If you are committed to bringing about excellence, not just to making up for deficiencies, you will have the most fruitful relationship with the consultant. Take tennis, for example. When you take a tennis lesson, the coach transfers skills. When you are satisfied with your skill level, you stop taking lessons. However, if you are a pro, you never stop learning new skills. You go from solving problems to realizing new opportunities. You are also likely to get the best work if you challenge the consultant with opportunities to do difficult and creative work.

In addition to support on the job, the consultant also needs care and feeding during off hours. When you bring someone in from out of the city, try to help him or her feel as comfortable as possible. Find out if the consultant prefers to drive a rental car or to be picked up at the airport. Explain the local terrain and arrange for a hotel room. The consultant will need time to be alone and doesn't have to be entertained every night. On the other hand, consulting can be a lonely business. Be sensitive to needs for social companionship.

Monitoring and Review

The difference between a good and a poor consulting job is often how well it is monitored. If you have already set up communication links and built review checkpoints into the work plan, your job will be easier now. Your single most important task is to give and receive feedback and to use the information to modify the course of the project. These review sessions will allow you and the consultant to adjust or revise your "present intent" as necessary.

Do not depend entirely on the consultant to learn how the project is going. Gather your own information from those affected by the project. If you hear distress signals, try to find out how widespread the discontent is. If the consultant is doing team building or process consultation, request regular feedback from participants, either through direct questions or feedback instruments. The more the project's success depends on interactions among people, the more frequently you should check to see how people feel about the progress of the work.

Of course, you should also give and receive feedback with the consultant. This should be done at regular meetings. You may also want to request interim reports if the project is long and a written record is advisable, but a written report is not a substitute for face-to-face reviews. A review meeting serves several functions. It gives the consultant an opportunity to test the acceptability and relevance of what is happening or planned. It allows you to solve problems of implementation as they arise. It permits additional planning when that becomes desirable.

Ask how the consultant feels the consultation is going. Does that appraisal coincide with your own observations and feedback you are getting from participants? If not, you may have a problem. Find out how many people are perceiving the situation differently from the consultant. Give the consultant both positive and negative feedback about how the work is affecting people. Be gentle and don't assume you have the whole truth. Let the consultant check out negative feedback and come back to you for a discussion of what should be done.

The problems that may arise depend a great deal on the kind of consultation. In a process consultation, people may perceive the consultant taking sides instead of maintaining an objective, mediating role. In an organizational development project, personal behavior or professional methods may be rubbing people the wrong way, despite your best efforts to guard against it. There may be a host of other possibilities. It's your job to tip off the consultant about problems that may arise so that he or she can make effective strategy decisions. Keep on talking when things get rough. That's the time when the consultant needs help the most.

During a checkpoint review, find out if cooperation and other resources are forthcoming. The consultant cannot exert the pressure of authority on your people, so make sure needed resources are there. Take direct action to solve relationship problems that may arise, so the consultation can progress constructively.

Use checkpoint reviews as an opportunity for revising the plan. Bring the consultant up-to-date on organizational changes that may affect the course and outcome of the project. Are the scope and purpose still seen as desirable and workable? Unforeseen difficulties or changes in the organization may change what is wanted and feasible. Your purpose is not to stick to a rigid plan but to get results. There must be freedom for both client and consultant to question how the project is going and to change the plan by mutual consent if need be. Talk over alternatives to the question, "Where do we go from here?" Encourage the consultant to use you as a sounding board for testing alternative strategies. Ask questions, test, explore, and challenge. Take an active stance; don't sit back and let the consultant do all the planning. If you think a change is needed, get an explicit agreement. At this point, you may be recontracting for part or all of the project.

Review meetings are an opportunity for mutual stimulation and thinking. You benefit and the consultant benefits. The meeting should be constructive, but it may not always go smoothly if you are really communicating openly. If the meetings are too easy, you may not be getting the best from the consultant. Are you being placated or challenged with new alternatives or perspectives? The most productive relationship is characterized by creative conflict through which client and consultant come up with optimal solutions to problems. A consultant who believes you are off-track should tell you so. And you, in turn, should not swallow the consultant's pronouncements at face value, out of deference. Ask for the data and rationale for statements you are not sure about. You know your organization best—what may work or not. Your judgment is as important as the consultant's expertise.

A checkpoint review should address the following questions.

—What planned activities have been completed?
—What conclusions have been reached?
—What are the benefits to date?
—What has been spent to date in relation to the total budget?
—What problems are occurring, and what can we do to solve them?
—What should be done next?
—What assistance is needed?

Keep the top authority and the organization as a whole informed of the progress of the consultation through phone calls, memos, newsletter articles, and other available media.

When It's Not Working Out

No matter how carefully you have gone through the steps of selection and contracting, you have to gain on-the-job experience with a new consultant to see whether you have a real or only an apparent agreement. Despite your best efforts to specify objectives and methods, the consultant may not act as you expect nor as the project requires. You may have to recontract if the discrepancy is very wide. The following story is typical of this kind of problem.

A consultant was hired to provide training in communication theory and skills for staff members of a social services agency. He was to use case studies of typical work situations as the context for skill exercises. The consultant came highly recommended by a staff person who had attended a previous workshop. He presented an excellent resume and talked intelligently about his subject area. At a planning session, he provided handouts he would use, but did not cooperate in explaining how he would run the practice activities. The sponsor was mildly concerned but felt that the consultant would be good. At the workshop, the consultant soon established rapport with the participants. He was skilled in modeling communication skills. However, he did not keep the focus of the work clearly on skills training using the case studies. He tended to get off on nonwork issues and situations brought up by the participants. When questioned by the sponsor, the consultant replied that he was only responding to the expressed needs of the participants. The sponsor acknowledged that the consultant was meeting personal growth needs, but pointed out that professional skills were not being developed as promised by the workshop objectives. The consultant agreed but continued to get off the track frequently. The participants enjoyed the workshop and liked the consultant. However, the sponsor felt they had not acquired the necessary skills.

In this situation, the consultant's professional values (work with the expressed needs of participants) were different from those of the sponsor (train participants in needed job-related skills). The sponsor used this same consultant in several more workshops. However, she was very explicit in specifying what the consultant was to do in order to keep the job. Also, the sponsor did not use the consultant when she suspected that expressed needs of participants might lead the workshop in an unintended direction.

There are a number of issues that may require the client and consultant to renegotiate, terminate, or substitute a new contract. Basically, they can be reduced to four situations.

1. The consultant fouls up in an obvious way, such as nonperformance of scheduled activities, nondelivery of a promised product, or breach of a clearly stated contractural agreement.
2. The client misjudges the consultant's abilities, professional beliefs, ethics, or values.
3. The client organization changes. The budget is cut, personnel are laid off, or new management changes the direction of the organization.
4. The client organization misjudges what is important to it. Through experience, it becomes clearer about what it wants to do.

When a project is not going well for any of these reasons, it's time to stop and find out what is wrong. Have an immediate session. Do not wait until the situation deteriorates. Be willing to stick in there to see if the situation can be corrected. If you think the consultant is not delivering as promised, ask for the reasons. There may be one that makes sense to you. Whatever you do, don't fire a consultant in the middle of a situation that involves risk or requires continuity. Instead, recontract to change the course of the project. Agree on what you and the consultant will do to get back on course. You may have to modify your roles. The following story illustrates this point.

A personnel director was given the responsibility of designing a selection system for a new police chief. Because the previous chief had resigned under a controversy that had brought a cloud over local government, the personnel director was instructed to make the selection process as fair and clearly explainable as possible to the public. After considerable research, she determined that a competency-based selection system did not exist and would have to be created. She settled on a procedure that combined interviews with written tests of police knowledge and psychological maturity. Each event was to be designed to test for specific competencies. She hired two consultants, a police expert and a personnel consultant to help design the system and the test for police knowledge. After the first session of work, the director realized that the personnel consultant was not working out. He had a traditional background and lacked appreciation of the importance of a careful overall selection design. He wanted to get down to formulating test items without being clear what they would measure. The director took over the design of the system himself, using the police expert as a resource. Once the competencies had been specified, the personnel consultant was able to help in generating test items. The client got the best use of the consultants in this situation by becoming very directive and supplying the missing expertise herself.

If recontracting doesn't work, do your best to come to a mutual agreement to stop. Talk about what went wrong and why. It's best if parting is by mutual accord. Don't fire the consultant if you can possibly help it. Firing is a one-sided action that indicates you haven't done a very good job of communicating or building a trust relationship with the consultant. Firing can take a number of forms. Some clients just let the consultant finish out the project, but they write off the work and don't hire the consultant again. Others duck out before the end with an excuse such as a sudden budget cut. Still others become involved in shoot-outs, accusing the consultant of failing to deliver the promised services. The consultant may then make counter accusations, saying that the client has withheld staff or data or had hidden agendas. These are "no win" situations. Whether firing is direct and accusatory or indirect and face-saving, it prevents you and the consultant from learning by the experience. Instead of firing, recontract to uncontract, and use the uncontracting process to learn how to do better, not to place blame for water already under the bridge.

If you decide to uncontract, pay the consultant fairly for the work performed, whether or not it is satisfactory to you. If payment is made by unit of time, pay for time spent up to the point of uncontracting. If a product was delivered but you are really unhappy about its quality, you may want to renegotiate the price and reach a settlement you both can live with.

Fredric H. Margolis is an independent consultant in Washington, D.C., specializing in the application of adult learning principles to technical-professional areas.

Chapter 19

The Client-Consultant Relationship in Organizational Transition

Leonard Nadler
and Zeace Nadler

Most consulting results in some kind of change in the organization and in the individuals who are part of that organization. Most of this book focuses on the change process, but it can be noted that there is one aspect that has generally received too little attention in the literature. It was only in recent years that we began to find material in the literature relating to transition.

As used here, transition is that period between the present state and some future state. That state presents an interesting dilemma. The consultant will have been working with the client to diagnose the current state and to develop a vision of the future state. In some situations, the consultant will stay with the client until that future state is reached, and where there has been a long time interval between the current and future state, the client-consultant relationship may have been mutually and successfully terminated. However, the client is then left to cope with the transition period without the consultant.

The consultant's leaving is not necessarily bad, but it requires that the consultant, before departing, do what is necessary to enable the client to cope with the transition period, as well as the current and future states. Recognizing that the transition period is a natural and expected state, some consultants build activities for the transition into the response phase of the consulting process. This training definitely should be part of the disengagement and closure phases.

Stimulus for Change

To explore transition, we must start with the change process. Transition is a result of change, but there are many sources of change. Some of these arise from internal stimuli, while others are the result of external factors. Change can generally be categorized as "anticipated" or "unanticipated", as seen in Figure

19-1. (Note that we and you, the readers, will be building a model through these figures.)

Anticipated changes are those that are expected or can be planned. Some examples of anticipated change for organizations are:

—New product line
—Expansion or downsizing
—Mergers or splits
—New but expected technology
—Replacement of personnel

Among unanticipated changes can be found:

—Destruction of plant or equipment
—New and previously unknown competitor
—New but unexpected technology
—Key personnel leaving without prior notice
—New government regulation

From just these brief lists it can be seen that for the most part the anticipated changes can be planned for prior to the actual change. Even some of the unanticipated changes could be planned for, but the actual occurrence might come at a time when the organization was not anticipating it. It is not possible for organizational planning to anticipate every eventuality. Managers (clients) are required to make decisions as to which changes they will plan for, or they would spend their entire work life planning, although most of the plans might never be used. In any manager's life there is some of that frustration, planning without using, but there are limits.

Concerning individuals, we are accumulating research data that enables us to move some of the unanticipated changes along the continuum, closer to antici-

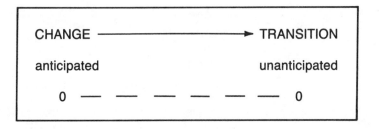

Figure 19-1. Model showing how change can be categorized.

pated. Levinson has helped us understand that just being alive brings changes, some of which could be anticipated—should be anticipated.[7]

There is not a dichotomy between anticipated and unanticipated, but rather a continuum. (See Figure 19-2.) Each change occurs someplace on that continuum. To the degree that a change can be anticipated, the client and the consultant can develop plans and have processes ready to activate, to implement that change. To the degree, on the continuum, that the change is unanticipated, there may be additional requirements for some ad hoc or immediate planning. Of course, it is possible for a consultant to work with a client to develop a list of possible unanticipated changes and to have contingency plans ready. The actual event, however, may occur in a form much different from what was anticipated during planning, and that is part of what makes it unanticipated.

Let us look at two changes, one focused on an internal stimulus for change and the second arising from an external stimulus for change.

Not too many years ago, in some large organizations, people were seen as chess pieces to be moved about at the convenience of the organization. Indeed, this is one of the characteristics of the Theory Z organization, as depicted by Ouchi.[12] Therefore, those in a position to make such personnel decisions could decide that Manager A should move from New York to San Francisco. Before the mid-1970s this would be an anticipated change on the part of the organization and the individual. Despite being anticipated, this was significant, as a study by Naismith indicated.[10] His research produced an "Organizational Readjustment Rating Scale" and the most traumatic factor was "Transfer against one's will to a new position or assignment."

Then came dual career couples! Manager A would now have to respond that "I must first talk this over with my spouse." This was unanticipated change for the organization! What had earlier been considered an accepted and traditional personnel action became controversial. It was further exacerbated when Manager A responded that the move could not be made as the spouse did not concur! Again, there was an unanticipated change. Many large organizations did not

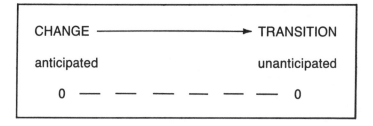

CHANGE ——————————→ TRANSITION

anticipated   unanticipated

0 — — — — — — 0

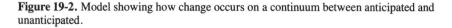

Figure 19-2. Model showing how change occurs on a continuum between anticipated and unanticipated.

have any contingency plan in place to deal with this behavior that on the part of a manager had previously been unknown or, at the very least, rare.

This discussion of the individual is not a digression, it is intentional. Almost any change in an organization requires change in individuals. It is too easy to be trapped into thinking of the organization itself as a living organism. This suffices as an analogy, but the reality is that an organization is composed of people, and despite organizational acculturation, people still remain differentiated.

A second example of unanticipated change is one that happens more frequently now than in the past. An organization is involved in manufacturing. With little or no notice, they are informed that one of the components in the manufacturing process has been determined to have cancer-causing implications. Therefore, that item can no longer be used.

It can be argued that the organization should have anticipated this. But such a position would indicate that the organization had some knowledge of the possibility that one of the elements they were using could cause cancer. If so, they could have anticipated the change, but that also means that they would have knowingly been using an item about which they themselves were suspicious. There have been examples of such a practice in some organizations, but most organizations do have a higher level of social responsibility.

The client, in such a case, may be seeking a technical consultant who can provide some alternatives so that manufacturing can continue. It may also be necessary for the client to seek the services of a behavioral consultant to cope with some of the personal and interpersonal factors that will arise from that unanticipated change.

Movement

Change requires movement. We can assume that most consultants, and many clients, are familiar with Lewin's model of:

$$\text{freeze} \rightarrow \text{unfreeze} \rightarrow \text{movement} \rightarrow \text{freeze}$$

A good deal has been written about unfreeze—getting the organization and the individuals ready to change. Movement has generally been in terms of the various interventions that can bring about change. Less has been discussed about what happens during that movement, which is here called transition.

To add to our model, change requires movement from a current state to some future state. The period between these two states is transition, as shown in Figure 19-3.

It is possible and generally essential to define the current state. This can be accomplished as part of entry and definitely as an aspect of diagnosis. Then, the client and consultant must identify the future state to which they wish to move.

Note that in Figure 19-3 the vertical line moves from solid lines into broken ones. This connotes that the future state is vague. Of course the client and consultant devise plans and models to depict that future state while recognizing that the future state may never be reached as planned. During the transition period (that interval between the current state and the future state) many things can happen that can alter the configuration of that future state.

One obvious possibility is that a new unanticipated change may take place and the planned future state is no longer relevant. Or, as the transition is taking place, new facts or information indicate that the originally planned future state should be altered. The client should not see this as a failure on the part of the consultant. The consultant is not an infallible machine, merely a human being, with the normal limitations of humans. Our increased sophistication with futuring has taught us to remember the advice of the philosopher Pogo, that "the future isn't what it used to be." As Toffler keeps reminding us[13] change takes place too rapidly to allow us the option of planning a future state that probably will be altered before we get there.

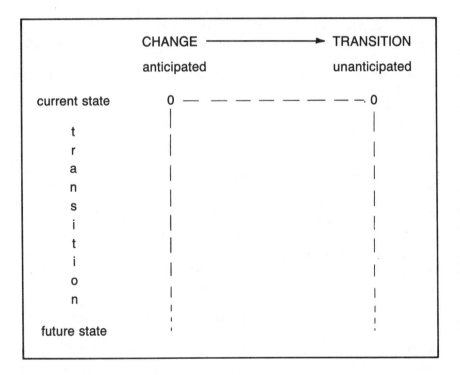

Figure 19-3. Model showing the transition period between the current state and the future state.

We need to recognize that transition takes up a good deal of our lives. Sometimes it seems as though we spend more of our life in transition than in either the current or future state. The longer the period of transition, the greater the probability that the planned future state needs to be reexamined.

What can significantly complicate the situation, is the possibility that there are several transitions occurring within the organization at the same time. The client and the consultant need to be aware of this. The client may be aware of this complication, for the client is actually living in the organization. The consultant, who is external to the organization or the actual situation, needs to be alert to avoid the tunnel vision that focuses only on that particular change → transition with which the consultant is involved. In a large organization, there can be several internal and external consultants involved in change, at the same time, in different parts of the organization. These parts are not insular, so that change in another part of the organization can affect the particular part with which a consultant may be working.

Future State Redefined

It is not often that the client and consultant can fully predict the future state. There are too many unpredictable factors that can take place while the organization is in transition. To plunge ahead to the future state, ignoring those influences, is almost to ensure disaster.

Both the client and the consultant should be able to envision the future state. It may even be something akin to imaging,[5] but it is essential that they put their perceived images into words. Even as they do this, they must also recognize that their image of the future state is subject to change. They should not allow themselves to be trapped into pushing ahead only to that future state. There are always possible alternatives that should not be completely disregarded.

Once they have configured the future state, it must be adequately communicated to all concerned. The more information shared about the future state, the greater is the possibility that it will be reached successfully.

The client-consultant relationship itself can also have an impact on the transition period and on the future state. The consultant should use those approaches that will avoid making the client dependent upon the consultant. This is a usual caution in a client-consultant relationship. It becomes even more important during the transition period when the client may feel insecure while trying to work in a state in which the signals are unclear and constantly changing.

Conversely, if the consultant disengages and reaches closure too early, the client may not be adequately prepared for the continuous alterations needed to complete the transition period and move into the future state. At the time the consultant leaves, the future state will have been agreed upon. The contract will have been completed to the satisfaction of both parties. But during the transition period the client may be faced with those forces that require a different future state. It may be necessary to recall the consultant, not because of failure but because there is the need to create a new future state and to plan for a different transition period.

The client must be helped to see that this interruption in the change process is possible. The client should not blame the consultant for not anticipating a future state that was essentially undiscernible at the time of the conclusion of the consulting assignment, and the consultant should not feel that the client has withheld anything during the earlier relationship. They are both trying to cope with change → transition → change and the need for a new transition.

Both the client and the consultant must accept the reality that the desired future state can change during transition.

The Transition Period

Transition has been defined as the period between the current state and the future state. As will be described later, under the heading of "kill," it is important to differentiate, to separate the current state from the transition period. This can be done for anticipated change, but specific events and behavior are required to make that distinction.

For unanticipated change, the movement from the current state into transition is generally abrupt and obviously unplanned. It is not uncommon for an organization to find that it is in transition without knowing it. This may be the reason why the help of a consultant is required. The client is aware that something has happened, but does not know what it is.

At any point on the continuum, the movement from the transition period to the future state is gradual. Sometimes, if the movement from the transition period to the future state has been carefully planned and carried out, it is not even possible to identify just when that future state was reached. It is important to note that some people need evidence that the transition has been successfully completed. It may be necessary to have an activity to signify that the future state has indeed been reached.

The transition period should not be seen as a hiatus. The organization cannot afford that. During the transition period, the organization and individuals must continue to function at the highest level possible. The transition period should be understood as a period that presents exciting opportunities and challenges. It is a time for experimentation within the plan that will lead the organization from the transition period into the future state.

The transition must be planned. This may seem obvious, but too often attention is focused on the future, desired state rather than on the period between the current and the future state. Beckhard and Harris[2] have provided significant insight into this, with further interpretation by Nadler.[8] As part of the overall plan, attention must be given to: a transition manager, resources for the transition, the transition plan, and the transition management structures.

The Transition Manager

The consultant should *not* be the transition manager, although this is a tempting role, particularly to an external consultant. It is even questionable whether the transition manager should be the client. Preferably, the transition manager should be somebody in the client system who has the authority and power to make things happen.

There are situations where a transition team is desirable. This may be preferable where there are complexities that are beyond the capacity of one single person. The transition might require people with technical, legal, or some other expertise that the transition manager does not possess. Also, given our renewed interest in participative management, a consultant may be able to help the client see the advantages of involving a number of people in planning and implementing the transition period.

The transition team should be headed by the transition manager, but exercise of power and authority will be the result of the team endeavor. Membership on the team must be planned carefully. In some situations it may be essential to include those who are functioning as managers in the current state. In that situation, the consultant can help the client anticipate the resistance to change that will be expressed by the current state managers. They must be helped to understand that the transition state will bring changes, but that the future state will bring benefits. If there will not be any benefits to the current state managers, however, it may be desirable to transfer or terminate them as rapidly as possible to reduce hindrance to an effective transition period. In some situations this is done by an outplacement approach where the organization assists the current state manager in finding a suitable position outside the organization.

If possible, the membership of the transition team should include at least some of those current state managers who will have responsibilities in the future state. Where these will be essentially the same people, the composition of the transition team is readily definable. Where they will be different people, the composition of the transition team requires very delicate handling. The very process of organizing the team affects the transition and certainly the future state.

Resources Required for the Transition

The transition manager/team cannot function without adequate resources—physical, financial, human. The team may require a specific place to meet. Depending upon the nature and extent of the transition, the meeting place could be just somebody's office or it could be an elaborate "war room." The importance of the physical resource should not be underestimated. During transition, the physical aspect is what many people in the organization will be able to observe. If the transition manager is provided with space that is considered undesirable in the organization (for example, in an outlying building, or next to the boiler room) a message about the transition period and the future state is being sent throughout the organization, without a memo being written or a sentence being uttered. If the team is forced to scrounge for a meeting place, the message may well go forth that this transition is too insignificant to be worthy of the allocation of physical resources. It can also communicate that upper levels of management are not supporting the transition effort.

Some financial resources are usually required by the transition manager. The manager, for example, may want to hire an external consultant. Whose budget should this come from? This will affect to whom the consultant is responsible. It is desirable to have a specific budget for the transition effort. If the transition manager/team feels the need for an external consultant, they should have the financial resources to engage one. If they want to use an internal consultant, there may still be the need for the availability of financial resources depending upon how the time of the internal consultant is charged.

The human resources are equally important. If a manager is to head up a transition team, that manager may have to be relieved of some other duties. Other members of the team must likewise have some flexibility if they are to participate actively. The transition team may require some other temporary human resources both from within and outside the organization.

Transition Plan

Transition planning should start as early as possible. For an anticipated change, the transition team should be identified in enough time before the transition period is to commence to allow for sufficient planning. For unanticipated change, the organization will not have the luxury of planning beforehand, but will have to start planning while already into some aspect of the transition period.

The consultant who is asked to work on change → transition must be able to determine the point of entry. It is not uncommon for a consultant to be invited in after some planning has started. Identifying the type of change (anticipated or unanticipated) is a crucial determination during the entry phase. The consultant must also ascertain whether there has been any planning prior to the entry of the consultant.

If a plan is already in motion, the consultant first goes along with the plan. This is not a ploy but a recognition of the fact that some person or group developed the plan and has ownership of it. If the consultant attempts to halt the plan, even temporarily, the resulting hostility could destroy the client-consultant relationship. The plan may have been conceived by the client, or by some other individual or group in the organization. It might even be a very good plan and this provides a problem for the consultant who has a need to have his own fingerprints on the plan.

During transition, the expectations and responsibilities of all the members of the transition team must be clearly specified. Some of the team members will probably be functioning in more than one role in the organization. As they approach the future state, the team and individual roles can be expected to change. Provision should be made for recognizing this, so that people will not hold on to roles that were relevant and needed during transition, but unnecessary in entering the future state.

Transition Structures

The transition team must recognize that the structures that are appropriate for the current state will probably not be those needed for the future state. As the organization moves into and through transition, it may be necessary to establish some temporary structures and relationships.[3] In the planning it may be intended that some of those temporary structures will be modified and will become part of the future state. Other temporary structures are just that—temporary—and there is no intent that they survive beyond transition. If this is not made explicit, individuals may devote energy to sustaining the wrong temporary structures to the detriment of the transition state and the hindrance of the future state.

Characteristics During Transition

As noted earlier, there has not yet been enough research, model building, or thoughtful writing about this transition state. It is possible however, to indicate some of the characteristic behaviors and conditions that will occur during transition. This does not suggest that every organization or individual going through transition will manifest all of what will be discussed below. Each transition is different. Organizations and individuals have differences. Despite this, it is still possible to identify some of what may occur during transitions.

Transitions take time. For some change → transition episodes the calendar time may be quite short. When that is the case, the future state that is reached will probably be very much like the future state that has been envisioned and planned. When the transition period must occur over a period of many months, or even years, the original planned future state may not remain valid. The need to modify the planned future state, during the transition period will become a necessity. This should not spread gloom among those involved in the transition. Rather, it should be seen as another opportunity to plan for the most desirable future state imaginable.

Transitions produce a 'cost' to the organization and the individuals in that organization. The client and consultant should be working together so that there is no undue cost to those concerned. The costs may arise in areas such as enthusiasm, morale, productivity, interpersonal relationships, as well as some direct economic costs. Those factors must be considered during the transition period. Building recognition of those costs into the transition period may enhance the possibility of rapidly recovering those costs when the organization reaches the future state.

In discussing these elements with clients we have frequently observed the "aha phenomena." That is, the clients light up and comment on how they have experienced some of these characteristics but had hesitated to discuss them. They had perceived that experiencing these characteristics meant that the organization or the individuals were sick, or not functioning effectively. They were surprised to learn that this is normal behavior—while in the transition period. If it occurs in the current or future state it is a matter for concern and further exploration.

The items are discussed separately, but it should be obvious that there are numerous interactions. Unexpected events during the transition period can produce ambiguity, and that ambiguity can breed anxiety.

Anxiety

It is very common for individuals and organizations to develop various kinds of anxiety symptoms during transition. This is not surprising—but somehow too few clients have been apprised of this by their consultants. Indeed, if there is no anxiety that could be dangerous.

The lack of anxiety may indicate that people in the organization do not recognize that change is occurring. If they do recognize that transition is taking place, perhaps they don't care! In either event, lack of anxiety can be a problem.

More common is unexplained or unexamined anxiety. While working in Zimbabwe with a multi-national company, we found that the anxiety level was so high that we could not work on the consulting task for which we had originally contracted. The anxiety was produced, in part, by the shifting political scene in that country. As Zimbabwe grew out of what was formerly Southern Rhodesia one could anticipate the black/white problems. Indeed, one government minister announced something to the effect that, "before the advent of the present government there were 150,000 whites, now there are 100,000 and in the next three years there will only be 50,000." How then, could the white managers be expected to take part in a transition period which envisioned a future state without them? How could they be expected to actively support that transition period?

In working through these questions, we used the model presented here and emphasized to the client system that they were in a transition period. Under the circumstances it was to be expected that people would experience anxiety. Particularly so in this situation, when the various public and private organizations had not yet clearly defined the future state. Unfortunately, this uncertainty would probably continue since the government was also in transition and unclear about its future actions. Once anxiety was recognized and accepted, we explored ways to deal with it. The Managing Director (MD) had informed us that expatriate employees of the company could be readily transferred to other countries as the need arose. However, it was the policy of management to maintain present operations and personnel as consistently as possible, with the one significant variation of including more blacks in management.

Nevertheless anxiety was exacerbated, producing more anxiety than would be expected in this situation, due to a number of different expectations of the transition period and the future state in the same organization. The MD and his group were going through a transition period with the government. Other management level employees were aware of this, but at the same time were unclear about what would happen if they had to relocate, or if any other changes were to be required. They had not been informed that there were transition plans already drawn up by the organization for their movement, if needed. The upper management levels did not want to make their plans known, as that might indicate a lack of faith in their transition program with the government! The result—an unnecessarily high level of anxiety.

Ambiguity

During the transition period, things appear unclear and ambiguous. Some clients, and even some consultants, strive to make things as clear as possible—and it is not possible. The very state of transition means ambiguity. There are plans, but they are generally contingent on many factors, some of which may not have been foreseen.

The transition plan may have been excellent—at the time it was developed. To stick to the plan without alteration can deprive the client of the possibility of moving into previously unknown areas, some of which may be much more appropriate than those that had been planned.

Ambiguity should not be seen as a lack of planning, direction, or commitment by upper levels of the organization. Clients sometimes overreact to feelings of ambiguity by seeking a closed plan for the future state, with no possibility of variation or influence during the transition period. This may meet the need for less ambiguity at the present time but produce a need for another transition period, hard on the heels of the first one.

There is one aspect of the client-consultant relationship that is most appropriate here. Consultants know that they must establish a high level of trust if the resulting relationship is to be helpful to the client. There are many ways to do this and perhaps this is one place where the consultant can share some of those with the client. Trust will not erase ambiguity, but it will make it easier to deal with. If those involved in transition can be helped to develop a high level of trust with each other, ambiguity will be less frightening and anxiety producing.

If all concerned can be helped to recognize the legitimacy of ambiguity, it can be allowed to remain as a normal part of the transition period.

Authority and Power

There are many ways to look at these twin aspects of behavior in organization. For purposes of our discussion here, authority is seen as the *right* to influence behavior, while power is seen as the *ability* to influence behavior.

The movement of the organization from the current state into the transition period is usually accompanied by a change in authority. This can be evidenced by various observable behaviors, such as new organization charts, different offices, reassignment of support personnel (such as administrative assistants and secretaries), or being included/excluded in specific management level meetings. Shifts in authority are readily discernible.

It is much more difficult to track the shifts in power. As authority and relationships change during transition, so does the ability to influence, that is, power. Some of the shifts of authority may create temporary vacuums and produce a struggle for power. If recognized and handled appropriately, such struggles can contribute to the strength of the change → transition and the future state. If ignored, or dealt with ineffectively, the power struggle can thwart the achievement of the future state and even weaken or destroy the organization during transition.

All organizations are involved in some kind of politics as a normal part of organizational life.[6] During the transition period, it can be expected that there will be an increase in political activity. Previous alignments may be altered or destroyed. The client should recognize that such increased politicking can be expected during the transition period. The political maneuvering is part of shifts in authority and power.

Recognition of and effective coping with the characteristics discussed in this section can produce orderly change during the transition period.

The "Kill" Phenomena

There is an element of the transition period that has, as yet, received little attention in the literature as it pertains to organizations. There is an excellent book dealing with this event as it pertains to individuals.[4] As we are dealing with a model, but not with research, let us include this element with the caution that there is the need to do a good deal of exploration before it can be retained as an essential part of the model. Despite that 'caveat,' it is too important to be put aside until there is further evidence.

Bridges notes that transition cannot begin until there has been an ending of the current state. It can be called the "kill" event as shown in Figure 19-4.

First, let us explore those situations that, on our continuum, would be closer to anticipated change.

This kill event is extremely important. It is not possible to stand with one foot in the current event and move the other through transition. Of course, one cannot

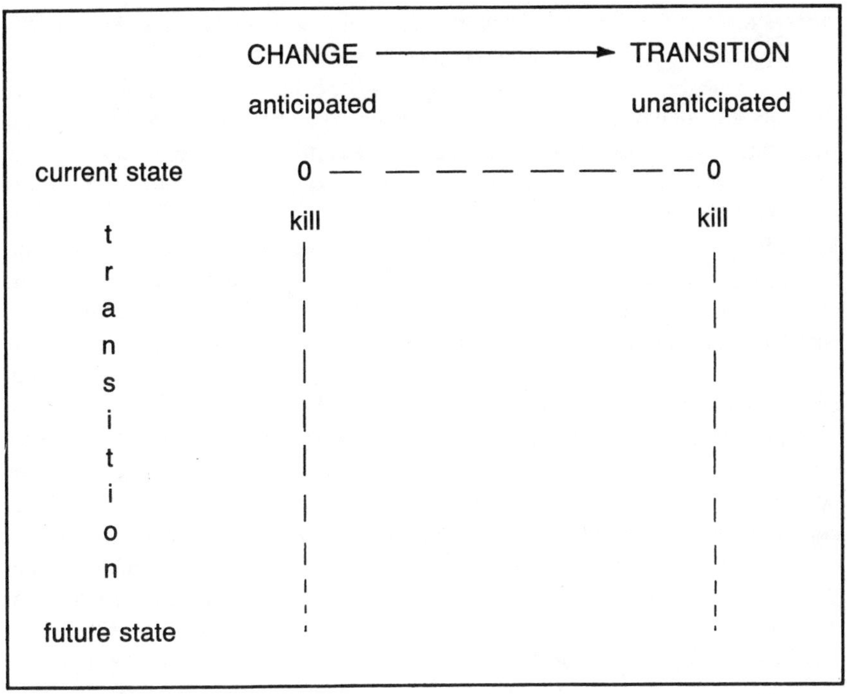

Figure 19-4. Model depicting the "kill" event ending the current state.

wipe out all of the past and still survive, nor is it necessarily desirable. It is essential to identify that element of the organization that is to be changed and then proceed to "kill" the current state. Some may see that word as too harsh, but it is chosen on purpose. It is not enough to plan to allow it to wither on the vine and slowly disintegrate. That can happen, but at the cost of damaging the movement into and through the transition period.

The kill event does not happen automatically. It must be planned and carried out. Bridges likens it to a "rite of passage." There must be some kind of observable experience that signals the change to all concerned. The rite must be directly related to what is to be left behind. This means focusing in on those elements of the current state of the organization whose life will be extinguished. This prevents regression on the part of those who still wish to hold on to the past rather than deal with an ambiguous future or the twilight zone of the transition state.

There are various ways to carry out that rite. The examples given below are only that—examples. The actual rite must be directly related to the part of the current state that is to be left behind and must conform to the organizational norms or culture related to what is being changed.

One way to do this, using a cautious approach, is for those in authority to issue a memo. This generally does not suffice to serve as a rite, since people in organizations are flooded by so many memos that the significance of the kill memo can easily be lost. Also, it is more a rite for those who send the memo, than it is for those who receive it.

We frequently find that an organizational change means new relationships among various people in the organization. This means a new organization chart, or some kind of statement that reflects the new relationships. Too often the old chart or statement is retained until the new is in place. As a result, during the transition period some people are confused, not knowing which depiction of relationships is operational. A rite can be designed to indicate to all that the old relationships are no longer valid as the organization moves into making the new relationships operational. It can be dramatic, such as a meeting during which the organization charts are "destroyed" in some appropriate ceremony. Everybody concerned takes part in the event and is involved in killing the current state and entering into the transition period. This area, of appropriate rites, is where consultants who consider themselves creative and innovative can be very helpful to the client.

A change in the organization can involve physical movement of individuals from one place to another. It can be within the same site, or to another part of the city, country, or world. Too often the focus is on the magnitude of the change, rather than on recognizing that any physical change requires a kill activity and entry into a transition period.

Let us assume that the client and consultant have worked together on planning the physical change. Of course, others in the client system would have been involved in diagnosing and planning for the physical change that is to take place. If it involves heavy moving, the actual move is generally signified by the appearance of those who will physically move the furniture and equipment from one place to another. That is *not* the rite, for the behavior is that of the movers, not those being moved. There should be a rite performed by those being moved, to signify that they no longer recognize the previous physical arrangement. The extent of that rite would, once again, depend upon the culture of the organization. The consultant should work with the client to develop an appropriate rite for that move, for the people involved, and for the organization.

On a simpler level, what of the move of an individual or small group of individuals? Too often this is done, after planning by the client-consultant-involved individuals, but carried out in almost a surreptitious manner. Secrecy seems to be the keynote of such moves. One result is that the informal communications network reads all kinds of negative implications into the move. There may be intimations that this is the result of a power play and those being moved lost, while the reality is that it is a win-win situation. A rite can be used to confirm the positive elements of the move and can take the whole effort out of secrecy and into the normality of everyday operations.

Situations that encompassed both of these were experienced during the early 1980s with the introduction of computers for managers. Resistance of managers to computers in their offices could be anticipated. Previously, computers were for "lower level" employees. Managers complained that they did not want to be secretaries—they refused to type or to learn simple finger manipulations to access the computer. What if there had been a rite including something symbolic to show that the secretary would still be there? What was being replaced was the "information float" as Naisbitt called it.[11] A balloon could have been used to symbolize that float, with the manager puncturing that balloon with a large symbolic computer key. (I recognize that this might be too dramatic for some organizations, but it is not too difficult to think of variations appropriate to a particular organization.)

This rite would be followed by the transition period. During this time, the manager would have participated in some planned activities—alone and with others—while learning how to use this new management tool. Too often it was expected that the manager would move directly from the current state (no computer in the manager's office) to the future state (actively using that computer) without planning for and recognizing the rite and the transition period.

Learning as Part of Transition

It has been contended that transition requires learning.[1] As it is different from the current state, people in the transition period generally need skills, knowledge, and attitudes that were not previously required. This is shown in Figure 19-5.

Anticipated Change

The closer the change is to the anticipated side of the continuum, the greater the possibility of providing the learning experiences that can enable people to cope with the complexities of the transition situation.

There are three types of learning that can be provided.[9] The first is training or learning to improve performance on the present job. In transition situations, some jobs will not change. People will be doing the same work but, for example, reporting to different people, or working in new configurations. Training can be used to prepare people for the changes, even though their own jobs will basically remain the same.

The second area is education, which has the objective of preparing people for jobs that are different from those held in the current state. Where the change can be anticipated, it is a waste of resources to provide learning after the change has

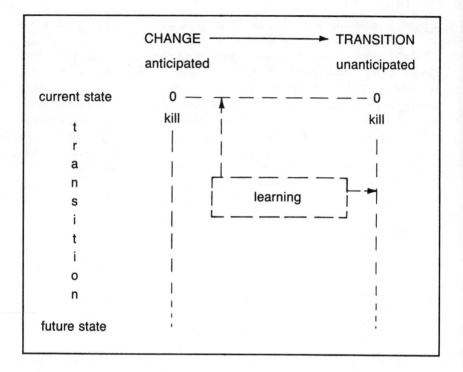

Figure 19-5. Model depicting the need for learning in the transition period.

already taken place. Indeed, providing education for those whose jobs will change can be an aspect of the kill phenomena discussed earlier. This also has the advantage of lessening the ambiguity and thus reducing anxiety.

The third area is development, which is not specifically job related. Its value in the change → transition picture may not be as clear as the other two types of learning to some people. It is not directly job related, and organizations tend to focus heavily on the present and future job. Therefore, they ignore development even though it has a significant contribution to make in facilitating transition.

Development learning activities keep people constantly alert to the possibilities of change → transition. The concept that organizations are constantly changing is not new. Those organizations that are most susceptible to change should be providing development for all employees on an ongoing basis. This will keep them intellectually and emotionally ready for change, for that is one of the things that learning can do. Development can reinforce the pervasiveness of change and can create an organizational climate that perceives change as a normal part of behavior in that organization.

Unanticipated Change

Where the change is unanticipated, learning sometimes occurs after the change has been initiated. In other words, the current state is in the past and the kill phenomenon has already taken place. People are already into new situations that require some new behaviors. When people are already into the transition state, with no opportunity for prior learning, the focus is on training. This occurs, unfortunately, when new equipment is introduced requiring significantly different job behaviors of the incumbents without any prior learning effort.

An organization can recognize that there will be unanticipated changes and therefore prepare the work force generally. For the unanticipated, it is not possible to prepare specifically.

Time for Learning

Difficulty arises when a transition plan, whether individual or organizational, does not provide the time and opportunity for learning. This forces those involved in transition to attempt to cope by trial and error, and that can be a very costly way to change behavior.

It may be necessary for the consultant to convince a client to provide learning time even though the immediate results are not discernible. This can be extremely difficult when an organization is trying to cope with either internal or external forces that require changes.

If the client has not utilized learning (Human Resource Development) as part of the regular organization behavior, the first responsibility of the consultant may be to make this need clear. This may not convince the client until much later, but the consultant will have performed ethically in pointing out the need.

Conclusion

The transition period is not new. It has been with us since we have been dealing with change. What is new is our recognition that organizations and individuals spend a great deal of their lives in transition and that behaviors during transition are different from those required in the current state or future state.

The exploration of the transition period presents an interesting challenge and an opportunity for clients and consultants. By handling the transition period effectively, both the client and the consultant can have the satisfaction of contributing to the growth and change of individuals and organizations. Acknowledging the problems that can occur in the transition state is the first step in doing something constructive about them.

The transition period presents a challenging opportunity for uncovering new resources among individuals and within organizations. When routine behavior is being replaced, previously overlooked individuals and opportunities can surface.

To bring about effective change, both the client and the consultant must give significant and intense attention to the transition period. It is possible for the transition period to be successfully accomplished for the benefit of all. It is possible to reach future states with a healthier organization, one that is more viable and energetic as the result of having passed through a successful transition period.

References

1. Aslanian, Carol B. and Henry M. Brickell, Americans in Transition: Life Changes as Reasons for Adult Learning, New York: College Entrance Examination Board, 1980.
2. Beckhard, Richard and Reuben T. Harris, Organizational Transitions: Managing Complex Change, Reading: Addison-Wesley, 1977.
3. Bennis, Warren G. and Philip E. Slater, The Temporary Society, New York: Harper and Row, 1968.
4. Bridges, William, Transitions: Making Sense of Life's Changes, Reading, MA: Addison-Wesley, 1980.
5. Bry, Adelaide, Visualization: Directing the Movies of Your Mind, New York: Barnes and Noble, 1979.
6. Kakabadse, Andrew, The Politics of Management, Aldershot, England: 1983.
7. Levinson, Daniel et al, The Seasons of a Man's Life, New York: Alfred Knopf, 1978.
8. Nadler, David, Concepts for the Management of Organizational Change, New York: Organization Research and Consultation, 1980.
9. Nadler, Leonard, Corporate Human Resource Development, New York: Van Nostrand, 1980.
10. Naismith, Douglas, Stress Among Managers as a Function of Organization Change, (unpublished dissertation), Washington: The George Washington University Library, 1975.
11. Naisbitt, John, Megatrends: Ten New Directions Transforming Our Lives, New York: Warner Books, 1982.
12. Ouchi, William, Theory Z: How American Business Can Meet the Japanese Challenge, Reading: Addison-Wesley, 1981.
13. Toffler, Alvin, Previews and Premises, New York: William Morrow, 1983.

Leonard Nadler is a professor of human resource development and adult education in the School of Education and Human Development at George Washington University.

Zeace Nadler is vice president of Nadler Associates, a consulting firm in Washington, D.C.

Chapter 20

The Consultant's Role with Entrepreneur-Owners

C. William Webb

Entrepreneur-owners of small- to medium-sized businesses are both fascinating and difficult clients—fascinating because of their creativity, complexity, and charm; difficult because they seldom seek a consultant until they are in deep trouble. Their grand sense of self-confidence often leads to the belief that problems lie anywhere except within themselves. Furthermore, since their personalities are so strong, and their intuitions about what is right for their business are so sound, they can take on the mystique of a wizard. When they come to believe, as they sometimes do, that they can pull off anything, they may not even be reachable until the inevitable crash.

Entrepreneur-owners appear to have a number of common characteristics. Knowing these characteristics can lead to better and quicker understanding of an individual client even though, in many respects, each client also will be different from others. Being alert to these common characteristics, identifying them in an individual, and observing their positive or negative impact upon the client's business can improve the accuracy of diagnosis as well as the effectiveness of cure.

What is an entrepreneur? Peter Drucker defines him in this way: "He has to redirect resources from areas of low or diminishing results to areas of high or increasing results. He has to slough off yesterday to render obsolete what already exists and is already known. He has to create tommorow."[1] An entrepreneur enjoys developing goals which are important, significant, and even heroic and can be defined as a businessperson who has a concept and a drive for creating tomorrow. That definition is grandiose: a *touch of grandiosity* is a distinguishing characteristic of the true entrepreneur.

Entrepreneurs are also *innovative.* Creative ideas flash out of the unconscious at regular intervals, like strobe lights. They are not straight line, logical thinkers, but enthusiastically dance around a problem. Good ideas arise from patterns they see in the material.

They are *intelligent,* grasping ideas quickly, and possessing the capacity for excellent retention. In whatever they are involved, they bring a *complete investment of their powers* and energy. Some are workaholics, but some love to play, playing with the same intensity that they work. A client went to London and became fascinated with St. Paul's Cathedral. He came home an expert on St.

Paul's, buying beautiful antique books containing old architects' drawings and descriptions. He spoke to me about it eloquently for perhaps twenty minutes. "What else did you do?" I asked. "Well, let's see," he said, "we ate at some good restaurants."

A fifth characteristic of the entrepreneurial personality is that they are *risk-takers*. Hercules is the archetypal hero who accomplished tasks against incredible odds in order to achieve a personal goal. Having achieved his goals, he became a god. Entrepreneurs aspire to be Herculean! One client climbs difficult mountains as a hobby. In his office is a spectacular photograph of himself scaling the last precipice of Mt. Rainier, reaching the summit "against all odds."

Related to their risk-taking and the touch of grandiosity is a *sense of the dramatic*. Entrepreneurs have a capability for catching employees up in dramatic scenarios, getting their energy focused on some project, and motivating them to achievement. They can excite the imaginations of investors or bankers who will commit investment capital in their projects.

They typically radiate *abundant self-confidence,* although this is sometimes a cover for poignant fears that their power is inadequate for their needs, fears that they might make a gross miscalculation, fears that an associate may make a fatal error, fears (the worst of all) that they may in the end be a crashing failure. These fears have a powerful and destructive effect upon interpersonal relationships in the business.

Related to risk-taking and the confidence/fear factor, an entrepreneur prefers a chain-of-command, *military-style organizational structure,* often assuming the aura almost of an emperor as he pursues his heroic goals. Of course, to do what he does, his body must deliver a *high energy output.* Several younger entrepreneurs with whom I work have a seemingly laid back, laissez faire manner, but beneath that they are wound tight and driven.

Entrepreneurs *manage interpersonal relationships by wooing.* With their dynamic, magnetic personalities and sense of the dramatic, they are very powerful and can persuade sensible people to invest energy or capital in projects they would not dream about, even in their wildest fantasies.

Finally, entrepreneurs *love money.* Money becomes a method of keeping score in the great game of life. The more they accumulate, the better their score is. Some enjoy spending it, some don't. But all want to be recognized as a significant champion in the great American game of financial empire-building.

The interaction of these entrepreneurial personality characteristics with an organizational system, provides the dynamic which tests the knowledge, creativity, and skills of the consultant. For example, consider the issue of heroic goals. All human beings have a powerful internal drive to gain attention. Most of us learn to gain attention in constructive ways, building our own self-esteem, enjoying being esteemed, or helping others build self-esteem. However, in this pursuit, we tend to see our merits with clarity, even exaggeration, while being only dimly aware of our shortcomings.

Ernest Becker, author of a Pulitzer prize-winning book on this subject, expressed this concept in a rich, dramatic manner. "It is not that children are vicious, selfish, or domineering. It is that they so openly express man's tragic destiny: he must stand out, be a hero, make the biggest possible contribution to world life, show that he counts more than anything or anyone else."[2]

In contrast with an entrepreneurial personality, a managerial personality pursues heroism through the maximization of his coordinating skills. He enjoys goal-setting, developing processes for reaching those goals, and regulating and controlling those processes. Managers enhance and strengthen their sense of self-worth by seeing the processes produce the goal. They like strengthening existing institutions and enjoy taking on and dutifully discharging specific responsibility. They build teams and take pride in minimizing risk (or taking only measured, moderate risks).

Entrepreneurs, however, are a very different breed of cat. Innovative, they develop a grand concept and become almost obsessed with the realization of it. They are charismatic and can catch others up in the excitement of achieving the grand concept. They are strong-willed and can pursue their heroic goal with a conviction that they count "more than anything or anyone else," as Becker puts it.[2] Such feelings are perhaps felt by everyone, but in the entrepreneurial personality, they are less overlaid with acculturation processes, less constrained by fears of retaliation. He does own the company and is not going to be reprimanded or worse dealt a humiliating termination.

She is, however, motivated by the fear of humiliation of a much more personal and poignant nature. Her grand concept may crash, bringing her both financial ruin and the public knowledge that either she or her concept was a loser. To compound this problem, the typical entrepreneur-owner takes considerable risks in developing and marketing her product or service, calculating the outcomes substantially alone. Because risk-taking means opening her grand design to humilating failures and because she typically operates from a low trust that others will really hustle, as she would, to get the results she needs, she has a high drive to control the performance of other people, right down to the minutiae. In a high-risk situation, the minutiae can be significant.

This leads the entrepreneur-owner to display another aspect of the "heroic" principle expressed succinctly by Becker: "It is one of the meaner aspects of narcissism that practically everyone is seen as expendable except ourselves."[3] Thus, managers working for entrepreneur-owners feel constantly under the gun to deliver a perfect result on time with no margins for shortfalls—or else! This is a tough environment in which to live, and many managers wilt and die in it.

The pattern is like this: The entrepreneur-owner is preoccupied, sometimes even obsessed, by his grand project. The risks are large and frightening. The fear is repressed and overlaid with abounding confidence. Errors by his managers or workers open the grand goal to failure. Failure is intolerable, even unthinkable. If an error does occur, the error-maker is attacked out of proportion to the deed, as the error is seen as affecting the grand goal's realization. After several episodes of over-reaction by the entrepreneur-owner, managers begin to experience stress, which makes them more error-prone and less willing to take risks. The problems of the business increase as a consequence, and a blow-up, after which the manager is fired or resigns, becomes a probability. Most, although not all, entrepreneurs, in my experience, do have unnecessary turnover of good personnel.

This pattern of action also produces the worst problem entrepreneurs typically face—inadequate or distorted feedback of reality. Apprehensive managers don't feed back the bad news. They cover it up or distort it or blind themselves to it. Even if the bad news is fed back, the entrepreneur, caught up in his heroic goal and sense of personal power, can become deaf to words of warning or information which implies impending serious problems. When he is no longer confrontable, his doom is sealed, and the great powers which led him to success have been exaggerated into hubris.

Because of the uniqueness of the entrepreneur-owner's personality, some consultant interventions work better than others. Competent consultants with varying styles and methods of operation can be effective with these clients. However, I believe a consultant can increase his effectiveness by being sensitive to opportunities to use one or more of the following strategies.

The Use of Stories

We live our lives through stories; deleting, distorting, and reworking the experiences of our lives so that events appear to support and fulfill our stories. Entrepreneurs have very dramatic, even melodramatic stories. Frequently the theme of their stories can be captured in a phrase, such as "building an empire," "winning against all odds," or, in the case of a medical doctor entrepreneur, "gaining the undying devotion of my patients." Frequently, in order for the entrepreneur to achieve the effectiveness he has hired a consultant to facilitate, he has to see the world with greater clarity and enrich his story.

One of the most powerful ways to enter the client's world and bring to it greater reality-orientation is through the use of stories which are presented as fables and which contain essential elements of the client's mythology so that the story being told can be easily fitted into his own story.

A client who was "building an empire" was having a difficult and humiliating problem with the leading marketing executive in his company. This man produced nearly half of the sales of the company and had been developed by the entrepreneur from ignorance in sales to the competent, professional executive he had become. The entrepreneur wanted gratitude and loyalty from his executive. What he got was thinly disguised criticism, backbiting, negotiations with other possible employers, and demands for special treatment.

The executive proferred loyalty if the special demands were met. However, the executive was always able to find fault with the entrepreneur's response and made further demands before the loyalty would finally be forthcoming. These transactions were being consummated substantially at an ulterior, hidden level, and neither was fully aware of their game. If the entrepreneur was to be free of the energy drained by this relationship, he needed to understand the nature of the transactions and develop a strategy to cure the problem. Here is the story I told him.

"Once upon a time, there was a powerful king who had taken an impoverished land and through his genius, dedication, and hard work had built it into a rich kingdom. The land overflowed with milk and honey.

The king called in a young nobleman and said, "I will teach you how to be a great emissary to other lands, and you can go forth and trade our riches with other nations. You can bring back wealth to your country and for yourself. Will you do that?"

The nobleman was overjoyed and learned all that the king taught him and became wealthy. The king made him ruler over a small principality. Soon the emissary began to think that his principality was more powerful than the kingdom in which it resided. He began to think that the king was not generous enough with him and that he deserved more gifts than he was getting. He saw the king as unappreciative and lacking in good judgment of emissarial capability. He was sure other kings appreciated him more.

Meanwhile, the king, who cared about his emissary, pondered ways to have a genuine and lifelong alliance with him. The emissary had a beautiful daughter. "I will marry the emissary's daughter and we will live together in peace forever as members of the same family."

So the king asked the emissary for his daughter's hand in marriage and the emissary said, "If you will do three special things for me, I will give you my daughter's hand in marriage." The king did them and returned to claim his bride, but the emissary said, "You did not do them very well. However, if you will give me three gifts, which I will name, I will give you my daughter's hand in marriage." The king gave the gifts and came to claim the bride, but the emissary said, "These gifts were not of the quality I expected. So you must do more. If you give me these three honors, I will give you my daughter's hand in marriage."

The king realized he was never going to get the daughter's hand in marriage. He went home sorrowing and began to raise a large army.

The entrepreneur understood the metaphor. He decided to confront the loyalty issue with his executive to demand support and cooperation, to offer to respond as he could one last time to whatever specific needs the executive had in order to feel secure, affirmed, and rewarded, and to develop plans for strengthening and expanding his sales team. The executive submitted a written want list and, as had been the consistent pattern in the past, began to develop dissatisfaction with the entrepreneur's response. The entrepreneur was decisive and firm about what he would do and was clear that if the executive could not find this response satisfactory, he should find employment where he could be happy and loyal. Eventually, the executive resigned. However, by this time a sales team was in place to cover the needs of the company, and the great energy drains of dealing both with this executive and the small fires he built throughout the company were over.

Stories can communicate quickly what hours of analysis and rational thought may communicate less well. This story, with visions of kingdoms and royal power, fit the world view of the empire-building entrepreneur. The courtship motif fit another aspect of the entrepreneur's personality and illustrated how the continuation of courtship had become inappropriate for a powerful king to continue. The consequences of that inappropriate strategy were that the king (entrepreneur) was being rendered helpless. While the story communicated a potential solution, the metaphor was sufficiently general that the entrepreneur was not constrained by it.

Having a bias for persons choosing to work together cooperatively, I was disappointed that the emissary-executive did not alter the story ending by choosing to give his daughter's hand in marriage. Having talked with the executive in several interviews, however, his history indicated a therapeutic intervention might be in order before he gave loyalty to anyone.

The Use of Truth-telling

Another strategy effective with entrepreneur-owners is truth-telling. Because their personalities are strong, their energy high, and their power in their business virtually absolute, their executives often find it difficult to confront them even when truth is on their side. The consultant, however, after first gaining the trust of the client, is in a much different position. The consultant is established as the client's ally, not a rival in any sense. Most consultants gain power by truth-telling, never risking the loss of total income, pension, and other benefits as an employee would. The consultant is also well-versed in coping with angry feedback and is difficult to intimidate.

A client was engaged in strategic planning with a group of his senior officers. The process had become mildly tedious. The entrepreneur also had experienced the group's deciding against several of his ideas, and he was having difficulty with such opposition. Nevertheless, in each case, the group's decision had been based on sound data and wise probability-estimating, and he had ultimately agreed to each decision. In time, however, the entrepreneur stood and pronounced, "This is too damned slow, and we aren't getting anywhere. What the hell are we doing this for anyway?" In a very low-key, matter-of-fact manner, the consultant said to the entrepreneur, "We are doing this because this company lost over a half-million dollars last year and it can't afford to do it again this year."

This type of simple, straight truth-telling cuts through the entrepreneur's heroic mystique and enables him to keep himself rooted in reality, a feat he must do in order for his vast personal resources to be effectively used.

I was recently the recipient of an elegant bit of truth-telling which instantly and radically changed my thinking. I enjoy tennis and play often. Gradually over a period of months, I began to experience pain down the back of my leg from hip to knee. I had difficulty sitting for long periods of time and began to have strange sensations in my calf and foot, tickles, pin-pricks, the sense of gravel in my shoe when none was there.

I went to an orthopedist, who couldn't make a precise diagnosis without more data or tests and sent me to a neurologist. The tests would cost around $700, and since my major medical insurance has a $1,000 deductible feature, the cost was all mine. I began to think of all the enjoyable things I could do with $700 and recalled how many physical problems I had had over the years which healed themselves. I attributed the pain to my weekly yoga class. Finally, I related the situation to a friend, who is a psychiatrist and business consultant, and told him I thought I would take a holiday with the money and cure my problem by dropping out of yoga. His response was, "Bill, you are at the age when the next illness you get may be the last one you ever have. Don't you want to know what it is?" I got the tests. Fortunately, this was not the last illness I'll ever have, and the yoga classes were not the cause but became part of the cure.

The Use of Empowering

The third strategy which works well with entrepreneur-owners can be called "empowering." Successful entrepreneurs have built their businesses or professions with their genius and their sweat. They have done it in a hands-on manner, controlling most of the activities of the enterprise, calculating and assuming the risks, putting in the long hours when a hole developed in the dike, literally carving out their success as Michelangelo carved and polished "David."

However, as the business grows, the entrepreneur herself can't do or control it all. She has to delegate. Yet delegating is frightening as she loses the absolute control she enjoys and thinks she needs. Also, delegating is personally threatening, as she both loses power and sets up the potential for errors she can't control. The concept of "delegating" to an entrepreneur, in my experience, means setting up somebody to do something less well than she can do it, someone who neither recognizes nor cares about the risks. She has given away personal power and is less than she was.

Of course, entrepreneurs must either delegate or give up their heroic dreams. The potent question then is how to enable them to delegate and still feel their power to influence outcomes.

Here is a strategy that has worked well. Target the department or unit where delegating is both feasible and desirable. Engage the entrepreneur in considering how he could free up some of his own time for more creative activities by "empowering" the head of the target division to do more for him. Engage the entrepreneur and executive in a strategic planning session for the division. Of course, the entrepreneur and executive both know how to run the operation, so this session generally produces broad agreement and understanding. In a private session with the entrepreneur, show him how regular, periodic meetings with the executive on the subject of the game plan will enable him to empower the executive to be effective in running the department and enable him to check on whether the level of performance presents any significant risk. At this point, propose that he meet with the executive, "empower" him to effect the game plan and set up the feedback and checking-out meetings. Note the use of the word "delegate" is avoided as it seems to be anathema to most entrepreneurs. Afterwards, congratulate the entrepreneur on increasing his own power through empowering to a colleague to run a department, thus freeing up time the entrepreneur can invest in his great gifts as an entrepreneur. And, in truth, he has become more powerful.

The Use of Strategic Planning

Finally, entrepreneurs are prone to get themselves involved in the fatal game of "Emperor." The game is elegantly described by Dr. Martin Groder in his book *Business Games*. When the entrepreneur's quest for his heroic goals gets out of control, when he stops carefuly weighing the pros and cons of a business venture and is concerned with its potential for adding to his grandeur, when he "is consumed by his vision of an empire in which he will reign as a benevolent despot over forever grateful subjects,"[3] he is over the hill. The key to perceiving whether a client has become an emperor is whether he can be confronted.

For entrepreneurs to be at their best, they must be confronted regularly and must do strategic planning. As consultants, we must concentrate our powers upon leading entrepreneurs to protect themselves against grandiosity by developing feasible goals and strategic plans in a group setting with their best colleagues. With the entrepreneur focusing his prodigious creativity and energies upon feasible plans, protected by confrontation and feedback from his best managers, his capabilities for reaching his heroic goals will be at their fullest. The organization and the customers will benefit.

In conclusion, entrepreneurs conceive innovative and useful projects and get them executed. They organize, direct, and bring to successful achievement the lives of many people while delivering to their customers products and services which are both creative and wanted. They are the shapers and movers of our socio-economic system. They both deserve and will demand the best consultation capabilities we have to give them.

References

1. Drucker, Peter, *Management, Tasks, Responsibilities, Practices,* New York: Harper & Row, 1974, p. 45.
2. Becker, Ernest, *The Denial of Death,* New York, The Free Press, McMillan Publishing Co., Inc., 1973, p. 2, 4.
3. Groder, Martin G., *Business Games,* New York, Boardroom Books, 1980, p. 65.

C. William Webb is an independent consultant in Charlotte, North Carolina and specializes in working with small- to medium-sized, closely held companies.

Chapter 21

Managing the Consultant

Marie S. Nock
and Alex L. Moore

There is something about the word *consultant* that conjurs up illusions of, as well as expectations of, an "all knowing expert," and frequently clients and consultants act as though this is the reality. But in fact, the consultant is a person with areas of expertise who needs guidance, parameters, outcomes, and feedback just as others in the work place do.

One may think that there are a number of circumstances that are unique in the client's management of the consultant, and perhaps some are, but essentially, good management practices that are used with internal professionals are the basis for managing the consultant. This chapter will focus on effective practices for managing the different stages of the consultant relationship. Specifically, it will focus on managing the consultant through the stages of contracting, setting goals and objectives, implementation, accountability for results, and closure. The pitfalls that can occur, and actually are more likely to with poor consultant management, will also be delineated.

Contracting

The tone for the way the consultant will be managed is set during the contracting stage. This stage broadly refers to the way that the client contacts the consultant, interviews, describes the assignment, sets the parameters, negotiates the fees, selects the consultant and ultimately writes the contract. The steps sound simple enough but provide ample opportunities, if mishandled, to shift the management responsibility from the client to the consultant.

Generally, an organization determines that a consultant should be brought in when the internal staff does not have the time or expertise to address an organizational need. In other words the management of the organization makes a decision that the need is a priority, that the need when addressed will contribute to the efficiency and effectiveness of the organization, and that external rather than internal resources should be used. A search process is then begun to identify a consultant with the expertise, style, industry background, if appropriate, and inclination to get the job done. Checking with professional colleagues for referrals or going to consulting groups and universities are good ways of identifying potential consultants. Following through with interviews, checking references with prior clients, making a selection based on the consultant's ability to fully address the organization's need, and finalizing the relationship with a contract that is very explicit about the results to be achieved, the time frame, and the fee for services, are the next steps.

Throughout the process the client does his or her best to ensure that a qualified consultant will be selected, that the organizational needs are the agenda, and that the consultant will be able to enhance and extend the organization's ongoing efforts. The client is in control even though assistance is being sought. This is important.

Pitfall #1—*Hiring consultants who do their thing not your thing.*

Be wary of selecting consultants because of their sales efforts when no organization need exists or that need is not a priority. Consultants are aware of an increase in their contracted time that is proportional to their time and efforts in marketing their services. This is a good business practice for them, but not the way for the client to determine that a consultant should be retained.

Setting Goals and Objectives

As a representative of the organization, the client manager is responsible for assuring that the organization's goals and objectives will be enhanced by the consultant's intervention and that the consultant's objectives relate to the ongoing efforts of the organization.

The next stage, setting goals and objectives, refers to specifying the results that the consultant will be responsible for achieving through his/her relationship with the organization. This stage is begun during the contracting stage so that the full scope of the assignment may be explored before the contract is set. If the manager does not explore the expected outcomes fully enough, the wise consultant will begin the consultation process with the manager to clarify the expected goals and objectives. This structures expectations on both sides and provides the basis for later satisfaction when the desired results are met.

Just as in setting goals and objectives with internal staff that are specific, measurable, and achievable, it is important for the consultant's goals and objectives to be equally specific, measurable, and achievable. If they are not specific, the consultant is at a disadvantage in planning the course of action. If they are not measurable, the organization has no way of knowing that it is getting what it is paying for. If they are not achievable, the consultant has no way of meeting the contract. So important are the goals and objectives in the client/consultant relationship that they may be written into the contract. They should, as written, represent the purpose for the relationship.

Pitfall #2—*Retaining a consultant for the process, rather than the result.*

Sometimes the purpose of the client/consultant relationship is process oriented. Team building, process consultation and conflict resolution are all process activities. When done in the organizational context, however, they are done for a purpose—for a desired result. It is this purpose or result that should be specified in the goals and objectives, not the process.

Implementation

Managing the consultant through the implementation stage is the most critical stage; here it is important to use the "art" rather than the "science" of management. Implementation refers to the consultant's activities that lead to the achievement of the contracted goals and objectives. These activities are many and varied and include all consultant actions and interactions within the organization.

The key to the successful client manager/consultant relationship is to manage, not control. To do this it is important for the manager to build trust, respect, open communications, and a shared sense of mission with the consultant. The basis for the relationship has its foundations during early interactions, typically during the contracting stage. The relationship is built, however, after the contract is signed.

The best way for the manager to build trust with the consultant is to trust. It is important to disclose not only the assignment, but the potential barriers to its achievement, the hidden agendas of different groups in the organization, organizational culture, and individual idiosyncrasies; in other words, the entire scope of the issue or problem without holding back. By bringing the consultant into the manager's confidence, a number of aspects are being managed simultaneously. Time is being saved by sharing with the consultant all information pertinent to the issue.

This is assuming of course, that the purpose of the assignment is not to verify the manager's perceptions. If this is the purpose, information that could affect perceptions may be held for a later time. By being open, the manager is also modeling the trust and communication expected from the consultant. Also being communicated is the value of the assignment and of the client/consultant relationship.

It is important for the manager to identify key players and to pave the way for planned interactions the consultant will have with them. Assuring access and information is essential. In consultant interactions with individuals in the organization, a frequent purpose is gathering data that relate to the assignment. The consultant must build trust with those given individuals so that they will be comfortable being as candid as possible with him or her. Important to this is guaranteed anonymity for the sources of the information. In introducing the consultant to the organization, it is important for the manager to communicate the purpose of the consultation as well as to support the anonymity individuals will have as information is fed back by the consultant. This is one of the guarantees that enables the consultant to be effective.

It is important for the manager to schedule periodic meetings with the consultant during implementation for purposes of planning next steps, debriefing, and giving feedback. Throughout, the manager is assuring that the organization's mission is being served. If it is not, redirection is appropriate.

During implementation it is important for the client manager to be open to new information and new perspectives and to be nondefensive about problem areas that are identified. A manager with an authoritarian style may want to "control" the consultant at these times. This control, however, will have a limiting effect on the potential outcomes. A better approach is to explore fears or catastrophic expectations with the consultant and to join him or her in managing the situation.

Pitfall #3—*Controlling, not managing the consultant.*

Pitfall #4—*Being managed by the consultant.*

Throughout the consultation, the consultant needs to be linked to the manager. The manager is charged ultimately with the accountability for the results and must be in a position to assure continuity and follow-through. The manager must always be aware of this responsibility and thereby avoid the pitfall of being managed by the consultant.

Accountability for Results

Managing the consultant throughout accountability for results is similar to managing individual employee accountability. This is begun with the setting of objectives that later will be evaluated. If the agreed upon objectives are specific and measurable, the manager has an easier task in evaluating the evidence and documenting that the desired results have, in fact, been delivered. If the set objectives were fuzzy, the evaluation will be an uncertain measure.

The manager may want to get written progress reports from the consultant on a scheduled basis. The weekly, bi-weekly, or monthly reports would be scheduled based on the anticipated length of the consultation. Depending on the nature of the consultation, it is entirely possible that data gathered by the consultant will cause the manager to want to retarget the objectives.

If it becomes apparent that the objectives need to be revised or that additional objectives need to be set, it is appropriate to do so during the progress review.

A final report should be requested from the consultant that specifies the differences in place as a result of the consultation. This report may include points for ongoing monitoring as well as recommendations for further steps. This report is a summation for the organization of the effectiveness of the consultant dollars spent.

Pitfall #5—*Not monitoring the consultant's progress toward the results.*

Consultants are professionals and do a lot of self-monitoring. The manager's role in monitoring is made easier because of this, but the manager must continue to ensure that the organization's interests are being served.

Closure

When the consultation has gone well and the consultant has been managed effectively, closure will be a time filled with feelings of accomplishment and a job well conceived and delivered. The stages mentioned throughout the chapter, if handled properly, will lead to ending well a relationship that has been handled well by all concerned.

Marie Nock is assistant vice president and manager of human resources at Southeast Banking Corporation headquartered in Miami, Florida.

Alex Moore is Vice President and director of human resources at Southeast Banking Corporation headquartered in Miami, Florida.

Part VI

Disengagement and Closure

In our original thinking, and in the model we propose, there are two different phases. One is disengagement, and the other is closure. Little has been written which is specifically labeled disengagement. The phase does exist, but is generally combined with closure in most writing. We feel disengagement should be discussed as a separate phase and it is hoped that writers and practitioners will give more consideration to making it a distinct phase.

Disengagement

During disengagement, the relationships between the client and the consultant begin to change. The purpose of disengagement, as the name implies, is to start the process in which the consultant leaves the situation. At this point in the relationship, the problem or purpose of the consultation will have been resolved or well on its way to solution. It is often a tentative phase where the consultant might have to recycle back to response, and even to diagnosis. Disengagement is characterized by a period of testing whether or not the client and the client system are able to function in the new situation caused by the response, and whether they can cope with the new relationships which have emerged.

An analogy, although a harsh one, is to compare disengagement to the practice of certain colonial powers in the past half century as they granted freedom to colonies. In some cases, the granting of freedom (i.e., the allowance for new behavior) was done with too little preparation and only the briefest time for the novice nationals to become acquainted with their new system. Often, the result of this abrupt transition was civil war and chaos during ruthless struggles for power, as factions competed to fill the gap left by the departing colonial power.

The departure of the consultant may not produce such dramatic and world shattering results, but it certainly can create a power vacuum, the need for new, untried behaviors and development of fresh emerging relationships.

An abrupt departure by the consultant can be quite threatening to the client — an unnecessary distraction sure to impact the project's effectiveness. Fortunately, it is possible to alleviate this problem. The departure of the consultant can be carefully planned and recognized by both the client and the consultant. The reduced involvement by the consultant in the life of the client system — at least for this particular assignment — can be envolved.

Unfortunately, the consultant who wishes just to emphasize the need for his or her services can easily demonstrate this need by departing in an unplanned and precipitous manner. The consultant might even tell the client that it is "for his or her own good," or "that it's time for the client to stand on his or her own feet." The result can be an insecure client, unsure, and highly dependent on the consultant. An anticipated result is that the client asks for more, even though the need for the consultant is no longer essential. If so, the consultant will have put the client in a position where he or she thinks help is still needed, rather than concluding this particular assignment and leaving a client who is able to function independently of the consultant.

The tendency to overlook a carefully planned disengagement can also occur when the consultant is on some kind of retainer. There is the implication that funds are still available and the temptation to continue until those funds are exhausted. In that case, disengagement will reflect the money available, rather than the completion of the assignment.

An internal consultant may have more difficulty in disengaging than an external consultant. The internal consultant is still evident within the total organization and may even have some geographic proximity to the client. This requires even more attention to the disengagement phase to ensure the relation does not limp along until actually forced to terminate by some external force demanding closure.

During disengagement the process of evaluation should be very evident. There may be some evaluation during response but that will be more of the formative kind of evaluation designed to influence the situation while in progress. By the disengagement phase, however, the evaluation should become the focused, summary type to determine specifically if the response has met the needs of the organization as identified during diagnosis.

As the consultation unfolds, changes may have occurred which render the earlier diagnosis either partially or completely invalid. To push ahead is to court failure. If the situation has changed, it may be necessary to go back to diagnosis or to alter the response. Hopefully, this has occurred. If not, it should be addressed during disengagement.

Consultation frequently produces new behaviors, relationships, or processes within the organization. At disengagement, the client and the consultant should verify whether the organization has the resources to continue in the preferred direction. If there are new relationships, determination must be made regarding whether these are to be supported so they will continue after the consultant leaves. During disengagement, the consultant may be available on an "as needed" basis while the client system tries to work with the changes which have been introduced.

Closure

Assuming disengagement has proceeded successfully, it is then time for closure. This should be distinctive and both the client and the consultant should acknowledge that they are now moving into this final phase. They can continue their relationship, but it should be based on other problems or concerns. It is important that each task or problem be brought to some kind of finality. Where the consultant is working with more than one client within the same client system, this process can easily become obscured. Closure should not be seen as a rejection of the consultant, but rather as a signal of the successful completion of a particular assignment and relationship.

Evaluation was mentioned earlier. It should have been planned in some fashion during the early stages of the response. During closure, the results of the evaluation should be shared. However, there are many times when the final effect of a consultation may require several months or even years before a meaningful evaluation can be conducted. Both sides should recognize this and understand that closure can take place, and that the final evaluation can come later. Meanwhile, it should be possible to agree on what would constitute an acceptable evaluation before the consultant departs.

If the evaluation discloses that the objectives of the consultation have not been met, further work might be needed. This should have surfaced during disengagement, but it is possible for it to become evident only in this final stage. Frequently, there is little that can be done about working further at this point, which is why it is crucial to do the evaluation during the disengagement phase. If the summary evaluation is done during closure, then both sides must agree that all they can do is to live with the data and the situation as presented. It may raise the need for further consultation, or the need for a different consultant.

Reducing the involvement of the consultant during disengagement should also bring about reduced dependency by the client. It is always desirable to keep dependency at the lowest possible level. Still, dependency does occur. If it has not been adequately dealt with by disengagement, it can become a horror during closure. The client may present excuses and see reasons why the consultant should continue. We have known clients who have suddenly discovered new financial resources just so the relationship could be sustained. Or, the problem suddenly changes, creating a desperately renewed need for the consultant. Such actions on the part of the client can build the bank statement and ego of the consultant. But if they are reflections of contrived client–dependency, then the behavior of the consultant becomes suspect. They should both be working toward closure as the normal, expected stage of their relationship. That does not prevent either from exploring the possibility of working together on other problems or in other relationships.

The physical aspects of closure take several forms. Frequently, a written report is required. This ranges from a brief memo to a comprehensive analysis or log. In consulting with the federal government, a written report is almost always required. However, this direction may not be stipulated in the initial discussions or subsequently in the contract, purchase order, or other legal obligating documents. Some of our colleagues have negotiated a contract, blocked their time, and made the necessary preparations for the consultation. When the written contract arrived, they found it mentioned a written report which was not previously mentioned or implied. The report, of course, entailed additional costs not anticipated. The consultant should query early in the contracting phase, if a written report is required by the terms of the contract.

Working with the private sector does not present this kind of problem. There are other problems, however, which differ from organization to organization. For example, some organizations require a written report when an external consultant is used, while there may not be the same requirement for an internal consultant. Generally, we have found that most organizations do not require a formal written document on closure of the consultation.

There should be a clearly identified closure meeting. Both parties should have agreed that this particular meeting is for the purpose of closure of this assignment. If all has gone well, and both parties are satisfied, the closure meeting is frequently in the form of a social experience. It may take place in a restaurant or some other environment conducive to social as well as business activities. This signifies that both parties are satisfied and there is nothing substantive which needs to be discussed at this time. Others might be invited to this meeting, as appropriate. It is a form of farewell to the consultant — at least for this assignment — and can become a warm occasion in the relationship.

At the same time, this would be when the consultant presents the final bill for services and related expenses. The client should have the assurance that no other financial requirements are outstanding. The consultant can expect that payment will follow and that no additional bills can be charged to this activity.

Some people consider it unprofessional or beneath their dignity to discuss the financial arrangements. This can be very unrealistic. It is not necessary to belabor the financial aspect, but to ignore it is to court financial disaster, particularly by the consultant. If the consultant has used a group, they must be paid. In some cases, they may require payment early, even before the lead consultant has been paid by the client. For those who consult with the federal government, the expected time lag in payment can cause severe cash flow problems. Such a situation has encouraged many good consultants to avoid contracting with the federal government.

Private companies usually present no problem here, but there are times when the client may have forgotten to push the right buttons or to put the appropriate paper into the system. By having a closure date, the consultant can follow-up the payment from a specific given date.

And so, closure is final. The particular assignment is completed. Neither the client nor the consultant is foreclosed from continuing with other tasks or from creating new relationships. Some clients keep going back to the same consultants time after time. This may be due to the successful work of the consultant, or the client's comfort with the relationship which has developed. There is nothing unethical about a consultant following up, at a later date, to determine whether the client has any additional needs which the consultant can help resolve.

If all has gone well, closure should bring a feeling of satisfaction to both the client and the consultant. They should feel they have been mutually helpful and have a high personal regard for each other. With great satisfaction, we have experienced, as have others, that old clients can become new friends.

Chapter 22
"Evaluating the Consulting Process"
Donald Swartz and Gordon Lippitt

The authors offer some sound, specific questions which should be asked as part of evaluation. They present a model, and areas to be evaluated. We do have a minor difference with one aspect of their material. They write of the "consulting/ training" event. Within this book, we separate consulting from training as two different kinds of activities. Despite this distinction, the material they present can be very useful for evaluating consulting activities.

It is important to note that Donald Swartz and Gordon Lippitt encourage evaluating the client–consultant relationship. Too often, this is an overlooked area, though the results of this evaluation can be extremely helpful to both parties. Note, too, their use of a "contractual agreement for consultative services." Such a document proves extremely helpful during disengagement, as it provides the basis for identifying whether the mutual expectations have been met. Of course, it is always possible that the expectations have changed since the initiation of that document. Reference to the expectation of written reports could improve the utility of the document for the closure phase.

Chapter 23
"Disengagement: Reducing Involvement with the Client System"
Edgar H. Schein

This is one of the few sources we have found which specifically discusses disengagement. Schein emphasized the need for both parties to agree that disengagement is actually taking place. When the point is made that "involvement not zero" it does raise the question of whether this is rightly disengagement or another part of the response phase. For process consultation, which the author clearly espouses and is noted for, it is probably acceptable to describe disengagement as he does.

Note particularly his last section about reinvolvement with the client. This comes closer to what we are describing as part of the closure activity. This article is taken from Schein's book *Process Consultation*.

Chapter 22

Evaluating the Consulting Process

Donald Swartz
and Gordon Lippitt

There are some key questions to ask about evaluation —These questions should be asked as part of the contract-setting discussion with the client:

1. What should be evaluated?
2. Why is this important to you? What will you gain from measuring it?
3. How will you measure it? Can you use existing data sources and processes?
4. Who will do the measurement data collection and analysis?
5. Who will do the evaluation based on the data?
6. When will the measurement be done? How often?
7. Who will/should see the results of the evaluation?
8. What will it cost in time and dollars to do this evaluation?
9. Are the benefits of the evaluation worth the cost?

It's easy to ask questions. It's quite another thing to get good answers that will result in a realistic and relevant evaluation system for the client. The model in Figure 22-1 has helped our clients to focus on possible areas of evaluation and appropriate levels of measurement sophistication for their projects.

Explanation of the Evaluation Model

The model points out four interdependent elements to consider when designing an evaluation system:

— Evaluation areas
— Evaluation criteria
— Sources of data
— Methods of data collection

Some brief explanations and definitions of these elements will lead us into a more detailed look into each evaluation area later in this article.

Reprinted from *The Journal of European Training*, Vol. 4, No. 5, copyright 1975, M.C.B. Publications, Ltd., Bradford, England.

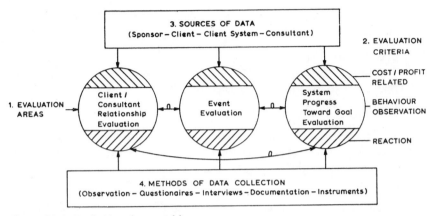

Figure 22-1. Evaluating the consulting process.

Evaluation Areas

Client – Consultant Relationship. This area relates to the evaluation of the personal and professional relationships between client, client system, and consultant. These behavior relationships often have a major impact on the final outcome of the consulting process.

Consulting/Training Events. This area relates to the evaluation of significant consulting interventions such as survey-feedback meetings; skill training; conflict resolution meetings and other important "milestone" activities. Assessing the impact and contribution of each of these types of event on the overall project can provide important information for designing future projects with the client — and for improvement of similar events that will take place in the current project.

Progress Toward Specific Goals. This area relates to the client system's progress toward achievement of pre-stated goals and the possible contribution that the consultation help made to this progress. Overall results evaluation helps to answer the client's question, "Was the money I invested in consulting help at least returned by the results achieved?"

Evaluation Criteria

Cost/Profit-Related. These "hard measure" criteria are developed to determine as directly as possible the effect of consultation on the achievement of specified results. Some examples of cost/profit-related specified results are:

— Consulting time and expense estimate vs. actual
— Consulting event outcomes resulting in increased sales, decreased costs, etc.
— Trend changes in safety record, grievances, turnover, absenteeism, theft

Within the cost-related evaluation criteria there are three approaches to measurement that can be considered:

— Specific goal attainment by a specified time
— Trend tracking vs. plan or estimated performance
— Spot checks of performance vs. hoped for change, e.g. down-turn trend has been reversed

Behavior Observation. These criteria call for documentation of significant factual observed changes in individual and in organizational behavior that resulted directly from the consulting process or from an event influenced by the consulting process. Some examples of observed behavior change are:

— Client much more relaxed and functioning in a more assertive manner
— Change in organization structure, simplifying lines of communications
— Event participants' demonstration that they can plan for and conduct problem-solving meetings

Reaction. These criteria relate to the reactions of client and client system to the consulting process. They report feelings, attitudes, points of view, as these change over time. Some examples of reaction criteria measurements are:

— Client's expressed feelings about the consulting relationship
— Participants' evaluation of a training event
— Client system's reactions as expressed through a series of attitude surveys during the course of the consulting process

Sources of Data

There are four sources of data for an evaluation system. We define each of them as follows:

The Sponsor. A person or persons who can significantly influence the consulting process; who has (have) strong interest in the initiation, progress and final outcome of the consulting process. In some instances the sponsor is the client's "boss." Many times (particularly when working at the top of the organization) the sponsor is the client, e.g. the President. The sponsor could also be a group of people such as City Council, advisory board, executive committee, board of directors, etc.

The Client. The person who makes the "go or no-go" decision about events and directions within the project scope.

The Client System. Any person or group directly involved in or affected by the consulting project.

The Consultant. The helper(s) whose expertise has been contracted for by the client. Helpers may be internal to the client system or external to it. They may be a combination of internal and external helpers.

Methods of Data Collection

Data can be collected in a wide variety of ways. The following five methods are most frequently used to collect data for evaluation of the consulting process:

— *Observation*. The observation and recording of individual and group behavior as it relates to the job to be done. Also, the observation and recording of the way systems are functioning; e.g. flow-charting, decision trees, PERT charting, etc.

— *Questionnaires*. Specially designed or standardized formats that ask for individual written responses concerning attitude, viewpoints, opinions, perceptions.

— *Interviews*. Face-to-face or telephonic live interviews with individuals or groups to gain in-depth perceptions, specific examples, ideas and feelings.

— *Documentation*. The use of archival records, current records, and specially recorded data to show trends and changes resulting from the consulting process.

— *Instruments*. Specially designed data collection devices whose purpose is to stimulate individual feedback about a situation and to provide a framework for evaluation discussions between client, client system and, consultant.

We'll next illustrate how the four evaluation elements interact by looking at evaluation examples in each of the three "evaluation areas".

Evaluating the Client–Consultant Relationship

The success of the consulting relationship is not just a matter of consultant competency and/or creativity. The trust and acceptance of client–consultant are key factors along with appropriate definition of roles. Some guidelines in assessing the consulting relationship are as follows:

1. *Does the consultant form sound interpersonal relations with the client?* A consulting relationship is based on trust developed by effective interpersonal relations. Does the consultant allow time for exploring this relationship in sufficient depth so both parties feel that changes are likely for developing confidence and trust?

2. *Does the consultant build dependence on his resources with the client?* A responsible and ethical consultant does not make the client dependent on him, or his methods. Instead, he recognizes the need for people to develop their own competence and capabilities, while he assists only when needed. He can do this without creating dependency.

3. *Does the consultant focus on the problem?* Beware of the consultant who so much wants to please everyone with his work that he glosses over problems and conflict. The realities of organizational life and interpersonal dynamics mean that there will be people who feel threatened, upset and unhappy about the results of any organizational change. The problem or need, however, must be confronted or we are dealing with "flight", not coping behavior.

4. *Does the consultant respect the confidences of his clients?* Another sign of a professional consultant is his ability to keep confidential his dealings with clients.

5. *Does the consultant achieve influence appropriately in the organization?* The professional consultant makes every effort to build the resources or the department or person who brought him into the consultation. His influence is by expertise and he does not put on a political show to impress others.

6. *Does the consultant indicate the skills he possesses relative to the client's problem?* Many consultants who are good in one field may not be expert in the resources required to help an organization to investigate the total aspects of its structure, finances, technology, and human processes. Be wary of the consultant who may be venturing far beyond the limits of his actual skills and abilities.

7. *Does the consultant clearly inform the client as to his role and contribution?* A consultant should clarify his role with the potentials and limitations inherent in such a clarification.

8. *Does the consultant express willingness to have his services evaluated?* One sign of the non-professional consultant is an unwillingness to have his work reviewed or evaluated by persons in the organization. He will muster up comments such as: "My kind of services cannot be evaluated," or "The nature of my work is so scientific and technical that there is no way it can be accurately measured." Exercise caution with the consultant who is reluctant to get "feedback" on his own performance.

These suggested assessment guidelines are based on our experiences from both the sending and receiving sides of consulting services. Of course, this is not meant to be an exhaustive list, but is indicative of some of the concerns which should be brought to the attention of managers and organizations that use consultants and wish to evaluate the process.

In Table 22-1 we have attempted to illustrate a number of possible ways to organize the evaluation of the relationship between consultant and client and between consultant and client system. Most of the criteria are dependent upon behavior observation and reaction data.

Evaluating the Consulting/Training Event

Most consulting interventions include key training and group process events. It is often helpful to client, client system, and consultant to evaluate these events so

Table 22-1
Evaluating the Client-Consultant Relationship

What to Evaluate	Why Evaluate	How Evaluate	Who Will Evaluate	Who Will Get Evaluation	When Evaluate
Client-Consultant Contract Agreements: Role Clarity Commitments Schedule Cost vs. Estimate	Project success depends on it. May need to re-negotiate due to changes	Open discussion	Client or consultant	Consultant or client	As desired by either party or between phases
Interdependency or Dependency	To determine if client is becoming too dependent on consultant	Open discussion	Sponsor, client or consultant	Client and/or consultant	As desired by either party
Consultant's Influence	To determine if the consultant is exerting too little or too much influence	Instrument observation	Other consultant, sponsor or client	Consultant	As desired by the client
Consultant's Ethics	To determine if consultant's behavior is helpful to the project	Observation Client system reaction	Client system, client, sponsor, other consultant	Consultant	As desired by client
Consultant's Arena	To determine if the consultant is staying within the bounds of his expertise and competence	Observation Client system reaction	Client system, client, sponsor, other consultant	Consultant	As desired by client
Consultant's Ability	To determine if the consultant's work is performed adequately	Reaction interviews with client system Observation Questionnaire	Other consulting professional	Client, consultant	As desired by client

that learning reinforcement and needed corrective action take place. Much has been written about event measurement. We have included here the methods we have used most frequently.

Post-event Measure (only)
Use this method when:

— There is no opportunity or little need for comparative pre- and post-measurement.
— The trainer/consultant is interested in the immediate reaction to the content and methodology of the event.
— Consultant and client are satisfied with reaction data as the main basis for evaluation.
— The event is not designed to result in a specific measurable behavior change. Rather, its purpose is to create awareness, internal motivation, inform, educate.

Evaluation Criteria

— Behavior observation: consultant/trainer's observation of behavior changes in participants during the event
— Reaction data: post-event questionnaire is frequently used for these data
— Post-event interviews of individuals or group by consultant or client

Pre-event and Post-event Measure
Use this method when:

— The event is designed to help to cause a specific observable behavior change in the participants.
— The event is designed to increase the participants' knowledge or understanding of a subject area and it is worth measuring the degree of improvement.

Evaluation Criteria

— Cost/profit related: summaries of decisions made and problems solved as a result of the event, including cost/benefit estimate of each. This summary should be made by the participants and *they* should report it to the client or sponsor.
— Behavior observation: documented observation of participant behavior by consultant and/or client before and after the consulting event. For example, participant ability to plan and conduct effective staff meetings.
— Reaction data: participant response to a pretest and to a posttest, demonstrating an increase in knowledge and understanding; or expressing a change in attitude about an issue with which the event was concerned (e.g., attitudes about minority employment).

Table 22-2
Performance Data Summary

Condition	Premeasure Bags/Man-Hr	Postmeasure Bags/Man-Hr	Change	Cost Difference
Control Group	0.1027	0.1020	− 0.7%	-0-
Continuous ($2)	0.0813	0.1081	+33.0%	−$4.14/Bag
VR-2 ($4)	0.1010	0.0929	− 8.0%	+$3.61/Bag
VR-4 ($8)	0.1151	0.1359	+18.1%	+$0.15/Bag

Pre-event and Post-event Measure with Control Group

| Group A (Trained) | Measure Performance | Training | Measure Performance |
| Group B (Not Trained) | Measure Performance | ——— | Measure Performance |

This is a more sophisticated method of evaluating the payout from consulting events in terms of performance on the job. All three Evaluation criteria could be used as under "Pre-event and Post-event Measure" above.

Table 22-2 illustrates the use of this method for evaluating the performance change of tree planters in a large wood products company in a consulting event versus the performance of those who had not participated.

The Control Group method can also be used for comparing Post-event measurement between training group and control group.

The Control Group method should be used when:

— It is possible to identify a control group who are experiencing similar variables as the training or consulted group (e.g., working conditions, supplies, tools, climatic conditions, terrain, etc.).
— The Control Group and the training group each contain 15 or more persons, so that the results are statistically reliable.
— The consultant and/or client need good comparative performance data.
— Identifying a "control" group will not create a "have" and "have not" feeling in the client system.

Time Series Pre-event and Time Series Post-event Measure with Control Group

In this design, a series of performance measures are taken prior to and again following the consulting event.

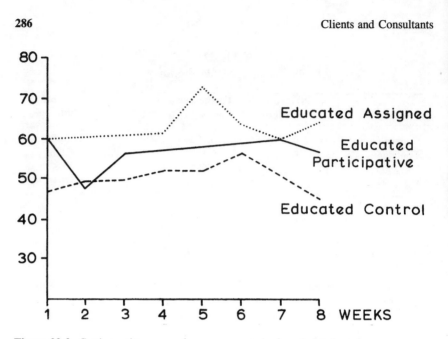

Figure 22-2. Cutting units per manhour across weeks for educated workers.

	Design		
Group A O_1 O_2 O_3 Event	O_4	O_5	O_6
(Trained)			
Group B O_1 O_2 O_3	O_4	O_5	O_6
(Not Trained)			

where 0 = Observation, reaction or cost/profit measure data.

Figure 22-2 demonstrates the use of this type measure design used to determine the effectiveness of goal setting practices as related to production rates of educated wood workers.

The charts in Figure 22-2 show the comparative effects of a consulting event with occured in weeks 4 and 5 of the time series.

The time series can also be used without control group. Figure 22-3 illustrates the use of time series without control group in measuring the effect of a goal setting consulting event on the productivity of truck drivers in a logging operation.

The time series method should be used when:

— Sample sizes of training or control groups are less then 15.
— When there are a great many variable factors that could cause an actual decrease in performance during the measurement period (for example, bad weather may cause a decrease in productivity for all outside operations).

Figure 22-4 illustrates the value of using time-series, control group measure.

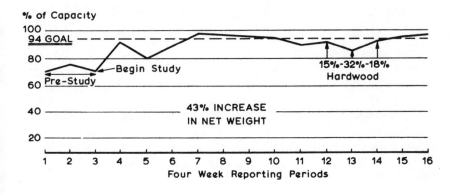

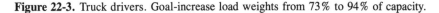

Figure 22-3. Truck drivers. Goal-increase load weights from 73% to 94% of capacity.

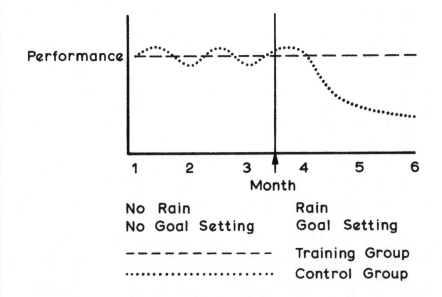

Figure 22-4. In this hypothetical situation, the control group's performance dropped significantly, while the training group maintained production despite the rain. Since the employees were randomly assigned to the two groups and their performance was approximately the same prior to training, and since both groups were exposed to the same factors prior to and again during training (with the exception that the control group did not receive training), the only logical conclusion that can be drawn is that training maintained production.

Evaluating Progress Toward Specific Goals

In evaluation of the overall system's progress toward specific goals it is usually difficult to isolate the effect of the consulting process. The cost in time and money to isolate the consulting process to show its contribution to the end result may be higher than the value returned to the client.

One way to evaluate progress is for the client and consultant actually to develop a written "contract" between the client and consultant so expectations on goals, terms, and roles are spelled out for all parties concerned. An example of such a form used by internal consultants in a large voluntary agency is indicated in Table 22-3.

Our experience indicates that it is good practice to review the overall measurement possibilities with the client and then to determine the level of sophistication in measurement he can live with. Regardless of the level of sophistication or methods chosen, they must be part of the initial understanding between client and consultant — even if the cleint says, "I'll know if this consulting has helped because I'll feel better."

Here are some examples of Evaluation Criteria methods as applied to evaluating client system progress toward goals:

Cost/Profit-Related Criteria

Specific Goal Attainment by a Specified Time. Example: To have a career development system in operation by 1st January 1976 at a cost not to exceed $15,000 for printing, training, and outside consultation. To attain an annualized production rate of 15 tons per hour by reducing downtime required for maintenance through a concentrated continuous training and problem-solving process for maintenance employees between 1st January 1976 and 1st July 1976.

Trend Tracking vs. Plan or Estimated Performance. Figure 22-5 shows how historical performance and projected estimates might be used as a base-line performance against which to track client system performance over time.

Trend Tracking and Comparative Analysis with Similar Systems

Table 22-4 shows a sophisticated comparative analysis of the safety performance of a large pulp mill as compared with the performance of other similar mills in the area. Note that the statistical analysis is accompanied by a documented account of significant planned and unplanned events which the consultant considers to have had an impact on the safety performance change.

(Text continued on page 293)

Table 22-3
Contractual Agreement for Consultative Services

Client _____ Consultant_____

Duration: from _____ 19____ to _____ 19____

Reason for Requested Service:

Client Expectations/Time Frame:

Description of Service: (estimated number of days _____)

Goals and Evaluation Method:

Personnel Involved:

Signatures:

client_____ date_____

consultant _____ date_____

project manager _____ date_____

Instructions for Completing Contractual Agreement

Client: Name of group or individual requesting service.

Consultant: Name of person designated to render service.

Project Manager: Name of Staff Member co-ordinating project services.

Duration: Total length of agreement for services, to include preparation, on-site and follow-up service.

Reason for Requested Service: (completed by client) Give statement of situation or problem for which consultant services are requested.

Client Expectations/Time Frame: (completed by client) Define expectations and give time frame for results of service to be provided by consultant.

Description of Service: (completed by consultant) Describe design of service as related to fulfillment of client expectations.

Goals and Evaluation Method: (completed by consultant) Describe anticipated results of service, method of measuring results, follow-up required by client or consultant.

Personnel Involved: (completed by client and project manager) Designate groups or individuals within client complement with whom consultant will work. Identify person(s) to receive written report if required.

Distribution: Client   2 copies
                       Client   1 copy
                       Consultant
                       Project Manager
                       File

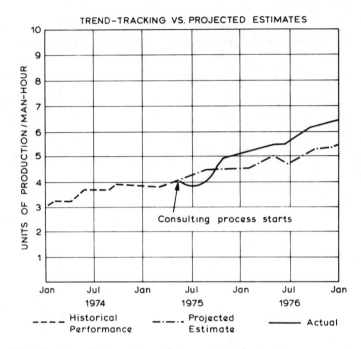

Figure 22-5. Tracking client system performance over time.

Table 22-4
Cost-Related Criteria

Measurement Area No. 1: Safety Results

The purpose of this analysis was to *test* the hypotheses that (a) the number of accidents in Mill A was significantly higher than that of the BC pulp and paper industry average *prior* to the OE intervention; and, that (b) the number of accidents decreased significantly after the OE intervention.

The null hypothesis* was that the difference between the number of accidents in Mill A and those that occurred in the industry in general would remain relatively constant. A Mann-Whitney U test was used to test this hypothesis. This test combined the scores from Mill A and those reflecting the industry average and ranked them in order of increasing size.

Data were collected from January, 1973 until August, 1974. The OE intervention process was completed in November, 1973. The data were analyzed by comparing the preintervention data for Mill A with the preintervention data for the industry. Similarly, the postintervention data for Mill A were compared with the postintervention data for the industry.

---

*The null hypothesis assumes that no significant differences or changes occur as the result of an intervention.

(Table continued on pages 291 and 292)

Table 22-4 (continued)
Premeasure—Safety

Month	Mill A Accident Frequency	Rank	BC Average Frequency	Rank
January	70.87	22	18.82	11
February	64.18	21	15.15	10
March	50.66	20	14.61	4
April	44.20	19	14.30	3
May	41.77	18	14.28	1
June	40.92	17	14.95	7
July	38.04	15	15.03	9
August	38.15	16	14.90	5
September	36.56	14	14.87	5
October	35.79	13	14.29	2
November	34.02	12	15.02	8
$p < .001$	$R_1 =$ 187		$r_1 =$ 66	

Postmeasure — Safety

Month	Mill A Accident Frequency	Rank	BC Average Frequency	Rank
December	30.30	17	15.45	10
January	10.07	8	12.65	9
February	9.39	7	15.55	11
March	8.94	6	16.08	13
April	7.28	3	15.96	12
May	7.76	4	17.04	14
June	8.03	5	17.54	15
July	6.82	1	18.13	16
August	7.19	2		—
$p < .001$	$R_1 =$ 53		$R_2 -$ 100	

Conclusions: The odds are 1 in 1000 that these results are due to chance†. The Mill A accident frequency is significantly lower than that of the BC industry average.

†Odds of 5 in 100 (or 1 in 20) are considered sufficient in science for assuming that the results are not due to chance. The present results exceed even this stringent criterion.

Table 22-4 (continued)
Significant Interventions/Events—Safety

November 1973
1. Top management commitment to establish a comprehensive safety program.
2. Safety co-ordinator job position filled by a respected "line" management employee.
3. Supervisors meetings held with mill manager to fix accountability for safety at first line supervisor's level.
4. Arranged schedules, etc., so that every employee attends at least one departmental safety meeting/month.
5. Safety work order system revised and published to all employees. (See Appendix 1 for effect on work orders received and processed in December 1973 and January 1974).

December 1973
6. Revised safety induction procedure.
7. Ceased hiring "casual" labor.
8. Revitalized and reconstituted Labor-Management Safety Committee.
9. Established environmental protection joint committee.

January 1974
10. Revised and posted mill safety rules.

March 1974
11. Revised Tag Out procedure and trained crews in its applications.
12. Instituted new accident investigation procedure.
13. Instituted new "near miss" investigation procedure.
14. Instituted monthly safety themes and methods for departmental meetings.

July 1974
15. Reviewed and standardized safety equipment in mill.

Behavior Observation Criteria

There are two ways to use behavior criteria measurements:
— To test an assumption about what changes will be observed in individuals and groups as a result of the consulting intervention
— To demonstrate the effect of the consulting process based on observations made after completion of the process

Some examples of preprocess assumptions about expected behavior change are:

— The average time for coffee breaks will decrease from 25 minutes to within 15 minutes.
— Employees will make greater use of industrial relations counseling services.
— Engineering and production will work more collaboratively in new product development activities.

An actual example of an observation measurement made after the process was completed is shown in Table 19-5. These observations data and conclusions were jointly developed by the internal consultant and the client.

Table 22-5
Behavioral Observations

Observable change in individual and organizational behavior was the second set of criteria used to measure the effectiveness of the OE intervention. The seven observations reported here can be related directly to various OE intervention events such as Survey-Feedback decision/action meetings, team development sessions, personal consultation, productivity and effectiveness study, etc. In many instances, the "interventions/events" contributing directly to the observed change are themselves direct results of a specific OE intervention activity.

Observation No. 1 — Mill Supervisors' Unionization Attempt

Observed Behavior Change	Interventions/Events Contributing to Change	Transferable Learnings
Before: March 5, 1973 Mill supervisors filed for certification to unionize. **After:** Nov. 1, 1974 No threat of supervisors unionizing.	Corrected inequities in salaries and compensation for overtime worked during construction and start-up phases. (July-August 73).	Develop controllable S.O.P's and conduct performance/reward reviews against these standards vs. giving across-the-board "merit" increases.
	Conducted objective salary reviews (August 73). Disclosed salary ranges.	Do not reward extra work with trips of dollars is the expectation. At least give a choice.
	Instituted performance bonus plan (July 74).	Do not allow unrewarded overtime to "pile up."
	Team-building meetings to socialize front-line supervisors into management (November 73 — April 74).	Over-staff with supervisors during start-up to reduce fatigue and provide adequate training time.
	Heavy involvement of supervisors in labor relations strategy and procedures (November 73 forward).	Be absolutely open related to salary administration plan and details. Any other behavior creates suspicion and distrust.

Reaction Criteria

As in the other evaluation criteria methods there are multiple levels of sophistication. Some examples of these levels are shown here:

Sponsor/Client Reaction. The sponsor and/or client are invited to make spot-check observations of the project, and record their reactions in writing. (We are noting an increasing tendency for sponsors and clients to be satisfied with this level of sophistication as a measure of the value of the consulting process to their project).

Client System Reaction. This can be obtained through spot-check interviews by client or an evaluation consultant. Client system reaction can also be determined through the multiple application of attitude questionnaires. These questionnaires can range from homemade one-pagers to highly sophisticated and validated computerized attitude surveys (e.g., Survey Research Centers at University of Michigan and University of Chicago). Figure 22-6 illustrates the use of an employee survey to indicate attitude changes related to 11 work climate dimensions and issues. The base document from which these data were summarized on the chart was designed for use as a diagnostic instrument during the consulting process. By collecting data from the client system at the beginning of the consulting process, again at 6 months after the start, and again at 18 months after the start, the consultant and client were able to see attitude trend changes that were consistent with behavior observation and cost/profit-related changes.

Summary

Evaluation of the consulting process must always be considered as part of the initial contract between client and consultant. Ideally, evaluation will serve several important purposes:

1. Give the consultant feedback that will support professional growth.
2. Give the consultant feedback so that corrective actions can be made during the consulting process.
3. Give the consultant accomplishment feedback necessary for his psychological needs.
4. Provide progress and final accomplishment data as positive reinforcement for client behavior, or as a basis for needed change in the behavior.
5. Justify the time and expense of the consulting process (and this should be the least important reason of all).

Evaluation should be helpful to the projects goals, not hindering. The time and money expenditure for evaluation must be weighed carefully by the client against expected payout.

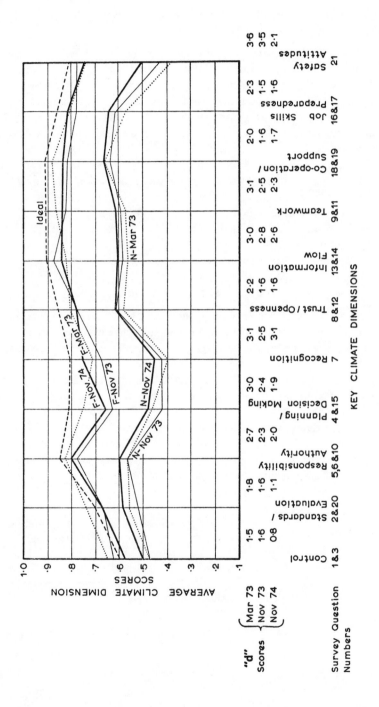

Figure 22-6. Organization climate profile.

The following questions give some of the criteria for determining whether a particular consultation lends itself to evaluation:

1. *How complex is the consulting problem?* If the problem is really a number of problems, or is very complex, it may not be possible to evaluate the process.
2. *How much time will be required to get the information?* If a consultation covers a scope of years, it may not be possible to do evaluation.
3. *Is the question one of values or operations?* If a question is a matter of policy rather than measurable operations, it may raise a question of whether evaluation is possible.
4. *What will be cost demands in securing the facts?* If the financial demand of such an evaluation is too great, it might make data collection impractical.
5. *What will be the nonfinancial demands on the consultant and client?* Any consulting relationship should assess such matters as need for support, time, possible public relations, stress tolerance, etc., in determining the possibility of doing evaluation.
6. *How feasible is it that consultation success can be answered through the obtaining of evidence?* If the data are difficult or impossible to obtain, it might make it questionable that evaluation will be possible.

This may sound as if we are making evaluation difficult. No, our point is that in *some* cases evaluation may be difficult but that a subjective evaluation of consultation will *always* take place, and we suggest that *some* attention be given to make it an objective part of the process as frequently as possible.

There is no "one right way" to evaluate. Consultants and clients need to "invent" evaluation systems appropriate to their needs and based on proven principles of evaluation.

It is our hope that this article provides internal as well as external consultants with some bases upon which to develop some useful evaluation processes with their clients, so that consultation becomes a professional part of the improved effectiveness of individuals, groups and organizations.

Donald H. Swartz is president of Effectiveness Resource Group in Federal Way, Washington.

Gordon Lippitt is professor of behavioral science in the School of Business Administration, George Washington University.

Chapter 23

Disengagement: Reducing Involvement with the Client System

Edgar H. Schein

The process of disengagement has, in most of my experiences, been characterized by the following features:

1. Reduced involvement is a mutually agreed-upon decision rather than a unilateral decision by consultant or client;
2. Involvement does not generally drop to zero but may continue at a very low level;
3. The door is always open from my point of view for further work with the client if the client desires it.

Let me comment upon each of these points and give some examples.

Joint Decisions

In most of my consulting relationships there has come a time when either I felt that nothing more could be accomplished and/or some members of the client system felt the need to continue on their own. To facilitate a reduction of involvement, I usually check at intervals of several months to see whether the client feels that the pattern should remain as is or should be altered. In some cases where I have felt that a sufficient amount had been accomplished, I have found that the client did not feel the same way and wanted the relationship to continue on a day-a-week basis. In other cases, I have been confronted by the client, as in Company A, with the statement that my continued attendance in the operational group meetings was no longer desirable from his point of view. As the president put it, I was beginning to sound to much like a regular member to be of much use. I concurred in the decision and reduced my involvement to periodic all-day meetings of the group, though the initiative for inviting me remained entirely with the group. Had I not concurred, we would have negotiated until a mutually satisfactory arrangement

---

Edgar H. Schein, *Process Consultation*, ©1969, Addison-Wesley, Reading, Massachusetts. Reprinted with permission.

had been agreed upon. I have sometimes been in the situation of arguing that I remain fully involved even when the client wanted to reduce involvement, and in many cases I was able to obtain the client's concurrence.

The negotiation which surrounds a reduction of involvement is in fact a good opportunity for the consultant to diagnose the state of the client system. The kinds of arguments which are brought up in support of continuing (or terminating) provide a solid basis for determining how much value and skill change has occurred. The reader may feel that since the client is paying for services, he certainly has the right to make unilateral decisions about whether or not to continue these services. My point would be that if the consultation process has even partially achieved its goals, there should arise sufficient trust between consultant and client to enable both to make the decision on rational grounds. Here again, it is important that the consultant not be economically dependent upon any one client, or his own diagnostic ability may become biased by his need to continue to earn fees.

Involvement Not Zero

If the client and consultant agree on a reduced involvement, it is important that both should recognize that this does not necessarily mean a complete termination. In fact, a complete termination is not desirable because the diagnosis on which reduced involvement is based may not be accurate enough to warrant termination. A more desirable arrangement is to drop the level to perhaps a half-day every three or four weeks, or attendance only at certain kinds of special meetings, or an interview with key members of the client system once every two or three months. Through this mechanism it is possible for the client and the consultant to reassess periodically how things are going.

In Company B, there was a period where I felt that a plateau had been reached. At this point I suggested that I reduce my involvement to a half-day every other week, and even then only if specific individuals wanted to have some time to talk over problems with me. After a few months at this reduced level, a number of events made it more important than ever for the top management group to increase their level of effectiveness. The group decided to have more meetings and asked me to become reinvolved at an increased level. This decision was much easier to negotiate from a reduced involvement than it would have been from a situation where I had terminated the relationship completely.

In my relationship with Company F, there are long periods where I do not pay any visits, but it is understood that as problems or issues come up the client is free to call on me with the expectation that I will respond positively. The only problem with this kind of arrangement is that it makes it difficult for the consultant to plan his time. Obviously if several clients decide to increase their involvement all at the same time, it may be impossible for the consultant to respond. If this occurs, the consultant has to be open about his dilemma and determine from the various clients whether or not they can wait for a month or so. I have found from experience that I can carry about four clients at any given time, with two of them being more active (one half-day every week), while two others are "dormant" (an occasional visit every three weeks to a month).

Reinvolvement Is Always Possible

This point is closely related to the previous one, but I want to separate it to bring out a special aspect of the obligation of the process consultant. In any P-C consulting relationship with a client, I think the consultant should make it clear that the door is always open to further work once the relationship has begun. The reason for this obligation is that a good relationship with a consultant is difficult for a client to develop. Once both the consultant and the client have invested effort in building such a relationship, it does not terminate psychologically even if there are prolonged periods of lack of contact. I have had the experience with a number of clients of not seeing them for many months and yet being able to tune in on the group very quickly once contact has been reestablished.

As a general rule it should be the client who reestablishes contact, but I would not advocate sticking to this rigidly. I have, after some period of no contact, called a client and asked if I could talk with him to find out what was going on. In several cases such a call was welcomed and served as the basis for some additional counseling or process observation. The consultant must be careful not to violate his role by selling himself back to the client. It must be an honest inquiry which can comfortably be turned down by the client should he desire to do so. I have been turned down often enough to know that there is nothing inherent in the situation to force an artificial contact. Rather, it sometimes helps a client who wanted help anyway to ask for it in a face-saving way.

Edgar H. Schein is professor of organizational psychology and management in the Sloan School of Management at Massachusetts Institute of Technology.

Part VII

Issues

One way of defining the word "issue" is "a point of view subject to dispute." The propensity for dispute is generally a function of the relative value placed on the point of view. We get some sense of valuing occurring when we hear phrases like, "That's an issue for me" or "I take issue with you on that."

Conventionally, issues come in continuums; the larger the crowds at either end, the more likely a point of view will come to be labeled an issue. While our Eastern neighbors encourage us to transcend duality and experience a reality in which all views are part of a larger framework, our Western heritage entices us to define values as a collection of continuums and dichotomies — for every up, there must be a down; for every left, a right.

Issues are borne out of values; values give our lives meaning, purpose, and parameters. They provide a type of control aimed at fostering freedom without anarchy; fairness without apathy. The comparative judging of people, things, and ideas insures diversity, creativity, and progress.

Conventional issues in the client–consultant relationship generally have to do with rightness, goodness, and openness. Few words have more quickly recognizable opposites. Since the definition of right–wrong, good–bad, and open–closed is solely in the eye (value) of the beholder, the three continuums make a useful framework for exploring conventional issues.

Rightness

If issues spring out of valued points of view, the greatest recoil is from those viewpoints dealing with rightness. At their greatest breadth, right–wrong continuums are legal or ethical boundaries; at their narrowest, they revolve around our sense of fair play. Gross and flagrant misrepresentation of professional skills by a consultant, for instance, is clearly unethical and in some circumstances illegal. Subtle misrepresentation of some minor skill (the ability to use a particular training exercise) is, at a minimum, unfair to the client.

Consultation in the behavioral sciences has yet to achieve the kind of professional stature which is accompanied by enforceable codes of conduct. Nevertheless, even the most casual client is concerned with malpractice. Just as the use of inappropriate drugs can be physiologically damaging, using an inappropriate technique on a naive client can be as psychologically damaging.

Sex and money are frequently regarded within a right–wrong context. The consultant who allows the client–consultant relationship to evolve to a point incorporating sexual behavior is clearly courting charges of unethical, if not illegal, behavior. Likewise, inflated consultant fees which are negotiated via the inexperience of the bargaining client are unfair and potentially unlawful.

The list of issues which can fall on a right–wrong continuum are numerous. They can be short-circuited best by consultants employing codes of conduct which favor the client and by facilitating a client–consultant relationship which is built on honesty, effectiveness, and a keen sense of fair play.

Goodness

The road to goodness in the consultation is paved with standards, competencies, and qualities. The continuum relates most to the worth or value of the effort to parties involved. A consultative relationship falling on the good side of the continuum connotes congruence of expectation and outcome, mutuality of purpose, and interpersonal satisfaction. The bad side is laden with labels of conflict, confusion, and ambiguity.

The worth of the consultant in the client–consultant relationship is largely shaped by the qualities and competencies he or she possesses. Many writings have offered a taxonomy of consultant competencies. Central to most are (1) the ability to see things with minimal bias, (2) awareness of personal needs and motives and their potential impact on the effort, (3) an understanding of a body of knowledge related to the consultation, and (4) skill in solving problems and helping others solve problems. Other qualities include such things as trust, imagination, intuition, honesty, and flexibility.

Little has been written about client qualities and competencies which effect the goodness of the client–consultant relationship. Essentially, they are the same qualities required of a consultant, viewed differently. An honest consultant and a dishonest client, for instance, are likely to make rather uncomfortable bedfellows.

A client may not be expected to have diagnostic ability, but nevertheless may be expected to exercise resourcefulness and responsiveness in helping the consultant obtain the required data for an accurate organizational diagnosis. Client self-awareness increases the chances the consultative intervention will be implemented smoothly during the response phase. Disengagement and closure will be made smoother if the client has warded off consultant dependence by maintaining sufficient humility to learn from the relationship.

Whether client or consultant, the goodness of the relationship is typically a function of the commitment of both to consistently stay sensitive to relationship tensions. Likewise required of both is the willingness to test the authenticity of each other by confronting disruptions and uncertainties with caring candor and ruthless integrity.

Openness

Chris Argyris, *Intervention Theory and Method,* stated that if consultation is to be helpful in an ongoing sense, it is critical the client have "free, informed choice." For such choice to be possible, it is important the client have a cognitive map of what he or she wishes to do. Provision of a cognitive map requires a relationship characterized by openness.

Few people relish being coerced or having things done to them in mysterious ways. The relational climate needed is one in which members of the client system find increasing options open to them and a perpetual high return from their personal employment of behavorial science knowledge.

The openness of the relationship is increased as the consultant discovers ways to be helpful to the client rather than cementing the client's dependence on the consultant. The client has the responsibility of being honest in a manner which confronts any real or perceived deception in the relationship.

Consultants are often drawn to the behavioral science field out of personal needs for relationships, affiliation and social acceptances. This magnetic force, left unchecked, can lead to consultant action incompatible with consultant belief. The consultant's failure to function with congruence and genuineness dooms the client-consultant relationship to something less than authentic. Not only does it fail to provide the client a solid example to model, the lack of authenticity seduces the client into perpetual dependence on the consultant.

The client–consultant relationship marked by the spirit of collaboration and cooperation is likely to be right, good, and open to those touched by that relationship. The challenge to client and consultant is to construct their agreements with appropriate feedback loops which allow effective monitoring by each, or timely renegotiation by both.

Chapter 24
"Toward a Philosophy of HRD Consulting"
Chip R. Bell

An issue which cuts across all three types of client–consultant relationship issues (rightness, goodness, and openness) is the role of belief in impacting consultant behavior. A psychoanalyst friend once stated, "Every action a person takes is to them the best action they could take at the moment. No one ever does anything they personally label stupid or wrong. Given a person's self-perception, their world view, and their desire to meet personal needs, the behavior taken was the best choice of action at the time."

This perspective is useful in replacing blame with insight. It is likewise helpful in better managing the client–consultant relationship. Each party has responsibility for continually assessing the impact personal belief has on behavior in the consultation. The Bell article describes a number of issues in which belief can bias what behaviors occur. Several suggestions are provided as means for tempering the weight of prejudice on practice.

Chapter 25
"Ethical Considerations in Consulting"
J. William Pfeiffer and John E. Jones

The Pfeiffer and Jones article makes the point that, while some consultant behavior is clearly ethical, other behavior may be ethical but may be irresponsible, imprudent, unprofessional, or incompetent. Many issues dealing with a variety of consultant misbehaviors are organized into four areas of consideration: (1) self and colleagues; (2) individual clients; (3) training groups; and (4) organizations.

The article is particularly useful for better understanding the rightness dimensions of the client–consultant relationship. As earlier discussed, the nature of consultation is such that the level of trust between client and consultant directly impacts the probability of success. That trust is enhanced if the client senses that the consultant operates from a code of conduct which has the welfare of the client as its primary fabric.

Chapter 26
"Organizations as Phrog Farms"
Jerry B. Harvey

Consultant competence lies at the heart of the goodness issue. The Harvey article slices caustically to the core of the issue by allegorically outlining ways consultants prostitute their competence by being seduced into responding to the client's desires rather than the client's needs.

Few articles have dealt more provocatively with the client–consultant relationship and the competency issue than the Harvey article. Already a classic in behavioral science literature, it stimulates reassessment of how honestly consultants utilize their skills to facilitate improvement in the client system. Likewise, the article enables clients to determine how the consultant may be enticed to affirm the client's beliefs rather than, more appropriately, supplying valid information which provides the client with choice of action.

Chapter 24

Towards a Philosophy of HRD Consulting

Chip R. Bell

A popular line we frequently hear in our society today goes something like, "When you understand where he's coming from, then what he does makes sense." The implied message is that a relationship exists between belief and behavior; that is, the assumptions we have about life color our perception of our environment and shape our actions in our environment. The importance of the linkages among assumptions, perceptions, and action cannot be overstated.

Assumptions, beliefs, or personal philosophy are derived out of our previous experience of making sense out of the world around us. We build up certain constants we learn to depend on to bring order to chaos and to help us to predict occurrences. These learned constants become our personal philosophy and determine what we perceive in our world. For example, one of the functions of the brain is to protect us from being overwhelmed and confused by the mass of data we daily encounter. As a reducing valve, the brain selects in and selects out information based on the constants we have learned. In the words of Goethe, "Every man takes the limits of his own vision as the limits of the world." Adam Smith in his book *Powers of Mind* implies that if one learns (believes) purple cows do not exist, one is not likely to report seeing one even if the purple cow is truly a part of one's immediate environment.[1]

Elements in perception include: some external stimulus, some process by which the external stimulus is transmitted into psychological experience, and some meaning of that psychological experience given by the person. Because they play an active role in giving meaning to stimuli, different people will see the same thing in different ways, depending on their personal set of constants, beliefs, or philosophy. It is how a person "sees" that determines his/her behavior. In brief, we learn assumptions which shape perception which determine action or behavior.

For the human resource development (HRD) practitioner functioning in a consultant role, the recognition of the connection between personal philosophy and possible consultative response is critical to objectivity. The purpose of this

Reprinted with permission from the *Journal of European Industrial Training,* Vol. 1, No. 3, Copyright 1977, M.C.B. Publication, Ltd., Bradford, England.

article is to discuss varied HRD philosophies and how a particular philosophy can bias what the HRD consultant "sees" during the problem diagnosis and can adversely influence what the HRD consultant recommends as the appropriate response for dealing with the problem. It is hoped this article will create a greater awareness of the potentiality of consultant bias enabling the consultant to take precautionary steps to minimize bias which can inadvertently reduce the accuracy of HRD consultation.

There are many studies on the effect belief has on behavior. A team of Stanford psychologists raised groups of kittens, some in only vertically striped environments, some in only horizontally striped environments. Even after they were adult cats and placed in normal environments, the vertical stripers thought the world was vertical, the horizontal stripers thought the world was horizontal. The horizontal stripers literally could not see the vertical world and vice versa. The neural connections had been totally modified by external stimulation[2].

"That's very interesting," you say, "but what does it have to do with people?" Research done by Toch and Schulte found that the training policemen received increased the probability that they would see themes of violence in ambiguous pictures[3]. Hadley Cantril reports research conducted in South Africa by Gordon Allport. A stereogram is an instrument in which the right lens has one picture (e.g., a photograph), and the left lens has a different picture (e.g., a different photo). Using a stereogram with photographs of an equal number of black and white faces, South Africans tended to see more black faces. Indians saw more Indian faces when viewing paired Indian and white photos. In both research efforts, people perceived what was personally significant to them.[4]

The HRD Consultant

There is a myriad of ways one can divide the major roles performed by HRD practitioners. They include such roles as learning specialist, administrator, program manager, and others. Most writers who have dealt with the HRD roles issue indicate that a key HRD role which has emerged in the last decade is that of HRD consultant. The complexity of organizational problems increasingly requires solutions broader than that furnished by the usual learning programs, methods, and technology.

The present era of tight economics has caused HRD practitioners to become more results-oriented in their responses to organizational needs. Learning programs are increasingly more relevant; program delivery, more practical. In this era of pragmatism, HRD practitioners are realizing they have diagnostic competencies and behavioral science-based orientations not only unique in their organization, but needed by their organization in order to cope with complex human system problems.

Practitioners are becoming increasingly reluctant to employ skill deficiency medicine as a cure for will deficiency maladies. Many are realizing their charter is not only to facilitate learning, but to stimulate improvement in the quality of work life. Some practitioners have donned an organization development hat as an important extra garment needed for the achievement of their HRD goals. No longer just the teacher of workshops and overseer of the tuition refund program, the HRD practitioner spends a growing amount of time as a consultant to managers on how best to manage and optimize the human resources for whom they are responsible.

An HRD consultant is a person who, because of competence, experience, status, reputation, or a combination of these, is contacted by a client to provide help in solving a current or potential problem which involves or is concerned with human resources. The HRD consultant is usually external to the client's area of responsibility but may be internal to the organization in which the client is an employee.

Leonard Nadler, in his book *Developing Human Resources*[5], divides the HRD consultant role into four subroles.

1. Advocate: takes a position and attempts to have management adopt his/her views.
2. Expert: responds to management questions regarding the use of HRD, supporting his/her response with research and other evidence.
3. Stimulator: raises questions for management consideration as it explores directions and actions concerned with HRD.
4. Change Agent: assists management in diagnosing and planning for change focusing primarily on the process of change rather than the goals.

Gordon and Ronald Lippitt[6] divide the HRD consultant roles along a directive to nondirective continuum and include the role choices of advocate, technical specialist, trainer/educator, collaborator in problem solving, alternative identifier, fact finder, process specialist, and reflector. The appropriate choice of role is determined through dilemma analysis, an effort aimed at discovering the nature of an organizational dilemma and the determining of the real causes of that dilemma.

The HRD Consulting Process

There are numerous ways of perceiving the HRD consulting process. Like the HRD roles, writers differ on their labels of process steps and on the models or conceptual frameworks they utilize. They do agree that there is entry, some type of diagnosis, some action or response taken based on the diagnosis and at some point, disengagement, closure or termination of the consultation. Most writers agree there is some type of contract agreed upon by client and consultant. Figure 24-1 reflects yet another way of outlining the process and is included to provide visually a simple overview.

Because of some psychological pain or disequilibrium experienced or expected to be experienced by the client and/or client system (e.g., the advent of a new product, employees not sufficiently skilled, supervisors not working as a team,

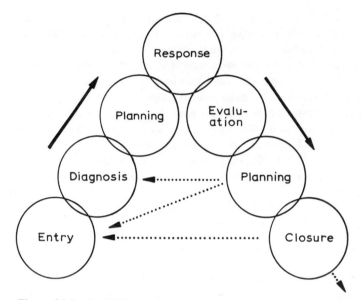

Figure 24-1. The HRD consulting process.

morale or productivity lower than it should be, etc.), a consultant is called onto the scene. During the *entry* phase, problems are jointly explored; roles defined; relationship clarified; goals, objectives, time and budget parameters identified; and a contract (written or psychological) is negotiated. The consultant conducts a *diagnosis* of the situation using one or more data collection methods such as survey, interview, observation, etc.

The results of the diagnosis are fed back to the client (and/or client system); alternative responses are explored discussing the pros and cons of each alternative; priorities are established; and a course of action is *planned,* spelling out goals, roles, and strategies.

The *response* or action phase includes the engagement of structured activities or interventions employed to bring about the needed system improvement. Response could include such activities as workshops, serving as catalytic advisor to the client, survey feedback to the client system, MBO, career planning, team building, job redesign, technostructural changes, intergroup activities, confrontation sessions, process consultation, and many others. Response could also be the action plan itself to be later carried out by the client alone or with a different consultant.

Utilizing procedures to elicit feedback about change progress, the effort is *evaluated* to determine if the consequences of response are consonant with the goals and objectives established at entry and if there is need for response revision or additional resources. Based on that evaluation, *planning* for continuous process maintenance is conducted to insure permanent integration and lasting change.

A part of the postresponse-planning component may include agreement that other aspects of the client system need some type of change process which came to light as a result of the current response. Under this condition the process recycles to diagnosis. For example, in a team building effort, the client and consultant may discover that supervisors in the client system need formal training in decision making and problem solving. A career planning intervention may uncover need for performance appraisal process revision.

The postresponse planning may likewise indicate the need for entry into a different subunit under the jurisdiction of the current client but a subunit not impacted directly by the current response. Other units, not a part of the client system but interfacing with the client system, may require the consultant to work simultaneously with two or more interlocking client systems. Finally, there may be *closure* and termination of the client–consultant relationship with or without a rider or agreement for entry again at a prescribed point in the future.

Admittedly, the HRD consulting process is much more intricate and complex than may be apparent in the overview discussed here. The reader, unfamiliar with the process, might do well to review books which treat the process in more depth. Works by such writers as Fritz Steele (*Consulting for Organizational Change*), Robert Blake and Jane Mouton (*Consultation*), Gordon and Ronald Lippitt (*The Consulting Process in Action*), Ed Schein (*Process Consultation*), Chris Argyris (*Intervention Theory and Method*), and Richard Walton (*Third Party Consultation*) may be particularly helpful.

HRD Consulting and HRD Philosophy

Regardless of the consultant subrole or process used by the HRD consultant, there is difficulty in escaping the impact personal HRD philosophy has on consultation effectiveness. Each of us will tend to hold a primary philosophy regarding how best to understand the dynamics of relationships and organizations. Like the Stanford cats, we have learned cause-and-effect relationships and paradigms which may or may not reflect reality. These learned beliefs predispose us in our diagnosis and recommended responses. While congruence of paradigm and practice is vital, a more critical issue is the relative ease with which consultant philosophy clouds consulting objectivity, resulting in a prejudice inappropriate in meeting the true needs of the client.

What follows is a discussion of the more frequent HRD philosophies and their potential influence on diagnosis and response. Conflicting philosophies are presented as polar opposites, recognizing there is likely greater allegiance to points along the continuum than to those at the extreme ends. Also, the resultant influences discussed are not givens, although they may appear to be in this article. The influences are rather propensities or inclinations of which one should be aware in order to counterbalance their impact.

Helping Others vs. Helping Others to Help Themselves

There is a measure of ego gratification in the expert subrole. Most of us derive some degree of satisfaction in being needed and in being perceived as a person with good solutions to tough problems. While appropriate in some cases, the expert helper risks seeing only problems which he/she can solve framing diagnosis feedback in a way in which the consultant is the only key to response. Another risk is that the response will be conducted in a manner which reinforces the consultant's expertness reputation. The fallout of client dependence is obvious — the consultant potentially stacks the deck to keep the client forever knocking on the consultant's door for assistance.

The flip side of the coin is the philosophy of "Give me a fish and I eat for a day; teach me to fish and I eat for a lifetime." Diagnosis tends to be collaborative; response, participative. It is the philosophy that true consulting is helping the client and the client system to become better able to learn from their experience. As altruistic as the philosophy is, the real need may be for timely expert advice or research-based advocacy. It is like the HRD consultant whose client exasperatingly said, "I want to learn and you are a great teacher, but right now I just need your recommendation; that's all!"

Process vs. Content

Process-oriented HRD consultants tend to view all organizational dysfunctions as due to maladaptive relationships. They typically focus on the lack of interpersonal communication, lack of shared power, ineffective use of delegation, and interunit conflict. Response takes the form of highly experiential workshops, sensitivity training, process consultation, team building, weekend retreats, etc. Workshops may be designed around simulation exercises and off-the-shelf games rather than developed around the terminal job behaviors needed. They often overlook the fact that problems are sometimes due to inadequate skill training, obsolescent methods, or lack of task knowledge.

Content-oriented consultants see the source of most problems as being lack of clarity regarding organizational goals, absence of or inadequate use of feedback, incomplete information, and skill deficiencies. They believe most problems happen because people do not know what they are required to do or how best to do it. Response is likely to include elaborate orientation programs, technostructural changes, extensive job training, job redesign, work simplification, MBO, and management information systems. Workshops designed by content-oriented HRD consultants are often high on structure and information dissemination, making heavy use of movies, slides, and lectures. Missing from their diagnosis and response are the process factors described above.

Individual vs. Group

There are HRD consultants who view their role as facilitating the meeting of the needs of individuals. They often speak of the enhancement of individual power and freedom, and they fear technocratic control and loss of individuality. Viewing organizations as a collection of individuals, they zero in on such areas as counseling, career and life planning, performance appraisal, boss–subordinate relationships, role clarification, behavior modification, and transactional analysis. They sometimes overlook the synergistic effect of work groups or the role of group norms and pressures. Consultation often centers on the relationship with the client and never directly interfaces with the client's unit.

Group-oriented HRD consultants get lost in the group process and forget the importance of individual needs. They see their primary task as group catalyst and process observer. Responses are likely to be very group-oriented activities such as confrontation meetings, survey feedback, organizational mirroring, family T groups, and third-party peacemaking at group levels.

Behaviorist vs. Humanist

No doubt one of the most hotly debated issues among social scientists is the conflict between behaviorism and humanism. Behaviorists draw their arguments from the works of such people as Watson, Thorndike, Hull, Dollard, and Skinner; humanists from the works of Maslow, Rogers, Allport, May, and Goldstein. Behaviorists tend to believe man is flexible, malleable, and a passive victim of the environment, which determines his/her behavior. While not denying the existence of emotions, feelings, and attitudes, they discard them as unobservable and unmeasurable, and therefore immaterial. Ethics, morals, and values are only the result of associative learning. Diagnosis by behavioristically oriented HRD consultants focuses on reinforcement systems and the quality of feedback; response is built on system feedback, leadership behaviors of supervisory personnel, and the establishing of positive consequences or rewards for appropriate behavior.

Humanists, while not totally rejecting behavioristic theory, assume the human species to be more than just a higher form of animal, but with unique characteristics. It is a belief that we can learn a great deal more about human nature through consideration of the subjective as well as the objective. Humanism stresses the dignity and freedom of the individual. A gestalt approach, the humanistically oriented HRD consultant's diagnosis focuses on barriers to openness, lack of empathy, inclusion, trust, and growth. Response is usually non-manipulative and takes the form of group experiences designed to enhance leveling, honesty, affiliation, and freedom.

Philosopher King vs. Participative Manager

Perceiving leadership parameters in organizational disharmony is likewise subject to consultant bias. The recommended leadership response can easily reflect the style of leadership personally preferred by the HRD consultant. While participative management and adaptive leadership are the "in" prescriptions, a growing number of HRD consultants are leaning more toward leadership with an air of enlightened self-interest; Machiavelli has been resurrected. The era of assertiveness and power is causing some to reconsider the importance of charisma and influence. While not with the rawness of bygone days, the age of uncertainty has created a new homage to the strong, decisive, courageous leader. HRD consultants with philosopher–king orientations tend to work primarily with individual managers and focus on a leadership skills recipe with a twist of politician added. The danger lies in potentially subverting follower opinions, talents, and ultimately their followership.

The shift from hierarchical to horizontal organizational structures carries its own special bias. Caught up in the popularity of matrix organizations and participative management, the HRD consultant may inappropriately see the client's unit as a fertile entree for a novel structure. Diagnosis tends to reveal the need for adaptive and organic structures with the manager serving as the co-ordinator or "linking pin" among various temporary task forces. Response likely includes the alteration of organizational charts reflecting project groups rather than stratified functional groups. Employees and supervisors most probably would be trained in project management with liaisons identified to provide interteam continuity. The danger in such an orientation is that the matrix form may be inappropriate for the people or nature of work and/or introduced too rapidly for effective integration and adaption.

Conclusion

There are other dichotomies which could be included. Proactive creator versus reactive buyer, centralization-oriented versus decentralization-oriented, thinkers versus feelers, grass-roots rebel leaders versus executive suite diplomats are all categories with potential for belief-based bias illustrations. Those discussed in this article are only a few of the major sets.

Most HRD consultants would indicate they are more eclectic, subscribing to a variety of beliefs and philosophies. Granted, some are commonly linked together. Humanists, for instance, are often process, individual, facilitative, participative manager oriented. Some readers will disagree with the manner in which their favorite philosophy has been here described.

My own beliefs no doubt peek through. The crucial point is, however, that we all are tied to certain beliefs or assumptions which shape what we see and how we respond. Think of the interventions you have recommended in the last year. You will no doubt recognize a pattern. If I am a process-oriented consultant, I will very likely see process problems and recommend process solutions.

Guarding against the encroachment of bias is no easy task. Being aware of its likelihood, however, is a useful step in reducing its exaggerated influence. The use of a shadow consultant, a professional peer who can serve as consultant to the consultant, is often helpful in countering the influence of a particular paradigm. A related method is collaborative consulting, that is, working with colleagues who have a slightly different philosophical bias. Choice of perspectives is the first step toward reality-based diagnosis and need-fulfilling response.

It is probably no accident that the word "vision" has connotations regarding both the eye and soul of mankind, for it is through vision we derive meaning and decide direction in life. Yet, our vision and its seductive effect on behavior can deliver a heavy blow to the objectivity foundation of HRD consulting. Widening the brain's reducing valve entails constantly punctuating our declarations of reality with question marks instead of exclamation points. It requires a deliberate search for truth and a never-ending state of personal growth. At stake is not only our personal effectiveness and credibility, but the mental health and productivity of the client system we serve.

References

1. Smith, A., *Powers of Mind,* New York: Random House, 1975, p. 24.
2. Spinelli, D.N., H.V.B. Hirsh, R.W. Phelps, and J. Metzler, "Visual Experience as a Determinant of the Response Characteristics of Cortical Receptive Fields in Cats," *Experimental Brain Research,* Vol. 15 (1972), pp. 289–304.
3. Toch, H., and R. Schulte, "Readiness to Perceive Violence as a Result of Police Training," *British Journal of Psychology,* Vol. 52 (1961), pp. 389–393.
4. Cantril, H., "Perception and Interpersonal Relations," *American Journal of Psychiatry,* Vol. 114 (1957), pp. 119–126.
5. Nadler, L., *Developing Human Resources,* Houston, TX: Gulf Publishing, 1970, p. 235.
6. Lippitt, G., and R. Lippitt, "Consulting Process in Action," *Training and Development Journal,* Vol. 29, No. 5 (May 1975), pp. 48–54; and Vol. 29, No. 6 (June 1975), pp. 38–41.

Chip R. Bell is an independent consultant in Charlotte, North Carolina.

Chapter 25

Ethical Considerations in Consulting

*J. William Pfeiffer
and John E. Jones*

As the field of human relations training grows and the number of human relations consultants and group facilitators increases, it becomes more important than ever to face the question of ethical behavior. It is necessary to consider with care what is ethical, what is not ethical, and what may be ethical but irresponsible, imprudent, unprofessional, or incompetent.

In this article we discuss 19 issues that pertain to human relations consulting. Some of these issues are clearly questions of ethics; other topics do not fit into the ethical–unethical category but rather concern themselves with the responsibilities of prudent, competent professional consultants. We have divided these 19 issues into four areas of consideration, relating to (1) self and colleagues; (2) individual clients; (3) training groups; and (4) organizations.

Self and Colleagues

Presentation of Professional Qualifications

A major ethical issue relating to the individual consultant is the presentation of the consultant's professional qualifications. If a consultant is inaccurately represented by someone else as having extensive experience in a particular area, it is categorically incumbent on that consultant to correct the misrepresentation. The consultant has an ethical responsibility to clear up all actual or implied inaccuracies of qualifications, experience, and/or education.

For example, if someone introduces you as a person who knows a great deal about organization development in government (*nobody* knows a lot about OD in government), you might say, "That sounded good, and I wish I could say that about myself, but it isn't literally true. I have done some work with government trainers, and I have done some work with government departments, but most of my work has been in educational settings."

Reprinted from John E. Jones and J. William Pfeiffer (Eds.), *The 1977 Annual Handbook for Group Facilitators,* San Diego, California: University Associates, 1977. Used with permission.

It is, of course, possible for facilitators to dwell too much on their limitations. If you give excessive emphasis to your inadequacies, you may severely erode your clients' confidence. It is important to balance the representation of your professional competence in a way that gives equal weight to both your strengths and your limitations.

It is essential to recognize that if you allow *implicit* misrepresentations to stand, you are promoting and encouraging an inaccurate perception of your competencies. A prudent test is to imagine that your most severe critic is present when you are presenting your qualifications to a client or prospective client. Ask yourself if your imaginary critic would take issue with the manner in which you have represented yourself. If you can pass this "test," it is highly likely that you have made an ethical representation of your credentials.

Fees

There are several potential issues concerning consulting fees. It seems to be a fairly common practice for consultants to vary the amount they charge according to their clients' ability to pay. It is clear that, in general, business and industrial clients are used to paying substantially higher consulting fees than either education or government agencies. A free market exists in consulting, and fees seem to reflect a balance between the value that clients place on services and the value that consultants place on their time and contribution. If consultants set their fees too high, they will price themselves out of the market.

Fee setting is a matter of prudence — demand what you are worth and deliver what the client pays for. It is unethical to pad your expenses or to charge the client for either time or materials not delivered. It is your responsibility to see that your agreement with the client is *explicit* in terms of professional fees and agreed-upon expenses.

It is unprofessional to undercut your competition's fees in order to secure a consultation. However, while it is generally a poor professional practice to allow a client to negotiate a reduction in your fee, there may be times when you should weigh the longterm payoffs of a consultation against the immediate budgetary limitations of the prospective client.

The Consultant's Health

Particularly important as it relates to the individual consultant is the issue of health. Consultants are responsible for monitoring their own physical and mental health. If, for any reason, you are emotionally "stretched," your consulting work is going to be affected. There may be times when you have to decline, postpone, or cancel a consultation. You need to recognize that if you are physically ill or emotionally chaotic, you cannot adequately attend to your responsibilities to your clients. If you cannot pay attention to people, you cannot be empathic, and you cannot teach. You may need to take a vacation for a while and "get your own act together."

Because consultants work with other people, it is a major imperative that they keep themselves healthy. Working with people is taxing if you do not maintain yourself; dealing with emotions all day long, every day, can take its toll. Human relations consulting makes special demands on its practitioners. To help others effectively, you must be in good emotional and physical shape. If you are below par, you cannot give the client your best. We believe that you are responsible for delivering the best consultative services of which you are capable.

Meeting Your Own Needs

Not only must consultants be concerned about their own health; they must also be aware of their own needs and whether those needs will be imposed on their clients. Consultants usually get their needs met; it is simply a matter of who is going to "pay." If, for example, you have a big need for power, you are apt to meet that need through your clients, possibly at their expense. If you are first concerned with your own needs, your groups are going to suffer.

Most consultants can recall examples of other consultants forcing their needs on people. If you are very unhappy in your job and/or your marriage, it is very likely that in your groups you will manipulate the members into giving you emotional support. They will be forced to soothe and console you. If you find yourself in such a situation, perhaps you should stop leading groups until you get yourself together. If you do not, you will be jeopardizing the development of your groups. One person should not be allowed to manipulate an entire group to that person's sole benefit — and of course this applies to you, the consultant, as well as to any other individual.

Promises

Consultants are faced with a dilemma: selling their skills but not doing it blatantly. Selling professional services takes a special approach. Business-oriented people who work for consultants may not see that selling skills is different from selling shoes and that it operates according to a different set of rules. Brochures, flyers, advertising copy—all have to fit the professional image the consultant wants to project.

Regardless of the kind of consultation to be performed, consultants cannot ethically promise that they will be able to bring about certain types of outcomes. Nothing can be guaranteed in working with people. You cannot promise people what will happen as a result of your efforts. You cannot imply that people are going to be different when you leave or that you will "set them free." People may be unable or unwilling, and you cannot force them to achieve any specific outcomes or learning. You can simply state that they may learn some things they will be able to use.

What consultants can promise to do, in effect, is to be interventionists, to work hard, and to be sensitive and resourceful in any given situation. That is the basis on which a defensible contract can be built.

Public Criticism of Other Consultants

Consultants must be concerned with ethical issues regarding themselves and the way they present themselves, charge for their services, perform their work, meet their own needs, and offer promises. But ethical issues relate also to consultant's behavior toward their colleagues.

If you talk with anyone about other consultants, you should either comment in a positive vein or not comment at all. You should not, either subtly or directly, put down any other professional or consulting organization. It is unethical for a professional to criticize another professional either to another colleague or to the general public.

You may not like what you hear about another consultant or what the consultant does, but you are not obligated to pass judgment; you can simply decline the opportunity to comment. Be sure, however, that you do not, at the same time, give contradictory nonverbal signals. The best test you can apply in this situation is to imagine that the individual concerned is present. If what you say could be said in front of that person, your comments probably pass the test of being ethical.

Confronting

If you do have serious reservations about the competence or behavior of another consultant, you are ethically responsible for confronting that individual. You should let that person know exactly what behavior you believe is unethical. You might say, "in my judgment you're behaving unethically, and I will not lend implicit support to what you are doing." If the person's behavior is not modified, you must register your concern with an appropriate professional organization. That may be an uncomfortable decision. But consultants cannot afford to have their effectiveness undermined by someone else's incompetence or unethical behavior. It is a difficult problem. The strong tendency is to *collude*, not to confront — just to "let it go." But failing to confront when a confrontation is called for can be irresponsible. "Not to decide is to decide."

One slogan a consultant can use is, "When in doubt, confront." As professionals, we must attempt to regulate ourselves, just as bar and medical associations do.

Individual Clients

Ethical issues also exist in relationship to individual clients. Consultants have an obligation to behave in a responsible and professional manner with those who are relying on their expertise.

Evaluating Participants

Doing training for the purpose of evaluating people — the "assessment center" method — can be ethical if everyone understands the rules. But if, on the other hand, a consultant conducts communications training and later is asked how a particular person performed, the only position that is ethically defensible is for the consultant to tell the inquirer to talk directly to the individual concerned. If evaluation is not the purpose of the training, it should not be the result. The consultant may have a great deal of information about individuals and may even have counseled them privately. It would be unethical to reveal such information without a clear previous understanding between the consultant and the participants.

It goes without saying that ethically you must not give specific data about any participant or client to that person's supervisor; be sure that the participants understand that you will not do this. As for giving information to people outside the group, you may generalize or report anonymous data, but you may not be specific or give particular, identifiable details.

Confidentiality

Violating confidentiality is an obvious ethical breach. If someone asks you to keep information private, and you agree to do so but do not, you are being unethical. Very often you, as a consultant, can find yourself caught in a trap. Someone has confided in you, but you cannot use that information, although its disclosure would clearly affect the situation. You have to be very careful about letting yourself be the recipient of a great deal of confidential data. It can tie your hands and stifle your effectiveness. If someone wants to give you confidential data, you can say that you do not accept confidential information — and explain why. You can tell the person that, instead, you are willing to keep the data anonymous. Our experience is that people will still give you the same data — although obtaining it should not be your hidden intent. Refusing to accept information if it is labeled "confidential" makes it much easier for you to deal authentically with a situation.

Sexuality

Consultants and group facilitators, like teachers, therapists, and counselors, have potent roles. That is, participants in human relations training respond to the facilitator differently from the way they would respond to the same individual in a peer relationship. If you, as a consultant/facilitator, use your role to establish a sexual relationship with a participant, you have clearly violated the standards of ethical behavior.

This issue is somewhat complicated; if you are involved with a participant, you are not in a good position to differentiate objectively between your personal attractiveness and your role potency. One test to apply is this: if, as a facilitator, you start a training event with identifiable sexual needs, you will *probably* meet your needs at the expense of someone else.

Logically, a consultant's colleagues should be good sources of balanced judgment on this question, but collusion is common — especially among colleagues who are open to (or seeking) sexual relationships with participants.

The reality is this: if you are heavily involved personally with a participant (either sexually or emotionally), you are (1) less able to attend to your professional commitments and (2) less available to be responsive to other participants. Most participants sense it if a special relationship between the facilitator and a participant exists. Such a situation often generates counterproductive energy that is experienced as jealousy and resentment.

A practical solution is to establish a clear ground rule: observe a cooling-off period of three to six months to allow the relationship to evolve and your role potency to fade before you become involved in a sexual relationship with a participant.

Perhaps it is worth mentioning briefly that engaging in sexual relations with *colleagues* while co-consulting is, at a minimum, likely to be distracting to the work at hand. Your major commitment has to be to your contract with the client, and anything that jeopardizes your effectiveness should be avoided.

Training Groups

In addition to their personal behavior and their behavior toward colleagues and other individuals, consultants must also be concerned with their professional responsibility toward their training groups.

Deception

Sometimes structured experiences and other training techniques involve deception — withholding information from trainees for strategic teaching purposes. If consultants do purposely deceive their training participants, they must be careful to undo the effects. Some structured experiences, for example, require that the facilitator not discuss the goals before the activity. They must, however, be made explicit later. A general training rule that we have found useful is "no surprises."

Cooptation

If a consultant coerces people into doing something they really do not want to do, that consultant is involved in unethical cooptation. For example, in a workshop, part of whose purpose is to involve people in giving each other feedback, someone may not want to participate. You, the facilitator, might put pressure on that person by suggesting the the activity will be harmless. That is coopting the person. Groups, too, can become tyrannical; they can pressure someone to participate when that person does not really want to participate. You should protect the right of individuals not to take part in an activity if they do not want to — particularly if the activity involves their talking about themselves or receiving feedback and even more so if it requires their talking about their emotions, feelings, values, beliefs, and wants.

Inappropriate Techniques

A consultant should be aware that in some settings particular techniques, such as activities that involve physical touching, may be very inappropriate. For example, asking a group of first-line supervisors to explore each other's faces would probably be altogether inappropriate and would undoubtedly create unnecessary anxiety. We believe that you have to be sensitive to the norms of the context in which the training takes place and not use methods that deviate markedly from participants' behavior expectations.

Inattention to Application

It is irresponsible for a consultant to conduct training without paying attention to the application of that training. The integration of learning cannot be left to chance. In using experiential learning, the facilitator must be careful not to cut short its full cycle. Participants should be directed to answer the questions "So what?", "What am I going to do with this learning?", "What implication does this have for new behavior?" Part of your responsibility as a trainer is to help people come to grips with the ways in which they want to change toward more effectiveness.

Rehashing

If consultants do the same training over and over again, by rote, not learning anything new or improving their professional skills, that behavior may be "ripping off" their clients. When you conduct a particular workshop many times, you have a professional obligation to keep it vital. You have to keep yourself generating new ideas, content, and methods. You should strive to experiment, to improve your style, to rethink your procedures — you should not "lecture from old notes." Otherwise, you become stilted, and what you do becomes unimaginative and mechanical. You will not be bringing your best to the people who need what you have to offer.

Organizations

In dealing with organizations, the consultant has similar problems of ethical and responsible behavior, although the applications of the issues are different.

Accepting Organizational Goals

Consultants need to determine what the values of a client organization are, and if they cannot accept those values, either they have to get out or they have to try to change the organization's values. If you are working for a unit whose leader has a philosophy that you cannot accept, then you must either confront that person's values or not work with that unit. In helping a leader to achieve better, you, the consultant, are, in effect, accepting the client's goals by helping to further them. A consultant's techniques are very powerful; they can be used to manipulate people, or they can be used to free people. Techniques themselves are "value free" — it is the purposes for which they are used that determine whether they are ethical. It is you who must decide in which direction you will lend your expertise.

Guerrilla Warfare

If you decide that you cannot accept a particular organization's goals, it is clear that you should not work for that organization; it is even clearer that you must not agree to work for it and then surreptitiously undermine it. If you engage in covert activities that are not correlated with the goals of the organization or that are antithetical to them, you are engaging in unethical behavior. For example, a high school counselor may not like the school system she works in, and she meets with the officers of the student government to reinforce their fight against the system. That counselor is working against the system in a clandestine way, and that is unethical. Besides the fact that consultants who behave that way sooner or later will be "caught," they are not meeting their obligation to be direct in promoting change, and they are not modeling appropriate confrontive behavior.

Assessing Outcomes

After conducting their interventions, facilitators must follow through to identify the effects of what they did and to determine further needed work. That is a difficult task, especially in working with people. In dealing with an organization, consultants are aware of the complex political, environmental, and leadership pressures, inside and outside; they know that the effects of their work may not be immediate or obvious. But even though much of what they do in organization development cannot be specified with any scientific accuracy because of the subjectiveness of the data, they still have to try to determine, in whatever terms they choose, whether they made a difference. Although you will have to live with ambiguity in terms of outcomes, you must ask yourself such questions as these: Did a team-building session improve the work group's meetings? Does the group seem to be cooperating better? Are the training participants improving their supervisory skills on the job?

Hatchet Jobs

Doing someone else's dirty work is neither ethical nor prudent. If consultants do, they will soon gain unsavory reputations. Your image or reputation as a consultant is critical; if you carry out the unpalatable tasks of management, your image will be sullied and your effectiveness will be jeopardized. If, for example, you suspect that a manager's "real" motivation for requesting a team-building session is to provide a basis for firing someone, that suspicion needs to be confronted before you agree to do the work.

Conclusion

Although the consideration of ethics in human relations training is imprecise at present, we believe that the key to understanding the issues lies in a few pertinent words: *power, sensitivity, responsibility, motivation,* and *caring.*

You, as a trainer or a consultant, are in a position of power, simply by virtue of your role. You need to be sensitive to the fact that prople will have different expectations of you than of anyone else in the consulting situation.

Because of these heightened expectations, you must be clearly aware of your responsibilities. Facilitators are responsible for monitoring the climate of the groups with which they work; for facilitating openness, so that people will feel free to explore and experiment; for providing sufficient structure so that learning can take place; and for helping the groups to maintain themselves. You are responsible for *yourself* and the effectiveness of your own helping behavior; you are not directly responsible for the behavior or the learning of others.

Motivation and caring are critical final determinants of ethical behavior: you are less likely to be unethical if you are concerned with benefiting the client than if you are thinking of taking care of yourself at someone else's expense. Too great a desire for contracts, for example, puts your motivation in doubt; a good rule might be that if you cannot say "no" to a proposal, you should not say "yes." In the end, a decision based on your sincere concern for people is likely to be an ethical decision.

J. William Pfeiffer is president of University Associates in San Diego, California.

John E. Jones is a human relations consultant in San Diego, California.

Chapter 26

Organizations as "Phrog" Farms

Jerry B. Harvey

A short time ago I received a telephone call from a friend of mine who was employed as an OD specialist in a large corporation.

"Jerry, I've just been fired," he said.

"Fired? You mean you are out of a job completely?"

"Well, not completely," he replied. "I'm just no longer an OD specialist. In fact, the whole function has been wiped out. They have given me a make-work job in salary administration. It's a nothing job, though. I hate it, I was really interested in doing OD. All I'm doing now is scutt work and drawing a paycheck."

"Why were you fired, Hank?"

"I'm not really sure. I've never heard the reason directly. My boss's boss was the one who really did the firing. He told my boss to do it."

"Why did he tell your boss he wanted you fired?"

"My boss was vague about it. He just said his boss had said I wasn't powerful enough to do the job."

"What did your boss's boss say to you when you asked him about it?"

"I haven't talked with him."

"Why not?"

"That would be violating the chain of command. You don't do that around here."

"Why not?"

"You can get fired for that."

"But Hank," I said, "You *have* been fired."

"Oh!"

And then, perhaps because I had recently read my children the fable of *The Princess and the Frog,* I said, "Hank, your boss's boss is correct. You aren't powerful enough to do the job. In fact, for all intents and purposes, he has turned you into a phrog. I can almost see you in a big phrog pond with your boss's boss sitting on a willow stump saying to himself, 'I think I'll turn ol' Hank into a phrog.' And then he waves a magic wand, mutters some mystical-sounding incantation

Reprinted by permission of the publisher from *Organizational Dynamics,* Spring 1977, © 1977 by AMACOM, a division of American Management Associates.

and concludes with, 'Hank, you are a phrog,' and suddenly you have web feet. Hank, you are now a phrog."

The silence at the other end of the line was seemingly interminable.

Finally, out came the poignant, one-word reply that echoed down the line, "Ribbit."

Organizations as Phrog Farms

After talking with Hank at some length about his life in the phrog pond, I got to thinking that most formal organizations are, metaphorically speaking, phrog farms. By phrog farms I mean that they turn a lot of good people into phrogs. In addition, if we accept the metaphor of organizations as phrog farms, we might conceptualize organization development as the process of draining the swamp. Therefore, building upon that metaphor, I would like to suggest a number of hypotheses, to make some generalizations, and to conceptualize some issues of organization, management, and organization development within the framework of life in the swamp. These various statements are provided, in no particular order of importance and in no conscious linear sequence, as follows:

1. All organizations have two essential purposes. One is to produce widgets, glops, and fillips. The other is to turn people into phrogs. In many organizations, the latter purpose takes precedence over the former. For example, in many organizations, it is more important to follow the chain of command than to behave sensibly.

2. *Phrog* is spelled with a *ph* because phrogs don't like to be known as frogs, and they try to hide their phroginess from themselves and others by transparent means. In short, once one has been transformed into a phrog, one likes to attempt to hide that fact. For one who has been a person, it's a great come-down to be a phrog.

3. Phrogs tend to live a solitary life in the swamp, or as one phrog said, "It's a lonely life on the lily pad." Phrogs compete with one another for insects, vie for the right to head the flicking order of the swamp, and are ultimately evaluated for what they do in their own mud flats. Furthermore, phrogs don't really get rewarded for how well they sing in the chorus. Given that, is it any wonder that a common phrog maxim is, "You can't get involved with other phrogs in the swamp; someday you may have to appropriate their lily pads"?

4. Phrogs speak the Language of Ribbit. The language is simple because it contains only one word, but it doesn't communicate very well. When all the phrogs in the swamp croak "Ribbit," the swamp is noisy as hell, but not a lot of real information is ever exchanged. You see, accuracy of information is not very important in the swamp. In fact, any time a person enters the swamp, he or she is generally told why the Language of Ribbit is the only possible language of the swamp, despite the fact that phrogs don't learn much from one another when they

use it. For that reason, people have a difficult time talking with phrogs. In fact, they seldom talk with phrogs at all.

5. Most phrogs spend more time flicking flies in the fog than in draining the swamp. As best I can tell, their behavior is circular. If they were to spend time draining the swamp, there would be no flies to flick and no phrogs. For that reason, it's very important to phrogs to maintain the swamp as it is rather than to drain it.

6. In phrog farms, bullphrogs generally get to be fresident. Stated differently, the better a phrog can tolerate the loneliness of his lily pad, the more competent he becomes at speaking the Language of Ribbit, the more facile he becomes in flicking flies, the more skillful he becomes at appropriating other lily pads, and the more adroit he becomes at maintaining the swamp, the more likely he is to become fresident.

7. Bullphrogs are greatly revered in the swamp. In fact, other phrogs assume bullphrogs have magical powers because of their unusual abilities to turn people into phrogs. In one sense, such reverence may not be misplaced. They are apparently instrumental in the process of phrog production. It is strange to me, though, that we have devoted so little effort to understanding the role that humans play in permitting phrogs to attack them in the swamp.

8. The magic exercised by bullphrogs comes from humans' belief in it. The tyranny of bullphrogs stems not from the reality of the bullphrogs' power, but from the belief of humans in the Myth of Bullphrog Power.

9. Belief in the Myth of Bullphrog Power prevents one from having to take responsibility for the fog and mud and moss that make up the atmosphere of the swamp.

10. Bullphrogs — particularly fresidents — frequently feel very trapped in the swamp. Many of them are destroyed by it.

They feel trapped because they are trapped. Mr. Nixon was not an aberration.

11. One of the peculiarities of the swamp is that the masses of swamp phrogs both worship and destroy bullphrogs for the very qualities of phroginess that resulted in their becoming fresident.

12. Darwinians say only the strongest go to the top of the phylogenetic scale. Phrogologists say only the weakest go to the top of the same scale. Both say only the fittest survive. One is incorrect.

13. Another perculiarity of the swamp is that cowphrogs seldom become fresident. Cowphrogs apparently don't have the capacity for loneliness, the Language of Ribbit, fly flicking, and swamp maintenance that bullphrogs have. If, by chance, they do develop that revered capacity, they become cowphrogs in bullphrog's clothing, and their croaks deepen.

14. The process of producing phrogs is not sexual — it's magical.

15. OD generally consists of phrog kissing, which is magical, harmless, and platonic.

16. Any activity designed to facilitate phrog kissing is an example of ODD behavior — cosmetic organization development or organization development by deception — or OD as practiced by phrogs. Activities such as phrog chorus-building, interlily-pad conflict resolution, phrog sensing, phrog-style assessment, marsh groups, tadpole development, and phrog coaching in the absence of swamp drainage and area reclamation are examples of phrog kissing by ODDITIES.

17. Phrog kissing is a seductive activity. Frederick Herzberg claims that being seduced is ultimately less satisfying than being raped, because when we are seduced, we are, in fact, part of our own downfall. Stated differently, and in our context, ODD specialists are frequently seduced into phrog kissing, an activity that seldom leads to love-making but frequently adds to the warts on the kisser's face.

18. Many organization members belong to Phrognarian Networks, and Swamp Maintenance Associations. The purpose of such networks and associations is to meet and exchange information regarding the nature of the fog in each member's respective swamp. Since the Language of Ribbit is employed, such exchanges seldom allow one to differentiate one swamp from another. Phrogs seem to get reassurance from noting the similarity among their swamps. Or, as one bullphrog put it, "Misery loves company and miserable phrogs love miserable companies."

19. Occasionally, during meetings of Phrognarians, a phrog pharts in the fog. When that happens, that phrog loses some of his or her phroginess and therefore represents a great threat to the balance of the swamp. Phrog pharts are seldom sanctioned by Phrognarians. They are too real. They put holes in the fog and ultimately threaten the atmosphere of magic required to maintain the swamp.

20. There is a myth on the part of phrogs that kissing another phrog turns that phrog into a prince. I think it should be noted that, in general, kissing a phrog only produces skin irritations. For those who decide to kiss anyway, I think they should also realize that, in all that fog, it is very difficult to determine which way a phrog is facing.

21. Phrogs frequently try to set traps for one another. Phrog traps have a peculiar quality because they catch only the phrogs who set them. Stated differently, if you have to set a phrog trap, there is no need to do so. You are already in it.

22. So that the technology of setting phrog traps is not lost to future generations, phrogfessors of marsh management are hired by Schools of Swamp Maintenance to research and teach. (Phrogfessors of marsh management are not limited to Swamp Maintenance Schools. In fact, they are on the faculties of all kinds of teaching organizations, defined not by what they teach but by the attitude and approach with which they teach it.) The work of such phrogfessors is governed by the underlying credo that is frequently displayed on their respective lily pads. It goes something like this: "If the tadpole hasn't learned, the phrogfessor hasn't taught."

The underlying rationale of that credo is rather peculiar if subjected to close scrutiny. To explain, it clearly implies that the basic responsibility for the tadpole's learning belongs to the phrogfessor. Consequently, if the tadpole does a lousy job, the phrogfessor is at fault. Likewise, following the same logic rigorously, if the tadpole does competent work, the phrogfessor must also get the credit. For all intents and purposes, then, the tadpole doesn't exist, except as some sort of inanimate, passive receptacle for the phrogfessor's competence or incompetence.

23. Given that such a teaching attitude implies that students have no animate existence, is it any wonder that students seem to fit so well into the lonely parallelism of the swamp? Is it also any wonder that when someone accepts responsibility for another's learning, that person ceases to be an educator and becomes a phrogfessor, whose primary job is to prepare tadpoles for life in the swamp?

24. People frequently become phrogs in other kinds of organizations by the same process. After all, a common swamp saying is, "You can delegate authority but you can't delegate responsibility." Translation: "You are responsible for your subordinates' performances. If your subordinates perform competently, it is because of you. If they perform incompetently, it is because of you, too. Like students, they don't even exist, except as extensions of you. They are objects you must manipulate in the best interests of the swamp."

If phrogs don't feel they are responsible for the performance of their subordinates, then why do so many of them go to training programs designed to help them alter their styles of phrogging? As I see it, they do it because they believe they are responsible for their subordinates' performances and that their style (as opposed to their essence) has something to do with how effectively their subordinates perform.

25. All of us are phrogs at one time or another. All have the potential to develop webbing between their toes. All have experienced the terror of the trap, and accepting responsibility for others actions is the bait with which phrog traps are set.

26. Many bullphrogs can't laugh at the absurdity of their lives in the swamp. Such phrogs tend to become steerphrogs and are very poignant creatures. Bullphrogs frequently die laughing, but I have never seen a steerphrog laugh. They just croak.

27. The seat of our government is located in Washington, D.C., in a swampy area of the city known affectionately to some as "Foggy Bottom." For many, it is also the locus of the "bureaucratic mess." Perhaps it should be renamed, "Phroggy Bottom."

28. *Making Waves in Foggy Bottom,* by Alfred Marrow, is a book about an OD effort to clean up the bureaucratic mess in the U.S. Department of State. In its essence, the book is about the failure of that effort. Should you decide to read it, you might come to realize that making waves — in any organization — is a very different process from draining the swamp.

29. The size of the swamp is growing; the world may ultimately be inhabited by phrogs. Air pollution is not really a great a threat to future generations as phrog pollution.

30. The swamp is ultimately evil. Hannah Arendt described how phrog farms, despite their benign appearance, tend to develop bullphrogs with an enormous capacity for evil. Adolph Eichmann was not an aberration either.

31. The job of most swamp mannagers is to maintain and enhance the swamp, not to drain it. For example, Winston Phroghill said, "I was not made marsh minister to preside over the draining of the swamp."

32. The purpose of swamp consultants — in the eyes of swamp managers — is to help the swamp operate effectively, not to drain it.

33. Most OD literature is designed to facilitate swamp management, not area reclamation. Most managers are phrog farmers. Most OD specialists and phrog-fessors of marsh management are phrog farmers' helpers. The relationship is symbiotic.

34. Most phrog farmers and their helpers are aware of their lots in the swamp. Most have about all the consciousness they can bear. May God have mercy on their souls.

35. God does have mercy on their souls. Otherwise, God would be the greatest phrog farmer of them all.

Alternatives to Life on the Phrog Farm

With all those objects around, it is indeed a lonely life on the lily pad.

"What is the alternative to life in the swamp?" you ask. After all, isn't that my job as a responsible phrogfessor, to provide some answers to the problems of the dismal swamp?

The temptation is great.

Suddenly, though, I see that sign on my lily pad and realize that another feature of phrogs is that they are frequently afraid to think. It's not that the thoughts are not there. In fact, in the swamp, there are plenty of thoughts to be thought. But who is to think them? Certainly not phrogs, because thinking is as dangerous to the ecology of the swamp as passing gas in the fog.

Not thinking, or getting someone else to be responsible for thinking one's thoughts, is not without its advantages — as long as a phrog can get someone else to take responsibility for changing the climate of the swamp.

I do know, though, that noncosmetic organization development involves swamp drainage and area reclamation and is done by humans, not phrogs. Ultimately, that process of drainage and reclamation destroys the swamp and includes such modifications in the swamp's environment as building habitats that allow people to cooperate — rather than compete. Such habitats allow people to:

- Get paid as pairs, teams, organizations rather than as individuals. If two individuals get paid for working as a pair, it is amazing how much interest they take in helping one another succeed.

- Work in nonzero-sum climates when it comes to promotion, layoffs, salary, performance appraisal, and grades. For example, during bad times, phrogs lay others off in terms of seniority. People don't lay one another off at all. They all take proportionate pay cuts and therefore learn that they can rely on one another during both good and bad times.

  People with zero-sum attitudes believe that the outcome of any interpersonal encounter is zero, that is, "If you get a pay off of plus one, I must get a payoff of minus one, and the outcome is zero." Stated in day-to-day language, people with that attitude say, "If you win, I must lose." People with nonzero-sum attitudes believe that the outcome of any human encounter can be other than zero, that is, we can both win and, if we do, under certain conditions, it is not one plus one equals two but rather, with synergism, three.

- Leave the environment when they lose interest in it. For example, when it comes to vesting (of rights), people don't wear vests, phrogs do.

- Accept personal responsibility for their own activities in the habitat. Phrogs, for instance, demand that bullphrogs take responsibility for the swamp. People will not permit others to take over their responsibilities for the habitat and its operation.

- Trust one another in a wide variety of situations. Phrogs distrust 'most everybody. Given their distrust, they put in time clocks which say, "We don't trust you to do an honest day's work, so prove that you did." They demand doctors' certificates when someone calls in ill. They have private offices so that others access to them is limited and so that their conversations and work with other phrogs can't be observed and overheard. They demand close verification of expense accounts because "Everyone knows those slick swamp salesmen would rob the marsh blind if a bullphrog doesn't keep tabs on them." They keep just-in-case (JIC) files to protect themselves from other phrogs' poisons.

  People have, by contrast, very few rules and procedures that question the honesty of others. In fact, they assume other people can be trusted and live with the reality that in a few cases such trust will be violated.

- Be treated as subjects — not objects. R.D. Laing has pointed out that one way to make others mentally ill is to treat them as depersonalized objects or things, (that is, objectively) rather than as "personalized" subjects (that is, subjectively). Bullphrogs try to treat others objectively. They try to gauge the performance of others objectively, and they try to "keep their feelings out of the situation." However, when you treat another objectively (that is, as an object), you should know that the price of being objective — eliminating one's feelings from the situation — is that you become an object yourself, since you have denied the very essence of your own humanness. Thus are bullphrogs born.

Humans don't treat one another as objects. They try instead to build a work environment in which human subjectivity is accepted as an integral part of the habitat's problem-solving process.

"You still haven't answered the question of "What do we do to save ourselves from the swamp? You are too vague, too idealistic and too impractical. You certainly have not fulfilled your responsibilities as an article writer."

I hope you don't feel that way, but if you do about all I say is: "You're right. I haven't tried."

"Ribbit."

Jerry B. Harvey is professor of behavioral science in the School of Business Administration, George Washington University.

Bibliography

Alderfer, C. P., "Organizational Diagnosis from Initial Client Reactions to a Researcher," *Human Organization*, Vol. 27 (1968), pp. 260–265.

Argyris, Chris, *Intervention Theory and Method*, Reading, MA: Addison-Wesley, 1970.

Baker, John K., and Robert H. Schaffer, "Making Staff Consulting More Effective," *Harvard Business Review* (January–February 1969), pp. 62–70.

Barber, William H., and Walter Nord, "Transactions Between Consultants and Clients: A Taxonomy," *Group and Organization Studies*, Vol. 2, No. 2, (June 1977), pp. 198–214.

Bazerman, Max, and Roy J. Lewicki (Eds.), *Negotiating in Organizations*, Sage Publications, 1983. Contains the basic concept that every manager is a negotiator. Includes material on use of a third party, achieving agreement, evaluating outcomes.

Beckhard, Richard, "A Leader Looks at the Consultative Process," Leadership Resources, Inc., Washington, D.C., 1965.

Beene, Kenneth D., "Some Ethical Problems in Group and Organizational Consultation," *Journal of Social Issues*, Vol. 15, No. 2 (1959), pp. 60–67.

Bell, Chip R., *Influencing: Marketing the Ideas that Matter*, Austin: Learning Concepts, 1982.

Bell, Chip R., "The HRD Managers 'Rules for Living,' "*Training and Development Journal*, Vol. 30, No. 12 (December 1976), pp. 38–39.

Bennis, Warren G., Kenneth D. Benne, and Robert Chin (Eds.), *The Planning of Change*, New York: Holt, Rinehart, and Winston, 1979, Third Edition. A good book of readings on various aspects of planning change, particularly change in organizations.

Bion, Wilfred, *Experiences in Groups*, New York: Basic Books, 1961.

Blake, Robert R., and Jane S. Mouton, *Consultation*, Reading, MA: Addison-Wesley, 1976.

Block, Kenneth L, "The Professional Consultant," *The Office* (January 1972).

Blumberg, Arthur, "The Consulting Function of Leadership," *Adult Leadership*, Vol. 8 (1960), 265–266.

Boehm, W., "The Professional Relationship Between Consultant and Consultee," *American Journal of Orthopsychiatry,* Vol. 26, No. 3 (1956), pp. 241–248.

Boyatzis, Richard E., *The Competent Manager,* John Wiley, 1982. Based on a study of 2,000 managers, this book documents the essential characteristics of the competent manager.

Bradford, Leland P., "How to Diagnose Group Problems," *Adult Leadership,* Vol. 2, No. 7 (December 1953), pp. 18–26.

Brandon, David, *Zen in the Art of Helping,* New York: Dell, 1976.

Bridges, William, *Transitions: Making Sense of Life's Changes,* Reading, MA: Addison-Wesley, 1980. This book is essentially concerned with the changes (transitions) in the life of individuals. There are direct counterparts in transition in organizations.

Brown, David, *Managing the Large Organization: Issues, Ideas, Precepts, Innovations,* Lomond Press, 1982. A provocative book challenging some of the traditional ways we have organized and suggesting some alternatives.

Brown, T. H., "The Business Consultant," *Harvard Business Review,* Vol. 21 (1944), pp. 183–189.

Browning, Larry D., "Diagnosing Teams in Organizational Setting," *Group and Organization Studies,* Vol. 2, No. 2 (June 1977), pp. 187–197.

Burke, Warner W., (Ed.), *Contemporary Organization Development: Conceptual Orientations and Interventions,* Washington D.C: NTL Institute for Applied Behavioral Science, 1972.

Carkhuff, Robert R., *Helping and Human Relations: A Primer for Lay and Professional Helpers,* New York: Rinehart and Winston, 1969.

Carkhuff, Robert R., *Sources of Human Productivity,* Amherst, MA: Human Resource Development Press, 1982. Models developed by the author covering various aspects of productivity within organizations.

Carr, Rey A., "Principal-Centered Preventive Consultation," *Group and Organizational Studies,* Vol. 1, No. 4 (1976), pp. 455–473.

"Consultation as a Training Function," *Exploration in Human Relations Training,* Washington, D.C.: NTL Institute for Applied Behavioral Science, 1953.

Deal, Terry, and Allen Kennedy, *Corporate Culture,* Reading, MA: Addison-Wesley, 1982. Decribes, through case histories, how culture evolves in an organization and how it is maintained and communicated to new employees.

Dyer, William G., *Contemporary Issues in Management and Organizational Development,* Reading, MA: Addison-Wesley, 1982. Includes planning and organizing, team building, relationships between managers and organizations.

Dyer, William G., *Team Building: Issues and Alternatives,* Reading, MA: Addison-Wesley, 1977.

Egerton, Henry C., and Jeremy Bacon, "Consultants: Selection, Use and Appraisal," *Managing the Moderate-Sized Company, Report No. 13,* New York: National Industrial Conference Board, 1970.

Frederiksen, Lee W., *Handbook of Organizational Behavior Management,* John Wiley, 1982. Some specific techniques from the field of behavior science dealing with productivity, strategic planning, absenteeism, health, etc.

Fordyce, Jack K., and Raymond Weil, *Managing With People: A Manager's Handbook of Organizational Development Methods,* Reading, MA: Addison-Wesley, 1971.

Fox, Robert S., Richard Schmuck, Elmer Van Edmond, Miriam Ritvo, and Charles Jung, *Diagnosing Professional Climates in Schools,* Fairfax, VA: NTL Learning Resources Corp., 1975.

French, Wendell L., and Cecil H. Bell, Jr., *Organization Development: Behavioral Science Interventions for Organization Improvement,* Englewood Cliffs, NJ: Prentice-Hall, 1973.

Friedlander, Frank, "A Comparative Study of Consulting Processes and Group Development," *Journal of Applied Behavioral Science,* Vol. 4, No. 4 (1968), pp. 377–399.

Gluckstern, Norma B., and Ralph W. Packard, "The Internal-External Change Agent Team: Bringing Change to a 'Closed Institution,' " *Journal of Applied Behavioral Science,* Vol. 13, No. 1 (1977), pp. 41–52.

Goldman, Samuel, and William Moynihan, "Strategies for Consultant-Client Interface," *Educational Technology,* Vol. 12, No. 10 (October 1972), pp. 27–30.

Gollessich, June, *The Profession and Practice of Consultation,* Jossey-Bass, Inc., 1982. The focus is mainly on human service organizations, but the book contains good material on various models for consulting.

Goodman, Paul S., et al., *Change in Organizations,* Jossey-Bass, 1982. Discusses various ways of bringing about change in organizations.

Goodstein, Leonard D., *Consulting with Human Service Systems,* Reading, MA: Addison-Wesley, 1978.

Green, Howard L., "Management Consultants: How to Know What You're Getting and Get What You Pay For," *Management Review,* Vol. 52, No. 12 (December 1963), pp. 14–17.

Greiner, Larry E., and Robert O. Metzger, *Consulting to Management: Insights to Building and Managing a Successful Practice,* Prentice-Hall, 1983. Includes: marketing, writing proposals and contracts, implement change.

Guder, R. F., "How to Choose, Abuse and Misuse Consultants," *Management Review* (December 1963).

Guss, L. M., "Consultants Need Client's Cooperation," *Chemical and Engineering News* (April 1965).

Harris, Philip R., *New World, New Ways, New Management,* New York: AMA-COM, 1983. Explores the changes taking place in the work place, organizational relationships, and the need for a new kind of management person.

Harrison, Roger, "Role Negotiation: A Tough-Minded Approach to Team Development," in *Interpersonal Dynamics* (Warren G. Bennis et. al., Eds.), Homewood, IL: Dorsey Press, 1973.

Harvey, Jerry, "It's Not My Dog: Eight Myths OD Consultants Live and Die by," *OD Practitioner,* Vol. 7, No. 1 (February 1975), pp. 1–5.

Harvey, Jerry, and Richard Albertson, "Neurotic Organizations: Symptoms, Causes, and Treatment" *Personnel Journal,* Vol. 50, No. 9 (September 1971), pp. 694–699; Vol. 50, No. 10.

Harvey, Jerry, "The Abilene Paradox," *Organizational Dynamics* (summer, 1974), pp. 63–80.

Haslett, J. W., "Decision Table for Engaging a Consultant," *Journal of Systems Management* (July 1971).

Havelock, Ronald G., and Mary C. Havelock, *Training for Change Agents,* Ann Arbor, MI: Institute for Social Research, 1973.

Herzberg, Frederick, "One More Time: How Do You Motivate Employees?", *Harvard Business Review,* Vol. 46 (January–February 1968), pp. 53–62.

Hultman, Kenneth E., *The Path of Least Resistance: Preparing Employees for Change,* Austin: Learning Concepts, 1979. Recognizes that people have to be prepared for change and indicates ways of doing this (HD 58.8 H.84).

Hunt, Alfred, *The Management Consultant,* New York: Ronald Press, 1977.

Huse, Edgar, *Organization Development and Change,* New York: West Publishing, 1975.

Kaplan, Robert E., "Stages in Developing A Consulting Relation: A Case Study of a Long Beginning," *Journal of Applied Behavioral Science,* Vol. 14, No. 1 (January–March 1978), pp. 43–60.

Kelman, Herbert C., "Manipulation of Human Behavior: An Ethical Dilemma for the Social Scientist," *Journal of Social Issues,* Vol. 21, No. 2 (1965), pp. 31–46.

Kintzer, Fredrick C., and Stanley M. Chase, "The Consultant as a Change Agent," *Junior College Journal* (April 1969).

Kolb, D., and A. Frohman, "An Organization Development Approach to Consulting," *Sloan Management Review,* Vol. 12, No. 1 (fall 1970), pp. 51–65.

Kubr, M. (Ed.), *Management Consulting: A Guide to the Profession,* International Labor Office, 1983, Second Edition. Although focused on the international scene, provides a great deal of information on the consulting process, models, and organizing to consult.

Lawler, Marcella R., "The Role of the Consultant in Curriculum Improvement," *Educational Leadership,* Vol. 8 (1951), pp. 219–225.

Levinson, Harry, *Organizational Diagnosis,* Cambridge, MA: Harvard University Press, 1974.

Lippitt, Gordon, and Ronald Lippitt, *The Consulting Process in Action,* La Jolla, CA: University Associates Press, 1978.

Lippitt, Gordon, "Operational Climate and Individual Growth: The Consultative Process at Work," *Personnel Administrator,* Vol. 23 (1960).

Lippitt, Gordon, "The Criteria for Selecting, Evaluating and Developing Consultants," *Training and Development Journal,* Vol. 26, No. 8 (August 1972), pp. 12–17.

Lippitt, Gordon, *Organizational Renewal: A Holistic Approach to Organization Development,* Prentice-Hall, 1982, Second Edition. Explains how changes in social responsibility, moral standards, economic pressures, school requirements, and the search for quality of life are causing disequilibrium in modern organizations.

Lippitt, Ronald, "The Dimensions of the Consultant's Job," *Journal of Social Issues,* Vol. 15, No. 2 (1959), pp. 5–12.

Lippitt, Ronald, J. Watson, and B. Westley, *Dynamics of Planned Change,* New York: Harcourt, Brace and World, 1958.

Lippitt, Ronald, "On Finding, Using and Being a Consultant," *Social Science Education Consortium Newsletter* (November 1971).

Lorsch, Jay W., and Paul Lawrence, "The Diagnosis of Organizational Problems," *The Planning of Change* (Warren G. Bennis, Kenneth D. Benne, and Robert Chin, Eds.), New York: Holt, Rinehart and Winston, 1969.

Luke, Robert A., Peter Block, Jack M. Davey, and Vernon R. Averch, "A Structure Approach to Organizational Change," *Journal of Applied Behavioral Science,* Vol. 9, No. 5 (1973), pp. 611–635.

Lundberg, C. C., and A. P. Raia, "Issues in the Practice of Organizational Development Consultancy," in *Proceedings of the Academy of Management,* Thirty-Sixth Annual Meeting, Kansas City, MO, 1976.

Mager, Robert F., and Peter Pipe, *Analyzing Performance Problems,* Belmont, CA: Fearon Publishers, 1970.

Margolis, Fredric H., and Chip R. Bell, "Making Organization Development Work at the Department Level," *Training: The Magazine of Human Resources Development,* Vol. 18, No. 9 (1981), pp. 116–119.

Marguiles, Newton, "Implementing Organization Change Through an Internal Consulting Team," *Training and Development Journal,* Vol. 25, No. 7 (July 1971), pp. 26–33.

Martin, Shan, *Managing Without Managers,* Sage Publications, 1983. Proposes the elimination of redundant supervisory jobs and allowing employees to design and supervise their own work. Focus is on the public sector.

Merry, Uri, and Melvin E. Allerhand, *Developing Teams and Organizations: A Practical Handbook for Managers and Consultants,* Reading, MA: Addison-Wesley, 1977.

Mink, Oscar G., Majes M. Shultz, and Barbara P. Mink, *Developing and Managing Open Organizations,* Austin: Learning Concepts, 1979. Contrasts open and closed organizations. Provides case studies and instruments for developing organizational potential.

Mintzberg, Henry, *Power in and Around Organizations,* Prentice-Hall, 1982. Looks at external coalitions, internal coalitions, organization goals, and power configurations in organizations.

Mitchell, M. D., "Consultant Burnout," in *The 1977 Annual Handbook for Group Facilitators,* (J. E. Jones and J. W. Pfeiffer, Eds.), La Jolla, CA: University Associates Press, 1977.

Morris, Jud, "Why Management Consultants Are Not Needed," *Manage,* Vol. 20, No. 8 (June 1968), pp. 50–55.

Nadler, David A., *Feedback and Organization Development: Using Data-Based Methods,* Reading, MA: Addison-Wesley, 1977.

Nadler, David, J. Richard Hackman, and Edward E. Lawler III, *Managing Organizational Behavior,* Little, Brown and Co., 1979. Discusses individual and organizational behavior, the design and management of organizations, and effective management of organization behavior.

Nadler, Leonard, *Developing Human Resources,* Houston, TX: Gulf Publishing Company, 1970.

Nadler, Leonard, "How is Your Organizational Health?" *Management of Personnel Quarterly,* Vol. 9, No. 1 (spring 1970), pp. 18–28.

Paine, Whiton Stewart (Ed.), *Job Stress and Burnout: Research Theory and Perspectives,* Sage Publications, 1982. Outgrowth of what is claimed to be the first national conference on this topic. Emphasizes where clinical and industrial psychology intersect.

Paster, Irving, "So You Want to be a Consultant," *Personnel Journal,* Vol. 50, No. 11 (November 1971), pp. 827–833, 871.

Peters, Thomas J., and Robert H. Waterman, Jr., *In Search of Excellence: Lessons from America's Best-Run Companies,* Harper and Row, 1982. Report of a study on various companies and how they function. Important information for consultants.

Rapoport, Anatol, and Albert Chammah, *Prisoner's Dilemma,* Ann Arbor, MI: Ann Arbor Paperbacks, 1970.

Redding, William J., "Confessions of an Organizational Change Agent," *Group and Organization Studies,* Vol. 2, No. 1 (March 1977), pp. 33–41.

Reiff, Robert, "The Control of Knowledge: The Power of the Helping Professions," *Journal of Applied Behavioral Science,* Vol. 10, No. 3 (1974), pp. 451-461.

Schmuck, Richard A., and Matthew B. Miles, *Organizational Development in Schools,* La Jolla, CA: University Associates Press, 1971.

Schroder, Marjan, "The Shadow Consultant," *Journal of Applied Behavioral Science,* Vol. 10, No. 4 (October-December 1974), pp. 579-594.

Steele, Fritz, "Interpersonal Aspect of the Architect-Client Relationship," *Progressive Architecture,* Vol. 50, No. 4 (1968), pp. 32-133.

Steele, Fritz, "Potter Unearthed for the Consultant," *Journal of Applied Science,* Vol. 8, No. 5 (1972), pp. 513-526.

Steele, Fritz, *The Role of the Internal Consultant,* CBI Publishing, 1982. A practical approach to coping with staff conflicts, working within the organizational structure, exercising personal influence, gathering information, and motivating people to listen, question, and implement solutions.

Steele, Fritz, and Stephen Jenks, *The Feel of the Work Place,* Reading, MA: Addison-Wesley, 1977.

Swartz, Donald, "How Not to Sabotage Your OD Consultant," *Successful Meetings Magazine* (October 1973).

Swartz, Donald, "How to Use an OD Consultant," *Organization Renewal Newsletter,* Vol. 4, No. 5 (July-August 1974), pp. 1.

Swartz, Donald H., "Similarities and Differences of Internal and External Consultants," *Journal of European Training,* Vol. 4, No. 5 (1975), pp. 258-262.

Terreberry, Shirley, "The Evolution of Organizational Environments," *Administrative Science Quarterly,* Vol. 12, No. 4 (March 1968), pp. 590-613.

Tichey, Noel, "An Interview with Roger Harrison," *Journal of Applied Behavioral Science,* Vol. 9, No. 6 (1973), pp. 701-726.

Tichey, Noel M., Harvey Hornstein, and Jay N. Nisberg, "Participative Organization Diagnosis and Intervention Strategies," *Academy of Management Review,* Vol. 1, No. 2 (1976).

Tichey, Noel, and Jay Nisberg, "Change Agent Bias: What They View Determines What They Do," *Group and Organization Studies,* Vol. 1, No. 3 (September 1976), pp. 286-301.

Tilles, Seymore, "Understanding the Consultant's Role," *Harvard Business Review,* Vol. 39, No. 6 (November-December 1961), pp. 87-99.

Titles, S., "Ideas for a Better Consultant-Client Relationship," *Business Horizons* (summer 1963).

Van De Van, Andrew H., "A Framework for Organization Assessment," *Academy of Management Review,* Vol. 1, No. 1 (January 1976), pp. 64-78.

Varney, Glenn H., *An Organization Development Approach to Management Development,* Reading, MA: Addison-Wesley, 1976.

Walton, Richard E., *Interpersonal Peacemaking: Confrontations and Third Party Consultation,* Reading, MA: Addison-Wesley, 1969.

Weisbord, Marvin R., "Organizational Diagnosis: Six Places to Look for Trouble With or Without a Theory," *Group and Organization Studies,* Vol. 1, No. 4 (1976), pp. 430–447.

"What to Do Before the Consultant Comes," *Management Review,* Vol. 58, No. 6 (June 1969), pp. 14–19.

Woody, R. H., and J. D. Woody, "Behavioral Science Consultation," *Personnel Journal,* Vol. 50, No. 5 (May 1971), pp. 382–391.

Author Index

Subject Index

NOTES

p 64
Begin role clarification by looking at
expected behavior & label behavioral roles.

p 80 a-l
may want
consultant take observer role

1. try figure what problem is
2. begin c̄ statement of what problem going to
   focus on

3. try to
   a. solve particular problem
   b. teach client how to solve prob.
      for self next time

all wants legitemite

Try achieve
   · confidence, warmth, acceptance
   · inquiry, exploration, quest
   · mutual growth
   · shared problem solving

Consultant
   · professional behavior
     leadership

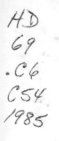

HD
69
.C6
C54
1985

A.L. OLIVEIRA MEMORIAL LIBRARY

3 1782 00027 0591

HD69 .C6 C54 1985
Clients & consultants : meeting
and exceeding expectatio 1985.